Presented by the Virginia Founda
For the Humanities
September 16, 2004

T.H.
Isaiah 55:1-3

Published for the Margaret Grattan Weaver Foundation by the
Virginia Foundation for the Humanities
145 Ednam Drive
Charlottesville, Virginia 22903

Text ©2003 Robert R. Hewitt, III

Library of Congress Control Number 2003106665

ISBN 0-9668919-5-3

Book Design by Wood & Associates, Inc.

Printed in the United States of America
by Good Printers, Bridgewater, Virginia

where the river flows

Original illustrations by Bob Kirchman, Kirchman Associates, Staunton, VA – Schriesheim, 11; The Palatinate, 13; Early Virginia settlement, 21; Augusta Stone church, fort and stockade, 52; Tunker House mechanism, 78; Burkholder's meetinghouse, 128; Cook's Creek Presbyterian, 138.

Original photography by Eli Moore, Waynesboro, VA - Cover, 1, 2, 17, 24, 29, 34, 40, 41, 43, 45, 53, 88, 92, 113, 126, 130, 132, 160, 162, 165, 171, 182, 183, 190, 194.

Special thanks to the following individuals and institutions for allowing permission to photograph and/or scan items in their possession for use in this publication: Casey and Cathy Billheimer, Elkton, VA, ElkRun/Liberty Meetinghouse, 143; Randy and Janet Shank, Broadway, VA, The Shank House, 188; Augusta Stone Presbyterian, Fort Defiance, VA, Communion tokens, 34; Lutheran Archives, Salem, VA, Thomas Giffin communion cup, 40, 41; J.B. Yount, Waynesboro, VA, painting of Tunker House, 130; Brethren Archives and Reuel B. Pritchett Museum, Bridgewater College, Bridgewater, VA - Alexander Mack's Bible, 29; Greenmount love feast items, 92; Wittenberg Chapel, 166; John Kline's saddlebags and hat, 183; Menno Simons Historical Library, Eastern Mennonite University, Harrisonburg, VA, *The Martyrs' Mirror*, 53.

The following have been reproduced from original, previously published sources: Footwashing, 91, and Kiss of Peace, 131, from *Scribner's Magazine,* "Among the Dunkers," November 1901; Union Church, 137, from Benson J. Lossing, *Pictorial History of the Civil War in the United States of America.* Hartford, CT; Thomas Belknap, 1880; John Bear portrait, 142, from James Edward Armstrong, *History of the Old Baltimore Conference,* Baltimore, MD, 1907; Bishop Glossbrenner, 189, from A.W. Drury, *The Life of Bishop J.J. Glossbrenner,* Dayton, OH; United Brethren Publishing House, 1889; "A Service Interrupted," 180, from J. William Jones, *Christ in the Camp,* Richmond, VA; B.F. Johnson & Co., 1888; Kentucky Harmony advertisement, *Knoxville Register* (26 May 1818 from microfilm), 124.

The following have been reproduced with permission from the collections named: THE METHODIST COLLECTION OF DREW UNIVERSITY LIBRARY, MADISON, NJ - William Otterbein, 60; Martin Boehm, 59; Long's Barn, 61; Francis Asbury, 84; Asbury's powder horn, 85; Love-feast tickets, 89; leather purse for love-feast tickets, 90; Camp meeting, 118. THE VIRGINIA HISTORICAL SOCIETY, RICHMOND, VA - Bishop Madison and Bishop Madison's seal, 87. THE WESTERN RESERVE HISTORICAL SOCIETY LIBRARY, CLEVELAND, OH - sketches from James E. Taylor, *With Sheridan Up the Shenandoah Valley,* "Fort Harrison," 94; Harrisonburg Court House (detail), 140; Harrisonburg Main Street, 178; Dunkers, 184, JOHN W. WAYLAND COLLECTION, ARCHIVES ROOM, HANDLEY REGIONAL LIBRARY, WINCHESTER, VA - Joseph Funk's print shop, 157; Bethlehem church, 176, THE EVANGELICAL AND REFORMED HISTORICAL SOCIETY, LANCASTER, PA - Johannes Braun (digitally repaired), 98. The Albert and Shirley Small Special Collections Library, University of Virginia Library, Charlottesville, VA - page from Joseph Funk's *Genuine Church Music* (Winchester [,VA], 1832), 158; battlefield map from Jedediah Hotchkiss Civil War Maps (#38-403), 181.

Layout and Design - Jennifer Wood, Wood & Associates, Inc., Staunton, VA

Jacket Photography - Little Dry River, Brocks Gap. Photograph by Eli Moore.

preface

Margaret Grattan Weaver always had great interest in the history and genealogy of the people who settled the Valley of Virginia. In order to preserve that history she created a charitable foundation, "The Margaret Grattan Weaver Foundation," which was directed to focus on preserving the historical and religious heritage of the City of Harrisonburg and the County of Rockingham, Virginia.

She was aware of the great diversity of faith in God and the practice of religion among the people of this unique area of the Valley of Virginia. Many had come to the Valley expressly for the opportunity and freedom to worship in their special ways. As a result, some of the groups such as the Mennonites, Brethren, and Presbyterians, among the earliest, established their churches when the Valley was first settled, and have continued to this day. Now, almost every faith and denomination has its place among the citizenry of Harrisonburg and Rockingham County.

Because Margaret Weaver herself had a strong faith in God, she knew the value that faith had for a permanent and lasting settlement of pioneer peoples and their descendants. It was because of her insight and interest in the historical and religious heritage of this area that her foundation was able to produce this work, a work which honors Margaret Grattan Weaver and our faithful forbearers in Harrisonburg and Rockingham County.

George G. Grattan, IV

Baptist Brethren themselves in official documents to the Virginia legislature as late as 1863. Dunkers and Mennonists often referred to members of their own groups as "Brethren," but that term would have caused confusion with a group known as the United Brethren in Christ, now in part subsumed within the United Methodist Church. All considered, I thought "Dunker" the most appropriate and least confusing label to use for the German Baptist Brethren before 1880.

But for all this explanation about labels, I found them of little use in advancing the story. Though there were often similarities among people who called themselves by a certain name, whether Presbyterian or Dunker, Lutheran or Methodist, Baptist or Anglican, these were sometimes more akin to cultural likenesses.

The real story is told not by affixing labels, but in seeking to understand individuals and their relationship to God. Here is where the records often fail us. Thankfully, every now and then we are given a glimpse of someone, whether through their own words or the words of others. As with our own lives, even more telling are their actions.

Rob Hewitt
Albemarle County, Virginia
August 2002

I can only begin to acknowledge all of the people who have offered their help, encouragement, advice, wisdom and patience. I am sure there must be several who are absent from the record below. Please forgive me for not keeping a better list or having a better memory. Your help was often so timely.

Before I ever began working on this project, the Margaret Grattan Weaver Foundation had hired Cathy Baugh, a Harrisonburg resident with a Master's degree in history to begin the research. Not only did she begin, she continued, wanting to see it through. I have often called her with an obscure question about some long-forgotten group, and she has proven to be a diligent and resourceful colleague. My work began with the Virginia Foundation for the Humanities, which oversaw the project for the Weaver Foundation. Through a 22-month fellowship, I had the opportunity to talk and think and laugh with many very fine scholars working along similar lines. In addition, there were many good conversations with their very gracious staff. I am grateful for their support and trust, especially for that of VFH director Rob Vaughan who gave me a broad place to grow and learn. Martha Caldwell of the Weaver Foundation was also a tremendous support throughout.

Especially, I would like to thank my family. It is sometimes difficult to understand how a big person can be very busy when they are sitting in a chair, or to talk with them when you don't know if the person they just casually mentioned was someone at the grocery store or a person from the 18th century. I hope I have not been as grumpy as I think I have been sometimes, and I hope my lap was not in front of a computer too much.

Most important, my family reminded me that this project could be completed - not in my own strength, which can accomplish nothing of lasting value, but in the strength of the eternal God whom I serve. I cannot tell you how many times I was looking for a certain piece of information, or had a specific question and was able to find the answer very quickly and often "out of the blue." The amount of material was frequently overwhelming to me and I was sometimes quite discouraged, but He could see the entire picture from start to finish. I was honored to be a part of the process. May He alone receive all praise.

acknowledgements

Nelson Alexander, Diane Stephens
Cooks Creek Presbyterian

Fred Anderson, Darlene Slater
Virginia Baptist Historical Society, Richmond, VA

Marie Koontz Arrington
Mountain Valley United Methodist Church, Rockingham County, VA

Terry Barkley, Ruth Greenawalt, Lisa Wilson
Bridgewater College Library and Archives

Gary Bauserman
Luray, VA

Debbie Bear, Mary Taffet
Gibbons, Yancy, Bear Family Letters

Dick Berg, Dianne Russell
Evangelical & Reformed Church Archives

Nina Mae Bible
Mt. Zion Church of the Brethren

Casey and Cathy Billhimer
Elkton, VA

Charles Blair
Mossy Creek Presbyterian Church

Emmert Bittinger
Bridgewater, VA

Lois Bowman, Harold Huber
Menno Simons Historical Library

Dorothy Boyd-Rush, Clive Hallman
James Madison University

Leila Boyer
Glen Burnie Museum, Winchester, VA

Keith Brown
Virginia Synod Lutheran Archives, Salem, VA

John M. Burner
Brown Memorial United Church of Christ

Becky Chapman, Doug Hill
Asbury United Methodist Church

Lynn Conway
Georgetown University Archives, Washington, DC

Fred Cooper, Nelson and Mary Belle Dove, Tom Reynolds, Neil and Mildred Showalter, Evelyn Stiteler
Harrisonburg Baptist Church

LaMar Crosby, Dorothy Harpine
Fellowhip United Methodist Church

Dane David
Good Printers, Bridgewater, VA

John B. Davis
Augusta County Court House

Warren Denton
Harrisonburg, VA

Tracey Del Duca, Jocelyne Rubinett, Mark Shenise
Drew University Library, Madison, NJ

Janet Baugher Downs, Jane Wenger
Mill Creek Church of the Brethren

Robert & Lois Emswiler
Linville United Church of Christ

Michael Erkel
Crozet, VA

Ellen Eslinger
DePaul University, Chicago, IL

Betty & Charles Foltz, Clifford Allen and Georgia Foltz
Shenandoah, VA

Mrs. Nancy Garber
Harrisonburg, VA

Edith Garrison, Virginia Miller
Port Republic Methodist Church, Port Republic, VA

Edith H. Good
First United Methodist Church, Broadway, VA

Karen Grindal, John Sellers, Faye Witters
Harrisonburg-Rockingham Historical Society, Dayton, VA

June Good Hulvey
St. Jacob's/Spaders Lutheran Church

acknowledgements

Al Keim
Eastern Mennonite University, Harrisonburg, VA

Bob Kirchman
Staunton, VA

Kenneth Kite
Elkton, VA

Mary Elizabeth Kite
Elkton United Methodist Church, Elkton, VA

Ken Kline, Keith May
Kline & May Realty, Harrisonburg, VA

Jim Lehman
Virginia Mennonite Conference

Jean Lindsay
Broadway, VA

Dale MacAllister
Singers Glen, VA

Mrs. Ollie McWilliams
Rockingham County, VA

Jody Meyerhoeffer
Dayton, VA

Gordon Miller
James Madison University, Harrisonburg, VA

Melvin L. Miller
St. Paul's Lutheran Church, Shenandoah, VA

Kristen Mitrisin
American Tract Society, Garland, TX

Max Moeller
Historical Society of Pennsylvania, Philadelphia, PA

Eli Moore
Waynesboro, VA

Sara Mummert
Lutheran Theological Seminary at Gettysburg, PA

Gail Nardi
Bremo Bluff, VA

Randy Neuman
United Brethren Historical Center, Huntington, IN

Deborah Pugh
Methodist Archives, Randolph-Macon College, Ashland, VA

Pat Turner Ritchie
Winchester, VA

Jason Robson, Graphic artist
Waynesboro, VA

Jim Rush
Zion Mennonite Church

Anne Salsich
Western Reserve Historical Society, Cleveland, OH

Edwin Schell, Suni Johnson
Archives of the Baltimore-Washington Conference, Baltimore, MD

Ted Schulz
Shepherd of the Valley Lutheran Church, Bridgewater, VA

Nan Sellers
Bethlehem United Church of Christ, Tenth Legion, VA

Nancy Sorrels
Augusta County, VA

Warren Souder
Martin Luther Lutheran Church, Bergton, VA

Bruce Souders
Shenandoah University, Winchester, VA

Jewell Spangler
University of Calgary, Alberta, Canada

John and Nancy Branner Stewart
New Market, VA

Dan and Julia Stickley
Cross Keys, VA

Garnett R. and Lela A. Turner
Fulks Run, VA

William "Herb" Warble
McGaheysville United Methodist Church

acknowledgements

Agnes Weaver
Edom, VA

Jennifer Wood, Beth Fauber, Cathey Morton
Wood & Associates Inc., Staunton, VA

J. B. Yount
Waynesboro, VA

and also to the many helpful people at

Alderman Library, *University of Virginia*

Augusta County Court House, *Staunton, VA*

Augusta County Public Library, *Fishersville, VA*

Carrier Library, James Madison University, *Harrisonburg, VA*

Library of Virginia, *Richmond, VA*

Massanutten Regional Library, *Harrisonburg, VA*

Museum of American Frontier Culture, *Staunton, VA*

Presbyterian Historical Society, *Philadelphia, PA*

Rockingham County Court House, *Harrisonburg, VA*

Shenandoah Presbytery, *Harrisonburg, VA*

Virginia Historical Society, *Richmond, VA*

Waynesboro Public Library, *Waynesboro, VA*

table of contents

HEADWATERS
ORIGINS TO 1750

CONFLUENCE
1750 - 1800

table of contents

RAPIDS
1800 - 1850

CATARACTS
1850 - CONCLUSION

HEADWATERS

ORIGINS TO 1750

Every stream has its source, its open spring.
The settlers who came to the Shenandoah Valley
were no exception. Each brought with them
a distinct culture and understanding of faith,
one which would be shaped and molded
in their new Virginia home.

OUT OF THE FIRE

Perhaps it was summer. By then, barring a sudden thunderstorm, the streams would be safely within their banks, having sent their fullness from the spring thaw well on its way to the Atlantic. The travellers would take the paths plodded out long ago by small herds of buffalo and large, red deer in search of fresh pasture — trails used by the men, women and children who were here before them. And they would follow the river.

There were probably some who thought Adam Mueller a bit foolhardy for venturing far from the growing Pennsylvania communities, out into the wild Virginia frontier. Yet here, beyond the great blue ridge of mountains, the valley had seemed to open its arms in welcome. Even the river here seemed in no hurry to leave, wandering north with carefree turns, dragging its wide footprints in the sweet, dark earth.

After a journey of several days, the Muellers had found themselves not far from the broad south fork of that river. A large creek fed by generous springs presented a wide meadow, promising a good return for their efforts with the fallow bottom land. Come spring these grasslands would be a

HAWKSBILL VALLEY
in present-day Page County, Virginia, where the Mueller family first settled.

field of color and motion, a welcome tribute to new life. This is where they would start again. This was finally home.[1]

Standing on the valley floor, they could watch the long, rolling lines of the blue ridge meet the edge of eastern sky, descending quietly into cool, green hollows, then reaching to the bare ledges of a great stony mountain. To the west, the peaked head and almost straight-ridged back of another range separated them from the broad valley beyond as far as the eye could see.

In some ways, this place with its open land and gentle back of mountains was like another Adam Mueller had known, distanced not so much by thousands of miles, but by an almost irresistible liberty from the conflicts that had driven thousands away from it. Though he had left that home, he carried its story with him, a story that had shaped the lives of many who would join him, on both sides of the peaked mountain.

———

Adam Mueller was born in 1703 in the tiny German village of Schriesheim, a col-lection of homes and ruins spilling over the western edge of a mountainous plateau. Here was "the garden of Germany," where spring came a few weeks earlier than for the rest of the country. The old mountain road — The Bergstrasse — passed through here, skirting the quickly rising slopes of vineyards and orchards at a perfect level, at just a height to offer a broad view of the well-tended Rhine River valley stretching far into the west.[2]

The Romans had built this road. Beyond it to the north and east ran their 330-mile earth and stonework barricade, raised against the threat of barbarian invaders.[3] The legions had been forced to retreat from this valley centuries ago, but even in the year of Adam Mueller's birth, its people were confronting a more enduring and tenacious legacy of that rule — the Holy Roman Empire.

When Constantine and his co-regent Licinius ended the vicious persecution of Christians throughout the Roman Empire in 313, they began a commingling of church and state that would propel the future of Europe and its colonies for the next fifteen hundred years. Before long, Christianity was not merely tolerated, it had become the exclusive religion of the Empire, and those who dared to differ from it would face an undetermined punishment by the state.[4] Seemingly emboldened by the new policy, at least one church bishop used a civil leader to have someone put to death on charges of heresy. The bishop was excommunicated from the church, but his use of force to settle issues of faith was merely the beginning of a long and vicious affair.[5]

Applying Christian principles did bring a solution to some of Rome's more public moral issues — giving greater dignity to women and bringing an end to the murderous gladiatorial contests — but under threat of force, it is questionable how many Roman citizens truly responded to the message of Jesus Christ. "For by grace are you saved through faith," the first Christian missionary to Rome had preached three hundred years earlier, "and this is not your own doing, it is the gift of God." All the laws and powers of earth would not be able to make it otherwise.[6]

Only thirty years after Christian practice had been commanded throughout the Empire, in A.D. 410 the Germanic Goths breached the Roman defenses and laid waste to the imperial city. As the new political capital moved hundreds of miles to the east, the Roman bishop took increasing responsibility for the care of the city and its people. Eventually, he assumed the title of "Pope" — father. Yet despite his position of authority and the respect he received from so many, the Pope remained vulnerable to the armies of power-hungry leaders.

Schriesheim likely began as a settlement of the Franks, a Germanic people who had once been a threat to the Romans. In the middle of the eighth century a Frankish king forced the nobleman in that area to "donate" all of his lands, goods, and vassals to the local monastery, Ellwangen.[7] Although this compromised the position of the monastery as a place to renounce earthly cares and seek greater devotion to God, it simply reflected the newest assertions of the church hierarchy, namely that the palace, crown, lands, and authority of the old Roman Empire had been given to the head of the church of Rome, a gift from no less than the Emperor Constantine himself.[8]

Not long after Ellwangen took charge of the lands at Schriesheim, the armies of the Frankish King Charlemagne restored the exiled Pope Leo III to his position in Rome.

In gratitude for his efforts in promoting the spread of Christianity — though often with military force — on Christmas Day of the year 800 Leo crowned Charlemagne emperor of a "holy" Roman Empire.

After Charlemagne's dynasty came to an end, the title of "Holy Roman Emperor" was claimed by a continual progression of German kings. Eventually, by the mid-fourteenth century, the wearer of this lofty crown had to be voted in by a handful of politically powerful electors. Schriesheim had come under the charge of the Elector Palatine, who ruled an area of the Rhine and Neckar River valleys northwest from Heidelberg.[9]

By then, the monastery of Ellwangen had well secured its position in Schriesheim. Generally speaking, the Roman church's hierarchy had become quite good at maintaining both money and power, and some of its own priests began to speak out against it. "In the present day nothing is sought throughout the whole world save presents and profits, gains and honors, marks of favor and carnal lusts," declared Stephen, a priest from Prague speaking before an official council. "Ignoramuses, incapables, and worthless men are promoted to the highest spiritual offices."[10]

Despite his unadorned candor, it was not Stephen who found the ire of church leaders, but his bishop — Jan Hus. The bishop's book, *De Ecclesia*, criticized the clergy for liking to rule as secular lords, and suggested it might be the prerogative of civil authorities to withhold the clergy's tithes, public taxes collected for their maintenance. In many respects, Hus was echoing the ideas of a priest across the English Channel, John Wyclif, so much so that he and his followers were known as "Wyclifites." Though supported by the Holy Roman Emperor, in 1415 Hus was called before a church council in Rome and burned at the stake. Some of Hus's followers tried to repel force with force, but they were physically outmatched.[11] Three years later in a letter to the Palatine Elector Lewis, the new Holy Roman Emperor affirmed his intentions "to root out the novelty which has arisen in that place from the Wyclifites."[12]

By the end of that century, the parish of Schriesheim began complaining about its own clergy. They were neglectful in things relating to the Mass — the worship service

5

— and frequently were not present at all, the parishioners cited. One priest, Peter von Bolanden, was an active participant in the fashionable humanist circle at nearby Heidelberg.

In just a few years the unrest would spread so rapidly, the Pope himself would mourn the "fire with which…all the world is now ablaze!"[13] In Schriesheim and the Palatinate, they would feel the flames twice.

———

One fall day in 1517, a professor at Germany's Wittenberg University posted some ideas he wanted to publicly debate. Mainly, they concerned the sale of indulgences — written pardons from the Pope that were said to remove the penalty of sin — now actively being hawked to raise money for the construction of St. Peter's Cathedral in Rome. As the professor had watched peasants spend their last coins purchasing these so-called pardons, he tried approaching the priests about it, but with no results. Public debate was a logical next step.

Though the writings of Wyclif and Hus might be burned to suppress their circulation, the invention of Johannes Gutenberg had forever altered that possibility. With the aid of the printing press, Martin Luther's "Ninety-Five Theses" spread throughout Germany with amazing speed. "It is a miracle to me," Luther wrote in a letter to Pope Leo X the following year, "by what fate it has come about that this single disputation of mine should…have gone out into very nearly the whole land."[14] Still, he would not recant what he had written. Luther did not challenge the Pope's authority, but he did call into account the priests who used the Pope's name and the threat of heresy to cow people into belief.

For Luther, the issue was not academic, but deeply personal. Throughout his early life, like the peasants who had impoverished themselves purchasing indulgences, he had sought to earn God's favor through the prescriptions of the Roman church. Going without food, performing good works, even becoming a priest had not calmed his doubts. One day, while reading Paul's letter to the Romans, he saw the answer: "the just shall live by faith." Faith *alone*, Luther added, not cold assent to doctrinal formulas, but an active, living trust in the God of mercy and faithfulness.

Despite Luther's apologetic letter, the Pope declared him excommunicated from the church, and Holy Roman Emperor Charles V convened the Imperial Council at the Palatinate city of Worms to carry out the sentence.[15] At his defense, Luther made clear another key principle of reform. "Unless I am convicted of error by the testimony of Scripture…and my conscience is taken captive by God's word, I cannot and will not recant anything."[16] *Faith alone* and *Scripture alone* — these were the rallying cries of reformers throughout the turbulent years to come.

For the next several decades, Germany was restless. The peasant revolt of 1526 — condemned by Luther though doubtless inspired by the new challenge to traditional authority — was only the beginning. Several German princes embraced Lutheran reforms, gaining control of properties and powers in their territories long claimed by the Roman church. These kinds of stakes brought their sincerity into question, and with German unity seriously at risk, war broke out among the fractured states. Finally,

in 1555, the Peace of Augsburg declared that each local ruler could allow the type of worship he himself chose — either Lutheran or Roman.[17]

The following year when the new Elector Palatine took office, Schriesheim began to make a switch to the Lutheran camp. Interestingly, very little changed, at least on the surface. The church, the clergy, even many aspects of the worship service were kept the same as they had been all along. Luther was not interested in getting rid of any ritual or belief in the Roman church that Scripture did not specifically prohibit. Yet there were many essential differences, each spelled out in a written explanation of Lutheran beliefs called the Augsburg Confession. Centuries later, in Germany as well as in Adam Mueller's new home in Virginia, it would remain the standard for defining Lutheran orthodoxy.[18]

One central point of departure was the Lutheran understanding of the Eucharist, the meal shared by Christ with his disciples which represented his sacrificial death for the forgiveness of sin. Since Jesus had directed his followers to celebrate this meal until His return, the Eucharist was a central ele-

Reforming or reviving the Church was not original to the day of Hus, Luther, or Menno Simons, not even to those we call "Protestants," but at the heart of almost every reformation or revival was a call to personal faith, a living trust in a living God. Even during the Reformation, such faith could easily become supplanted with adherence to a creed or by the performance of religious duty.

Martin Luther found the answer to his own dissatisfaction with religious duty by reading the Bible. In particular, he found special joy in Paul's letter to the Romans, which he considered "the chief part of the New Testament...the purest gospel." In the introduction to his commentary on Romans — a selection that would have an impact on many, including Methodist leader John Wesley and Shenandoah Valley missionary preacher Paul Henkel — Luther gave a clear sense of the kind of faith that he believed makes one right with God.

Faith is not the human notion and dream that some people call faith. When they see that no improvement of life and no good works follow — although they can hear and say much about faith — they fall

ment of the Roman Mass. For several centuries now, the Roman church had declared that as the priest consecrated or set apart the bread and wine, those elements became in substance the actual body and blood of Jesus, a view called transubstantiation.[19] Luther took issue with this, saying that the body and blood of Jesus were *mystically* present in the bread and wine, but the idea that a substantive change took place was Scripturally unacceptable.

The Eucharist — or communion service — was at the heart of Christian fellowship, and the Lutheran departure from the Roman view was not simply a matter of doctrinal hair-splitting. Roman priests by this time had stopped offering the wine to their parishioners, claiming that only they themselves could receive this element — the blood of Jesus for the forgiveness of sins. Holding this back, just as they held back the Scriptures by keeping them preserved in Latin, was to Luther just another of several ways the Roman church attempted to block people from the means of grace.

Luther understood that the Roman church had insulated itself from reform by masquerading its hierarchy as the "spiritual estate," aloof from the judgments and rule of the "temporal estate" composed of princes, lords, artisans and farmers. According to Scripture, Luther countered, every Christian believer is part of the "spiritual estate." What was more, in the words of St. Peter himself, long held by the Roman church as the first Pope, every believer is a priest: "You are a royal priesthood, a priestly kingdom."[20] It was the right and responsibility of every Christian — not just those whom the Roman church chose — to read and understand the Scriptures, and to apply it actively to daily life. This renewed understanding of "the priesthood of all believers" almost guaranteed the variety of beliefs and expressions of faith that would continue to emerge, and which Luther could scarcely have imagined.

Lutheranism did not last long in Schriesheim. Within just a few years the village had changed its affiliation yet again, not back to the Roman church, but to an expression of the reformation long growing on the borders of the Palatinate. In France, a young man by the name of John Calvin, seemingly on his way to becoming a priest in the Roman church, had come to many of the same conclusions as Martin Luther. For a time, the reformers held secret night meetings in France, and Calvin published some of his ideas. Doubtless encouraged by the lack of official response, they distributed circulars referring to the Mass as "pompous and conceited" in which "our Lord is so outrageously blasphemed," boldly posting one on the bedroom door of the French king himself, Francis I. Enraged, Francis stormed into church carrying a blazing torch and ordered thirty-two of the heretics to be burned alive at the four most public places in the city.[21]

In the aftermath, Calvin fled his native France and sought refuge in Basel, just across the French border in the Rhine Valley of Switzerland. There, a similar reform had been taking place largely under the leadership of Huldreich Zwingli, a priest whose contact with Luther's ideas had caused him to see the need for reform — first personally, then in the Church at large. By 1529, the Swiss principalities of Zurich and Basel had abolished the Mass altogether.[22]

The Reformed ideas of Calvin and Zwingli did not differ all that much from Luther's. At the Colloquy of Marburg, where Zwingli and Luther met to hammer out their differences, the two agreed on fourteen of fifteen points, but on the fifteenth — the Eucharist — they parted company. Zwingli considered it a memorial meal, but Luther believed there was a true spiritual presence in the elements.[23] From that time on Luther considered Zwingli a heretic.

Though their differences in theology were not great, there was a vast difference in appearance and forms of worship. Unlike the Lutherans who held to many of the Roman church's traditions and styles not expressly forbidden in the Scriptures, Reformed adherents rejected all of the old traditions the Bible did not specifically initiate. In Schriesheim, though the move to Lutheranism signaled their alignment with the reformers, the switch to the Reformed position was far more visible. Now all decorations were removed from the church — candles, votive pictures and altars, crucifixes were suddenly gone. Gone also were the bells that used to call people to church, and familiar rituals such as the blessing of the fields. Even dancing and games were frowned upon as the life of parishioners was doctrinally proscribed to match the simple, unadorned interior of the church building itself.[24]

into the error of saying, "Faith is not enough; one must do works in order to be righteous and be saved." This is due to the fact that when they hear the gospel, they get busy and by their own powers create an idea in their heart which says, "I believe;" they take this then to be a true faith. But, as it is a human figment and idea that never reaches the depths of the heart, nothing comes of it either, and no improvement follows.

Faith, however, is a divine work in us which changes us and makes us to be born anew of God, John 1. It kills the old Adam and makes us altogether different men, in heart and spirit and mind and powers; and it brings with it the Holy Spirit. O it is a living, busy, active, mighty thing, this faith. It is impossible for it not to be doing good works incessantly. It does not ask whether good works are to be done, but before the question is asked, it has already done them, and is constantly doing them. Whoever does not do such works, however, is an unbeliever. He gropes and looks around for faith and good works, but knows neither

9

From Roman to Lutheran to Reformed, the religious life of the people in Schriesheim remained tied to the directives of the Elector Palatine. In that sense there had been no real change from the policies of the Roman church. One form of dominance was replaced by another. The people "believed" what they were told, and "worshipped" accordingly.[25] Of course that was not real faith in the eyes of the reformers, but raising your head in the face of the established order only made you an easier target.

———

When the Elector Palatine Frederick III embraced the Reformed faith, he introduced a new and illegal element within Germany. His influence and prestige enabled him to carry out his plan without interference, and the Heidelberg Confession he had commissioned became as important to the Reformed church as the Augsburg would be to the Lutherans. But with politics and religious establishment still so entwined, the system had its serious flaws. In practice certain leaders might exercise tolerance, but disagreements of belief were tantamount to treason, and public expressions of anything other than the state-approved system were not to be considered lightly.

Not far from Schriesheim lived members of a group whose convictions had brought them into such a conflict. Like the Lutherans and Reformed, they believed in the essentials — faith alone and Scripture alone. But their study of Scripture had led them to one fundamental difference: baptism was for adult believers in Jesus Christ, not for infant children. This is the practice they observed in the New Testament, and this is what they believed was necessary for them as well. Since most had been baptized as babies in the Roman or Lutheran or Reformed churches, they received baptism again, earning them the name re-baptizers — "Ana-baptists."

Zwingli himself was initially sympathetic with the Anabaptist view of baptism, but he soon settled into an understanding that both adults and infants could receive the sacrament.[26] From 1526 on, many Anabaptists in Switzerland were executed by drowning, a contemptuous mockery of their deeply held belief.

In 1535, several who styled themselves

as Anabaptists took part in an overthrow of the government of Münster, an independent German city nearly two hundred miles north of Schriesheim. In response, armies under the leadership of Lutheran and Roman Catholic princes came against the city and crushed the rebellion, executing the leaders and leaving their decaying bodies to disintegrate slowly in iron cages suspended above the entrance to the established church. The stigma of Muenster and its would-be rulers would remain etched in the minds of religious reformers for centuries, an epic to the folly of human efforts to effect the plan of God on their own initiative.[27]

Many of their faith and practice were gathered together in the north of Europe by a former Dutch priest named Menno Simons. Yet still bearing the disgrace of the radical element who had attempted to usurp

Righteousness, then, is such a faith. It is called "the righteousness of God" because God gives it, and counts it as righteousness for the sake of Christ our mediator...For as no one can give himself faith, neither can he take away his own unbelief. How, then, will he take away a single sin, even the very smallest? Therefore all that is done apart from faith, or in unbelief, is false; it is hypocrisy and sin, Romans 14, no matter how good a showing it makes.[Side 1]

SCHRIESHEIM
Showing the steeples of the Reformed church (left)
and the Roman church buildings.

the authorities in Muenster, they were hunted down and killed in many places on the Continent. A bounty of a hundred gold coins was offered for Menno's arrest, but even severe persecution did not dampen their zeal for spreading their message.[28]

As the church grew, it was organized under bishops responsible for a certain area, and by the spring of 1544, Menno's "Brief and Clear Confession" began to give order and structure to the ideas of many who followed him in his desire to serve Christ with their whole heart.[29] In contrast to the state establishments, the followers of Menno — Mennonists[30] as they would be called — held that the Church of Jesus was made up of those who put their faith and trust in him for the forgiveness of sin, regardless of their geographical location or religious label. Though they were to obey the government, they themselves were never to go to war or use physical force against their opponents.[31]

Rather, they should overcome evil by doing good, by loving their enemies. In the ensuing decades, as the governments of Europe fought war after war for supremacy and the "true faith," Mennonists would have only too many opportunities to live out that truth.

One of the most contested cities throughout these many wars was Heidelberg, Schriesheim's close neighbor, the cultural and political capital of the Palatinate. In 1630, Schriesheim became the gathering place for Swedish and Palatine troops. In mid-September, as recorded in the Reformed church book, the opposing army overran Schriesheim from the mountainside, plundering and setting houses on fire, and blowing up the church tower. A counterattack restored order, but Schriesheim, like many other places throughout Europe, had felt the hard fist of war.[32]

In 1648, the struggle that would be

"Oh, how easy it is to be a Christian, so long as the flesh is not put to the trial, or nothing has to be relinquished; then it is an easy thing to be a Christian."
— *Maeyken Wens, Anabaptist martyr writing from her prison cell, 1573*

called the Thirty Years War finally came to an end. Now, three different confessions would be allowed — Roman, Lutheran, and Reformed. But if this was a victory, it was a bleak one. Friends, family and relatives had been sacrificed in this struggle for politi-

THE PALATINATE
and neighboring areas after the Thirty Years War

cized theology. Some villages were left completely uninhabited. In terms of population alone, it would take Europe more than a century to recover.[33] In 1652, as part of the growing immigration to fill these vacant lands, Adam Mueller's grandfather — the carriage maker Hans Müller — moved to the mountainside village of Schriesheim.[34]

The Muellers were Reformed, but many of the new immigrants were not. Anabaptists came too, perhaps joining those of a like mind already settled in the Lambsheim area a few miles to the west where Adam Mueller's father would one day settle. There were still some restrictions. Anabaptists were allowed to stay in the Palatinate only if they paid a special tax and kept their meetings to twenty persons or less.[35] But at least there was a measured degree of freedom, far more than they had enjoyed in their own homeland.

Now, for the first time in almost nine hundred years, Schriesheim would lack a formal, confessional unity. But even with the new immigration, Reformed policies tended to dominate. In another twenty years, the Calvinist minister would bring the town back together under a single confession. By

that time, another war would have found its way into the Palatinate.[36]

The French king Louis XIV's war with Holland began in 1672 and soon swelled to include much of Europe. In October of the following year, a group of twenty attacked some men with their cattle near Schriesheim. The cry of alarm brought out all armed men in town. Two of the attacking force fled, but the villagers were able to take eighteen prisoners to Heidelberg.

In the summer of 1674, the French Marshall Turenne returned with more troops, and for four weeks Schriesheim was overrun by the "unbridled hordes."[37] Entire crops were destroyed, houses plundered, cattle taken away. On July 10, as recorded in the church book, the bell from the church tower was stolen and all of Schriesheim burned. More than half the homes in the town were destroyed. Even as cold weather approached, many families had still been unable to rebuild, and the houses that remained were left without windows. With no harvest and meager shelter, the residents of Schriesheim would have a difficult winter ahead.

Across the border in France, Louis XIV

continued his repressive measures against the French Reformed, dubbed "Huguenots." In October of 1685, the king who had claimed rule by divine right eliminated all tolerance for his Reformed subjects, and French dragoons poured through the countryside. Those who refused to convert to the Roman church were tortured and beaten.

Of those who managed to flee, many sought refuge in the Palatinate, perhaps later finding their way to the Reformed state of Holland or elsewhere. From there they travelled to all parts of the globe, some to Cape Town, Holland's new colony on the southern tip of Africa, and some to Ireland and points west. Pamphlets announcing the beauties and benefits of the English colony called Carolina had been circulating in France for some time. A group of Huguenots had settled there near Charleston several years ago. Soon afterward, a story ostensibly written as a travelogue spoke of another possible destination in the New World — Virginia.

Arriving in Virginia nearly eighty years after its founding, Durand of Dauphné found a land whose frontier was no farther than the fall line of its major rivers, scores of miles from the valley Adam Mueller and his neighbors would settle. Although its border reached as far west as the English claimed it should, he realized that only the inhabited eastern part deserved the designation Virginia. "The rest," he remarked, "although belonging to it has no name."[38]

The account of the French exile's travel contained a little something for everyone — pathos, romance, even a caveat against opportunists eager to take advantage of the refugees. In the end, it was perhaps no more than an intriguing advertisement for land — "the most beautiful, agreeable, and fertile country in all the West Indies." Ironically, the parcels for sale were apparently owned by some members of the church of Rome who had emigrated a few years earlier.[39]

Virginia did hold hope for the Huguenots, not to mention other Protestant refugees in Europe, but it would be on her own terms, and not for some years to come. For now, a much celebrated Huguenot minister — one of the exiles — had written in most convincing language that the Reformed church in France would be restored in the year 1689, and for some that was hope enough.[4]

If the year of 1689 held any hope for the Huguenots of Europe, it must have seemed buried in the snows of that savage winter. Seeking to establish the new claims of Louis XIV for the next ruler of the Palatinate, French troops under General Melac had overrun the region and were now attacking ordinary citizens with a fierce brutality. When they arrived at Schriesheim, the soldiers dragged household goods and cabinets into the street and set them on fire. They "took away and destroyed all things, mingling Corn, Flowers, Feathers, and all things together, thereby to render them useless." Afraid for their lives, many fled to the hills and rocks, despite the snow. Melac sent for them, assuring them no harm. Grateful and exhausted, many fell on their knees before him.[41]

When the war had ended eight years later, the people of the Palatinate thought to rebuild and enjoy their land and religion as before. But as one correspondent put it, "though the War is ended, yet the Wild Boars are ravaging our Vineyards."[42] The reference was to the policies of the new elector, John William, who had lately become a member of the Church of Rome. In 1698 he gave all three confessions — Catholics, Lutheran, and Reformed — the right to share all church buildings. In Schriesheim, this meant that the two dozen or so Lutheran and Catholic families had equal access to the Reformed church, used by some 140 families.[43] The new arrangement was strained to say the least. The Reformed populace was angered by the new laws, including the one that forbade "on pain of Death" any discussion of the eightieth question of the Heidelberg Confession addressing the divisive issue of "communion."[44]

"A new fire is kindled in the Palatinate," the correspondent lamented, "so that we Protestants are in as ill a case, as the French Reformed are in France, and worse than you were in England under the late King James."[45]

This sort of talk had ready ears among the English who had only recently emerged from a century and a half of religious conflict. Their previous king, James II, had become vastly unpopular for his strong Catholic position, and was now living in exile in France. For the time being, it seemed, England was standing with its own national church — the Anglican — a peculiarly English version of the Reformation with an equally peculiar history.

Despite the influence of Wyclif and others seeking to reform the Roman church, England's initial break from the old religion had more to do with fealty than faith. In 1534, the year so-called Anabaptists took control of Muenster, King Henry VIII of England decided to divorce his wife, Catherine, to marry Anne Boleyn in hopes of

"supreme head on earth of the English church," established the clergy under the Archbishop of Canterbury, and had the whole affair taken care of in short order. That same year, Henry had Anne tried and beheaded on charges of adultery, and the infamous monarch went on to marry the third of his six wives.

Ironically, Henry retained the title of "Defender of the Faith," bestowed by the

fathering a male heir. Since the Pope disapproved of this, the king declared himself the

Pope a few years earlier for Henry's treatise indicting the upstart professor Martin

Luther. Doctrinally, it was fitting enough. Though there may have been initial concessions to change, the Six Articles passed by Parliament in 1539 plainly affirmed the basic doctrines of the Roman church.[46] But Henry's capriciousness provided the catalyst for England's political and religious unrest for the next several decades, as one by one his estranged line of royal heirs took the throne.

During the reign of Edward VI — Henry's son who was crowned at age eleven and died before his sixteenth birthday — laws were passed requiring ministers to use the Book of Common Prayer, a decidedly Protestant order of worship. The next regent, Queen Mary, was the daughter of Henry's first wife, Catherine, and a devoted Catholic. During her short tenure, she had three hundred Protestant heretics burned at the stake. Following Mary was Elizabeth, daughter of Anne Boleyn. Over the next forty-five years of her reign, from 1558 through 1603, England again severed ties with Rome and made definite steps toward Protestant thought, including passage of an Anglican confession of faith known as the Thirty-Nine Articles.[47]

When the English colony of Virginia was founded at Jamestown in 1607, the only form of worship authorized in the new settlement was to be "according to the doctrine, rights, and religion now professed and established within our realme of England," and the first and largest building within the Jamestown fort was the Anglican church. For a time at least, the colonists met daily for prayers, with full services and a sermon once every Thursday, and twice on Sunday.[48]

As Virginia grew, it developed according to the Anglican system, establishing parishes — local jurisdictions with their own church building and clergyman. Each parish was served by a twelve-man governing body called a vestry, responsible for everything from paying the minister's salary and seeing to the needs of the poor, to confirming land boundaries and collecting an annual tax, known as the parish levy. Typically the richest and most influential land owners in their district, these vestrymen often held additional positions as militia officers and justices of the peace, giving them power in matters of the church, the military, and the civil government. In no small way, Virginia was unofficially ruled by this aristocracy, where power and position were frequently passed down to succeeding generations within the same families.

During the next hundred years — even though the position of Anglicanism as England's sole church would be challenged by individual reformers, civil war, and finally by James II himself — England became a refuge for many Protestant dissenters from the rest of Europe. By the time James II reached the throne in 1685 when Louis XIV revoked the Edict of Nantes and sent the Huguenots flying, there were nearly three dozen French congregations already established in and around London.[49]

It would take an invasion by his son-in-law, William of Orange, to remove James from the throne and reestablish the Anglican version of Protestantism. But with the rise of William and his co-regent, Mary, to the English throne, there also came a new policy for those who dissented from the state's position on theology. The Act of Toleration passed by Parliament in 1689 made allowance for almost all varieties of Christianity except "Papist," that is, Roman Catholic. Though imperfect in many regards, it was at least a beginning.[50]

It would be another ten years before the Act of Toleration was even mentioned in the Virginia code. Besides the delay, it would suffer the same problems as other British laws in the colony, laws that were not always enforced in the frontier colony of Virginia as they were in merry old England.[51] This milestone of religious toleration would be debated in Virginia until the eve of the Revolution — not simply in its particulars, but whether the law had any force at all within Virginia's territory.[52]

Be that as it may, recognition of the Toleration Act came just in time for Virginia to receive its first official colony of dissenters, a group of French Huguenots arriving with the blessing of King William himself.

———

On July 23, 1700, the London ship "Mary & Ann" entered the mouth of the James River. On board were two hundred French Protestant refugees — Huguenots — sent by the express order of King William. They were quickly settled far from the main population, about twenty miles above the falls, a curiously inhospitable spot for those in search of refuge. "There is a great deal of good Land and unpatented, where they may at present be all together," wrote Governor Nicholson in defense of his decision, "which we thought would be best for his Majesty's Service and Interests, and that they would be astrengthening to the Frontiers."[53]

"Astrengthening Virginia's frontiers" was foremost in the minds of many early governors. As those responsible for the safety of the tiny outpost belonging to the mighty British crown, they were well aware of the colony's vulnerabilities. The Roman Catholic powers of France and Spain, notorious for their aggressive political policies and fierce persecution of Protestants, had established colonies of their own — France to the north and west in Canada and Mississippi, Spain to the south in Florida. Only two years after the Huguenots had settled on the James, word reached Virginia that Britain had declared war on both of these European rivals. In no way was the colony prepared. Though Virginia claimed over ten thousand militia, fewer than a quarter of them were suitably armed or had sufficient ammunition. Besides

that, they were living "at so great a distance from one another, and have so many Rivers & Creeks to pass," the colonial authorities bemoaned, "that it will be very difficult to gett any competent number together to make head ag[ain]st. an Enemy."[54]

In addition to her older European foes, Virginia had found fresh opposition in the New World. Conflicts with various tribes of Native Americans had existed almost since the beginning, and there showed no signs of change. Virginia had thus far subjugated a number of "tributary" tribes whose 250 or so fighting men were pledged to defend the colony's interests, but greater threats loomed in the south with the two thousand warriors of the Tuscarora nation, and the even larger five-nation Iroquois confederacy to the north.[55]

Governor Nicholson's choice of settlement for the Huguenots was a silent testimony to the ongoing antagonism. When a group of Monocans were charged with making raids on nearby English, a military contingent was sent against them and the village was destroyed. Perhaps only a handful of those from "Manakin Town" had survived. From the colony's standpoint, the land was no doubt easily cleared and in a strategic position as an outpost. Nicholson anticipated the Huguenots "would quickly make a settlement, not only for themselves, but to receive others when his majesty shall be graciously pleased to send them."[56]

More French did come, but whether or not they provided an intimidating military presence is uncertain. They were, however, industrious, and the land was eagerly productive. Though settled a score of

miles from the nearest river transportation, they had little trouble getting their goods to market. "Things that are grown are there in such abundance that many Englishmen come a distance of 30 miles to get fruit," observed the Swiss traveler Franz Luis Michel. As an emissary from the canton of Berne, Michel was searching for some suitable land upon which to settle a group of Swiss. He was especially interested in the freedom of worship and other liberties

EARLY COLONIES
of Anglican Dissenters in Virginia (Proposed & Actual)

allowed the French dissenters. Not only were these Reformed cousins of his exempt from taxes for seven years, they had "a preacher there paid by the king."[57]

True enough, King William had supplied the Huguenots with £3000 sterling in addition to their free passage, and despite some grousing by Virginians resentful of this intrusion upon their charity, many had added their own contributions. The Huguenots were set apart as a distinct parish named after their benefactor, King William. Their minister, Monsieur De Joux, like all other priests in the colony "was admitted into holy orders by my Lord Bishop of London."[58] In appearance, they would resemble the prescribed outline of the Anglican Church in Virginia, yet because of their distance from Williamsburg and the insulation provided by their French language, they doubtless had some latitude to hold to their own particular beliefs!

As a step further, the House of Burgesses passed a law to naturalize these new Virginians and grant them the rights available to all other British subjects in the colony. Though naturalization would not require the standard oaths of allegiance to the Crown, it did insist upon the litmus test for Protestant orthodoxy: renouncing the Roman Catholic doctrine of transubstantiation, the belief that the bread and wine served in the communion service became in substance the body and blood of Christ. As proof of their renunciation, all those who wished to be naturalized were required to present a certificate from a duly licensed Protestant minister that they had received communion *in the Protestant form* within the past six months.[59]

The new laws were not just for the benefit of the Huguenots, but more generally for the "speedy settling and peopling of Virginia by persons of different nations." It further promised a monopoly of trade for anyone who established commerce with native Americans west of the Blue Ridge.

By 1709, Michel and his associate Christopher deGrafenried were applying for a grant of land from the British Crown. Not only was the government of Berne interested in settling their own people, they were looking to "unload" several Anabaptist prisoners in the New World as well. Prisoners were transported as far as Holland, but the authorities there — sympathetic to the

a hope and a future

cause of the beleaguered Anabaptists —
would allow them to go no farther.[60]

About this same time, thousands of
Germans were leaving their homes for
England. Repeated destruction of their land
and livelihood had been followed by a fright-
eningly cold winter in which birds were said
to have fallen dead from the air, frozen in
mid-flight. With their prospects for the
future looking as beaten as their grape vines
and fruit trees, a handsomely published invitation to emigrate to England created an exo-
dus of perhaps as many as ten thousand
within a few months. Regardless of their
point of origin, all of these newcomers were
given the name "Palatine," a word long associated in England with misery and torment.
Now, the problem became where to put the
refugees. The Germans still had no home.
Some were sent to the English colony of
New York, many of whom eventually made
their way to Pennsylvania and points south.

Three years later, the Queen finally gave
the Swiss a grant of land for a colony of their
own above the falls of the Potomac. When
deGrafenried arrived, he found it claimed
not only by the Crown, but also by the pro-
prietors of Maryland and the "Northern
Neck," the latter a 6 million acre grant of land
between the headwaters of the Potomac and
Rappahannock rivers given by James I.[61]

Disheartened, deGrafenried returned to
London. There he found a group of Germans
collected to work a silver mine Michel had
told him about. In apparent confusion, the
miners and their families had been sent on
to England to await transport. But
deGrafenried had lost all confidence in
Michel, now. Since he had discussed the
issue before with Governor Spotswood, after
trying to secure some employment for the
miners in London, deGrafenried sent them
on to Virginia, representing matters as best
he could.[62]

When they arrived in the spring of
1714, Spotswood settled them at a place he
named Germanna, above the falls of the
Rappahannock River. From his first days as
governor, Spotswood had considered it "a
peculiar blessing to the country to have but
few of any kind of dissenters," and though he
apparently risked the "same Censure" as others had undergone for transporting foreign-
ers into the colony, for the governor the tim-
ing could not have been better. An agreement with the Tuscaroras to defend the fron-

tier against the northern tribes of Iroquois had just fallen through, and the new arrivals would fit the bill nicely. Spotswood built a fort at Germanna and furnished it with two cannons, which he figured would "awe the Stragling partys of Northern Indians, and be a good Barrier for all that part of the Country." Since he said it had cost him £150 to transport them in addition to two years subsistence, he did not think it wrong to put them to good work in beginning Virginia's first ironworks on land that he leased to them.[63]

Conditions in Germany did not improve, and in 1717 more fled their native land in the wake of famine. Moving down the Rhine toward Amsterdam, they took passage to London before making their way across the Atlantic. For one group of passengers, that stop proved disastrous.[64] Their ship's captain was arrested for bad debts and detained for weeks on English soil. Abandoned in a strange land, the Germans were forced to consume most of the ship's provisions during their long wait. At last, the captain was released and they set sail. With little left to eat, many starved on that dismal voyage. Those left alive were driven off course by a severe storm. Instead of landing in Pennsylvania, their port of arrival was Virginia.

As often happened, the ship's captain sold his passengers as indentured servants to whoever would take them. It wasn't slavery — Virginia knew that trade all too well — but they too would be forced to labor in exchange for their passage money. For almost eight years Governor Spotswood put the refugees to work, settling them near Germanna.[65]

For a time, these Lutherans shared religious services with the first colony of German Reformed. A trip to England two

a hope and a future

years after their arrival to look for a minister of their own nation netted them twenty-five copies of the Anglican Prayer Book in High German.[66] After seven years, Spotswood sued several of the settlers for non-performance of a contract they claimed to have never seen. Once freed from their alleged obligations to Spotswood, by 1725 they had moved west to a spot much closer to the Blue Ridge of mountains. There, on a beautiful rise of land not far from the Robinson River, they built a log church that became known as the "German chapel."[67]

Again, two members of the congregation went to Europe to bring back a Lutheran minister to serve in Virginia, and again they were unsuccessful.[68] It would be another eight years before someone would arrive to help them. By then, a pastor would not only be needed for themselves, but also for those who would settle west of the Ridge, their German neighbors from the colony of Pennsylvania.[69]

———

Pennsylvania had from the start been

a sort of experiment, a "Holy experiment" as its founder William Penn once put it. Unlike Virginia, a Crown colony owned by the British monarch, Penn's colony was a proprietorship — a land grant — and Penn was under no obligation to maintain the established church. In fact, he himself was a dissenter, a Quaker, and it was his plan "to lay the foundation of a free colony for all mankind," to serve God's truth and people "that an example may be set up to the nations."[70]

The Quakers, or Society of Friends as they called themselves, had arisen in England in the mid-1600's. Their leader was George Fox, a forthright man who proclaimed that formal religious services with their written prayer books and worship services were simply "talking with other men's words." Fox believed his own calling was to "bring people off from all the world's religions...which stood in forms without power."[71]

As part of his commission to treat all as equal in the sight of God, Fox felt restrained from giving deference to any one, "rich or poor, great or small." He believed it was wrong to take off his hat in the presence of

Pious Desires

The spiritual fires of reformation quickly chilled to the gray coals of formalism. German princes, enlisted to purge their lands of Roman traditions, ruled the church through official ministerial committees. For many, the reformation of the Roman church had resulted in a change in form without a change of heart. During hymns and prayers, people walked about the sanctuary sharing the latest news and gossip, and frequently they would fall asleep during long sermons that stretched their ability to comprehend, much less endure. In less than a century, the church had fallen right back into the patterns it had sought to escape.

From his boyhood, Philip Jacob Spener seemed to be headed in a different direction. The books he read insisted that the Christian life was not "mere science and theory," but an "actual practice of faith and godliness" dependent on the new life of Christ within the believer. When Spener became a minister, he realized the reformation of lives depended on more than sermons and singing. It required the extension and application of a biblical principal Luther had emphasized — the priesthood of all believers.

"How much good it would do," he preached in a 1669 sermon, "if good

25

his "betters," and spoke to people of all ranks using the informal "thee" and "thou" reserved for friends instead of the more circumspect "you." These were not the central points of Fox's faith and message, but within the strict hierarchy of seventeenth-century English society, they were perhaps the more irritating. One judge to whom Fox did not proffer the expected courtesies inquired whether Fox was insane or just a simpleton![72]

Though many may have had difficulty understanding some of Fox's expressions of belief, particularly his emphasis on the "inner light," Penn had taken those values and established a colony based on equality and freedom of religious expression to "all Persons living in this Province, who confess and acknowledge the One Almighty and Eternal God, to be the Creator, Upholder and Ruler of the World, and that hold themselves obliged in Conscience to live peaceably and justly in Civil Society."[73]

It was equality that distinguished Pennsylvania from Virginia. Just as the Anglican church supported the aristocracy who composed its governing vestries, legislature and council, so Quakerism, with its egalitarian ideals, supported the "common-

folk." Mennonists, who shared the Quakers refusal to take oaths and bear arms, began arriving only two years after the colony was begun and found a safe haven there. In a short time Pennsylvania became a diverse mixture of Quakers, German Reformed, Presbyterian, Mennonists, Lutherans, Huguenots, Baptists, and a variety of other religious persuasions. The New World, physically separated from the Old by a sea voyage of six weeks or more, lent itself to a spirit of independence from European traditions and authority in matters of belief. In free-minded Pennsylvania, small, almost unknown, denominations and sects proliferated.

Among these were a small minority known simply as the "Brethren," led by Alexander Mack, a native of Schriesheim in the Palatinate. His son, Johannes, was baptized in the Reformed church there in 1703, only months before young Adam Mueller.[74] Soon afterward Mack's family was attracted by a renewal movement known as pietism.

Associated with the writings of Philip Jacob Spener and others, pietists sought a revitalized and active relationship with Jesus Christ. The reformation churches, once so vital in promoting personal faith, now easily

a hope and a future

languished in ritual and doctrine as arm of the state. Some pietists sought renewal within their own church traditions. Others, sometimes called radical pietists or separatists, left to form groups of their own. But at the heart of every pietist group were the home meetings, the *collegia pietatis*, when people would gather to confess their sin, pray, read Scripture, and sing.

At Mack's invitation, the radical pietist leader Ernst Hochman and several of his associates had visited Schriesheim in the summer of 1706, preaching in the Mack's home and on the streets, distributing literature to any and all. The Mack name was among the most influential in that place — Alexander's father had served twice as the town's mayor and the family had for decades been leaders of the Reformed church. Needless to say, Alexander's support of Hochman was not welcome news to the Reformed Consistory in Heidelberg. Within a few days, Heidelberg's chief police officer arrived and broke up the meeting then going on at the Mack's house. That same evening, the Macks left Schriesheim, never to return.[75]

Eventually they found their way to Schwarzenau, a German principality known as a refuge for religious dissenters, which had welcomed the Huguenots in 1685. Hochman's home was here as well — the Friedensberg, "citadel of peace." Almost two years after their flight from Schriesheim, Alexander, his wife Anna, and six others were baptized in the River Eder, signaling the beginning of a new group. Pietism was not necessarily associated with Anabaptist principles, but the eight who joined in this "covenant of conscience" had a keen interest in imitating the practice of the first-century Christians. Specifically, these Brethren adopted the practice of "trine immersion," a baptism that required the individual to be submerged three times, once for each Person of the Trinity — the Father, the Son, and the Holy Spirit. In time, this distinctive practice would earn them the name "Tunkers," or as the English would have it, "Dunkers."[76]

There were only a few havens for pietists of any name or variety throughout all of Europe, and soon Schwarzenau began looking less and less like a long-term home. In 1720 the little group moved to Friesland on the North Sea, and nine years later took fifty-five families and their fortunes to the unmolested freedom of Pennsylvania.

by this mark, how difficult it will be to find even a small number of real and true disciples of Christ among the great mass of nominal Christians!

Instead of love, though, many affiliated with pietistic gatherings began to be critical of the national churches and their ministers. Refusing to worship with their "godless" neighbors in church, they left completely to form their own separate groups, a move Spener had never advocated. At the same time, rumors circulated among church people about the "wild goings-on" at house meetings. Hoping to stem these divisive tendencies, Spener decided that all collegia pietatis should meet in churches, but it would take more than a change of venue to heal the rifts already developed.

Ironically, one of the strongest leaders of these separate groups was someone who had been in close contact with Spener's pietist gathering at Dresden, a young fellow by the name of Gottfried Arnold. His book Die erste Liebe (The First Love), encouraged many to seek a new form of worship and practice based on the example of first-century Christians, considered by many as the benchmark for the true Church. Many separatists longing for a "back to basics" reform of the faith were attracted to Arnold's work. Among them

27

were Ernst Hochman and the "Dunker" Brethren led by Alexander Mack who drew notably upon Arnold's historical accounts of feet washing, the love feast, and baptism.

While at Dresden, Spener made the acquaintance of another who would help carry the ideas of pietism not just throughout Europe, but to the New World as well — Augustus Hermann Francke. By his leadership, the University at Halle would become a center of pietist thought in Germany. Perhaps most important, Halle would be a major source of German missionaries to the New World, and would at least provide encouragement for a missions-minded family who would leave a lasting impact on the people of Virginia's Shenandoah Valley.[Side 2]

When they arrived in Germantown, about two hours north of Philadelphia, they found a community much as they had hoped for, free from outward persecution, where an honest man could attain a considerable estate through good, steady work. But it was far from paradise. Religious groups walled themselves off from each other, perhaps seeking to preserve their identity in such a diverse society. Even Mack found difficulty working together with similar-minded "Brethren" who had arrived earlier.[77]

These were not the only problems. Even though Penn's "holy experiment" had encouraged diverse groups and sects to travel east across the Atlantic, it had also become "especially a gathering place for many hundreds of restless and eccentric people," as one early resident wrote. "One hears with horror what luxury prevails in Philadelphia," he continued, "and it only lacks licensing the houses of

"I bless the Lord in obtaining it…and desire that I may not be unworthy of His love, and do that which answers His kind providence, and serve His truth and people that an example may be set up to the nations, there may be room there, but not here for such a holy experiment."
— *William Penn, on his new grant for the land of Pennsylvania, 1681*

prostitution, then things would have reached the limit. The rapidly approaching judgment day will hardly spare our borders."[78]

It is no wonder that many who reached Pennsylvania found it to be a spiritual wasteland. "It is a grave matter," one church leader lamented, "that such people who were banished because of the Protestant religion and suffered great hardship can so easily grow indifferent in this country."[79]

In 1729, by the time Mack and the others settled in Germantown, the frontier was already slowly creeping west and south. Adam Mueller had moved his family to the valley lands of Virginia almost three years earlier. Others were sure to follow. Some were no doubt seeking a newer Eden, a place to live and grow far from the press of constant immigration. Some, like the German Lutherans in Virginia, who had been

28

forced to pay for their transatlantic passage through indentured servitude, had settled their obligations and looked for a place to call their own.

ALEXANDER MACK'S BIBLE

For religious worship, dissenting groups had an advantage over the more liturgically-oriented churches with their defined parish boundaries. Families and congregations quickly spread too far apart to be served conveniently by ministers following the European pattern. Even Virginia, whose gov-ernmental system was part and parcel with Anglican church order and the establishment of parish boundaries, found it difficult to supply those people along their western frontier. On the other hand, groups who were already forged into tight communities — often the result of intense persecution in Europe — and who may not have required a formally educated ministry, were uniquely suited to conditions on the frontier.

For the rest — Reformed, Lutherans, Anglicans, and others — it was difficult enough to find ministers eager to serve in the New World. What would become of those who settled in the valley beyond the Great Mountains of Virginia?

That question would be answered in part by two unlikely candidates — a theology student from Germany, and a Spanish priest.

3 INTO THE VALLEY

It was not long before hundreds of people from Pennsylvania made their way south through the rich valley of Shenandoah beyond the blue ridge of mountains. As was the practice in the Quaker colony, there must have been several who came unannounced, scattering along the open edges of streams and staking their claim.[80]

When Adam Mueller arrived here in 1726, the land west of the Ridge was hardly known by most Virginians. Curiosity had undoubtedly grown when Governor Spotswood's elaborately fitted expedition crossed the Ridge and camped on the south fork of the Shenandoah ten years earlier.[81] Then in 1722, the legislature created the first Virginia county to stretch just over the Blue Ridge — Spotsylvania County.[82] That same year a treaty with the northern tribes and the Tuscaroras sought to control the traffic of war parties through the colony. Together, these events helped create a semblance of stability for prospective settlers.[83]

It wasn't really until the year of the Mueller's settlement, though, that a wide interest in the lands along the western rivers began. Before long, the record of those holding patent rights read in part like a list of Virginia's bluebloods — William Byrd, Larkin Chew, Robert Carter, William Beverly. The name of the game was profit, and these wealthy landowners actively recruited non-Anglican Protestants to come purchase their thousands of acres.[84]

Never mind that Lord Fairfax, proprietor of the Northern Neck grant, claimed much of the same territory. The specifics of his title were in question, and the colonial legislature was eager to have the lands occupied as quickly as possible. Nor were "the Virginians" alone in their bid for Valley land. A number of German and Swiss — among them Samuel Tscheffely and Jost Hite — were also applying for large tracts of land west of the Blue Ridge.[85]

But there was one enterprising fellow who had bigger plans than them all. In 1730, Jacob Stauber, a native of Zurich, petitioned the English crown for a new colony west of the Ridge. It was to stretch from the southern end of the Peaked Mountain, then two hundred miles north to the western border of Pennsylvania. From those beginnings it would extend west all the way to the Mississippi River. Since the land was "so far separated from Virginia by the mountains," the petition observed, "tis humbly desired that it be a separate Colony and Government under the name of Georgia."[86]

Stauber and his colleagues argued that a colony rapidly populated with German and Swiss Protestants — "reputed to be a good militia" — would be the surest firewall between Virginia and the French colonies in Louisiana and Canada. To encourage the prospective settlers, they recommended the colony have "an Unlimited liberty of Conscience" with equal privileges allowed to the public profession of all religions "excepting Heathenism Jews and Papists" — in keeping with the current English law — who were to be utterly disqualified from ever holding "any office of Trust or Profit."[87]

Despite making a trip to England to present his appeal directly, Stauber never received his hoped-for colony. As a small consolation, he still had ten thousand acres west of the Ridge which he had secured separately, granted on condition that he settle at least one family for every one thousand acres within the space of two years.[88] With time running out, he was in danger of losing even that.

Competition for part of the prime acreage came from William Beverly, a powerful landowner and Virginia aristocrat who had his eye on some of the same land, including an "old field by the name of Massanutting Town" not far from the Mueller homestead. The "northern men are fond of buying land there," Beverly noted in a letter to his lawyer in April 1732.[89] Word was evidently spreading quickly about Mueller's find of plentiful, inexpensive land, and back in Pennsylvania, Stauber took up the stump. Still, it may have been more than a year before several men arrived from Pennsylvania to claim the land Stauber had promised.[90] That December, the Executive Council in Williamsburg dismissed Beverly's claim and awarded Stauber two patents of five thousand acres each, one to include the Massanutten field along the west bank of the Shenandoah River's south fork, the other further up the valley just south of the Peaked Mountain.[91]

In and around Stauber's Massanutten patent there were soon settled a number of families — Mennonists, Lutherans, Reformed, even some Separatists and Inspirationists — a typical Pennsylvania menagerie of religious persuasions.[92] For his

31

part, Stauber had married a young lady from an established Quaker family — Sarah Boone, the aunt of the legendary frontiersman, Daniel. Jacob and Sarah would have their home built on the upper patent, in the broad fields beneath the Peaked Mountain.[93]

Some of the families who settled Stauber's lands had gotten to know each other in Pennsylvania's Lancaster County, more than a day's ride west of Philadelphia. Matthias Seltzer and Ludwig Stein, two Lutherans in the group of original purchasers, had also become acquainted with a young minister there.[94] Caspar Stoever, a recent theology school graduate, had arrived in Pennsylvania with his father and sister in early fall of 1728.[95] By 1735, the twenty-seven-year-old Stoever had begun making missionary trips into the valley of Virginia to preach, baptize, and perform marriage ceremonies.[96] His father, who had described himself as a "missionary," had met up with the Lutheran colony along the Robinson River on the eastern side of the Ridge a couple of years earlier.[97] Now a community of about three hundred persons and still without a formally ordained minister, they had immediately prevailed upon him to stay and receive ordination. For several months now, the elder Stoever had been in Europe trying to raise money for the Lutherans to build a church, support a minister as well as an assistant, and of course, provide a German school for their children. By this time, the congregation was "compelled to contribute its share to the support of the English minister and his services." Voluntary support of their own minister on top of the parish levy was stretching their resources a bit too far.[98]

"Beware of sitting down contented with any Measure of Grace or Knowledge that you have attained, but still strive to grow in Grace, and in the Knowledge of our Lord and Saviour Jesus Christ."
— John Thompson, Presbyterian minister in the Valley, 1749

In May of 1738, with his father still in Europe, young Caspar paid what was probably his second visit to the Massanutten community, again to baptize one of Matthias Seltzer's children. This time, two Lutherans from the Robinson River community were present — John Heinrich Schneider and

Christoph Zimmerman.[99] For decades to come, the Lutherans east of the Ridge would support and encourage the smaller, more scattered communities in the Valley. One day, though, the favor would be returned.

Returning to the Massanutten area the following May, Stoever baptized three children born to Adam and Barbara Mueller — Catarina, Adam, and Anna Christina. The Muellers were not Lutherans, but with Catarina now five and little Adam almost three, according to the Reformed tradition their baptisms were long overdue. It was not just that Stoever was the only game in town, Lutherans and Reformed congregations shared their ministers, their church buildings, and their schools in the New World. That cooperation, born out of necessity, would also spell out a pattern for the years ahead.[100]

For Caspar Stoever, it had been a bittersweet visit to Virginia that spring of 1739. In March, he had received word that his missionary-minded father had died at sea on his way home. On April 29, just two days before he reached the Muellers, the younger Stoever had baptized his father's first grandson, John Koontz, at the Opequon settlement near the colony of Maryland.[101]

Caspar's little nephew born that spring would follow in his grandfather's footsteps. He, too, would be a missionary, and his visit to the Massanutten settlement would be talked about for years to come.

———

As the land at Massanutten was being settled, another group of people began moving into the Valley, taking the Indian road that ran west of the Buffalo Mountain, past the Peak, and further up another ten, twenty, thirty miles or more. Like Adam Mueller and most of the others who had settled on the waters of the Shenandoah during the last ten years or so, the current group of immigrants were dissenters from the Church of England. But at least geographically, these newcomers were a little closer to the Anglicans, for they aligned themselves with the Church of Scotland.

Like their English neighbors to the south, the people of Scotland had difficulty breaking their ties to the Roman church. Scotsman John Knox, a Protestant who had

33

close contact with Calvin in Geneva, brought many of the reformer's ideas back to his native land. Within time, Scotland's officially established church was nearly identical to other national Reformed churches throughout Europe, with a leadership structure based on "presbyteries," committees of ministers responsible to oversee several congregations.[102]

In the spring of 1738 the Reverend James Anderson of Donegal Presbytery in Lancaster was sent with an official letter to Governor Gooch "on behalf of a considerable number of our brethren who are meditating a settlement in the remote parts of your government...to ask your favour in allowing them the liberty of their consciences."[103]

The Church of Scotland, which shared the same island and the same king as the Church of England, was well aware of the political implications of dissent, and in their letter stressed their "inviolable attachment to the Protestant succession." Governor Gooch, though sworn to uphold the establishment of the Anglican Church, was still a Scotsman born and bred.[104] They knew their request was in good hands, but it was a necessary and safe precaution.

Just the year before the Governor had penned his approval for the Orange County court to license the first Presbyterian minister west of the Blue Ridge, the Reverend William Williams. Once he met the requirements of the Act of Toleration, Gooch had said, Williams was "not to be molested in the exercise of his ministry."[105] Williams took the proper oaths, abjured the doctrine of transubstantiation, subscribed "the Test" by taking communion in the Protestant form, and

COMMUNION TOKEN
Marked JCAC - "John Craig, Augusta Church"

agreed to thirty-six of the thirty-nine articles of the Anglican doctrine as the law required. The Act of Toleration required one thing more: he must register his stated places of meeting. With no Presbyterian meeting houses nearby, Williams "certified his intention of holding his meetings at his own plantation & on the plantation of Morgan Bryan," and accordingly, he received his license.[106] But before long he was back in court again, this time not under pleasant circumstances.

The next February, an "informer" complained against Williams for conducting a wedding without providing the couple a proper marriage license, or giving the required notice known as "publication of the banns." Marrying and giving in marriage might be agreed to by members of any denomination, but in Anglican Virginia, only an Anglican minister could officially tie the knot.[107] By the time the presbytery of Donegal wrote their letter to Governor Gooch, Williams was already the

---

A New Side minister reportedly decried an upcoming communion service as "Craig's frolick," yet communion was a time for thoughtful reflection, repentance and renewal. Craig, like other Presbyterian ministers, granted tokens like these as evidence of a person's good standing before God and man prior to the service.

---

target of "a certain Scandalous paper" signed by some one hundred people attacking his conduct.[108]

Despite the difficulties with Williams, of which Gooch may or may not have been aware, the Virginia governor replied that he had always been "inclined to favour the people who have lately removed from other provinces, to settle on the western side of our great mountains." Gooch repeated the terms he had offered Williams, granting freedom to practice their Presbyterian mode of worship as long as they agreed to conform to the letter and spirit of the Act of Toleration — to take the standard oaths and register their places of meeting, and "behave themselves peaceably towards the government."[109]

Most of these Presbyterians were not strictly Scots, but Scotch-Irish, who generations earlier had been sent to Ireland to populate the north on behalf of the British Crown. Displaced now because of increased tariffs on their goods and exorbitant rents, many had sought a better life in the freedom of Pennsylvania.[110] Virginia was a relatively new venture for them, but they found the lands and the conditions allowed by Governor Gooch more than sufficient. Because of the rapid influx of these Scotch-Irish, one road through the valley became known as the Irish path. But the corridor served another purpose as well — it was the "road to war" for Native American tribes.[111] When Adam Mueller and his neighbors first settled the land, there were peaceable and friendly interactions with the Native Americans. The Lutherans along the Robinson River had also worked at earning their trust and building friendships.[112] But along the warriors' path on the western side of the Ridge things could be different. War parties ranging in size from twenty to fifty could be expected to demand food at whatever house they chose. If refused, they would take what they would, a practice that proved "troublesome, expensive, and sometimes dangerous."[113]

The very day Gooch penned his reply to the Pennsylvania Presbyterians, Commissary Blair was reminding the governor's Council of their responsibility to provide security and safety for those west of the Blue Ridge. The Council's repeated measures to secure peace, he noted, had proven ineffectual, and the dispute with Lord Fairfax over the Northern Neck was still not resolved. Several petitions from the new Valley communities were read, but a bill for the better security and encouragement of Virginia's western lands eventually failed. As a consolation, the Assembly created the colony's first two counties completely west of the Blue Ridge — Augusta to the south, Frederick to the north. Until the population grew, they would have no courts of their own, but they at least would have a commission to organize themselves for defensive purposes.[114]

Within another year, the upper Shenandoah Valley had its first settled minister, thirty-one-year-old John Craig. As he described it, his new home "was without place of worship, or any Church order, a wilderness in a proper sense."[115] The people he had been called to serve were scattered over six hundred square miles and more, but he travelled far beyond that, to "neighbouring Congregations where God in his providence ordered his labours." Riding to homes and new meeting houses throughout the Shenandoah Valley, he preached and baptized, served communion and selected elders.[116]

Denominationally, Presbyterians were established in the New World long before other dissenting groups would have formal representatives.[117] For more than thirty years already they had maintained a synod — an organization composed of various presbyteries. Yet, according to a number of their ministers, even those Presbyterians who "had been pretty exact and punctual in the performance of outward duties" often showed no experience or understanding of "true practical religion." The result, in the words of Presbyterian minister John Blair, was simply religious behavior. He and others preached that it was first necessary to be "in Christ" through a living relationship with him, before the outward behavior could be pleasing to God.[118]

Tensions within the denomination had been building for a number of years, but shortly before Craig moved to the Valley, many Presbyterians were struggling with the appearance of "objectionable" behavior during worship services. In some Presbyterian gatherings, people began to cry over their need for God — sometimes quietly, sometimes not. Less frequently, someone might fall down in a convulsion-like fit. For Blair, these signs were not necessarily an indication of personal faith in Christ, but in a day when "Reason" seemed to prevail as the common god, many considered this sort of emotional response not only suspect, but contemptible. Ironically, they labeled it "enthusiasm," meaning "God within."

Besides the issues surrounding this revival — for that is what it was to those who saw it as a move of God to bring spiritual renewal — there had been an ongoing disagreement about the proper education for ministers. Those who supported the revival — the New Side or "New Lights" so called in mockery for their apparently new revelation — lobbied for the education of "gracious ministers," those who had a personal awareness of their own saving faith. Old Side adherents held fast to the need for a traditional theological education offered by the established universities of Europe.

Even before the denomination split, there had not been enough ministers to go around. Now, it would be even more of a strain, particularly on the frontier. Almost immediately the Old Side presbytery of Donegal licensed a man to preach who weeks earlier they had judged "dangerous to admitt...into Such a weighty and difficult office."[119] A year later, John Hindman was ordained as a missionary to the back parts of Virginia to baptize, and by that November he was admitted as a full member of the Presbytery. For at least the next three years, Hindman itinerated widely throughout the Valley of Virginia.[120]

Craig was personally opposed to the New Side way of looking at things, and to some in his congregation, this meant he was opposed to the work of God. A few in his churches began to invite New Side ministers to come and preach to them. From Craig's point of view, it was bad news. "[M]y moral character stood Clear & Good Even among them but they freely Loaded me with these and the Like: poor, blind, Carnal, hypocritical Damned wretch, this Given to my face by some of their Ministers." In the ensuing days the Presbyterians from "our own conduct, our Enthusiastick & uncharitable notions became the jest of the wicked and profane."[121]

Similar events on the eastern side of the Ridge heated things up to a boil. As one New Side preacher spoke freely about the lackluster character of Anglican ministers, curiosity seekers flocked to the meetings, and rumors began to fly. In response, Governor Gooch called upon a grand jury to prosecute these schismatics who railed against the established church and whose efforts could lead to the weakening of the colony.

Alarmed by potential fallout on their own work west of the Blue Ridge, the ministers affiliated with Craig and Hindman quickly distanced themselves from these New Siders with their "divisive and uncharitable doctrines and practices." The governor assured them of his continued "countenance and protection."[122]

Over the next several years ministers from both Old and New Side presbyteries itinerated throughout the Valley. At best, this sort of traveling about to various homes and meeting houses was a generous understanding of the Act of Toleration, but it was a necessary way of life on the frontier, perhaps made easier by its distance from the seat of government.

Travelling ministers, however, especially

those who spread their "enthusiastical knowledge" in the east, were no comfort to Virginia's leaders. These times were uncertain enough. In the aftermath of the suspicious burning of the Capitol building in Williamsburg in the winter of 1747, the Governor's Council declared the spirit of enthusiasm "more dangerous to the common Welfare, than the furious element, which laid the Royal Edifice in Ashes" and that in the past had "utterly subverted our excellent Constitution in Church and State." This was fire all right, and within the week the Governor issued a proclamation "strictly requiring all Magistrates and Officers to discourage and prohibit as far as legally they can all Itinerant Preachers whether New-Light Men Moravians, or Methodists, from Teaching, Preaching or holding any Meeting in this Colony: And that all Persons be enjoined to be aiding and assisting to that Purpose."[123]

If Craig didn't already have enough to trouble him, he was in for another surprise. Two days after the Governor's pronouncement, John Hindman showed up at one of Craig's services, "having turn'd his Coat," as Craig wryly noted, this time wearing the vestments of an Anglican minister.[124]

———

Whatever allegiance John Hindman had felt for the Presbyterians may not have ended in 1747, but at the very least it was transferred. Augusta County, for more than a year now large enough to have its own court and justices of the peace, needed to carry out the establishment of an Anglican parish as well. They had taken their time, though, as might have been expected.[125] In an area dominated by Presbyterians, Hindman, an avid horse racer who perhaps had always felt somewhat squeezed by the strict standards of behavior encouraged by the presbytery, seemed a likely choice to be the parish priest.[126] No doubt the offer of a fixed salary and relief from the traveling life of an itinerant missionary helped make the choice even easier.

The vestry made it clear from the beginning that they were not prepared to spend a lot of money. For the time being, Hindman would not have a church building. Instead, he would preach in people's homes and in the courthouse, a rugged log building with unchinked cracks so long and wide it was deemed "not finished nor fitting" to hold court in that winter or even the following spring![127] Nor would he immediately have a glebe, a reasonably-sized plantation required by law for the Anglican minister of a parish. They would supplement his annual salary of fifty pounds to take care of room and board. These were the terms, that is, "unless his Honor the Governor thinks Proper to Reverse the same which shall not be by Complaint of s[ai]d Hindman or any Person for him..."[128] Regardless of Virginia law, in Augusta County, this is the way it would be.[129]

This communion cup, (detail), a gift to the Robinson River Lutherans from Thomas Giffin in 1727, was most probably used by Samuel Klug when he served communion in the Massanutten settlement.

In many parishes, the Anglican ministry had become simply a religious form of government required by law. True, persons were still presented to the court for not attending church, but how that would be enforced on the west side of the Ridge remained to be seen.[130] A parish vestry was necessary to care for the poor and orphans, and to reaffirm property lines. In essence, the people who sat on the vestry were members of the more "prominent" families, the aristocracy of Virginia who often ruled in political and military matters as well.

For most of Virginia east of the Ridge, these "blue bloods" were Anglicans, at least by name, who agreed in official documents to be "conformable to the doctrine and discipline of the church of England." In Augusta, however, the vestry was composed of a few Anglicans at heart, but still more were Presbyterians. That detail didn't sit well with the Anglicans in the county, and they soon submitted a petition to have the dissenters "turned out." The petition was referred to the House of Burgesses who, after some deliberation, rejected it, and the dissenters remained.[131]

Even though the parish was brand new, Hindman was not the first Anglican to minister in the Valley of Virginia. More than ten years earlier, when Caspar Stoever was traveling through these parts, a missionary-minded priest by the name of Anthony Gavin

THOMAS GIFFIN
Communion Cup

made visits to twelve places from his home near the western waters of the James twice a year. Each circuit comprised four hundred miles and nearly a score of fords across the North and South rivers.[132] On his first trip alone, Gavin baptized over four hundred people, including several Quakers and two Anabaptists. More than two-fifths of those baptized were Africans.[133]

It was not unusual for Anglicans to baptize slaves, but Gavin's position put him at odds with other priests as well as his own parishioners. "[I]t gives me a great deal of uneasiness," he wrote in a letter to the Bishop of London, "to see the greatest part of our Brethren taken up in farming and buying slaves." As a former Roman Catholic

NEW LIGHTS, MORAVIANS, AND METHODISTS

Reacting to the troubling events of 1745-47, Governor Gooch's proclamation against Moravians, New Lights, and Methodists attempted to cover the full range of itinerant "enthusiasts" who refused to restrict their worship to the order and doctrine of the Anglican church. Actually, one of those groups — the Methodists — had not even set foot in Virginia, unless you count George Whitefield who had dined with the governor himself on his first preaching tour here about seven years before.

But the groups cited in the effort to prevent religious and political chaos had closer connections than the governor may have realized. Methodist founder John Wesley was on his way to Georgia to serve as the Anglican chaplain when he first met the Moravians. During part of their passage from England, the ship encountered violent waters that threatened to drag passengers and cargo to the bottom of the sea. In the face of death, the Moravians — even their children — were at peace. Wesley was taken with their composure. Sometime later, he had a conversation with one of the Moravian leaders, Augustus Spangenberg who would one day travel in Virginia as well.

"Do you know Jesus Christ?" asked Spangenberg.

priest who had fled Spain to avoid execution for his newfound Protestant faith, Gavin had not been inoculated within the Virginia system. At first, he had accepted the necessity of slave labor to supplement his own living. Now he was convinced that slave holding was "unlawful for any Christian and in particular for a clergyman. By this the souls committed to their care must suffer."[134]

A D A M   M U E L L E R ' S
Homestead

With his own church and glebe complete with slaves, Lutheran minister Samuel Klug was living the life of many Anglican priests. Secured in Europe to help Caspar Stoever's father with the Robinson River congregation, Klug was now their only minister. In addition to his duties east of the Ridge, two or three times a year he would visit Lutherans throughout the Valley and hold a communion service.[135]

Klug did not have a reputation for what some might call a "well-ordered life," and trouble would result from it. Like the Anglican priests, he lacked strong, direct spiritual oversight. Without a bishop in Virginia to oversee many issues of church discipline and order, much of the responsibility fell to the governor and his Council. On good terms with the Anglican clergy as well as the governor, Klug was a sort of unofficial spokesman for the eastern Virginia authorities. He was particularly diligent about the proclamation against itinerant Moravians, a group that had "snatched" a Lutheran or two in the past.[136]

The Moravians, or Unitas Fratrum as they called themselves, were German-speaking missionaries who traced themselves to fifteenth century Czech reformer Jan Hus.

first arrived in Pennsylvania, Zinzendorf tried to encourage an ecumenical gathering of German Christians throughout the colony, but squabbles, suspicions, and differences of belief got in the way. In the aftermath, some of the Moravian leaders made occasional missionary trips to German communities scattered throughout Virginia.[137]

GREEN MEADOWS
The 1741 homestead of Adam Mueller near present-day Elkton.

Persecuted throughout Europe, in the early 1700s they found refuge on the estate of Count Nicholas Zinzendorf, a wealthy noble who still considered himself in some ways part of the Lutheran connection. When he

On one occasion the Moravian missionary Gottschalk paid a visit to Matthias Seltzer, the wealthy Lutheran at the Massanutten community. Seltzer's generosity had earned him a great deal of influence and

he has Christ!" In 1739, Whitefield invited Wesley to join him in "field-preaching" in Bristol. But their close ties would loosen the following year.

In Whitefield's estimation, Wesley went too far in a published sermon against the doctrine of election — the understanding that God has already chosen or predestined those whom He will save. "Dear Sir...you plainly make salvation depend not on God's free grace, but on man's free will." Around the same time Wesley wrote to the Moravians, expressing his disagreement over some of their principles and practices. Though he said he harbored no animosity, Wesley would carry the heritage of the Moravians, but he would not have their fellowship.

While in Pennsylvania, Whitefield observed the spiritually poor state of the Germans and wrote to the Moravian leader Zinzendorf to send missionaries. The next year, Zinzendorf himself arrived in the Quaker colony, but his attempt to unite all Germans under one banner of faith failed under suspicions that Zinzendorf had sectarian goals of his own. Before long, the Moravians began sending missionaries to the scattered German colonies in Virginia.

Soon after the governor's proclamation of 1746, Augustus Spangenberg travelled to the Massanutten colony and over the ridge to *the Robinson River Lutherans. It did not bother him to be threatened with arrest or harassment. In his pocket, he carried a proclamation of his own — Parliament's recognition of the Moravian Church as legitimate and protected dissenters.*

"I am compelled to believe [the governor] confuses us and considers us one with the New Lights or Whitefieldians," he announced to the Lutheran minister.

It seemed that now a game of politics and theological rabbit holes had replaced what began as a close fellowship among New Lights, Moravians and Methodists in spreading a simple message of forgiveness. Amazingly, each in their own way would still reach the people of the Shenandoah Valley with that very message.[Side 3]

respect, and Gottschalk was hoping to learn something about the local people from him. Unfortunately for Gottschalk, Seltzer was also a devout Lutheran bitterly opposed to the Moravians and threatened to have the itinerant thrown in jail. In the end, it turned out to be nothing more than talk — *literally*. Gottschalk's only "imprisonment" was being forced to listen to Seltzer rail against the Moravians, a punishment he was compelled to endure since, besides his desire for information, he was "surrounded by water and terribly high mountains on all sides."[138]

The influential Lutheran warned Gottschalk that if he ever got over the ridge to the Germans on Robinson River, they would soon take him by the neck. The next morning after breakfast, however, Seltzer saddled up a couple of horses and led him to the shortcut through the mountains to reach Samuel Klug's house, guiding him quite a distance so he would not lose his way. Perhaps he thought the governor's wishes might be enforced with more diligence east of the Ridge.[139]

Several months later, Adam Mueller met up with the Moravians while on his way home one evening. Mueller had since moved from near the Massanutten colony, further up the river, to a place he would call Green Meadows.[140] This particular night, he found the German missionaries at the home of a friend, Mathias Schaub. Soon the conversation turned to a favorite topic of the itinerants.

"I would like to come to your house and preach," the Moravian ventured.

"Are you sent from God?" inquired Mueller.

The question may have seemed awkward, but the Moravians no doubt understood his intent. Mueller was only interested in hearing from ministers who understood their calling.

"Yes," they answered.

"If you are sent from God, you will be welcome," returned Mueller, "but there are at present so many kinds of people that often one does not know where they come from."[141]

Those in the Valley had been watching the bitter feuds between New and Old Side Presbyterians, the sometimes questionable behavior of the new Lutheran minister, and the uncertain allegiance of a Presbyterian-turned-Anglican parson. It is no wonder if many were fed up with "professional" ministers who presented a certificate or license as the main evidence of their authority to preach.

Mueller notified his neighbors of a meeting the next day. After travelling eight miles through the rain, the Moravians crossed the south fork of the Shenandoah to arrive at Mueller's home, now ten or fifteen miles further up the valley than where he had first settled. Here, at Green Meadows, one of the Moravians preached from John 7, "Whosoever thirsteth let him come to the water and drink." In his journal afterwards he reported that "a number of

thirsty souls were present. Especially Adam Mueller took in every word and after the sermon declared himself well pleased."[142]

Mueller likely based his assessment of the Moravians on the Bible. Though offering some room for different interpretations, for many this book was the reasonable standard for truth. What Luther had proclaimed over two hundred years earlier — Scripture alone, faith alone — was still the common thread among most Protestants, whether Reformed or Lutheran, Mennonist or Moravian.

In the decades to follow, that bond would be tried again and again.

TODAY'S SILVER LAKE
Near Dayton, covers the traditional site of the first meeting house for Presbyterians who settled in the neighborhood of Cooks Creek

CONFLUENCE

1750 - 1800

---

*Dissenters had already begun to deal with the
problems of living and worshipping in Anglican
Virginia. As their numbers increased west of the
Blue Ridge, they would also face the challenges of
getting along with each other, as well as
navigating a new course in a new republic.*

4

THE LOST BRETHREN

Not two dozen years had passed since the Muellers made their home near the Shenandoah River, and already the land south of the Fairfax proprietary was being busily settled. The valley to the west stretched twenty miles before its abrupt ascent at the North Mountain. Here ran an old Indian road, now dubbed the "Great Wagon Road." Before long, many of these creeks bore the names of those pushing their way south — Cook, Smith, Linville, Brock, and others.

For all the new immigration, the homes and farms of families were still thinly scattered in the early 1750s. Even along the Great Wagon Road there might not be a house for twenty miles at a stretch. The only town south of the Fairfax Line was Staunton, a fledgling settlement with a courthouse, twenty or so homes, but still no house of

COOK'S CREEK

worship.[1] Faced with more miles than ministers, a weekly worship service even for the predominant Presbyterians could prove difficult. Here on the frontier, the celebration of faith was often simply a matter of the heart and held within the province of the home.

As far as Samuel Newman's family was concerned, it's likely there was no one within a day's travel who believed as they did. Like Mennonists and Dunkers, they held that baptism was only for those who had made a personal decision to follow Christ. In the eyes of Europe's national Protestant churches, any and all of these groups were "Anabaptists" — rebaptizers. But in England and Wales, where this particular branch had grown, they were known simply as "Baptists." Before long the Newmans were joined by a not-too-distant neighbor. Close to sixty, and probably raised a Church of England man, John Harrison became convinced of his need for believers' baptism. With no Baptist minister nearby, Harrison travelled some five hundred miles or more to Oyster Bay, a little village on the northern coast of Long Island where he had once lived. There he was baptized, and returned another five hundred miles back to his home

in the Valley.[2]

Over the next ten years or more, Newman and Harrison saw a Baptist minister only once or twice. Very likely they practiced family worship — daily prayer, Bible reading, and perhaps singing — as well as "closet devotions," a personal time alone with God spent in prayer and study. By 1756, there were about a half dozen Baptists and their families in the Smith's and Linville's Creek areas where Newman and Harrison lived. Though a tiny group, they wanted a full-time preacher. Baptist minister John Alderson had paid them a few visits, but it would take more than good will to get him to move his family from Bucks County, Pennsylvania. To sweeten the offer, Newman divided his own farm in half, deeding Alderson two hundred acres.[3] In the fall of that year, the small group formally organized as a "congregational Church...of Christ, baptized on personal profession of Faith." Happily, they had their own meeting house, conveniently located on the main road that extended from beyond the western mountains all the way east to Williamsburg.[4]

In September of 1757, less than a year after Alderson's installment as minister, there

Today we think of the little group that began the Smith's and Linville's Creek Church in 1756 as Baptists, but that was not necessarily the name they used then. In their own records they describe themselves as one of "the three congregational Churches of Christ, baptised on personal Profession of Faith." Not exactly catchy, but this was more than a mere label. It was a statement of church government and belief, with a little history thrown in for good measure.

The "Baptists" of whom the Linville's Creek group were a part had begun in England as an off-shoot of the Congregational Church. As their name implies, Congregationalists believed in the authority of the local congregation as opposed to a hierarchical structure of priests and bishops. When John Smyth and his followers decided to no longer baptize infants, but only those who made a "personal Profession of Faith" in Christ as their Lord and Savior, the Baptists were born.

But these Baptists were only one branch of those who would settle in Pennsylvania, Maryland, and the Shenandoah Valley. Dunkers, Mennonists, and Baptists (both Regular and Separate) all agreed on the practice of believers' baptism. In fact, Morgan Edwards, who col-

"arose certain of the Favourers of that Scriptureless Practice, Infant sprinkling," the baptism of babies into the community of the church.[5] They called to their assistance the new Presbyterian minister, Alexander Miller, who had been requested just a few months earlier by congregations gathered at Cook's Creek and near the Peaked Mountain. Without permission, Miller opened up the Baptist meeting house, took

DANIEL HARRISON'S
stone house, circa 1747 along Cook's Creek

the pulpit, and began to "slanderously, falsely, and contrary to Christian Rule & Order, despitefully use both our Minister, and Brother, the Deacon of this place." Needless to say, the incident "occasioned Animosities," as the Baptist record keeper put it, and

served "to disturb the Churches Peace, and the Peace of the Neighbourhood, this being a Time of noted Peace with us, in the Midst of Difficulties elsewhere."[6]

Difficulties elsewhere was an understatement. In recent years the French had begun in earnest to push their claims for land in the New World farther towards the English settlements. They had enlisted the help of several native American tribes whose raids on the scattered frontier families had grown more frequent though still largely ignored by the Virginia authorities safely removed east of the Ridge.[7]

Two years ago, the politicians in Williamsburg had sent a twenty-two-year-old colonel by the name of George Washington to defend the exposed settlements, but his severely criticized defeat that year served as an impetus for more Native Americans to side with the French. The following year, in October of 1755, the overconfident army of British General Braddock met with disaster. With the English defenses shattered, the passages through the mountains were left open to the inroads of the French and Indians. Panic overran the scattered settlers throughout the Valley, filling the roads with bands of fleeing refugees carrying whatever they could manage.[8]

For almost two years since then, the settlements around Smith's and Linville's creeks had been undisturbed. Then, exactly one week after Alexander Miller had stood in the Baptist pulpit in support of infant baptism, the Indians attacked. The keeper of the church record for the Linville Creek Baptists saw this as divine retribution, "A just Retaliation for Such unheard of Proceedings, and Measures" taken the Wednesday before.

An Anglican himself, Harrison was given leave to build a "chapel of ease," though the vestry offered no financial support for it. These neighborhood chapels were traditionally offered as an alternative for those unable to reach the main parish church.

Throughout that fall, there was great discouragement and confusion. Those with enough money to leave and establish themselves elsewhere were interested in abandoning the frontier, but John Craig advised against it. Leaving now, he warned them, would be "a scandal to our nation, falling below our brave ancestors, making ourselves a reproach among Virginians, a dishonor to our friends at home, an evidence of cowardice, want of faith, and a noble Christian dependence on God, as able to save and deliver from the heathen; it would be a lasting blot to our posterity."[9]

With Craig's leadership, small forts were built throughout the area — palisaded buildings strong enough to protect against guns and small arms, each holding several families. One fort was the stone house of Daniel Harrison on Cook's Creek, where Anglican services were occasionally held.[10] Still another was the Stone Church of Craig's Presbyterian congregation, around which an earthen trench and embankment were dug

lected much information about these groups in the eighteenth century, did so in the hopes that it would foster an understanding and unity among them. Sometimes they did cooperate, but heated discussions could result from particular nuances lost on those outside of the groups.

Whatever their differences, all at one time or another bore the reproach of the name Anabaptist, a term connected with religious zeal run amok, the label worn by the fanatics who in 1535 had taken the German city of Muenster and held it by armed force. Calvin had written his first draft of the famed Institutes of the Christian Religion to distinguish the French reformers from the dangerous element "who substituted their own spirit for the divine Word, and held all civil magistrates in contempt." At that time there was perhaps little uniformity among these "rebaptizers," but they were easy scapegoats. To the north, Menno's followers quickly shed the Anabaptist label for the more innocuous "Menoists."

Ironically, though, the names of many groups spawned by the Protestant Reformation were not ones they chose for themselves. Neighbors, magistrates, and others — not caring to delve into the particulars of a nonconformist group — would typically bestow a name in mockery, usually based on outward *appearance or their most controversial practice. Since members of their group were immersed three times in baptism, Alexander Mack's small following became known as Dunkers, from a word meaning to dip food into sauce — in other words, sops. Yet as the eighteenth-century historian Morgan Edwards consolingly remarked, since "the term signifies Dippers they may rest content with the nickname, since it is the fate of Baptists in all countries to bear some cross or other." The Society of Friends who settled Penn's colony were Quakers since they were seen shaking during their meetings, or Broadbrims for their largish hats. The Dunkers "dunked," the Quakers "quaked," and the Baptists "baptized." What could be more simple? And the names stuck.*

Not surprisingly, these labels did little to promote understanding. The particular beliefs of those who dissented from state-supported churches were not necessarily well known among the general public. This was particularly true in eastern Virginia. When George Whitefield arrived there in 1739, he jokingly remarked, "If I talk of the Spirit, I am a Quaker! if I say grace at breakfast, and behave seriously, I am a Presbyterian! Alas! what must I do to be accounted a member of the Church of England?"

In the Valley, thanks to

in military style.[11]

By the first of the year, folks were beginning to adjust to the "Disorders that attended us, as that with Comfort and Peace, we could proceed." But the Indian incursions began again that spring. In May, "the Indians

into Forts or over the Mountains, to escape their Rage." In just four years, the population of sprawling Augusta county was cut in half.[12]

More than fifteen years earlier, the Mennonists of Pennsylvania had foreseen the possibility of war with the neighboring

AUGUSTA STONE CHURCH
Artist's rendering of stockade fence & possible blockhouse during the French & Indian War

murdered over fifty persons and more than two hundred families were driven away homeless." By June 1758, "the whole Neighbourhood [was] forced either to go

Indians. They had shared a tradition of difficulty. Now they would draw strength from it. In the face of death and persecution throughout their homelands in Europe, their history of non-resistance had been chronicled in a book known as *Bloody Theater or Martyrs' Mirror.* Knowing the test of war would require renewed courage for the "defenseless Christians," they sought to translate this massive tome from Dutch into their own German language. When help from Holland did not come, they secured the assistance of Peter Miller, a former German Reformed minister educated at Heidelberg who knew several different languages. When the Mennonists found him, Miller had become a leader in the Seventh-Day Dunker community at Ephrata.[13] Translating the 1,512-page volume took three years, with Miller catching no more than four hours of sleep each night. Still, when the largest book printed in colonial America rolled off the presses of German Christopher Saur in 1748, it sold for the minuscule price of twenty-two shillings.[14]

M A R T Y R S '   M I R R O R

their "common state of socia-bility" as Ireland put it, there was greater communication among various groups, but sometimes not much attention was paid to their differences. No wonder that in 1781 when Reverend Anderson Moffett of the Smith's Creek Church in nearby Shenandoah County paid a visit to the Rockingham Court, the clerk recorded that he was an "Anabaptist."

Maybe "The Congregational Church of Christ, Baptizing on Personal Profession of Faith" wasn't such a bad name after all.[Side 4]

There was at least one copy of the *Martyrs' Mirror* among the Mennonists of the Massanutten community, perhaps more.

The conclusion of the inspiring volume advised the reader to "consider the end or design of the creation of man...that such reflection may stimulate us to prepare ourselves resolutely to endure those calamities which equally befall the willing and the unwilling." Still, in one sense they were not prepared when trouble came.[15] Perhaps overconfident that the mountain would shield them, residents had ignored the warnings of Mrs. Brubaker, who said she had seen the fires of Indian encampments the night before. With only that warning, Indians crossed over the mountain, killing John Stone, his wife and infant child as well as John Holtzman's wife and children. Now joining the flight of refugees on the Wagon Road north, several Mennonist families returned to Lancaster, in Pennsylvania. There, a number of them, including Michael Kaufman from the Massanutten community, wrote their brethren in Amsterdam for help.[16]

"We were 39 Mennonite families living in Virginia," the letter read. "One family was murdered and the remaining of us and many other families were obliged to flee for our lives."[17]

The ties to Europe were still strong. England, Germany, the Netherlands — these were the places the New World settlers would continue to look to for guidance and help. Though they did not know these refugee Mennonists by name, the Holland fathers responded with a generous gift. Soon the community at Massanutten would return and grow. The next challenge would be altogether different.

"...I believe they are more encompassd by fear than by the Enemy..."
— George Washington, on the response of the regular militia during the French and Indian War, 1755

The Mennonists were not the only group in Europe to be served by Holland. The few German Reformed people in the valley of Virginia had been without regular ministers for thirty years or more, relying instead on the occasional services of Lutherans, Moravians, and their Reformed "cousins," the Presbyterians.[18] In 1748 Michael Schlatter, newly arrived as a representative of the Reformed Classis of Amsterdam, identified four Reformed congregations in Virginia — Shenandoah, "Misanotti," South Branch, and New Germantown.[19] Though these may have been the larger groups, there certainly must have been others scattered about in small numbers. Even in the year of Braddock's defeat, Christopher Saur was advising new German immigrants to take the Wagon Road south where the land was more affordable.[20]

At least since the Augusta Court was established, Jacob Herman had been settled in the southeastern shadow of the Peaked Mountain. A meeting house was built near his mill there on Stony Creek, and by 1762 a Reformed minister and his family were settled in the area — Philip and Mary Van Gemuenden and their children.[21] Probably from the beginning, this was a "union church," jointly held by Reformed and Lutheran congregations. Though distinctions between the two groups had been painfully clear in Europe, here in the New World this kind of cooperation was not uncommon. More than a practical solution to limited resources, it perhaps reflected a newfound freedom to start afresh. Quickly establishing a mutual appreciation with his Lutheran counterpart, Henry Muhlenberg, Schlatter remarked, "One may well desire that such traces of harmony might also be found in Germany."[22]

About the same time along a tributary of the North Fork, close to the Fairfax Line, another union church was underway near the home of Adam Röder. Van Gemuenden would serve that congregation as well. Even taking a shortcut across the Peaked Mountain, it was more than a half day's ride from Stony Creek to the group at Fort Run, but this was a short distance for a frontier preacher. Sadly, within two years, Van Gemuenden's death brought his earthly ministry came to an end, and the congregations were once again on their own.[23]

Interestingly, in the event his wife remarried, the Reformed preacher conditionally left his two sons to the care of Mathias Lehr and Colonel Peter Scholl, both members of the Fort Run congregation at Röder's.[24] Colonel Scholl had been an officer in the

Augusta militia for more than twenty years, and was one of the first justices of the peace for the county. More importantly, he was a leader in the Fort Run congregation. Van Gemuenden clearly wished his sons to have

this time the Lutherans' stepped forward. Joining hands with the Robinson River Lutherans in Culpeper County east of the Ridge — now without a minister after the death of Samuel Klug — they wrote to

VIEW WEST
from old Röder's Church (Fort Run congregation)

the best advantages and remain within the tradition of the German Reformed church.

To a large extent, it was concern for their children that prompted the Fort Run congregation's next call for a minister, but

Muhlenberg, informing him that "their children were falling into heathenism for want of holy Baptism." This was not mere hyperbole to plead their cause. The baptism of infants, for both Lutherans and Reformed, was the seal of their belonging to a "covenant community" of believers, a crucial element for the life of faith.[25]

The carrier of these letters for the three-hundred-mile trip to Philadelphia was Johannes Schwarbach, a forty-five-year-old itinerant schoolteacher. Schwarbach had served fellow believers on the frontiers of Pennsylvania by reading sermons and teaching children in the *Kinderlehre*, the Lutheran system of instruction. For some time now he "had been doing the same in the wilds of Virginia."[26]

The Fort Run and Culpeper congregations, aware of the different requirements for schoolteachers and ministers, hoped that Schwarbach might be found to have at least "moderate ability." They also wished the Lutheran ministerium would grant him authority to administer the sacraments of baptism and the Lord's Supper at least "until the Lord of the harvest sends more faithful and regular laborers into his harvest," when Schwarbach would again confine himself to the instruction of children and "feed them as lambs."[27]

Muhlenberg had long complained of the "half-baked schoolmasters" who came from Germany and went far out into the country to set themselves up as preachers, but Schwarbach had not been so presumptuous. He had even refrained from administering the sacraments altogether. His actions on the frontiers of Pennsylvania and Virginia revealed a heart of concern for both young and old, and the need of the congregations at Fort Run and Robinson River was great. He was ordained the day he arrived.[28]

For Schwarbach, though, ordination did not mean the end of his role as schoolmaster. Both he and his wife would travel throughout the state, ministering to the remote congregations. The Schwarbachs may have had no children of their own, but they had family and children to greet them wherever they went.[29]

Education was central to both Lutherans and Reformed. As soon as he reached Pennsylvania, Muhlenberg expressed a hope of having "a free school in connection with each principal church," and the Reformed felt similarly. Besides instruction in reading, writing, spelling, arithmetic, singing, and the catechism — the beliefs of the church — schools were vital in preserving the "dear German mother tongue," challenged by the

English churches and schools throughout the colonies.[30]

The curriculum for these schools included a book of arithmetic problems called the *Rechnung*, the Bible, and the *ABC und Namenbuch*, a collection of reading exercises which included Biblical quotations, hymns, prayers, and the teachings of the church.[31] Though separate editions were printed for Reformed and Lutheran students, there were editions prepared for use in the "union" schools as well.

Children were to be instructed in such a way that their thought "be well analyzed and made clear…that it will fill not only the memory, but also the other powers of the soul with pleasure and with life." Though the Bible was a primary text throughout all grades, schoolmasters were warned not to dull their students to its message by treating it as an ordinary reading primer. The Scriptures were their "richest treasure and most precious gem."[32]

After their education was complete, children were brought before the church and "confirmed." If baptism was the sign of belonging to a community of faith, confirmation was intended to be the evidence of that faith grown to a certain level of maturity. Along with the child and the parents, the entire congregation was enjoined to help build upon that faith, to encourage the young person to grow in service to Christ.

The goals of education were clear enough, but the reality of people scattered throughout "the wilds of Virginia" presented its own challenges. In the spring and summer of 1768 alone, Schwarbach instructed and confirmed young people in seven different congregations scores of miles apart. In short order, he was tired, overworked, and underpaid. The congregations knew they could not afford to pay him what he deserved, in part because they were still required to come up with the annual parish levy in support of the Anglican church.[33]

But this was not the time to discuss any relief from that quarter. Things between England and the colonies had begun to heat up considerably. In Culpeper, sixteen justices of the peace had resigned their positions in protest of the 1765 Stamp Act, a tax Parliament had placed upon the colonies to help pay for the recently concluded war with the French and Indians.[34]

Apart from the outrages of an insensitive

British parliament, another issue would prove taxing to many Virginians. More "New Lights" had begun filtering throughout the colony, and their impact would leave a lasting effect.

The early awakening in Virginia may have been encouraged by Presbyterians, but it would not end with them when Old and New Side groups officially reunited in 1758. Springing up among Congregationalists in Massachusetts and Presbyterians in New Jersey, and spread by the itinerant Anglican George Whitefield, the revival found its way to Frederick County just north of Augusta. There, preachers influenced by Whitefield began sharing their message of personal faith in Jesus Christ and repentance from sin.[35]

Not only had their preaching and emotional response caused concern among the Baptists in the area — a group associated with the congregation at Linville Creek — but among the Mennonists there as well. In 1761 the Mennonists called their Bishop Martin Boehm to advise those who were now worried about their own salvation. As one father put it, "all we can get them to say is, we are lost, we have no true religion."[36]

Boehm knew exactly how to respond. When first selected as a minister in his Lancaster Mennonist community, he felt

M A R T I N   B O E H M

completely inadequate to preach. One day he heard a voice within him say, "You pray for grace to teach others the way of salvation, and you have not prayed for your own

WILLIAM OTTERBEIN

salvation." It had never occurred to him before, but the impression would not leave. As he prayed, he felt and saw himself a "poor sinner."[37]

"Lost!" *Verlohren,* he had cried again and again plowing his field one day. Finally, at the end of a row, he sank down and called out to God, "Lord, save, I am lost!" With his knees pressed hard into the newly turned earth, he heard these words in his mind, "I am come to seek and to save that which is lost." Now a stream of joy poured over him. Praising God, he left the field and told his wife what had happened. He was never the same. His visit to Frederick County not only resulted in several religious people coming to faith in Christ, it became the place where Boehm himself obtained "New Light." When he returned to Pennsylvania, large groups of people gathered to hear the Word of God, even on weekdays. Boehm's zeal for telling others the story of Christ's love "displeased" some of his fellow ministers, and some of the Mennonist meeting houses were closed to him, but he easily found other places to preach.[38]

Sometime during the late 1760s, some of the Virginia New Light preachers attended a great meeting in Lancaster County at the farm of Isaac Long. While they were preaching in the orchard, Martin Boehm was holding forth in the barn. Among the many hundreds of Lutherans, Reformed, Mennonist, Dunkers, and others hearing him that day was the German Reformed minister William Otterbein. In many ways, he shared Boehm's story and especially his love for God. Before

60

the Mennonist preacher could take his seat, the much larger Otterbein wrapped him in a strong embrace and proclaimed, "*Wir sind bruder* — We are brothers." At a time when Anabaptists and Reformed still held on to the old tensions and bitterness, many wept

Frederick, Maryland, where there were "the greatest number of awakened and converted souls." Facing the next several months without a formally ordained minister, many in the Frederick congregation continued to meet together to read from the Bible or a book of

LONG'S BARN

for joy.[39]

Otterbein had only recently left the pastorate of a Reformed congregation in

sermons, as well as to talk about their faith, sing, and pray.[40] Ironically, they would find worship easier without a minister than with one.

Shortly after his arrival in America in 1766, Charles Lange's first preaching assignment was to that same Evangelical Reformed Church in Frederick. Alarmed at those "sectarians" who had been holding their own worship services, Lange became the catalyst for a bitter dispute. Appearing before the association of Reformed ministers known as the Coetus, he accused Otterbein of "despising religion, the sacraments, and ministers."[41]

But it was Lange who needed correction. "It is not against the teachings of our church," the Coetus noted, "when people sometimes come together to pray and read God's Word." In hopes that restoration would follow, Lange was directed to leave Frederick as soon as possible.[42]

STONY RUN
Site of early Lutheran church near Jacob Harmon's, present-day McGaheysville

Even before Lange's reprimand, he had visited several Reformed congregations in Virginia where he confirmed children and served communion. It wasn't until the month after the Coetus meeting, though, that he first appeared at the Peaked Mountain congregation — not the one near Herman's Mill, but the "lower church," not far from Adam Mueller's home. Not surprisingly, Adam Mueller's son, Henry, and son-in-law Jacob Bare were the two deacons in the Reformed congregation where Lange confirmed thirty-one and administered the communion to ninety-two persons altogether.[43]

The following spring, Lange visited the congregations at Röder's and Peaked Mountain at Harmon's mill. Within a few months, he had left Frederick altogether, settling among the Virginia congregations on his own authority where he refused to baptize any child unless he was first paid. This, along with administering the Lord's Supper "to unchaste persons, without the previous ecclesiastical censure" earned him the disapproval of the congregations.[44] A year later, in debt and disgrace, he left Virginia "for parts unknown." In light of the circumstances, the Coetus knew nothing else to do but consider Lange "among the lost brethren."[45]

That fall, their new building nearly completed, the Lutheran and Reformed of the upper Peaked Mountain and Stony Creek congregations drew up a new union agreement. High on the list was the issue of money. After concerns about Lange, and still no doubt struggling to provide for the Lutheran minister Schwarbach, the head of each household agreed to "support the minister and school-master and help to keep in repair the church and the school-house as far as lies in his ability."

Those who would not keep that commitment would pay for the "services" of the church, five shillings for every confirmation, communion, and burial, and half that for a baptism. All monies would go directly into the church treasury with the exception of the confirmation fee, which was paid directly to the minister.[46]

Left behind after Lange's departure was his wife Ursula, and their only child, a daughter by the same name.[47] Remaining on the property at Stony Creek, Mrs. Lange apparently won the respect and affection of her neighbors. Born into a wealthy Swiss family, she had brought quite an extensive library.

In the days when books were rare commodities — particularly on the frontier — it was not unlikely that many children received a rich education in her home. In her honor, the little community was first named Ursulasburg.[48]

Lange's rebound into the Valley was hardly the only influence the awakening among Germans and others would have for Virginians. In Frederick County, John Koontz was having an awakening of his own. Almost certainly raised a Lutheran like his grandfather, young John had probably heard the New Light preachers since he was a teenager. The year Lange moved into Virginia, Koontz was baptized for the second time. The first had been by his uncle, Caspar Stoever, the unconventional, itinerant Lutheran minister. This time, at almost thirty years of age, it would be in response to his own personal profession of faith in Christ.[49]

Two years later, Koontz was visiting his brother in the Massanutten settlement. At a familiar landmark known as the Whitehouse there had already been New Light preaching in English by many, including the fiery young Scotsman, Jamie Ireland from nearby Smith's Creek.[50] They, like Koontz, associated with a group known as "Separate Baptists" — *separate* because they had chosen to separate from the established churches in the colonies; *baptist* because they held to the doctrine of believers' baptism.

The Whitehouse was the property of Martin Kaufman, Jr., a Mennonist who would be immersed Baptist-style and take a lead in preaching the revival encouraged by the Separates. With Koontz present, there were now two who could preach in both German and English. By 1772, a Separate Baptist church had been established at the Whitehouse, and among their numbers were several former Mennonists.[51]

Alarmed by this dissolution of the brotherhood, those remaining true to their Mennonist heritage sought help from four or five Mennonists preachers from Pennsylvania. Their primary target was Koontz. Going to his home, the Pennsylvania preachers argued that the principal features of faith must include a refusal to go to war, and opposition to taking oaths or holding slaves — cardinal elements of their creed.[52] The Baptists left these issues to the individual's conscience, Koontz countered. But he "questioned them as to the reason of their hope in Christ; whether they had felt the power of godliness in their hearts, or whether they relied upon their nursery faith." It was clear they were not speaking the same language. Within a few days, after holding some meetings in the area, the Pennsylvania Mennonists returned home, unsuccessful in their mission.[53]

Opposition to Koontz, though, was far from over. Others would try different tactics. At first there were harsh words and threats. Later, at least twice, Koontz was met on the road and beaten, once until he was nearly disabled. On another occasion Koontz and Kaufman were in a home not far from Smith's Creek, preparing to preach. Hearing an unfamiliar voice in the next room inquire for him, Koontz suspected trouble and slipped away to hide. Unfortunately for Kaufman, the troublemaker did not know either man on sight. Bursting into the room, he fell upon poor Kaufman with a stick and beat him several times before he could be convinced he had the wrong preacher![54]

Kaufman's principles of non-resistance were consistent with his Mennonist upbringing. In personal matters, Koontz also followed Christ's instruction to "turn the other cheek." But a larger conflict was looming, and there the agreement would end.

FIGHTING OVER FREEDOM

The sort of beatings that John Koontz received for his itinerant preaching were in many ways out of character for the folks west of the Blue Ridge. James Ireland, a young Separate Baptist from Smith's Creek who preached at the Whitehouse and would later minister at Linville Creek, noted that the people of the Valley "lived in a common state of sociability," a situation that "gave them an opportunity of being acquainted with each other's principles and practices, by which their *ideas* became more enlarged, and their *judgments* more generally informed" than those to the east.[55]

Both Ireland and his Smith's Creek neighbor Anderson Moffett had spent time east of the Ridge in the Culpeper jail for their particular "principles and practices." Ireland's five-month stay had been particularly brutal. Opponents filled his cell with sulfurous smoke, poisoned him, regularly threatened public whippings, and tried to blow up the small, one-room jail. When the twenty-year-old preached through the bars of the cell window, men would ride horses at a gallop among his listeners, and at least once they urinated in his face.[56]

Virginia had nodded towards the Act of Toleration more than seventy years earlier, but in the absence of clear policies, mobs and county magistrates held sway. As the Whitehouse church was getting on its feet under Anderson Moffet's leadership in 1772, the Virginia House of Burgesses was trying to hammer out its own version of toleration, and a move was afoot to establish the office of bishop in the colony.[57] In the swirl of politics and personalities that caught Williamsburg up in its course, a young man from Augusta County would have his own say in the matter.

James Madison, cousin to the Orange County man who would become the nation's fourth president, had grown up not far from where the South and North Rivers joined to form the Shenandoah's south fork. His father, John Madison, had been the first clerk of the Augusta Parish vestry as well as county clerk, and his mother, Agatha, was the daughter of William Strother, a wealthy eastern landowner. Agatha's two sisters lived nearby — Jane Lewis, wife of county surveyor Thomas Lewis, and Margaret Jones, who had married the King's attorney, Gabriel Jones. The three men were among Augusta's most influential citizens, but it was their wives, born and raised within the patterns of the Church of England, that made this small area a sort of Anglican enclave.[58]

True to form, the Madisons had sent their son, James, to the College of William and Mary for a proper education. This year, he was to give a speech in commemoration of the college's founders, the same who had initiated toleration throughout the British realm. "The extent, as well as the duration of legislative power," insisted Madison, "ultimately terminates in the will of the people."[59] The spirit of revolution was in the air, and that spirit would affect the way people thought about the connections that had existed in Virginia between church and state.

"I am well aware," Madison informed his audience, "that even the idea of a free toleration, in matters of religion, has been a source of endless apprehensions, no less weak than inhuman." Many found the new law proposed by the burgesses too restrictive, far less than the toleration afforded in England itself. With the legislation's first appearance in the public papers a few months earlier, the Baptists were quick to protest. Madison, in words the Baptists would echo, urged that the duty of a magistrate extended only to civil concerns, while allowing room for the legislature to craft "a profession of faith purely social…considered, not as Articles of Religion, but as Sentiments which the good Order of Society requires."[60]

During that same session, the burgesses were attempting to jump start the vestry in Augusta, still dominated by dissenters more than twenty years after its beginning. They had already dissolved the vestry once on charges that its members were not entirely "conformable to the doctrine and discipline" of the Church of England, but for the last two years the people of Augusta had managed to avoid certifying a new group of twelve to carry on their responsibilities. Meanwhile, parish levies remained uncollected and their ailing minister, the Reverend John Jones, went unpaid.[61]

As the Augusta vestry languished, just to the north the newly created parish of Beckford in Dunmore County landed on a creative solution. Like much of northern Augusta, Beckford had a healthy share of German-speaking Lutherans, close cousins to Anglicans in both doctrine and mode of worship. Lutherans were even allowed the privilege of calling their houses of worship a church or chapel, instead of the typical "meeting house" reserved for non-Anglican groups. The new parish of Beckford wrote to Peter Muhlenberg, the son of the Lutheran leader in America, and asked him to consider becoming their first priest. After some thought, Muhlenberg accepted and set off to England to receive his Anglican ordination. By the fall of 1772, he was settled in Woodstock.[62]

gations fifty to a hundred miles away from his Culpeper home.[63] Peter Muhlenberg was asked to look into the situation, and perhaps as a result, that same fall the finally-assembled Augusta vestry set aside money for a reader to lead services at the "Dutch meeting at the Peaked

HONEY RUN

Mountain." Now it was the Anglicans' turn to help the Lutheran congregations.[64]

Besides Dunmore County, which now included the Massanutten community, Muhlenberg's ministry extended into northern Augusta where he visited Röder's church. Schwarbach, now older and weaker, was finding it impossible to visit the congre-

One of the first orders of business for the Augusta vestry was to hire an assistant — a curate — to hold services for Reverend Jones. His name was Alexander Balmaine, and not surprisingly, he was a Scotsman.[65] The vestry also ordered a chapel of ease to be built — a local place of worship that served those unable to reach the parish church. This chapel at Cook's Creek, just a short distance from the Presbyterian meeting house and Daniel Harrison's stone house, would be only the second Anglican house of worship financially supported by the Augusta vestry.[66]

But the brief renaissance of Anglican order in the Valley would come to a sudden end. War with England and civil independence would overshadow other concerns, and the Shenandoah Valley's two Anglican ministers helped lead the way. Peter Muhlenberg doffed his clerical robes for an officer's commission as commander of the Eighth Virginia "German" Regiment. Before the war had ended, he would reach the rank of general.[67] In Augusta, Alexander Balmaine — whose sentiments in favor of American independence had been nurtured in his native Scotland — became part of the county's committee of safety, a group of men elected by the freeholders to replace the justices appointed by the governor. Later, he would join the ranks of the Continental Army as chaplain.[68] Exactly six months after the famous midnight ride of Paul Revere to warn the sleeping towns of Lexington and Concord of the advancing British troops, Balmaine wrote to his family back in Scotland.

> *"If a peron was disposed to persecute a Methodist preacher, it was only necessary to call him a Tory, and then they might treat him as cruelly as they pleased. For in many places existing laws were little regarded.... Some of the Methodists were bound in conscience not to fight; and no threatenings could compel them to bear arms or hire a man to take their places. In consequence of this, some of them were whipped, some were fined, and some imprisoned; others were sent home, and many were much persecuted."*
> — Jesse Lee, Methodist historian, 1810

I comfort myself with hopes which I believe animate the hearts of all true friends to both, that America & Britain will soon be reunited in the bonds of Harmony & Peace. And I heartily pray the Almighty to hasten an event at which every good mind will most devoutly rejoice.[69]

Thomas Lewis, a friend of Balmaine and a delegate to the first legislature of the new Commonwealth of Virginia in the fall of 1776, realized that the colony's old establishment of religion could cripple their struggle for political independence. "[T]here is Nothing under Divine favour more Conducive to our preservation in our present alarming Situation," read a petition he and other citizens of Augusta sent to the Virginia Convention, "than a Union of the Strength & Minds of all orders & Degrees of Men amongst us." Presbyterians and Baptists supported the war, too, but in the frontier counties where an estimated one-fifth of the colony's population lived, it had fallen largely to the dissenters to support the Anglican church. "Such partial Discremenating Impositions," noted Lewis, a devout Presbyterian whose name appeared at the top of the list, "have a Manifest Tindancy to Allienate & Imbiter the Minds of those that are thus Imposed on." In other words, if the Anglican government wanted help from dissenters in waging war, it had best relieve them from the burden of paying taxes to a church they didn't support with their hearts.[70]

The legislature was only too eager to comply. For now, religious freedom would serve the interests of civil liberty. Vestries were allowed to collect monies only to pay outstanding debts and to continue to provide for the poor. For all intents and purposes, the parish levy as a means of supporting the established church came to an end.[71] Dissenting denominations were encouraged

to form their own companies under their own officers. The Baptists were among the

most eager, not only raising groups of soldiers, but also gaining permission to preach
to the Continental Army.[72]

But the willingness of Baptists to pursue
a military solution to religious freedom
caused grave misgivings for Martin Kaufman
and ten to twelve other Mennonists at the
Whitehouse church. They would not raise
their weapons in war, nor swear allegiance
to the new Commonwealth. Though Koontz
and others urged them to "yield the liberty
of conscience to others," Kaufman and his
friends declared "they could not in good
conscience hold fellowship or communion
with persons who allowed such unlawful
practices."[73]

That would cost something, but they
were not alone. There would be others who
listened beyond the clamoring demands for
independence.

On April 19, 1777, Alexander Miller again
stood up for something he believed in. "To
claim independence," he wrote to Augusta's
newest House of Delegates member John
Poage, "seems to me evidently wrong."[74]
Besides a violation of the oaths taken to
Great Britain, the assertion of American freedom could only come through force and
strength — means no better than piracy —

PEAKED MOUNTAIN

71

Valley that opened the way for other dissenting ministers to perform weddings. In the late 1750s and early 1760s another Presbyterian, Cook's Creek and Peaked Mountain minister Alexander Miller, kept a list of many couples he had united in holy matrimony. Philip van Gemuenden, the German Reformed minister, also married several couples about the same time. Strictly speaking, this sort of thing was illegal, but Virginia law sometimes seemed a little worn out after that long trip from Williamsburg. Besides the strength of dissenters, Augusta was a huge parish, far too large for any one minister to serve.

Yet, there was more to this than the laws of the established church. Weddings were an additional source of income. An Anglican minister received twenty shillings for each wedding performed by license. By marrying one couple a week, the parish priest of Augusta could theoretically double his annual salary of fifty pounds. If dissenting ministers were not allowed to collect those fees, it put an even greater financial burden on their congregations. Those Lutherans trying to support Reverend Schwarbach made a particular note of it.

In part, financial need could provide one motivation for non-Anglican ministers to travel to other churches scores of miles away from their own. Besides marriages and funer-

and pirates were apt to be robbed themselves, with no room to appeal.

"You see what will follow," the former Presbyterian minister at Cook's Creek declared, "either to avoid claiming independency or be subjected to the divine displeasure and punishment."[75]

Miller had written "with great cheerfulness, confidence, and freedom" as he put it, even giving Poage permission to print the letter in the paper, anonymously of course. He had written the same to Colonel Abraham Smith, in hopes that these two men would use their influence to change the course of events.

Ironically, Colonel Smith was in charge of the Augusta militia, where he was experiencing a few other difficulties regarding loyalty to the patriots' cause. About seven times each year since the conflict with England began, the county militia would be called together for a muster. Occasionally someone would be missing, but there were a few who never turned up at all. John and Christopher Brunk who purchased land west of Linville Creek were two. So were the Laymans, a father and son both by the name of John who lived just west of the Peaked

Mountain.[76] They were Mennonists.

At the start of the war, when members of the "peace churches" were exempted from serving on the militia completely, it had created some hard feelings among their neighbors who pointed out the injustice of subjecting the rest of the community "to the whole burthen of government." They suggested that if these pacifists refused to serve or provide a substitute, they should be fined just like other militia men who refused to serve. The legislature had agreed, and in tacit understanding of the solidarity of the Mennonists, had made their entire community liable to pay what was due. By their absence, it was easy to assume they were Tories, but non-resistance did not mean they chose sides. They simply did not choose war.[77]

There were a few Tories, though, not far from the Laymans. Their leader, William Hinton, declared that the British General Howe might as well go home with his finely tailored troops. "I can raise men enough to take the country and I will do it," he bragged, "for I am Captain of better men than they." Hinton and two other ringleaders, John and Martin Groeder, were rounded up and

fighting over freedom

brought to Staunton for trial. The day after, Poage turned Alexander Miller's letter over to the authorities. Within the week, Miller was standing before the court to answer for his words, characterized as "contrary to the safety, peace, and good order of the people" of Virginia. An earlier charge had confined Miller to his plantation until the end of the war. On that occasion, arresting officers had found Miller 120 miles to the south, apparently spreading his views on the piracy of independence and the importance of keeping oaths.[78]

Not far from the home of Adam Mueller, another bit of piracy had been in the making. Peter Mischler, "a so-called Lutheran minister," had edged his way into the congregation at the Lower Peaked Mountain church. Years earlier the Lutheran ministerium had rebuked Mischler for allowing himself to be "used by Satan and his followers as a wretched tool," dividing churches for his own ends. The Lutheran leader Henry Muhlenberg, Peter Muhlenberg's father, had held little hope for Mischler then, perhaps even less for church leaders who willingly allowed such "ignorant and shallow" ministers to serve their purpose. "For this is a free country," such leaders were said to argue, "where neither Pope nor Council, neither Synod nor Coetus has any authority over us."[79]

In a way, Muhlenberg's thoughts were prophetic. Even as his son was preparing to lead the Eighth Virginia German Regiment into battle, and he himself was making plans to flee Philadelphia ahead of the advancing British army, Peter Mischler was set again to divide and conquer.

Members of the Lower Peaked Mountain church appealed to the current minister of the Culpeper Lutherans, Jacob Franck, to restore peace. Franck wrote Muhlenberg the following day, but in these chaotic times, no response could have been expected. Within a few days, Franck travelled over the ridge to check on the situation. Apparently the damage had already been done.[80] On June 1, 1777, Peter Mischler and others dedicated a new Lutheran church, based on the "unaltered Augsburg Confession, etc." still a euphemism for Lutheran orthodoxy. The name would be Peter's church, ostensibly for the Apostle of Christ, but there were those who believed it was Mischler's sly tribute to himself.[81]

als, a dissenting minister might be able to earn a little extra income by confirming children or serving the Lord's Supper in congregations who did not have a regular preacher. Charles Lange, the German Reformed minister who briefly served the Peaked Mountain churches as well as Röder's, tried to make baptisms a source of income as well, but his insistence upon payment due before services rendered irritated more than a few parents.

When salaries for Anglican ministers were suspended at the beginning of the Revolution, it was their turn to look hard into the face of financial insecurity. Using his position as the only minister legally allowed to solemnize a marriage, Augusta priest Alexander Balmaine collected a thirty percent commission on every wedding performed by the new Baptist minister at Linville's Creek. The "Day of Settlement with the Curiot," as John Alderson, Jr. put it exactly one month before the Declaration of Independence was signed, netted Balmaine three pounds and five shillings all together, or six-and-a-half shillings per wedding. A few months later, Balmaine took a job that at least offered the hope of financial provision, a chaplaincy in the Continental army.

It wasn't until 1780, the year Harrisonburg was set apart as Rockingham's new county seat, that the Virginia *legislature passed a law allowing dissenting preachers to legally marry couples in Virginia. No more than four ministers from each sect could be licensed in any one county. In Rockingham, the first to apply was Anderson Moffett, the Baptist preacher at Smith's Creek once jailed for not having a license to preach. It had been a long wait, but finally the wedding game was coming to an end.*[Side 5]

Like the church nearby Herman's old mill on Stony Creek and the other at Röder's, Lower Peaked Mountain had been a union church, composed of both Lutherans and

county to be called Rockingham. To the west it would stretch through Brock's Gap and beyond. To the south, it would embrace the homes of the Madisons, Lewises, and

A ROCKINGHAM SKY

Reformed. Thanks to Mischler's new enterprise, the union was dissolved, at least for the present. In time, their friends would see another side of Mischler's character.

That fall, Peter's church and the land on both sides of the Peaked Mountain north to the Fairfax Line would be divided into a new

Joneses.[82]

Though the function of vestries had been reduced to a sole civic duty — to take care of the poor — there would still be a new parish as well, also called Rockingham. Unlike the old Augusta vestry, this group would not have to worry about religious conformity to the Anglican church. Now, *political* conformity was demanded. Every vestryman was required to swear an oath to the new Commonwealth of Virginia, "to support, maintain, and defend the constitution and government thereof."[83]

For some reason, the particulars of the division came as somewhat of a surprise. Not long after the first court met at Daniel Smith's home in the spring of 1778, the new justices of Rockingham requested the line to be redrawn. It seems that about two-thirds of the tithables had been left in old Augusta, putting a strain on the new county's finances.[84] Since the minister of Augusta parish, Reverend Jones, was no longer living, the justices requested the sale of his glebe. In addition, they wanted their share of the value of the courthouse, the jail, the Anglican houses of worship, as well as their portion of the last levy.[85] In some ways, Rockingham was ahead of the game on their request. Once the war was over, ownership of glebe lands and churches — valued throughout the colony at several hundred thousand pounds — became a hotly contested issue.[86] For now, it was simply a matter of making ends meet.

Throughout the war years, collecting taxes from people often struggling to feed themselves was never easy. Much of the money would go to support the rebellion, and on that count, at least one group of people simply refused to cooperate at all.

———

There were never many, but they stood together. John Layman was among them. So was another Mennonist, Nicholas Beery. They were joined by John Glick and Jacob Bowman, both members of the Dunker church whose numbers were now growing in the new county of Rockingham. These men and others like them refused to report their taxable property in 1780 and 1781.[87] Both groups had also condemned payment of the militia substitute fees — paid to the treasury in lieu of military service — which one Dunker church in the colonies had called "protection money."[88]

But fines for not attending muster and refusing to turn in their taxable property lists were relatively mild admonishments for non-resistance. In Pennsylvania, eleven

Mennonist families were stripped of their belongings, including beds, linens, books and Bibles. Some were left without food for their children, or warmth for the winter ahead.[89] In Frederick County, Maryland, there lingered the gruesome story of a treason trial in which at least one Dunker was sentenced to be barbarously executed, and his remains publicly displayed.[90] In a state that offered war as the sole hope of survival, it was sometimes impossible to be a peacemaker and not be considered a traitor.

Perhaps because of this lingering suspicion and fear of retribution from their neighbors, it is hard to know precisely how many members of the "peace churches" made their way south of the Fairfax Line during the war years.[91] All in all, the Valley of Virginia seemed a relatively safe place to be. Virginia's draft exemption laws were mild in comparison with those in Pennsylvania and Maryland, and though many from Augusta and Rockingham fought in the war, the Valley saw no major conflicts. Besides rounding up the Tories near the Peaked Mountain, there was another scare when the fleeing legislature came to Staunton and stayed over for a while, meeting at the Anglican parish church. Then the vigilant guarded the mountain passes in expectation that British General Tarleton's troops might follow, but nothing came of it.[92]

Still, as one later recalled, "the times were generally dismal during the war, what with the Indians on the one side and the British on the other."[93] There were plenty of battles elsewhere, and Rockingham had sent its fair share of men to fill the ranks of the Continental Army. Others in the county had helped to supply the troops as they travelled to face the British in the Carolinas.[94]

After the decisive victory at Yorktown and the eventual end of the war, the roads were filled with people headed both north and south. Among them were Mennonists and Dunkers, many bringing little with them but the hope of a new start. Those who had settled in Rockingham joined their voices in a petition for mercy.

The old burden of serving in the military, the signers reminded the legislature of the now-independent Commonwealth, often tended "almost to the ruin or at least greatly to the prejudice of many poor Familys amongst us.…[R]ather wishing to enjoy Peace of Conscience…we purchase it at the

Expence of our whole Estate."[95] The assembly responded by acknowledging their religious beliefs against bearing arms, but continued to impose the fine system that was in place throughout the war. Now, apparently, was not the time for the fledgling colonies to let down their guard.

Legislatively speaking, little had been decided regarding the role of religion and faith in the new government. With Anglican ministers depending on the voluntary support of their congregations, several in the legislature favored a general assessment, a collection to be distributed to ministers of all Protestant denominations. In the Valley especially, those were fighting words, and one of the earliest protests came from Rockingham.

"[A]ny Majestrait or Legislative Body that takes upon themselves the power of Governing Religion by human Laws Assumes a power that never was commited to them by God nor can be by Man," read the petition signed by 168 citizens. Here again was the threat of establishment, a burden that had made it financially difficult to support their own ministers. Though even some of their own ministers would stand to benefit financially from the proposed tax, the signers warned that here was a dangerous precedent for the new Commonwealth: "if you can do anything in Religion by human Laws you can do every thing." If the legislature could take five dollars from their pockets this year, they could just as easily take fifty the next.[96]

Taxes were already enough of a burden to these citizens. More than three-fourths of all Virginia counties were delinquent in paying their taxes, and Rockingham was one of the most deeply in arrears, owing more than £2638.[97] "The great scarceity and the large demand for Cash at this juncture is becoming most alarming," a group of prominent Rockinghamers noted. But the issue was more than a lack of hard currency. The people of Rockingham owned little or no property that they could sell to make up the difference. Before the war, cattle and horses had been the mainstay of their economy. Now there was hardly a demand for these animals. Ironically, it was tobacco, the staple crop of the east, that had retained its perennial ability to command cash. Even in Rockingham, traditionally a region for growing such useful and necessary crops as corn and wheat, a few made a small try to grow the old Virginia currency, and requested that the Legislature build a tobacco warehouse in Harrisonburg to properly store, inspect, and grade the produce before it was shipped east, but none was apparently built.[98]

Mennonists and Dunkers — along with

German farms gained a reputation for their simple prosperity.

Even though the barrier of language and culture distinguished them from their English and Scotch-Irish neighbors, perhaps they might live in peace in this new and

TUNKER HOUSE
Artist's rendering of mechanism

the other German-speaking communities — were generally farmers, both frugal and industrious. Women carried a large share of the responsibility, working long hours in the field to bring a crop to harvest. With everyone lending an honest hand to the plow, the

uncertain land. In Pennsylvania, the Mennonists had built several churches. Here, perhaps for lack of money, perhaps for fear of reprisal, there would be none in Virginia for several years. The Dunkers, too, had built at least one meeting house in Pennsylvania, but generally "they chose rather to meet *from house to house* in imitation of the primitive Christians."[99]

As a result, Dunker homes were designed to serve the purposes of their immediate family as well as their larger church family. A typical one-and-a-half story house would have a first floor divided into separate rooms either by homespun curtains or by sawn, wooden partitions. The heavier partitions hung "on a pivot and could be hoisted, or the lower half could be so manipulated as to throw the entire lower story into one room on meeting-day." Gathering for worship was appropriately a time for hospitality. After the meeting was over and the locations of the next meetings were announced, everyone was invited to stay for dinner at the expense and kindness of their host. Of course, even the horses were fed and watered.

6 A NEW LIBERTY

Throughout their years in the Valley, both Dunkers and Mennonists would gain a reputation for their generosity and kindness, not only to those within their community, but also to those without. Though they may not have understood it, it was perhaps a blessing they arrived during a time of such physical and spiritual poverty.[100]

With the end of the war came also the end of an era. The pioneer Adam Mueller, whose family had made this open frontier a home, died in 1783, the year the Treaty of Paris brought an official end to hostilities between Britain and her former colonies. It would be left to a new generation to grapple with the questions of freedom and conscience, and they would need all the wisdom they could get.

Within the first decade after the Treaty of Paris declared the colonists fully independent, denominations of every ilk began to reshape themselves in the light of their new freedom.

"I was met by an old German, who shook me by the hand, and said he wished he might be worthy to wash my feet. Yea, thought I, if you knew what a poor sinful creature I am, you would hardly look at one so unworthy; but Jesus lives — O precious Christ, thou art mine and I am thine!"
— *Francis Asbury, Methodist bishop, on his way north from Harrisonburg, 1793*

Among the first was the fellowship of Methodists, a renewal movement within the Anglican communion. Methodist preachers consistently refrained from administering the sacraments of baptism and the Eucharist, leaving these rites to the properly ordained parish priests, and held to the dictum, "He that leaves the Church leaves the Methodists." As itinerant ministers who "travelled to call sinners to repentance," their goal was to encourage and build up the Anglican church from within.[101]

All of this underscored their desire not to compete with the established church. Yet, because Methodists placed an emphasis on the words of Jesus, "Ye must be born again," they encouraged a faith in God not based on ritual, but on personal relationship, and Methodist leaders were open to expressions of emotion consistent with that worship of a personal redeemer. Their meetings — which sometimes included shouts of praise, crying, even falling down under the power of God's Spirit — were a far cry from the ordered pattern of traditional Anglican worship. To some observers, these gatherings were more closely related to those of the Separate Baptists and former New Side Presbyterians. "We are not dissenters," the Methodists clarified in a 1776 petition to the General Assembly, "but a Religious Society in Communion with the Church of England [and] do all in our Power to Strengthen and support the said Church."[102]

When war temporarily suspended the establishment, Methodist leaders in Virginia and North Carolina took it upon themselves to break not only with the wishes of their leaders but also with the order of their church. Though not officially ordained by the Bishop, they began baptizing and administering communion in the many vacant parishes.[103] But it was a decisive American victory that brought the ultimate issue to the table. To continue under the hierarchy of the Church of England would be awkward at best now that the colonies were free from the Crown. The American brethren were "now at full liberty simply to follow the Scriptures, and the primitive church," suggested Methodist founder John Wesley. "And we judge it best that they should stand fast in that liberty wherewith God has so strangely made them free."[104] At Wesley's initiation, by the end of 1784 those involved with the Methodist society in America separated from the Anglican church and became a distinct organization, the Methodist Episcopal

W I L L O W   T R E E
*by old spring at
Adam Mueller's house*

emotion in these meetings, Jarratt noted. "It requires much wisdom to allay the wild, and not damp the sacred fire."

Methodists did at least try to guide the emotional side of meetings from becoming indecent spectacles. One such method was hymn singing. "When the passions of the people were rising too high, and breaking through all restraint, the preacher gently checked them by giving out a few verses of a hymn."

This method, however, did not always work, even for the Methodists, as Benjamin Abbott discovered on a visit to Martin Boehm's around 1779.

When I came to my application, the power of the Lord came in such a manner, that the people fell all about the house; and their cries might be heard afar off. This alarmed the wicked, who sprang for the doors in such haste, that they fell over another in heaps. The cry of mourners was so great, I thought to give out a hymn to drown out the noise, and desired one of our English friends to raise it, but as soon as he began to sing, the power of the Lord struck him, and he pitched under the table, and there lay like a dead man. I gave it out again, and asked another to

Church. Francis Asbury, who had travelled throughout the eastern states since his arrival to America in 1771, was ordained as a superintendent, the highest office in the new denomination.

Only a year earlier Asbury had been in Winchester, the largest city west of the Ridge, second only to Staunton, 150 miles to the south. "[R]eligion is greatly wanting in these parts," he recorded in his journal. "The inhabitants are much divided; made up…of different nations, and speaking different languages, they agree in scarcely anything, except it be to sin against God."[105]

In some ways his remarks could have applied to almost any place north of Staunton. German-speaking people were clearly divided from their neighbors by barriers of culture and language. They, in turn, were divided by their own groups and denominations — Reformed, Lutheran, Mennonist, Dunker, and others. English and Scotch-Irish had their own share of cultural and religious distinctives among Presbyterians, Anglicans, and various styles of Baptists. A new nation did not necessarily mean a united one.

Independence had also left the land

with a grave uncertainty at a time when spiritual guidance seemed wanting. "The Sabbath had been almost forgotten, and the public morals sadly deteriorated," recalled one. "A cold and lukewarm indifference was manifest in all the ministrations of the gospel throughout all that region of the country, without exception, as far as known."[106]

Even the Baptists, who had most recently carried the spiritual fervor of evangelism, were themselves caught up in political pursuits. Meetings that had been filled with mutual encouragement against fierce opposition prior to the war now turned to establishing a significant position in the new social order. There had been no record of activity at Linville Creek Baptist since just before the Spring of 1777. Cook's Creek Presbyterian, and "Upper" Peaked Mountain Lutheran and Reformed churches were much the same. Peter's church, organized anew under the questionable leadership of Peter Mischler, had languished like the rest.[107]

The change came sometime around 1789, when effects of a revival at the Presbyterian college of Hampden-Sydney broke out in Lexington, further up the Valley from Staunton. Reverend William Graham told the story of the rapid and effective change brought about in many "determined to seek their Saviour," weeping as he exhorted his hearers to follow their lead. The revival spread to almost every Presbyterian congregation in the Valley.[108]

Revival had been spreading among the Baptists as well. From 1785 to 1789 this "glorious work of God" resulted in nearly six thousand baptisms throughout Virginia among the Baptists alone. A group of Baptists gathered near where Dry Run flowed into the North River in the southern part of the county. The church at Linville Creek had been thinking about closing its doors in 1788, but just a year later, they were celebrating communion with two veteran evangelists who had seen the worst of the persecution of earlier days, James Ireland and Anderson

NORTH & DRY RIVERS

raise it: as soon as he attempted, he fell also. I then made the third attempt, and the power of God came upon me in such a manner, that I cried out, and was amazed. I then saw that I was fighting against God, and did not attempt to sing again. Mr. Beam, the owner of the house, and a preacher among the Germans, cried out, "I never saw God in this way before."

The day's events reminded Boehm and Abbott of the day of Pentecost, when Jesus' disciples were filled with the Holy Spirit. Boldly going out into the streets of Jerusalem, they spoke in languages they had never learned. People from many nations were amazed to hear "the wonderful works of God" spoken in their native tongue by these Galileean fishermen (Acts 2:11). Others just thought they were drunk. Jarratt's description appears to have been right on target.

In some degree, these expressions of faith turned some people away from revival, split denominations, or resulted in the organization of new groups. There were no doubt cases of excess, pure emotionalism, as many leaders were known to observe. But whenever they occurred, revivals like these never seemed to stay within denominational boundaries. Congregationalists,

Presbyterians, Baptists, German Reformed, Dunkers, Lutherans, Mennonists, and Methodists were all subjects of this unusual outpouring. Though it might become out of place in the worship services of many congregations, emotion would never grow out of place between a child and his or her Heavenly Father. Side 6

Moffett. John Lincoln, at whose home the Baptists of that area had often been meeting, suggested that it would be a good idea to hold prayer meetings with his friends and neighbors on Sundays when there was no preaching. After Moffett's added support, "the Church agreed, that it might be or was expedient to hold such Meetings." From the sound of things, these Baptists were at least a little uncertain.[109]

The proposed Sunday prayer meetings may have been partly an expression of renewed zeal, and partly a response to the rapid growth of the Methodists, who by now were drawing from the ranks of the Baptists along Smith's Creek.[110] Despite Wesley's plan to retain a modified Anglican worship service, the Methodists were rather unattached to the Prayer Book. Many of their preachers had been used to praying extemporaneously, and were "fully satisfied that they could pray bet-

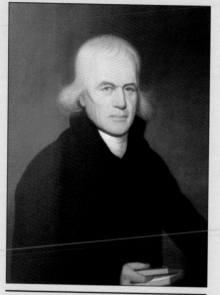

BISHOP ASBURY

ter, and with more devotion while their eyes were shut, than they could with their eyes open."[111] In fact, their trend away from a formal liturgy and their emphasis on personal faith were perhaps their closest points of agreement with the Baptists.[112]

Of course they agreed on the basics of the gospel: that God's Son, Jesus, had died for the sin of the whole world, that he rose again and offered forgiveness of sin to all who put their faith in him, that he would come again to reign on the earth. All of these were elemental. But there was one significant difference beyond these that seemed to eclipse all of their common beliefs, and that was "freedom of choice."

Essentially, it boiled down to who did the choosing in salvation. The Baptists in the main had followed what was called the Calvinistic plan, namely that God chose or "predestined" whom he would save and when. The Methodists held more to a belief known as Arminianism, that people were effective agents both in receiving as well as in "working out" their own salvation. In fact, the Bible said both, but by emphasizing certain Scriptures over others while losing some of their meaning in semantics and doctrinal formulas, it was easy to see why confusion and dissension flowed freely. More pointedly, one of the key issues centered around "final perseverance," whether those whom God saved were eternally secure as the Calvinists believed, or whether they could lose or somehow abandon that salvation, an Arminian viewpoint.[113]

In the midst of this conflict, the Baptists were growing, but it was the Methodists who seemed to have the stronger financial backing in the community.

In 1789, as the Linville Creek Baptists were still more than fifteen years away from getting a much-needed new meeting house, the Methodists were having their own completed in the county seat of Harrisonburg. They were enthusiastic not just for the gospel of Christ, but for their particular brand of it. No one besides Bishop Asbury or someone he appointed was "to have and

ASBURY'S POWDER HORN

---

enjoy the free use and benefit of the said premises" and no doctrine was to be preached other than that "contained in Mr.

John Wesleys Notes upon the New Testament and four Volumes of Sermons."[114]

The first amendments to the new Constitution of the United States, approved for ratification by Congress just the month before, declared there should be "no law respecting an establishment of religion, or prohibiting the free exercise thereof."[115] Denominational rivalries might have their own set of rules.

———

The First Amendment's assurance of freedom in religion was an echo of a Virginia law passed only a few months after the 1785 revival had begun. The Virginia Act for Religious Freedom — a modified version of

Thomas Jefferson's original proposal — proclaimed that all men should "be free to profess, and by argument to maintain, their opinion in matters of religion."[116] No longer could an individual's choice of faith determine his ability to serve in a civil capacity. Legally, the old Establishment was ended, but it had not entirely disappeared.

Scattered throughout the Commonwealth were the remnants of Anglican rule — glebes, poorhouses, churches, and chapels of ease — but there was very little in the way of public support. An act to incorporate the Anglicans under the new banner of the Protestant Episcopal Church in 1784 was repealed two years later, its language tasting too much like the bitter fruit of a defeated monopoly.[117]

Though weakened, the church did retain a number of strong supporters, clergy and parishioners who had stayed true to the American cause and to the English church. In 1785 about two-thirds of the parishes in Virginia were supplied by a priest, but in the Valley it was a different story. Rockingham, formed during the war years after the establishment had been suspended, never had an Anglican minister. To the north, Dunmore — now Shenandoah — had been relinquished by Peter Muhlenberg for the sake of American independence. Augusta's Alexander Balmaine, serving as the new rector of Frederick Parish, remained the only Protestant Episcopal minister for hundreds of miles on the western side of the Blue Ridge.[118]

But Rockingham did have one leader for

the ailing church. James Madison, who had served as president of William and Mary

BISHOP MADISON

College for the last several years, was appointed Virginia's first bishop of the Protestant Episcopal church. "I have consented," he wrote to the cousin who shared his name, "whether wisely or not I cannot say, to undertake it."[119]

Considering the state of affairs, his job was no romp through the park. For some

years to come, the citizens of Virginia would lobby to receive the old glebes as public property, and they would finally win. General sentiment leaned toward a more American expression of faith — or toward none at all. With no parish levy in effect, ministers and church buildings were forced to rely on the same means other denominations used to raise money. Generally that was by subscription, a voluntary commitment to contribute money over a given period of time. Plainly put, there were not enough former Anglicans to fill the coffers. The Staunton church — the only Anglican church ever built in Augusta and Rockingham — would sit vacant for twenty to thirty years, and the still new parish of Rockingham would not get on its feet for another fifty or sixty after

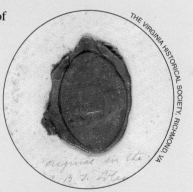

MADISON'S SEAL

that.[120]

Meanwhile, the Methodists were looking for places to gather. Besides their new church on the Southwest Square in Harrisonburg, they used the now vacant chapel of ease at Cook's Creek.[121] Many partisans of the old establishment had found a familiar ring to the Methodists, albeit with a rather different rhythm.

The year after the land for the Harrisonburg church was granted, Bishop Francis Asbury came to call.[122] Traveling down the south branch of the Potomac just over the North Mountain, he first stopped at the home of Michael Baker, "a pious German" as Asbury described him. Set among the broad, green fields of the North River beside the road that led east through Brock's Gap, in many respects Baker's 581-

acre estate rivaled that of Gabriel Jones, the former King's attorney and a neighbor of the Madisons.[123] Though Asbury was an Englishman holding a mid-week meeting for German farmers in the middle of August's sometimes thick heat, he reported he had "an attentive congregation."[124]

That weekend, the Methodist bishop was in Harrisonburg at the new church built for him on the hill. There, he said, was "the beginning of a good work....People came as far as thirty miles to preaching; and some found the Lord during my stay." Within a twelve-month period, the number of Methodists in the sprawling and newly established Rockingham Circuit more than tripled. In addition to Bishop Asbury's ministrations, there were one or two Methodist preachers assigned to the Circuit as well as a

MICHAEL BAKER'S ESTATE
along the north fork of the Shenandoah in Brock's Gap

number of local ministers.[125]

But these occasional visits and church meetings were only a part — in fact a small part — of what the Methodists were about. Accustomed to using the meeting houses and churches of other denominations in the years before and during the war, Methodist congregations — "societies" as they called them — had also gathered together in homes and elsewhere in smaller groups called "class meetings."

Each class was "placed under a person of experience and piety, who meets the others once a week, for prayer, and inquiry into the religious state of each, in order to administer exhortation and counsel."[126] It was important that the leader not only know each person on a friendly basis, but that he also understand their personal struggles, what temptations they might face, and whatever else might help this shepherd care for those in his charge. In the process, future ministers were prepared in the practical duties of their calling, an essential element for successful growth, especially on the frontier.

Classes also laid the foundations for new believers, including those who "found the Lord" during Asbury's visit. In the close, personalized setting of a class meeting, those who had only recently made a commitment

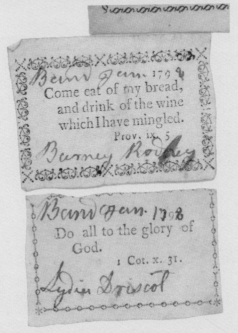

METHODIST LOVE FEAST
tickets

to Christ could be encouraged by the example and advice of older Christians and receive help to "oppose and subdue old habits and besetting sins." In many respects, the Methodist class was like an extended family, emphasized by their sharing a simple meal of bread and water known as a "love feast." A carryover from the Moravian practice, each love feast included a confession of sin and the reminder o f 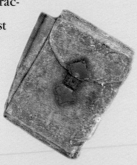 with his disciples just before he was crucified.

The first part of the love feast was footwashing. With men and women seated separately, someone would read the story of Jesus washing his disciples' feet which begins, "Now before the feast of the Passover, when Jesus knew that his hour had come that he should depart from this world to the Father, having loved his own who were in the world, he loved them to the end" (John 13:1). Footwashing signified not only the cleansing each believer needed, but also allowed the fellowship to serve one another in this simple, humbling way. The Lord's Supper that followed the footwashing was a simple meal of fellowship, often of beef, broth, and bread.

L E A T H E R   P O U C H
for Methodist Love Feast tickets

God's forgiveness. Clearly, here was a close-knit group that offered support as well as accountability in living out the Christian life.[127]

The love feast was a tradition of another group as well, the Dunkers. Like the Methodists, they desired to reclaim the spirit and camaraderie of the first-century Church, a legacy of their pietist heritage. For the Dunkers, the love feast included footwashing, the Lord's Supper, the kiss of charity and the right hand of fellowship, the holy communion (Eucharist), singing, and prayer. In many ways, the entire celebration was patterned after the Passover Jesus had shared

Finally, they shared the Eucharist, the holy communion meal of unleavened bread and wine. For the Dunkers, this was a memorial meal to be taken seriously. Perhaps days before the love feast, each member of the congregation might be visited by a deacon to ask if they were still "in the faith" and at peace with others in the congregation. They took seriously the words of Jesus to "be reconciled to your brother" before coming to the altar. To affirm this relationship, just prior to sharing the communion meal, the congregation would exchange the "kiss of peace" or the "right hand of fellowship" with at least one other person. Love for God meant nothing if it did not translate into love for your neighbor.[128]

When Virginia had considered eliminating the old Anglican establishment, some had been concerned that the absence of a state church would leave no moral foundation for the new republic.[129] But establishment or no establishment, many Virginians

FOOTWASHING
at Dunker Love Feast

cared little for a faith that required them to change in any way. The French Revolution may have brought soaring wheat prices and a partial solution to the Valley's bout with poverty, but in its wake spread deism — a philosophy of divine resignation and the fast-growing fashion of the educated elite.[130]

At its core, deism held that though there was a creator, he was a disinterested one, a god who has no effective power in human lives today. "Even they who still call themselves Christians have grown cold and languid," proclaimed Bishop Madison in his address to the people of the Anglican church, "while thousands availing themselves of that languor, treat religion as a prejudice which debases the human mind; deride its sacred obligations, and exultingly anticipate its obliteration from the earth."[131]

The cynicism with which many viewed religious faith was no doubt fueled by the divisions they saw among Christian believers. Perhaps as an antidote, Madison had appealed to his own church for unity with

Madison's cohort, Bishop Asbury, also grieved over these rifts among Protestant Christians. "How common is it for different denominations to ask each other of their distinguishing peculiarities," he remarked the year he first came into Rockingham, "and how very rare it is for them to talk closely of the dealings of God with their own souls."[133]

There was at least one group, however, who had landed upon a solution to that problem, and Asbury knew them well.

the Methodists and other Protestant denominations, but the Episcopalians did not seem at all interested.[132]

Asbury's focus was not unlike that of his close friend, Reformed minister William Otterbein. The informal gathering of Lutherans, Reformed, Mennonists, Dunkers, and others which Otterbein and Martin Boehm had helped organize — the United Brethren — closely resembled the Methodists with whom they had cooperated for years. United Brethren meetings were open to emotional expressions of faith often frowned upon in the more liturgical churches, and they "insisted on the necessity of genuine repentance and conversion, on the knowledge of a pardon of sin, and in consequence thereof, a change of heart and renovation of spirit." Perhaps their most visible distinction from the Methodists was that they tended to minister to the German-speaking people from which they had originated. As a result, they were often called "Dutch Methodists," a term that in those days was considered slanderous.[134]

One of the earliest United Brethren ministers to come into Rockingham was Christian Newcomer, a Mennonist from Lancaster County, Pennsylvania. In 1796, he conducted a meeting at Mr. Snider's on Linville Creek, and then went a short way to the home of his uncle, a Mennonist preacher in the area, where he "spoke with considerable liberty" from Psalm 34:15. The following year Newcomer returned to conduct a three-day meeting in cooperation with the German Reformed minister, George Geeting. The services would be at Peter Moyers' place, about five miles south of Harrisonburg on the Stage Road to Staunton.[135]

The meeting began on a Saturday morning at eleven o'clock, but it wasn't until the following day that they began to see visible signs of change. In the Sunday morning meeting, "Brother Geeting preached with remarkable power, from these words: 'Whoseoever will be my disciple, let him take up his cross and follow me.'" That night, a candlelight meeting was held at Mr. Klein's. There, "several young people were effected and prayed heartily to God for salvation." On Monday, the last day of the gathering, many people were so moved that they cried aloud.[136]

Of course, the United Brethren were still a very informal group. They had adopted certain practices — like footwashing and love feasts — from the denominations represented among them, but they were more interested in developing faith in Christ than establishing a new organization. Martin Boehm, in fact, urged those serious about their relationship with Christ to join with the Methodists.[137]

It would not at all have been surprising to find some of those associated with the United Brethren sending their children to the new Methodist school in Harrisonburg, which was set in order a couple of years earlier on June 23, 1794. Classes were held in the recently completed Methodist church on the hill, where students were required to attend public worship. The exception was Sunday, when all students seven years and older were allowed to attend any "publick service…wherever his or her Parents Guardians or Master may direct."

Beyond that freedom, the scholars were somewhat limited. School was to be held year-round, beginning around 8 o'clock in the morning, and ending sometime late afternoon, between four and six depending on the season. Recess was, however, generous — one hour in the winter, two hours in the summer. A "strict order of silence" was to be observed during school hours. If a student rebelled against the rules of the school, he or she could be dismissed. In the "case of Sinning against God, the trial shall be very serious, the facts proved, and the Sinner Properly dealt with, according to the Judgment of the Teacher."[138]

The following May, in 1795, Bishop Asbury visited Harrisonburg and read his "Thoughts on Education" to the Board of Visitors. Two years earlier he had noted that "Satan [had] been sowing discord here, and…hindered the work of God."[139] The Methodists were known to have been ridiculed for their sometimes boisterous gatherings, still seen by some as undignified spectacles. Perhaps he and the Methodists' "very respectable friends" in the community had hopes the school would

THOMAS HARRISON HOUSE

raise their esteem in the public eye.[140]

United Brethren faced the same possibility of censure as the Methodists. Both groups were new to the community and were drawing people away from the more traditional and established denominations. Two of the groups represented among the United Brethren — the Lutheran and German Reformed — would probably have struggled even without this challenge. Still facing the scarcity of well-qualified, ordained ministers, they had received several preachers "less than worthy" of their calling. George Butler had a rather tarnished war record, enlisting in Muhlenberg's German Regiment as well as in a regiment from Maryland, deserting both, and still claiming various bounties of land for his service. He began an irregular ministry in Pennsylvania, but the ministerium declared "he must forever be regarded incapable of serving in the ministerial office." Ironically, in spite of his perceived character deficits, Butler was "advised to serve as school teacher."[141]

Sometime in the early 1790s, Butler found his way into Rockingham where for a time he served the German Reformed church named Frieden's, from the German

word for "peace."[142] Located in the southern part of the county just a few miles southwest of the Peaked Mountain church, Frieden's had perhaps joined them in accepting the services of another controversial fellow, one Peter Ahl, a surgeon in Peter Muhlenberg's German regiment during the past war. Ahl had applied for membership in the Lutheran ministerium in 1791, but they "resolved [to]…have nothing to do with him." Both Ahl and Butler were gone by 1796 when the ministerium appointed John Foltz to visit congregations at Brock's Gap, Röder's, and St. Peter's.[143]

The Reformed also had to depend on the occasional visits of ministers passing through. Reformed minister John William Runkel, who ministered at Frieden's and Röder's in the early 1790s, complained of some people holding Otterbein's views who tried to draw "the religious portion of his members away from the church."[144] It would not be enough to have occasional leadership from transient ministers. What the Reformed church in Rockingham needed was someone of character who could go the distance, someone willing to walk the extra mile.

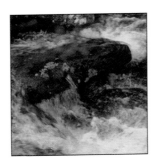

RAPIDS

1800 - 1850

---

*Along a river's rapids, the smooth, well-oiled surface
is broken up and brought to life in a majesty of
rolling white. It is a place of danger as well as beauty,
where many a traveller has become distracted, lost
sight of the rocks, and turned up shipwrecked.*

FANNED BY THE FLAMES

The roads were not completely safe, even on horseback. Robbers were a possibility, unless the cold drove them indoors to a warm fire. But the man with the walking staff seemed to have travelled a long way.

Where have you come from?

— York.

Pennsylvania? You've travelled two hundred miles on foot?

— Yes.

Johannes Braun was not far beyond his twenty-ninth birthday when he walked south, up the Shenandoah Valley and into Rockingham.[1] At first he had not planned to stay in America. It was only going to be a visit, a chance to see the land he had dreamed about as a child when he first saw German troops marching out to join their British allies. Then America had been only a word on the lips of a small boy. Now it held the faces of people who needed him.[2]

Not too long ago he had set sail from Germany for the first time, but when he landed in Baltimore that summer of 1797, it was already a familiar place. He had dreamed of it while still at sea. There among all the sights and sounds was the church on top of the

THE EVANGELICAL AND REFORMED HISTORICAL SOCIETY, LANCASTER, PA

JOHANNES BRAUN

hill, where in his dream he had gone in and worshipped with the people gathered — singing, praying, and listening to the sermon of the Reformed minister, William Otterbein.[3]

Braun benefited greatly from his time at the Evangelical Reformed Church of Baltimore, and it seems Otterbein's message impressed something deep on his young heart. In another year he was headed to central Pennsylvania to study theology. His mentor, Phillip Stock, had already visited the scattered German settlements in New Virginia, the name given to the land west of the Blue Ridge.[4] Within another two years, Braun would be coming back to stay, called by the German Reformed congregations in Rockingham to be their settled minister.[5]

Ministering in the back settlements of Virginia was not the young German's only opportunity in life. As the oldest of his father's sons, Braun was entitled to inherit his father's property, and when the elder Braun first heard of his son's thoughts about staying in America, "he urged him to return home and take possession of the homestead." But Braun had his hopes pinned elsewhere. His spirit was moved when he had seen the scattered German population "almost entirely destitute of the means of peace," and he decided his future would be here among them.[6]

Once a month, Braun ministered to four German Reformed congregations in Rockingham — Peaked Mountain, Röder's, Frieden's, and Weiss's, the latter just above the county line shared with Augusta, as well as to four congregations in Augusta itself. In addition, once or twice a year he made trips to the surrounding counties of Frederick, Shenandoah, and Pendleton, Rockingham's western neighbor.[7] During his four- to six-week stays with the more distant congregations, besides preaching in churches and homes, he would give a short catechism course covering the basics of the faith. On one of those visits, he taught and confirmed more than sixty people, young and old.[8]

The man they called "Father Brown" suited his name amiably. Braun was a minister with a childlike heart, and his great love for children was returned by them as well as their parents. For the next thirty-five years, the man whose "ruling desire was to do good to his people" was the only minister of the German Reformed in New Virginia.

Though he was spread thin among the many congregations, his stability was a welcome change, a hopeful sign of better things to come.

The same summer Braun entered full-time ministry, some other friends of William Otterbein were travelling in the Shenandoah Valley. On this trip, Christian Newcomer was accompanied by two more who had grown up in the Mennonite church, Martin Boehm and his son, Henry.[9] Their first stop in Rockingham that September was at the home of Captain John Peters, about three miles from New Market on the Valley Road.[10] This was a new preaching station for the itinerants, but when they arrived they "found a house full of people already assembled."[11]

All three preached — first Newcomer, then Martin Boehm, both in German, and finally Henry Boehm, who preached in English.[12] "The word," Newcomer reported, "made great impression. At the close of the meeting the people would not depart, but were standing about in groups, crying and mourning; indeed some cried aloud for mercy."[13]

Two days later, as Martin Boehm had just begun preaching to a large crowd at Mr. Strickler's house about sixteen miles away, several people all at once rose to their feet and began clapping their hands, "shouting and praising God with extacy of joy."[14] The evening meeting at Strickler's filled the house to overflowing, continuing past midnight. Before they returned home, the three also preached at Mr. Zimmerman's near Keezletown, about four miles west of Harrisonburg, and again at John Peters'.[15] The United Brethren had formed a denomination of their own that year — the United Brethren *in Christ* as they officially called it — but they still cooperated with their English brethren in the Methodist Episcopal church. No wonder that in the late summer of 1802, both groups were in Rockingham to reap the harvest.

Though the Methodists in Rockingham had made a decided place for themselves, they had grown bitter towards one another, so much so that by 1802 "prejudices among the members abounded much more than did the grace of God."[16] Joseph Travis, a fifteen-year-old boy who had joined the Methodist church the year before, well remembered the class meeting led by James Burgess in town one evening. Burgess opened the meeting with singing and prayer, then, unfolding the class paper, the Harrisonburg businessman broke down in tears.

"Brethren," he began, words laboring beneath his heavy grief, "go home, I cannot meet you in class tonight." Without waiting for a response, Burgess picked up his hat and walked alone out into the moonlit night. Slowly and awkwardly, the rest followed, going their separate ways.

Walking with the familiar limp he had had since the age of three, Joseph patiently made his way home along the quiet streets of Harrisonburg. *What made Mr. Burgess act so strangely?* he must have wondered. His route took him right by his class leader's place. Now he was almost there. Oddly, but unmistakably, he began to hear a moan coming from the Burgess' stable. This was no animal sound. It was a person. Curious and no doubt concerned, Joseph walked over and peeked through a crack in the boards. There, with the help of the moonlight, the young man saw Mr. Burgess on his knees, groaning and begging God to have mercy on the Church. Joseph always believed that what happened next was in answer to that man's deep and drawing prayer.[17]

That August, a three-day meeting was scheduled in "Rocktown" — the local nickname given to Harrisonburg — beginning Saturday, the twenty-eighth, at the Methodist church house on the hill. Bishop Asbury had come to preach along with two of his travelling companions, men who had reputations as powerfully effective preachers. On Sunday during the love feast, Asbury reported, "there was great shaking, and shouting, and weeping and praying." Asbury was

> *"The heads that are heaviest and best filled are not the tallest that out top and rise above the rest, but those that are short and bowed down, growing beneath their weight. So it is not the Christian who has high and exalted opinions of himself and that in his own estimation rises above his fellows, but he that like the head bowed down is humbled in the dust before God."*
> — *Johannes Braun, German Reformed minister, making a favorite observation on a ripened field of wheat*

101

scheduled to preach afterward, but since most everyone there was already earnestly seeking God, either for themselves or their friends, they decided to move the preaching elsewhere.[18]

The year before they had fought the heat and gone outside, but with the ground damp from the heavy thunderstorm two days earlier and no shade to ward off the August sun, those prospects did not look promising. Graciously, someone offered the use of the Presbyterian church just a few blocks away on the other side of the Court House.[19]

By the time Monday rolled around and the meetings had come to an end, there had been some crying, even some shaking among the people, but still no observable change in the lives of individuals or in the church.[20] The old divisions still remained. Asbury moved on to Augusta for his next appointment. Little did he know, the happenings in Rocktown had only begun.

That afternoon, Henry Shaver,[21] an apprentice to one of the Methodists, had been sent on a business errand to William Bryan's, a local Methodist preacher living about six miles north of Harrisonburg. Bryan asked Shaver about the meeting in town, and Shaver — although not a believer himself — told him they had had a *wonderful time.* What is more, Shaver added, perhaps as an afterthought (perhaps to please the preacher), there would be more preaching that very night! Taking Shaver at his word, Bryan quickly spread the news to his neighbors, and folks from five or six miles away started travelling to Rocktown for the "meeting."

Watching the wagons roll into town that afternoon was eighteen-year-old Leonard Cassell, one of the two Rockingham circuit preachers that year. This circuit was his first assignment, and it probably felt like an armful to the young boy from Maryland. But hearing the news about the mix-up, and seeing that so many folks had come in from so far away to hear preaching, he decided he would not them leave disappointed. He would preach for them.

That night, the church was filled with a sizable crowd. Cassell, still a little new to the pulpit, stood up to preach, but he wouldn't make it to the end. About halfway through his sermon, there was a sudden and unmistakable change — "quick as lightning from heaven, the power and presence of the great

fanned by the flames

Head of the Church was manifested in the midst."

Quite unexpectedly, many who were not Christians began crying aloud for mercy. Those living a half-hearted commitment to Christ began weeping and groaning, while many devoted believers were shouting for the goodness of God in visiting his people. People at odds with each other just a few moments earlier now found themselves in each other's arms weeping, begging forgiveness "for their hard thoughts and still harder words against each other, promising hereafter and for ever, to live in brotherly love, and to pray for one another."[22]

For the next eight days and nine nights, amazing things were seen in that little church on the hill. Business came to a standstill as people closed shop and spent time doing little else "but waiting upon the Lord."[23] Yet the town had its fair share of skeptics about these goings-on, as well as an ample supply of people who were just plain angry about it.

But even those most harshly opposed to the revival, who would walk through the door with looks of sarcasm and malice in less than ten minutes…would be stricken to the floor, as if shot by a deadly arrow, and for an hour or so remain speechless, breathless, pulseless, and, to all appearance, perfectly dead — then, afterwards, with a heavenly smile, look up, stand up, and shout aloud, "Glory, glory to God! my soul is converted, and I am happy."[24]

The scene became so familiar that many were afraid even to go into the meeting house, thinking they too would be affected, but that didn't mean they weren't curious. With little else to do, there apparently was a regular group who assembled at the tavern. One day, a challenge was thrown out for someone in their company to go in the church and bring back a report. A fellow by the name of Mackey — not particularly afraid of anything that might happen — willingly volunteered.

Casually stepping into the church, Mackey stood at the back and began counting the number of people on the floor. Before he reached six, he was down there himself. Young Joseph Travis was a friend of Mackey's, and stayed close by him.

After about an hour, Mackey awoke and began shouting "Glory to God! Glory to God!" Grabbing hold of Travis's hand,

Mackey tried to explain. "Oh!" he burst out, "had I known the power of God, I should not have resisted it, as I have done." Mackey was a changed man. Somehow, mysteriously to those around him, he had done business with God. When he finally returned to the tavern to give his report, he had a very different story to tell.[25]

About 130 people were added to the church during those nine days.[26] Writing more than fifty years later, Joseph Travis declared he never witnessed "before or since, such displays of divine power."

In another six weeks, the United Brethren began a quarterly meeting in Rockingham, at George Hoffman's barn just below Pleasant Valley.[27] What had begun a few weeks earlier continued. As the Reformed preacher George Geeting "spoke with tender compassion: the people began to cry aloud." Christian Newcomer went through the crowd, encouraging them to accept God's offer of forgiveness. A young man grabbed at Newcomer's neck.

"O, Mr. Newcomer! What shall I do?" the young man pleaded through his tears. "What shall I do to be saved?"

"Believe in the Lord Jesus Christ," Newcomer replied.

Two brothers fell to their knees. "What shall I do? I am lost forever. O, Lord Jesus have mercy on me."

Soon the barn was filled with the cries and moans of people calling out for mercy. "Never before have I witnessed the power of God in so great a degree, among so many people," Newcomer wrote in his journal. They began to sing and to pray, "and glory be to God many distressed souls found peace, and pardon of their sins, in the blood of the Lamb." The meeting went on till late that night.

The next day, a Thursday, the barn was filled even more than the night past. Lutherans, Presbyterians, Mennonists, Baptists, and Methodists attended that meeting, "all distinctions of sects lost in christian love and fellowship."[28] Appropriately, they shared the meal of the Lord's Supper together as an evidence of their unity.

———

It is not clear just how many of those in attendance at the unusual meetings in 1802 were African, but within a year about fifty had joined the Methodist ranks.[29]

Virginia had been a slave state almost from the very beginning, and the Valley had not escaped its pernicious influence. As might have been expected, those parts of the county with strong ties to English gentry owned the largest number of enslaved men, women and children laborers. In 1774, Gabriel Jones advertised for a runaway slave by the name of Bacchus, "a cunning, artful, sensible Fellow" whom Jones had trusted, now probably seeking passage to England and thereby his freedom. By 1790, one out of every ten persons in Rockingham was African, and every one of them was a slave.[30]

As a rule, Germans owned few slaves, if any. Habits of frugality and a strong work ethic typically predisposed them against the system, though some were willing to hire out someone else's slaves or accept their labor when work was traded between neighbors.[31] In the 1730s, however, when Caspar Stoever, Sr., had sought European help for the Robinson River congregation, part of the plan had been to buy slaves to help support the minister. But Stoever had an interesting take on the proposal, hoping that "If these slaves be kept better than those among the English people, and be instructed in the Christian religion…that thereby hundreds, nay even thousands of slaves, who are compelled to work for Englishmen, will be brought from heathen ignorance to Christ, indeed that much good could thereby be accomplished among the English."[32]

As far as Mennonists and Dunkers were concerned, slavery was simply wrong, a violation of Christ's command to "love your neighbor as yourself."[33] Slavery had been one of the issues dividing the Mennonists from the Separate Baptists at the Whitehouse church in Massanutten. The same man who helped organize that congregation, Anderson Moffett, now served the Linville Creek Baptists. There, since 1791, slaves had been allowed to attend business meetings, presumably with permission to participate. That in itself seemed an unusual liberty, but even in a democratic Baptist congregation, the real test was still to come.[34]

In 1794, Margaret Harrison, a member of the Linville Creek Baptist church, called to account "Mr. Moore's Joe (who is a Member of this Church) for propagating, as she says, a Scandalous Report as a Truth, against a

Member of Sister Harrison's family, which Report, it appears, can't be proven a Truth." The Harrisons had been one of the founding families of the Linville Creek Baptist church, and Zebulon Harrison's home had been their first meeting place after the war had ended. Upon hearing her accusation, the church issued an official rebuke of Joe's behavior and suspended his membership.[35]

The next meeting, though, when Joe's side of the story was heard, the church decided to suspend Mrs. Harrison as well. When it came to disciplinary action, Linville Creek had never played favorites with anyone — not "persons of quality," not even their own minister. As the Good Book said, "There is neither Jew nor Greek, there is neither bond nor free, there is neither male nor female: for ye are all one in Christ Jesus."[36]

The congregation at Linville Creek was eager to settle the dispute between Sister Harrison and Brother Joe, and a committee was appointed to speak to Mrs. Harrison. Finally, three months after the initial accusation, Margaret Harrison said she had forgiven "Brother Joe his Fault against her, or that which she viewed as a Fault in him," and was willing for both to be restored to full fellow-ship, but on one condition: that Joe would not have the privilege of her "wench, Dine, as his wife." Joe accepted the terms, however hard they may have been. Despite what the Good Book said, in this church a slave's membership evidently came at a price.[37]

The Methodist church had gone on record against slavery from their earliest days in the colonies. Such was their respect in the African community, that in 1800 when a violent slave uprising was being planned, the only whites they intended to spare were Quakers, French, and Methodists.[38]

Gabriel's Conspiracy, as it came to be known, involved hundreds of slaves throughout central Virginia. The intended massacre was averted in part by a sudden, torrential rainstorm, which overflowed creeks and turned roads into muddy obstacles. The political effects of the conspiracy were just as strong and immediate. Over the next several years, a host of laws were enacted against slaves, free blacks, and mulattos. Besides restricting more slaves from being brought into the state, legislators revived the law that every free black or mulatto must be registered, with a list of all such registered to be fixed upon the Court House door.[39]

By 1806, free blacks and mulattos were required to leave the colony within twelve months of being granted their freedom. It was unwise, lawmakers agreed, to have such

ty man. Perhaps from his first arrival, Peters, a saddlery maker who grew to have a sturdy reputation for industry and honesty, would take his role as a leader of an African class in

LINVILLE CREEK

"loose cannons" roaming about free to stir up trouble. The registration laws, however, were often ignored.[40]

In Rockingham, the first person on the register was Joshua Peters, a Culpeper coun-

the Methodist society.[41]

Methodists had ongoing class meetings attended by Africans, but the meetings were segregated, and "people of color" were required to sit in the gallery during the

church meetings.[42] But the Methodist discipline — a statement of their rules and prac-
to be saved from their sins," but those who
wished to continue in a Methodist society

M A D I S O N   R U N
along the Brown's Gap Road

tice — was clear. Those who wanted to join
a Methodist society need only have "*a desire
to flee from the wrath to come, i.e. a desire*
must exhibit the fruit or evidence of that
salvation. This included "avoiding evil of
every kind; especially that which is most

generally practiced: Such as…*The buying or selling the bodies and souls of men, women or children, with an intention to enslave them.*"[43]

In practice, this did not necessarily mean immediate freedom for enslaved Africans. There were economic considerations. In 1801 Rockingham Methodist William Hughes made a sacred promise to emancipate his slave, Samuel, in ten years "and as much sooner as I can make it conveinant." The following year, a few months before the revival, the question was asked whether any of the members had bought or sold slaves. Two people, Reuben Harrison — one of the strongest supporters of the Methodists in Harrisonburg — and William Dalton, were each instructed to free an adult slave by the slave's forty-fifth birthday. Children who were slaves were guaranteed freedom by the time they reached twenty-five.[44]

Though slaves were quite numerous in the area where the Lewis, Jones and Madison families had originally settled, Methodists had gained a strong foothold there. So it was that one muddy February day in 1809, Francis Asbury and his new travelling com-panion, Henry Boehm, crossed over the Blue Ridge Mountains on the Brown's Gap Road high above the plantations of the wealthy Rockinghamers. They were on their way to the Annual Meeting of the Baltimore Conference, held this year for the first time in Harrisonburg.[45] Their first stop, though, was the Methodist church at Port Republic, the new town situated where the North and South rivers met to form the south fork of the Shenandoah.[46] The day after the Sabbath, Asbury and Boehm travelled to Harrisonburg. It had been dangerous riding through the snow, and Boehm would ruin a valuable horse during the trip.[47]

From the north, another participant to the annual conference was soon on his way. Christian Newcomer left his home that Wednesday, the roads still "remarkably bad." Newcomer had long hoped that another road would be cleared during this trip, one leading to the union of the United Brethren in Christ and the Methodist Episcopal Church.[48] On Monday and Tuesday of the following week, several leaders met to try and bring the two groups together. Asbury's main concern was the lack of a formal, written order of discipline among the United

Even before the controversy over slavery erupted, George Bourne had continued his publishing career in Harrisonburg, largely in association with the Presbyterian minister at Mossy Creek, Cook's Creek, and Harrisonburg, the Reverend A. B. Davidson. As the Lexington Presbytery's 1811 delegate to the General Assembly meeting of the national Presbyterian church, Davidson had become interested in the potential benefits of Bible and tract societies. With Bourne's assistance, the Virginia Tract Society began on October 30, 1812, with 250 members.

The following year, Davidson and Bourne had established a publishing partnership in Harrisonburg, bringing in a German printer by the name of Lawrence Wartmann to operate their newly acquired handpress. By 1814, their company had published two of Bourne's sermons, a couple of tracts, and two books by Bourne — one on the importance of lifelong marriage, the other with the homey-sounding title, The Christian's Companion in His Field and Garden.

Besides these, Bourne was involved in at least two other publications not from his own pen. Perhaps the most successful was The Mountain Muse, the story of Daniel Boone told in verse by Daniel

Brethren. Though the German group had class meetings, attendance was not a requirement for church membership as among the Methodists. But the United Brethren were not ready for any regulations beyond what was set forth in the Bible. After a few years of correspondence, the idea of uniting the two groups was dropped, and each did their own work in their own way.[49]

The Baltimore Conference meeting in Harrisonburg that mud-thickened March decided on an another issue. In spite of the new Virginia laws on slavery, the Methodists would stand firm in their opposition, at least for now.[50] The fireworks on that volatile issue would not be ignited by the Methodists, but by a transplanted Presbyterian in Port Republic.

―――――

There were undoubtedly many who were uncertain how George Bourne, an Englishman and former newspaper editor from Baltimore, turned up in Rockingham County, but most everyone would know why he left.[51]

Sometime around the fall of 1810, the thirty-five-year-old settled at Port Republic and began to preach.[52] Though not a Methodist himself, Bourne agreed with most of their teachings. Just three years earlier, he had published a biography of Wesley with a short history of the denomination in America, but at heart he appreciated the efforts of "all striving to spread the savour of the Redeemer's religion," who had in their hearts a "missionary flame." A year later he applied to the Valley's Lexington Presbytery for permission to preach within their bounds.[53]

At first the Presbytery was reluctant, having heard "certain allegations unfriendly to Mr. Bourne's moral character," which had been "extensively circulated." Bourne had certainly gained a reputation for speaking his mind, sometimes bluntly. But by the following spring, with the charges against him apparently fading away, Bourne had formed a congregation eager to accept him as their new minister.[54] On Christmas Day, 1812, he preached a sermon at the opening of the South River Presbyterian church at Port Republic and was ordained as their new minister.[55]

fanned by the flames

In the process of clearing his name, Bourne had gained a new friend and colleague, fellow Presbyterian minister Andrew B. Davidson. Not only were both men about

tions. In addition to starting a publishing venture and working to build the Virginia Tract Society [see side], the two friends shared their ideas on a number of issues

PORT REPUBLIC
The first Methodist church building here was located near this spot on the south fork of the Shenandoah River

the same age, they had come into Rockingham about the same time, Davidson taking charge of the Cook's Creek, Harrisonburg, and Mossy Creek congrega-

important to both of them. For Bourne, one of those concerns was slavery.[56]

Living in Port Republic certainly gave Bourne a chance to view this "domestic

Bryan, a nephew of Boone with Rockingham connections. All of these ventures were published in tandem with Davidson, but at least one book out of Harrisonburg was published by Bourne alone. George W. Snyder's eighty-page book was released in 1815, the year Bourne made a bold stand against slavery. Snyder wanted to spell out how the Bible taught that Jesus Christ is God. The conclusion of this work is interesting not only from Bourne's personal struggles at the time, but also in light of the conflicts brewing among different denominations in Rockingham and throughout the Valley.

Reader, have you ever felt the pity and compassion of Jesus, your Lord and your God? And are you yet opposing, hating, and wrangling with those who differ from you in some indifferent points? know that no such unsocial passions can be harboured in celestial bosoms; no resentment can dwell in heavenly minds. The point of union is unalterably fixed; it is Jesus Christ, who is God our Saviou[r]; in him the whole multitude of the redeemed rejoice and to him alone they bring their songs of praise.

When the black clouds of adversity hang

111

arrangement" on a personal level. The largest slaveholders in the county lived in this neighborhood.[57] But what grieved Bourne the most was to see Presbyterians and Presbyterian preachers — the proclaimed leaders of Christian faith — taking part in this common mutilation of moral sensibility.

In 1815, George Bourne was appointed a third year in a row to be Lexington Presbytery's delegate to the annual, nationwide meeting of Presbyterians known as the General Assembly, an honor he received no doubt in part due to his respectability as an author and his keenness for debate. But this year Bourne had brought along a document of his own to be introduced onto the floor. Refused by the committee chair, he stood and read the paper himself.

"What ought to be done with a Minister of the Gospel," Bourne questioned his reluctant audience, "who tied up his slave, whipped her, left her tied, went to Church and preached, then came back and whipped her again?"[58]

Bourne did not stop there with his accusations, but when called upon to name those he indicted, he absolutely refused. It would already be difficult enough to return to

Virginia. He would at least refrain from personal attacks. Without names, though, the entire Virginia clergy bore the sting of his reproach.

Both the Bible and the Westminster Confession condemned *man-stealing*, and in Bourne's eyes, slavery was exactly that, no matter how benevolent the thief.[59] "How can a man be a Christian who steals souls?" he questioned. In Bourne's South River church, no slaveholders would be allowed to the communion table. "Our town is in war," Bourne wrote that summer. By mid-September, he and his congregation had mutually ended their commitments.[60]

Bourne's trial before the Presbytery was held two days after Christmas, 1815. After listening to testimony of Bourne's actions at the General Assembly and reading some letters he had written to his old colleague, A. B. Davidson, the Lexington Presbytery deposed Bourne of his office in the Gospel ministry. A few days later, Bourne left for Pennsylvania, never to return to the Old Dominion.[61]

Like someone pressing hard on an angry sore, Bourne had forced the debate on slavery to the surface. It was not that people were unaware of the cruel treatment of

112

slaves. That sort of behavior was often excused as a necessary means of maintaining domestic order. But abuse inflicted by church leaders — or any Christian for that matter — was impossibly difficult to square with Christ's command to "love your neighbor as yourself."

In the aftermath, the Methodists took a hard look at themselves. Despite rules prohibiting membership to those who

enslaved others for life or who were not merciful, slaveholders remained in their societies. And what was to be done with those who had inherited slaves? Though they had-

n't broken the letter of the law in "buying or selling," as long as they had no intention of freeing them, weren't they just as guilty?[62]

The national denomination had tried to walk the tightrope on the slavery issue, but the Methodists of t h e Rockingham circuit saw this as hypocrisy: "whatever is Morrally evil in the North must be such in the South; the laws of the States to the c o n t r a r y notwithstand- ing." Besides r e m i n d i n g their national conference of the rules already in place, they suggested that no one be admitted to an official position in the Methodist church without first freeing his

113

slaves when the laws of the state would allow. If state laws prohibited it entirely, slaves were to be granted the freedom to go to a state "that will receive and protect free people of Colour, whenever he or she may choose to go."[63]

On a more personal level, between 1815 and 1817 several Methodists like Joseph Cravens, Reuben Harrison, Jesse Sisson and Jeremiah Hansberger made written agreements to free their slaves after a given period of time. Rhetoric was nothing without action, or to put it in biblical terms, "faith without works is dead."[64]

But the most lengthy and thoughtful response to the slavery debate in Rockingham came from the pen of the Reformed minister, Johannes Braun. In 1818, he published a book of over four hundred pages, which he called a "circular writing," intended to be distributed throughout Rockingham, Augusta, and the surrounding counties. The final section — "A Treatise on Slavery and Serfdom" — was not completely in keeping with his theme, but it was by now an issue that had everyone's attention. The book was written entirely in German, for Germans, too, were involved in this destructive practice.[65]

It was first important, Braun urged his readers, "especially in matters of conscience and religious practice, when other men think otherwise than we…to seek counsel and proof in the word of God before we blunder into a conclusion." But even if God's word spoke clearly against a neighbor's actions, Braun said, "if we have the spirit of true Christianity, our judgment should be firm and fair, accompanied by pity, gentle correction, and intercession [prayer]."

After a careful examination of passages in both Old and New Testaments, Braun convincingly established that slavery was incorporated into Hebrew law and practiced in early Christian communities. Yet, for him, the practice of slavery was incompatible with the spirit of Christianity, and, he asserted, "the form of slavery which descends from generation to generation, in which men are born slaves…brings little honor to mankind, nor should it be established by the civil code of the realm."[66]

Unlike Bourne, Father Brown stopped short of directly calling slaveholding in and of itself a sin, but it was clearly a tree producing bad fruit.[67] There was evidence of it everywhere — in the laws of the Commonwealth, and in the manners and morals of the common people. Throughout his treatise, Braun maintains a sense of reason and dignity, but he did not hide his passion. "Oh America! Once so happy! So blessed! How luckless are now thy inhabitants, now that the greedy and Godless slave trade has brought here the wretched and pitiable African!"[68]

The final part of the treatise dealt with "the emancipation of the slaves with its benefits desirable to the human race." Braun believed that the Bible Society — distributing God's word among all people — would play an important role in the elimination of slavery. "We may, therefore, cherish the most confident hopes that the Christian religion in the future will be more generally known and followed, and that then slavery will have reached its limits of toleration."[69]

Like Bourne, Braun was convinced of the need to eliminate slavery, but the Reformed minister had lived among these people for eighteen years, and he knew the difficulties involved. Though Rockingham had seen no uprisings like Gabriel's, the memory of a Rockingham county slave who had killed his master must have lingered. The abuses of slave owners should be ended immediately, but how slavery itself should be abolished would need a careful plan to avoid further bloodshed.[70]

Perhaps more than anything else, Braun understood the need for truth to be mixed in full portions with grace, and to say what must be said in love. Bourne, whose self-admitted "irratible temper" and "undecorous expressions" had only caused more trouble, left after just a few years here. For Father Braun, this was home.

Braun's condemnation of slavery was directed toward the Germans, but not of course toward all Germans. Slavery had been one of the issues the Mennonist preachers from Pennsylvania had taken up with Baptist leader John Koontz, an issue that Koontz said the Baptists left to the individual conscience.[72]

The "conscience" of Mennonists and Dunkers seemed to be expressed collectively. As early as 1782, when many Dunkers were just moving or about to move into Rockingham, their General Conference unanimously refused to tolerate "the un-Christian negro slave trade" in any shape or form within their church.[73] A little over thirty years later, as George Bourne began his official ministry at Port Republic, Dunkers reaffirmed that stand. If any member refused to emancipate their slaves, "he would have to be considered as disobedient and we would have no fellowship with him until he sets them free." This 1813 declaration went even farther, urging parents as far as possible to restrain their children who were not members of the Dunker church from buying, selling, or even holding slaves.[74]

To many of their neighbors, this anti-slavery stand coupled with their refusal to serve in the militia was just another reason to view both Dunkers and Mennonists as out of the mainstream of society, even "Christian" society.[75] Language — and culture — further darkened the dividing line. It was easy for one observer of the day to characterize the farmers of the county as mostly *Germans*, and the lawyers, doctors, merchants, sheriffs, clerks, and others as *Virginians*.[76] And though the Germans must learn English to be able to live in a predominantly English society, their English neighbors were undoubtedly much less interested in learning German.

With insufficient communication, prejudice flourished, and the Mennonists decided to do something about it. In 1810, an important book rolled off the presses in New Market, just north of the Rockingham County line.[77] First printed in Pennsylvania about the time Adam Mueller moved into Virginia, this was an English translation of the Dordrecht Confession, a Mennonist statement of faith. As an appendix, there was added a short history of the Mennonist way. Both were intended to promote understanding of a group sometimes considered by their English neighbors as "almost worthy of all Reproach, Mockery and Trouble, and to be minded as nothing."[78]

Perhaps their English-speaking neighbors gained some understanding of their principals of non-resistance, but five years later Mennonists still faced "reproach and calumny" according to Rockingham resident

Peter Burkholder. This time, apparently, the abuse was not coming from the English, but from the Dunkers who lived nearby. Not far from Burkholder lived Dunker leader Peter Bowman. For the one hundred years of their existence, Dunkers had insisted on historically authentic expression of the ordinances of baptism, footwashing and the Lord's Supper.[79] Dunkers still held to the trine immersion formula for baptism, in which a candidate was immersed three times in the name of God the Father, God the Son, and God the Holy Spirit. The Mennonists' practice of baptism was to pour water over the head of the new believer. For the Lord's Supper, Dunkers believed it was correct to serve

Though Africans were present at many worship services and gatherings organized by whites, such as camp meetings, very few documented stories remain of what church life was like for Africans — both free and slave — in Rockingham during the early 1800s. While some stories attempt to poke fun at their experience, they fail to capture either the difficulty or the dignity of African church life. Two early accounts of African ministers, one Baptist, the other Methodist, provide an interesting contrast. The first is attributed in part to the pen of Presbyterian minister George Bourne.

Uncle Jack
An elder at Mossy Creek Presbyterian church "held as a slave the wife of a Baptist colored preacher, familiarly called 'Uncle Jack.' In a late period of pregnancy he scourged her so that the lives of herself and her unborn child were considered in jeopardy. Uncle Jack was advised to obtain the liberation of his wife. [The elder] finally agreed, I think, to sell the woman and her children, three of them, I believe for six hundred dollars, and an additional hundred if the unborn child survived a certain period after its birth. Uncle Jack was to pay one hundred dollars per annum

117

for his wife and children for seven years, and [the Presbyterian elder] held a sort of mortgage upon them for the payment....James Kyle and Uncle Jack used to tell that story with great christian sensibility, and Uncle Jack would weep tears of anguish over his wife's piteous tale, and tears of ecstasy at the same moment that he was free, and that soon, by the grace of God, his wife and children, as he said, 'would all be free together.'"

In time Uncle Jack did obtain the release of his wife. Maria Carr, whose recollections of Rocktown give a unique picture of early Harrisonburg, remembered both Jack and his wife as good people. Unfortunately, some in town didn't share her opinion. In Miss Carr's words, "some hard hearted wretches would arrest him when he was preaching and have him whipped at the Post, behind the Court House."

Not only was Jack a faithful preacher, he was a pastor as well. Across the street from his home on North Main lived a man named Cato. One evening, Cato was murdered. When the suspect was arrested, "Uncle Jack" visited him in the jail, trying to lead him along the path to eternal life. But though the accused seemed interested in Jack's messages, he had another path in mind — breaking through the jail wall.

lamb and eat the meal at night, after the Passover celebration.[80] Mennonists held that the Lord's Supper was in effect a new celebration of a new covenant, and the old details of the Passover feast did not need to

CAMP MEETING

be observed. To try and set the matter straight, in 1816 Burkholder published a treatise on water baptism and the Lord's sup-

per, written entirely in German.[81] He was not intending to "strive and dispute with words," he said, but "out of love to God and his Church," wanted to address those "opponents [who] accuse us as having no ground

or foundation, and as such cannot give any."[82] Once again, it seemed that the two celebrations intended for joining the body of Christ and staying in close fellowship were causing the greatest divisions.

These debates would continue in public and private for years to come, so it was perhaps fitting for Burkholder to put the entire issue in its larger Christian perspective. "So I Affirm that CHRIST JESUS THE SON OF THE LIVING GOD, is the ground and Foundation whereupon our Church is grounded and built," he emphasized in his preface. "[Y]et we do not expect to be saved by outward ceremonies; but though his precious grace in his blood in the remission of sins through Faith in his Name."[83]

Burkholder's treatise was printed by Lawrence Wartmann, the craftsman employed by Davidson and Bourne to produce their volumes and those of the Virginia Religious Tract Society. Probably that same year, Wartmann came out with another German volume by a Mennonist, Joseph Funk's *Choral Music*, the first German songbook to be printed in Rockingham.[84]

Despite the activity of Wartmann's press in producing German texts between 1816 and 1818, the early part of the 1800s actually marked the noticeable erosion of the German language in the Valley.[85] One Lutheran minister lamented the case of a man whose "folly drove him to babble everything in English to his son's children and to neglect the German School."[86]

But German ministers and families were not oblivious to the need to make accommodations to the English language — not at all.[87] As Virginia Lutherans met to discuss the need for supporting German schools, they also discussed the need for good hymn books printed in both English and German.[88] Yet the desire to hold onto the German language was much more than a matter of nostalgia and cultural pride. As one traveller through the Valley noted, the Lutherans had lost their religion as they lost the German language.[89] German-speakers of many denominations wanted to keep undesirable English influences out of the German community and church. The Lutheran *Evangelisches Magazin*, begun in 1812 as a publication of the Pennsylvania Ministerium, had two stated purposes: "conserving the German language and fighting rationalistic unbelief."[90]

German communities in Virginia were fast under pressure to assimilate within the dominant culture. Unlike Pennsylvania,

When Jack found out, he stopped the visits.

Joshua Peters
Joshua Peters, a free black man, had been an indentured servant in Culpeper County before he arrived in Rockingham sometime around 1807. By 1835, he was listed as one of the local preachers in Harrisonburg. About that time, there were almost 250 free blacks and slaves living in Harrisonburg, about thirty percent of the total population there. But, as was doubtless true for "Uncle Jack," it was likely that Peters' messages were attended by some of the "white" population as well. His honesty and skill in workmanship had given his saddlery shop on East Market a fine reputation, and he employed several white men in the business. One resident recalled that he "was highly respected by everyone who knew him."

Camp Meeting Liberty
Perhaps one of the more outspoken public preaching events by African Americans during this time occurred near Pleasant Valley on the farm of George Hoffman. In September of 1819, during one of the many United Brethren camp meetings held there over the years, the new presiding elder Samuel Huber was in charge of the meeting.

On Sunday I

"The wilderness and the solitary place shall be glad for them, and the desert shall rejoice and blossom as the rose."
Isaiah 35:1

preached in German. The Methodist Presiding Elder, who attended the camp, followed with a sermon in English. There was a great deal of weeping in the congregation that day. There were also a great many people of color on the ground. I told them, "that they should have three hours' liberty for their religious exercises." After I came down from the stand, a "Goliath"-like looking man, with a heavy whip in his hand, took me roughly by the arm, and said, "that I had subjected myself to a fine of twenty dollars for giving liberty to the colored people." "I told him I was not aware of having violated the Virginia laws — that I was a Pennsylvanian — that I preached the Bible doctrine, and that colored people had as much need of the Gospel as either of us." He still held fast to my arm, talking for some time. At length a Magistrate came to where we were standing, and after he became acquainted with the affair, said, addressing the man, "This man thinks he understands Virginia laws; but, Sir, if you don't let go your hold on the preacher, and cease further molestation, I will teach you some law which you

where more insulated communities would worship in the German language well into the next century, Virginia Germans were usually more interspersed among their English neighbors.[91] Change was coming fast, and in no small way the United Brethren helped to forge that change.

———

At their annual meeting in 1819, United Brethren planned for their first "camp meeting" in Rockingham County on September 9, to be held on the property of George Hoffman. Although their first gathering by this name had taken place in Pennsylvania four years earlier, the idea of these several-day meetings in the summer was nothing new. At least since the great meeting — the *gros versammlung* — at Isaac Long's barn some forty years earlier there had been meetings of this sort. Methodists, too, had been gathering like this for a long time, though they were not really planned at first. It began in part with their love feasts, the celebration of a meal that included the Lord's Supper, and also their watchnight services,

typically on New Year's Eve.[92]

In 1801, the crowds at the Methodist's September quarterly meeting in Harrisonburg had been too large to fit in the meeting house. Taking to the woods, they found neither shade nor sun suited to their taste. But undoubtedly what set the stage — or at least primed the pump — for camp meetings in Rockingham was the nine-day revival of 1802.[93]

Essentially, the camp meeting was really just an extension of the regularly scheduled quarterly conference for the circuit, when people might come from a day's journey away to attend. In the more scattered settlements in South Carolina, Tennessee, and Kentucky, such large crowds would gather that there would neither be a building large enough to hold them nor neighbors numerous enough to house them. Sometimes the meetings would go on all night. Not unlike the 1802 revival in Harrisonburg, sometimes people "were struck down by the power of God, and lay helpless most part of the night and could not be taken away."[94] When that happened, or when people were "in deep distress" seeking God for the salvation of their soul, both ministers and friends would

breaking camp

feel it their responsibility to stay with them, to encourage and pray for them.

Soon, people planning to attend began to anticipate the possibility of late nights and made their own tents, either out of cloth or bushes, and brought enough food to last for a few days. Eventually, organizers started to recommend those preparations, and the name "camp meeting" soon represented a well-understood and eagerly awaited event.[95]

Just a few months after the nine-day revival of 1802, the February 1803 quarterly meeting held in Harrisonburg "continued for four days and nights, with but little intermission." Perhaps thirty or more made a commitment to Christ, but another three hundred or more joined Methodist societies within a few months. At a quarterly meeting in June 1804 at Colonel Moffet's meeting house, about twenty-seven people were said to have been converted.[96]

"Next to the bible, we are indebted to this work for our views of the system of slavery. We pronounce it the most faithful and conclusive exposition of the cruelty and sin of holding the slaves in bondage, that we have ever seen."
— *William Lloyd Garrison, African American leader and publisher, on George Bourne's* The Book and Slavery Irreconcilable, *written largely while Bourne was living in Rockingham*

That August, the Rockingham circuit had scheduled probably its first camp meeting along Linville Creek.[97] Organizers may have cleared away underbrush from as much as four acres. All around the perimeter of this huge rectangle, on a line, would be set the fronts of the tents. Behind each tent was a place for the carriages, wagons, or carts, so each tent would have its own space for its own carriage. Just back of the carriages, the horses could be tied and fed.[98]

The committee responsible for the camp meeting also oversaw the construction of a preacher's tent and stand. Temporary plank benches — seats made from split pine — would be fashioned to accommodate everyone, the men on one side, the ladies on the other.[99] Cooking fires in front of each tent on the inside of the rectangle helped to illuminate the grounds.

do not understand." He let go my arm, hung down his head, and sneaked away.

The meeting continued six days, with great outpourings of the Holy Spirit. Side 8

121

There would be oil lanterns as well, placed on the preacher's stand and at other convenient spots.

Every morning at first light, a trumpeter would walk the inside perimeter of the grounds, in front of each tent, blowing a sort of reveille. About ten minutes later, he would repeat the journey, this time with one, long blast sounded over and over again. Now, people all over the grounds would begin to sing and pray, some just outside their tents, some from within.

By sunrise, the entire assembly would be gathered on the split pine benches, and the first sermon would begin. Breakfast followed, with more preaching at ten o'clock. By about one in the afternoon, everyone would be settling down to their main meal of the day. Preaching would start again at three.

Around sunset, the glow of cooking fires skirted the edge of the grounds like low-set torches. After supper, as the last signs of day slipped behind the North Mountain, preaching would begin one more time. Lanterns placed at the stage and at various places, along with the light of individual campfires, gave enough light to keep the entire camp-ground illuminated. As one early Methodist wrote, "These lights in a dark night, when the evening is calm, add greatly to the solemnity of the meeting."[100]

The camp meeting at Linville Creek began August 18, 1804, on a Friday, just like most camp meetings in those days, and was probably scheduled to end by mid-day Monday. But once again, schedules and plans didn't seem to matter. Just as the quarterly meeting in Harrisonburg two years earlier, this gathering continued nine days, though "some of the people tarried on the ground until the tenth day." At least seventy-four people were converted and there was "reason to believe that a good many more were the subjects of a real change."[101]

For a while afterwards, camp meetings shifted to Colonel Benjamin Harrison's estate, near the stone house he inherited from his father, Daniel. Perhaps the old chapel of ease was still standing, a convenient place for the planners to congregate. Colonel Harrison had hosted class meetings at his place for years now, for both black and white classes. By 1815, planners decided it was time for a more permanent site for the Methodist meetings and by the following year had made arrangements for a ten-year lease at Taylor Springs, about five miles east of Harrisonburg on the road to Swift Run Gap.[102] The Methodist camp meeting had made another step toward becoming a community institution.

In August of 1819, a few weeks before the first United Brethren camp meeting in Rockingham, the Methodists convened at Taylor Springs. For the Methodists and the many others who attended, it was another year to remember. This time, it began with the children. In "their astonishing fluency and unaffected simplicity in narrating the work of grace to their parents," they spread the revival through the entire county, wrote the Methodist leader in charge, "bringing whole families to the knowledge of the truth." Within six months, over two hundred had been added to the church, including many "vile opposers of religion" who "embraced the faith they once sought to destroy."[103]

The very next year, a Presbyterian music publisher in Rockingham by the name of Ananias Davisson put out a book especially for his "Methodist friends." Davisson had already experienced great success with his first publication, *The Kentucky Harmony*, soon to go into its fourth edition.[104] This new volume, *A Supplement to the Kentucky Harmony*, contained "a suitable and proper arrangement of such pieces as may seem best calculated to animate the zealous christian in his acts of devotion; that he may not only sing with the spirit, but with the understanding also."[105]

Whereas *The Kentucky Harmony* had been a collection of popular "fuguing tunes" intended for singing schools, *A Supplement* fit the bill for camp meetings and revivals. Lyrics were drawn from the spiritual songs of frontier preachers, and the music was a mixing bowl in which "military marches and fiddle tunes rubbed shoulders with murder ballads and love songs." Because of their origins, Davisson was well aware his selections may not meet with the approval of the "sacred musicians" of the day. One Valley resident, an author whose book Davisson had printed, had earlier criticized this type of music as "ballad tunes, vamped up with accompanying parts, and applied as vehicles of religious sentiment."[106] But Davisson drew consolation from the fact that his intentions were pure — to provide a useful and delightful music through which the world could grasp the meaning of the poet who addressed himself to God, "To spend one day with thee on earth, exceeds a thousand days of mirth." His honorable intentions were rewarded financially, as the *Kentucky Harmony* and *A Supplement* both went through several editions.[107]

Camp meetings, per-haps in part because of their success, had suffered a bad reputation in some parts of the country from the very beginning. "The spirit of persecution is waked up, whipping, fining, rioting, possibly imprisonments, and death, if we will not give up campmeetings," Bishop Asbury had written a few years earli-er in reference to the northern states. "But,"

This advertisement in the May 26, 1818, edition of the Knoxville Register is evidence of the wide audience Davisson found for his music books.

he added, "rather let us die."[108] The spirit of persecution, though, was not the only diffi-culty the Methodists suffered.

Camp meetings were easily the big event during a long summer, particularly as the crops were waiting for har-vest and the residents of Rockingham were eager for any cool breeze. This applied not only to Methodists and those seeking the Lord, but also to those looking for trou-ble. As Maria Carr remembered, "All kinds of things were going on back of the tents, such as trading horses, playing games and having a jolly time generally."[109] At night, most camp meetings posted a guard, several men who would take turns patrolling the grounds to keep troublemakers from disturbing both people and property.[110] Even during the

Sunday meeting in 1819 when the revival began, presiding elder Lewis Fechtig seemed surprised that it had not been "a day of dissipation," as he perhaps was used to seeing.[111] By 1821, though, the situation was quite different. Apparently, things at the meeting had not gone well, and Fechtig appointed a committee to petition the General Assembly of Virginia "to pass a law for the better protection of Camp meetings."[112]

Problems continued to grow year after year. Finally in 1825, with no support from the legislature, the Methodist men passed their own sort of law along in the *Rockingham Register,* the community's young newspaper.[113] They took the "opportunity to solemnly forewarn all who have neither religion, honour, nor breeding sufficient to restrain them from disorderly and wicked conduct." This time, they promised, "the utmost vigilance will be used to detect and bring to merited and prompt punishment all Violators of the Laws against retailers of spiritous Liquors, against Swearers, Drunkards, and Sabbath Breakers." It seems Maria Carr was right when she said that "it was hard to tell whether these meetings resulted in good or evil" overall.[114]

The "Sabbath Breakers" it seemed had developed quite a variety of retail offerings, including "Cakes, Beer, Cider, & c." At least at the perimeter, the camp meeting had taken on the characteristics of a carnival, complete with food booths. It would be a difficult task for the Methodists and others in attendance to keep this very public worship service focused on spiritual matters.[115] On that score, they would find some local sympathizers.

———

After George Hoffman moved on to Augusta, the center for United Brethren gatherings in southern Rockingham was at Peter Moyers, whose home built in the fashion of the Dunkers had a room large enough to accommodate their meetings.[116] Not far away lived Frederick Rhodes, one of eight Mennonist ministers in Rockingham and Augusta, who had bought a farm about five miles south of Harrisonburg on the Stage Road that led to Staunton.[117]

Mennonists were already feeling the squeeze of meeting in homes. So were the

Dunkers. It wasn't just that there wasn't enough seating room. Those left outside had been known to get into mischief, not to mention the orchard, the pantry, and the kitchen.

By 1823 or so, each group had built its first meeting house set apart for public worship. For the Mennonists, it was Trissels, named after Joseph Trissel whose property

TUNKER HOUSE TODAY

To allow these distractions was no way to teach their children to honor the Sabbath, and coming out of worship meeting to find the dinner already picked through or nearly gone just added insult to injury.[118]

west of Linville Creek in an area known as "the Brush" bordered the new meeting house lot.[119] For the Dunkers, it was Garbers, about two miles south of Harrisonburg, just a short jaunt from where Moyers and

Rhodes lived.[120]

This was a change that did not come without some wrangling. Though both groups had meeting houses in Pennsylvania, it was long a tradition in Rockingham to meet in homes, and some were reluctant to leave the family atmosphere it helped to accent. For Mennonists at least, the church building issue was only one part of a mounting dispute. What perhaps worried them most was the threat of losing their identity as a people. They had held together in the face of three wars, enduring as a community the fines and persecution they had suffered for their non-resistant stand. With the demise of home meetings, and the slow erosion of their German language, it must have seemed the walls of protection around them were crumbling. For some, the final threat came from one of their own.

Frederick Rhodes had been attending United Brethren meetings at least since the 1819 camp meeting at Hoffman's. During Otterbein's time, Rhodes testified, he "had been brought out of darkness into the light of the Gospel," and he came to the camp meeting to see for himself how the United Brethren conducted their meetings.

Afterwards he had invited the leader of the meetings, Samuel Huber, to stay with him. Convinced that what he had seen "was the work of the Lord," Rhodes exhorted Huber "to continue on in the good work, in the face of all opposition whatsoever, and not to give way one inch."[121]

Rhodes' continued attendance at the United Brethren meetings put many Mennonists on edge. Some said he had not participated in the meetings; others claimed he had prayed when asked.[122] This was no crime in itself. Mennonist and United Brethren ministers had travelled and preached together, but Frederick's father was Bishop Henry Rhodes, a leader in the church building movement. Besides, said some, Frederick Rhodes was starting to *sound* like a United Brethren preacher, "being often quite earnest and loud." They had no argument with his doctrine, but his delivery left plenty to be desired.

On Good Friday of the year 1825, several of the "offended party" got together at the home of Jacob Blosser and wrote a letter expressing their dissatisfaction with Rhodes' preaching style. When their ministers refused to circulate the letter to see who would sign it, Blosser and Gabriel Heatwole took the task on themselves. Eventually, about thirty members signed, close to half the membership in Rockingham and Augusta.[123] The "offended party" had about touch of good humor, they called it Moyers' Meeting House after the United Brethren leader.[124] In time, after the Stage Road became the Turnpike, it was known simply as the 'Pike Church.

B U R K H O L D E R ' S   M E E T I N G   H O U S E

ten places for meeting, leaving the group who sided with Frederick Rhodes very few. To remedy this, they built a meeting house on the road from Harrisonburg that ran west to Dry River Gap — Burkholder's Meeting House as it was first called. Later, they would build a second one south of Harrisonburg, right on the Stage Road adjacent to Peter Moyers' farm. Ironically, and perhaps with a

For the next three years, the two groups operated quite separately. Once every two weeks the "offended party" would meet for preaching in their homes in the German language. They also ordained two new ministers — chosen by lot as was the custom — Benjamin Wenger and David Burkholder. The Burkholders were not among the families initially opposed to Frederick Rhodes, and his ordination was just one instance of how "the strife and contention...waxed warm and the heat of argument between individuals frequently brought unhappy occasions between families of the same name." David Burkholder declared their group the true Mennonist church in Virginia, and that their letter would keep their descendants on "the right side of the division." To Peter Burkholder, the letter of the "offended party" had become their idol. To those on the other side, the sometimes exuberant style of Frederick Rhodes was an unseemly attraction. And so the debate continued, year after year, between the "letter party" and the "Frederick people."

Eventually, two Mennonist ministers from Pennsylvania came to try to restore unity, but they were unsuccessful. Sometime in the early 1830s, Bishop Peter Eby and three other ministers from Pennsylvania decided to try again. Somehow, they managed to get both parties together at Burkholder's Meeting House, just a couple of miles west of Harrisonburg, where each side was given a fair hearing.

In the judgment of the Pennsylvania ministers, Frederick Rhodes had not violated any Gospel rule by associating with the United Brethren who still were tied closely to their Mennonist roots.[125] It was still also common for Mennonists — or Mennonites as they were now called — to travel and hold meetings with United Brethren preachers "and sometimes commune together."[126]

Although the Pennsylvania ministers gave full recognition to the ministers ordained in the "offended party," they declared that all those who had joined in opposition to Frederick Rhodes and signed the letter had not only withdrawn themselves from the Mennonite church in Virginia, but the Mennonite church in Pennsylvania and elsewhere. This was hard news for the offended party to hear. It would mean swallowing their pride, and admitting their mistake.

Finally, Henry Shank, a bishop ordained with the "offended party," stepped forward.

"If that is the way it is," he began, "it is better to stand with the Church."

Bishop Eby quickly responded. "Now, that is a commendable step."[127]

During and prior to the division, at least four Mennonite meeting houses had been built. Besides Trissel's, Moyers' or Pike, and

Burkholder's (soon to be called Weaver's), there was Brenneman's, about six miles south of Trissels. Now there was a meeting house within five miles of most Mennonite families.[128] The United Brethren had built a meeting house as well, their first in Virginia. Known as Whitesel's, it was situated just a few miles east of the Pike on a beautiful hilltop overlooking Pleasant Valley.[129]

The Dunkers too, had begun building churches. In addition to Garber's, the Cook's Creek congregation built the Beaver Creek meeting house. The Linville Creek group, meeting at the "Tunker House" since early days, built a new meeting house as well.[130] Though the shift to build meeting houses for Dunkers was not entirely new, it was a bit out of their original plan to live and worship as did the first-century Christians, in one another's homes. Likely it caused quite a bit of discussion among them. In any case, the meeting houses helped solve the problems of overcrowding and related issues, but greater visibility in a more public setting would have its price.

TUNKER HOUSE, c. 1830
Artist's conception

At least since the end of the Revolutionary War, Dunkers had dressed quite distinctively from their neighbors. They had always tended to avoid showy styles and faddish trends, but wearing different clothes simply to draw attention to themselves was not at all a Dunker attitude. By now, though, the non-resisting people had also become the nonconforming people. Dunker men never shaved their beards, nor even rounded the corners of them, according to an Old

Testament regulation believed to have been followed by Christ.[131]

Certainly curiosity about Dunker dress added to the outside interest about their religious life, and in time their love feast celebrations became an attraction not unlike the camp meetings.[132] Once a year, beginning on a Saturday morning, several hundred Dunkers would gather to celebrate the Lord's Supper, including footwashing and communion — and they had company. Neighbors from miles around would join them, and whether invited or not, the outsiders were welcomed. The big midday meal on Saturday was open to everyone, and the local Dunkers helped feed their own as well as the onlookers. The Lord's Supper, with its main meal of bread, lamb, and gravy, fol-lowed by the Communion meal and foot-washing, were all still strictly reserved for the members of the Dunker community, but even then they allowed their non-Dunker friends to look on as room was available.[133] Curious also to the English visitors must have been the kiss of peace practiced among the Dunker community, a greeting that signified to Dunkers that there were no divisions among them in preparation to eat the Lord's Supper.

Division, however, was exactly where many churches in Rockingham were headed about now.

KISS OF PEACE

Despite the fact that they had built meeting houses, Dunkers would continue to affirm their distinctiveness, holding fast to their practice of "primitive" Christianity. And though their love feasts may have begun to attract outsiders as the camp meetings had, Dunkers were far from the Methodist viewpoint. They had suffered much for their particular stance on biblical doctrine, and had proved through their suffering that they were not willing to compromise. Perhaps meeting houses of their own, besides increasing their public presence, offered a sense of stability, a "home" from which they might make their own stand within their rapidly changing community.

Many different denominations, though, had witnessed how the revival of the early 1800s had brought about a special unity among believers in Christ, regardless of their denominational background. In 1823, the editors of the *Methodist Magazine* wrote of the breaking down of "the thorny hedges of sectarian prejudice and jealousy," and observed a growing openness among Christians to "not only look, but sometimes leap, into each other's folds, and partake of their respective pastures, without the danger of contracting a disrelish for their own." As far as they were concerned, as long as this inter-denominational activity did "not degenerate into indifference for the distinguished doctrines of Christ, nor produce the fatal spirit of lukewarmness," such cooperation and love would "command a powerful influence over the skeptical mind."[134]

Clearly this kind of unity was manifested in the 1802 meeting of the United Brethren at Hoffman's barn, where Lutherans, Reformed, Mennonites, Presbyterians, Baptists, and Methodists had all gathered around a single communion table and eaten together. And no doubt people from these same denominations had attended the nine-day meeting at the Methodist church in Harrisonburg, as well as the quarterly meetings and camp meetings held since then.

Nationally and locally, joint efforts

among denominations had already begun. The Virginia Tract Society, started by Davidson, Bourne, and others in Harrisonburg in 1812, was one example. So was the Rockingham Bible Society which Johannes Braun had advocated in his 1818 circular writing. Some were willing to carry the idea of cooperation even farther. "How happy it would be," wrote one Lutheran minister, "if all the churches could unite, and send deputies to a general meeting of all denominations, and there sink down upon the rock Jesus...leaving to each their peculiar mode and form."[13]

Attached to this hopefulness of Christian unity was another element. In the wake of revival, with many new Christians throughout the land, there was a surge toward social reform as well. Temperance societies, advocating a complete ban on all alcoholic beverages, were formed, so were abolitionist groups who pushed for an immediate end to all slavery.[136] In the flush of these activities, some imagined that such great social and personal reform would bring an entirely new day to the world and usher in the thousand-year reign of Christ known as the Millennium.[137]

Benjamin Bowman, the Dunker leader of the Upper Linville Creek congregations near Greenmount, had a problem with this type of theology.[138] In point of fact, Bowman noted, it was plainly unscriptural. The Bible spoke of a breakdown of moral foundations before the time of Christ's return and his millennial reign, a time as in the days of Noah. People continued blindly about their usual business, the suffering of their wickedness increasing until the day Noah entered the ark, when the flood suddenly came and took them all away. More than this, the days before the millennial reign of Christ would be a time of "great distress, unequaled from the beginning of the world until now," Jesus had said, "and never to be equaled again."[139]

If some thought "that by much preaching and the great excitement" they would bring about Christ's reign on the earth, they were sadly mistaken, said Bowman. There was no place in any attempted union of the Church "for strange worship and the commandment of men [that] contradict the ordinances of God and the example of Christ." He reminded his listeners of the failed attempt of Jan van Leyden and his so-called Anabaptist associates in Muenster who had

A Pleasant Alternative

Ministers typically took the lead in the division of churches during the 1830s and 1840s, and congregations were often polarized. Yet, the more vocal debates and uncharitable argument that often received wide circulation does not tell the whole story.

At the Harrisonburg congregation of Old School Presbyterians, one member requested to be dismissed from the congregation to join the Methodists at Port Republic. Her motives as recorded were quite simple. There wasn't a Presbyterian congregation close to her home. Still, she did not find any theological or spiritual impasse in worshipping with a group whose evangelistic practices were at the heart of the New School movement from which her church had separated. Except for the basic message of the Gospel, Methodists stood for almost everything to which the Old School was opposed. Apparently for this woman, agreement on that one issue was enough.

Pleasant Clarke was another case in point. He and his family lived in Mt. Crawford, near the southern end of Rockingham on the North River. A number of neighbors, like Henry Bear, were moving west, some to Missouri, some to Kentucky. He describes the town of thirty

sought to establish the millennial kingdom of Christ through physical force almost three hundred years earlier. Their defeat typified the futility of anyone who would try to bring Christ's kingdom to earth, Bowman said, for "Christ will establish it by his own power, and consequently no preparation by men will be necessary."[140]

It was perhaps the fear of a forced Christian unity — by human effort alone — that began to create a distinct suspicion in many denominations. Regardless of the opinion of the editors of the *Methodist Magazine*, how would a union culminate without the loss of their "distinguished doctrines of Christ?" Several began to pull away from denominational efforts to cooperate with other groups, resisting any ill-defined unity. In 1823, when Bowman's words were penned and those of the Methodists were published, Röder's church signaled the early signs of this division in Rockingham. In that year, they petitioned a new Lutheran organization — the Tennessee Synod — to provide them with ministerial services.

It really came as no surprise. Röder's had been served since the close of the Revolutionary War by the independent, high-

ly motivated itinerant Lutheran, Paul Henkel. He had preached his second sermon at Röder's in December of 1782, and the church had been one of four that had sent a representative with the young pastor to vouch for his credentials before the Lutheran ministerium in Pennsylvania.[141] His sermons at Röder's were always well received. The first Christmas he had preached there, people came from miles away, "unmindful of the snow and cold," their hearts "warm and eager for the word of truth." Soon, he was preaching every four weeks there.[142]

Henkel had always tended to distrust the revival and its adherents. From his earliest meetings with them, he was unimpressed with the teachings of the "New Reformed" as he called the group now known as the United Brethren in Christ. To him, they had turned their back on the power of the sacraments of communion and baptism, substituting instead "their own personal religious experiences…their own works," as he put it. For Henkel, Christian experience proceeded from patience, and patience came from faith.[143]

Just a few years earlier at Röder's, during

the 1806 special meeting of Lutheran ministers in Virginia, Henkel had decried the type of revival that Rockingham was experiencing as "exceedingly strange to those who were well acquainted with the order of salvation." Speaking of events in North Carolina where he had lived for a few years, he declared it a mystery "that true conversion should consist in such a way as declared by these people; that true faith should originate in such sermons, as caused such corporeal convulsions, such representations of the devil, death, and hell; the fearful and awful expressions of lightning, thunder, hail, fire, and brimstone against the sinner, deprived many of their senses, and prostrated them in fainting fits."[144]

Central to Henkel's concerns were questions of orthodoxy. How could someone — even someone opposed to Christ — collapse to the ground, remain seemingly unconscious for an hour or more, then revive with an expression of praise to God? What had transpired during those wakeless hours? What place was left for the creeds, the sacraments? Had there been any comprehension of theological issues? Soon Lutherans were asking their own pastors the question,

"Don't we have to experience the same thing in order to be saved?" Despite the changed lives of many who had received evidence of pardon for their sins, Henkel and other Lutheran pastors were unwilling to surrender orthodoxy to the distraction of what they saw as emotion.[145]

Henkel's comments on the issue were among the first words printed at his family's press in New Market, about seven miles to the north and east of Röder's.[146] For the next several decades, that small one-room print shop on the Stage Road would become a mainstay of Lutheran orthodoxy, printing numerous publications vigilantly defending the Augsburg Confession and other standards of Lutheranism. In addition, it turned out copies of the minutes of the Tennessee Synod, an organization that Henkel and others created to resist the growing swell of indiscriminate "unionism" within their own denomination.[147]

Peter's church — now St. Peter's — near Adam Mueller's old home was another of the churches under Paul Henkel's care who sided with the Tennessee Synod.[148] Despite the fact that one elder, Piedefisch by name, was disdained by Henkel "as a complete

opinions nor a round of duty but repentance toward God and faith in our Lord Jesus Christ alone that can stand the test. Notwithstanding, if we have faith, we shall conform our lives to the Gospel of Christ.

And now, my dear brother, whom I have never seen in the flesh, I would want to try by any means to escape the wrath to come and get to the haven of Eternal Repose where the Wicked leave from troubling and the Weary are a t rest. And Mary and her mother, who I regard as relations, who I also love because I hear that they are striving to follow the Lord. May they and you heartily join in the good work and may the God of all Grace guide us all in the way of Truth and enable us to overcome through faith in his name and bring us to inherit the kingdom prepared for the Faithful where we may join in singing praises to God and the Lamb forever. Side 9

enthusiast," there were at least three elders and eight church members who had elected Paul Henkel's son, Ambrose, as their representative to the new Synod of Tennessee.[149] Belying its name, within ten years of its founding, the Tennessee Synod included churches in nine states. In Rockingham, besides Röder's and Peter's, they would also embrace Friedens and Ermentraut's.[150]

The other Lutheran churches in Rockingham would go a different route. Siding with their pastor Michael Meyerhoffer, congregations at Peaked Mountain and the Union Church, near the site of the old Peaked Mountain Presbyterian meeting house at Cross Keys, they joined the brand new Virginia Synod in 1829. At the beginning of the October 1830 meeting in Union church at Cross Keys, Meyerhoffer was elected president, but things did not go smoothly. The next day, there was a debate — no doubt rather heated — about whether or not to join the new General Synod. The majority voted to have nothing to do with the new body, and after lunch, four of the eight ministers present did not return.[151] By 1837, the Virginia Synod looked all but gone. That year, with encouragement from several preachers who saw them as the best opportunity around, they sent a strong message to the Tennessee Synod ministers that they did not consider them true Lutherans for at least three reasons. For one, they opposed most of the benevolent groups and activities like Bible and Tract Societies, prayer meetings and revivals. For another, they were accused of

> "...*pride, and worldly manners and the spirit of the world have flooded almost every thing, so that like in Noah's time 'all flesh has corrupted his way upon the earth,' and will not be reproved by the Spirit of God. Again how is that true love of our neighbor shown forth, which is one of the greatest commandments? Christ says, 'Therefore all things whatsoever ye would that men should do to you, do ye even so to them: for this is the law and the prophets;' and Paul says, 'Love worketh no ill to his neighbor.' "Now where is this observed in truth at this our time?"*
> — *Benjamin Bowman, 1823*

"intruding themselves" into congregations that had once been part of the Virginia Synod. But their first and most serious claim was this: in the eyes of the Virginia Synod Lutherans, the Tennessee members focused on the importance of the rituals of the church as a means for salvation.[152]

UNION CHURCH
at Cross Keys

The lines were drawn, not to be crossed for the next hundred years.[153]

Lutherans and Presbyterians had shared the little brick church at Cross Keys known as the Union Church probably since the 1820s. By 1834, Presbyterian minister Abner W. Kilpatrick organized the congregation there as the Union and Port Republic church.[154]

The old building was still there at Port Republic, but the Presbyterian presence — particularly after Bourne's stormy tenure — would not re-emerge. At Cook's Creek and Harrisonburg, Kilpatrick's main charge, the story was different. Between the two congregations there were well over 150 members, a number of them newly added during a revival that had followed the Harrisonburg meeting of the Virginia Synod in 1831. Now they would face their own storm.[155]

As early as 1804, in the wake of camp

meeting revivals, some Kentucky Presbyterians declared that church doctrine

firestorm. Finney noted that those "ministers and Christians who had adopted the literal

COOK'S CREEK PRESBYTERIAN

was being used as a weapon to keep people from coming to faith in Christ.[156] Their sentiments were echoed some years later by Charles Finney, a Presbyterian minister often at the center of a spiritual and ecclesiastical

interpretation of the Presbyterian Confession of faith…found it very difficult to deal with inquiring sinners."[157]

Presbyterian doctrine came down rather heavily in favor of "predestination," the belief that God chose those who would be saved. Those holding to the creeds would tell "inquiring sinners" they must "use the means of grace, to pray for a new heart, and wait for God to convert them." Finney, on the other hand "discarded all this teaching" and called on people "to make themselves a new heart and a new spirit, and pressed the duty of instant surrender to God."[158]

In 1837, the General Assembly of the Presbyterian church moved strongly away from Finney and the revivals now centered mainly in the northern and western states. Specifically, they voted to dissolve a decades-old cooperative arrangment with New England Congregationalists. Originally intended as a way to help spread the Gospel throughout New England, some Presbyterians were beginning to feel invaded by Congregational practices and government. That September, the majority of the members of the Lexington Presbytery followed the lead of the General Assembly, affirming the polity and creeds of "Old School" Presbyterianism.

At Cook's Creek and Harrisonburg, the people would feel the bitter edge of the national debate. Abner Kilpatrick favored the agreement with Congregationalists, and so did his successor, James W. Phillips, who had earlier served the Salem Presbytery in Indiana. The same month the Lexington Presbytery officially sided with the sentiments in the national debate, Phillips was already serving as a "supply" minister for the Cook's Creek and Harrisonburg congregations. By the following spring, he had been "unanimously" chosen as their new pastor.[159]

Almost immediately Phillips and his church elders — known as the "session" — planned two "protracted meetings," a new innovation after the fashion of the Methodist gatherings.[160] To traditionalists, protracted meetings were emotional carnivals designed to bring people into church membership. They produced "converts" without conviction, and totally ignored the Presbyterian doctrine that God had already chosen those whom he would save.[161] The issue came to a head in the spring of 1838 at the national meeting of the General Assembly, which began in the midst of vocal protest. After a "short but painful scene of confusion and disorder," several presbyteries withdrew to form their own New School organization.[162]

The scene was nearly repeated in

1 8 3 4   C O U R T H O U S E

Harrisonburg that summer. Under Phillips' leadership, the session of Cook's Creek and Harrisonburg passed several resolutions favoring alignment with the New School party. The next Sunday, Phillips announed the decision to the congregation after the sermon. The news upset and likely confused quite a few people. Phillips could be less than diplomatic on occasion and most likely did not mince his words now. Following the benediction, John Kenney rose to make a statement, but Phillips ordered him to sit down, declaring he was not a member of the church. Several people from both sides tried to speak, but the confusion was so great the meeting was adjourned. As Phillips and the session left — knowing they had the majority of leadership in their favor — they pocketed the key to the old stone church. It was a sour beginning.[163]

If they could, the Lexington Presbytery wanted to avoid a schism within their own ranks. In "an affectionate letter" to the Cook's Creek and Harrisonburg congregation, they announced a special meeting of the presbytery to be held in Harrisonburg on Christmas Day, 1838, to try and resolve the differences. When they arrived, the doors of the stone church were closed to them, so they met a block or so away at the Court House where Philips handed them a declaration signed by 108 of the members, along with every elder but one. As the cover letter stated, the signatures represented a majority of the members who clearly supported the action of the session in withdrawing from the presbytery.[164] Phillips signed his name, "Minister of the gospel in the true Presbyterian Church in the U.S. of America."[165]

The day after, the Lexington Presbytery met at the Methodist church, dissolved the pastoral relationship between Phillips and the church, and declared the remaining members and their elder the "real" Presbyterian church of Cook's Creek and Harrisonburg.[166]

For a while, it seemed that this "real" church would not have a place to meet, but when emotions abated, the members of the "true" Presbyterian church agreed to let them keep the church in town, while they, the New School, would continue to meet at the property known as New Erection.[167]

Nearby, from his home in Mt. Crawford, Johannes Braun was following the proceedings of the spectacle, which had been circulated in the public papers.[168] The Reformed had started their own organization in Virginia about the same time as the Lutherans, and had soon embraced protracted meetings with noticeable results. But Braun's take on certain aspects of the new

excitement of new converts "under his belt," approached the older Braun, now nearing his seventieth year.

"Father Brown, do you think anyone has ever been converted by your preaching?"

"Well," replied Braun in his pleasant manner and decidedly German accent, "I don't know; when perhaps if you would go round among all my congregations and ask them, you might find one here and there who would say, 'Lord be merciful to me, a sinner!' and who would not say, like the boasting Pharisee, 'God, I thank thee that I am not as other men!'"

This gentle rebuke would be his only answer.[169]

Perhaps the most prominent Methodist in the Bear family was John Bear, who committed his life to Christ at the Elk Run Liberty meeting house which stood in what is now the town of Elkton.

---

evangelism was a bit different.

One day, one of the new evangelists, a younger fellow perhaps enthused with the

Rockingham resident Henry Bear had moved to Missouri in the fall of 1832, but he was still deeply concerned about his sister Betsy's husband, Jacob Brubaker. Both Henry and Betsy were Methodists, but Jacob had been raised a Baptist. Much to their relief, Jacob had joined with the Methodist society at a camp meeting.[170] Just before Henry left

Rockingham, though, things looked uncertain for Jacob's denominational affiliation. As Henry put it, "the Baptists were using their

For years now, there had been a rising antagonism between the Baptists and the Methodists. In large part, it stemmed from

E L K   R U N
Meeting House

influence to get him down into the water, and as they had made a side-step toward the Methodists in doctrine and working with their tools I don't know where he will go."[171]

the same issues dividing the Lutherans and Presbyterians. From the standpoint of some Baptists, even those among their own denomination seemed to ply the emotions

143

of prospective converts like a horse trader. As one observed, after the sermon the preacher would pass through the congregation singing a "hymn on some tender and affecting subject, with a tune of mournful sound, or if thought proper, of lively cheerful sound." It didn't matter which, critics said, just as long as it fit the occasion and reflected the mood of his listeners.

As he walked, the preacher would shake the hands of those he met "with a great appearance of affection." Some would ask for prayer. Others would be asked if they wanted prayer. While the person was on their knees, the prayer would be offered "with an air of solemnity...that it may affect all around."[172] To the Baptists, so strong in their Calvinistic belief that God would choose whom he would, this type of ministry was merely a device certain preachers used to ingratiate themselves with the people — a method of gaining church members, but not a sound way to cultivate true believers in Christ. In fact, they argued, it was not Christ, but "anti-christ [who] has been so successful in making proselytes by these means, that the honest and sincere have been ensnared."[173]

The reference to antichrist, the fiend who would appear near the end of the world to lead a destructive force against believers, was not mere exaggeration to make a point. The antichrist's purpose would be to bring a false unity of the Church, just the opposite of the true unity available only through the work of Christ. Methodists and others at the forefront of the new evangelism were seen as enemies, or at least tools in the hands of the ultimate enemy of souls.

As for Jacob Brubaker, he was in the balance, as far as Henry and Betsy were concerned. "As long as Betsy can fight," Henry confidently asserted, "she will keep him from joining the Baptists." All the same he asked that a friend warn Jacob about the Baptists "and try and stay his mind from their refuge of lies."[174]

Perhaps the Bears were mostly concerned about the goings on in the Salem Baptist congregation near a town soon to be known as Dayton, a community that had grown up near the Harrison's stone house. Salem, formed in 1813 as an offshoot of the Linville Creek congregation, originally met in the home of Joseph and Abigail Coffman. In 1832 and 1833, the little church more than doubled as fifty-five people were baptized. It was the largest and most rapid growth Baptists had ever seen in Rockingham, or would see for many years to come.[175]

Perhaps the Salem church had done a little "side-stepping" toward the Methodists in those days of revival, but Baptists in Rockingham would generally move toward the straight-walking ways they called the "Old School." The rest of the old Linville Creek congregation had been centered in the Brock's Gap area at least since 1824. By 1843, in keeping with the leanings of the association to which they and Salem belonged, thirty-seven people officially organized as an Old School Baptist church called Brock's Gap.[176]

The Old School, or "primitive" Baptists, were often characterized as being anti-missionary, anti-Sunday School, and anti-Bible societies, but that was only part of the story. Mainly they were opposed to the interdenominational aspects of the many new "societies" forming throughout the nation. They supported missions, but they believed a missionary should be sent out from his or her own church, not by a mission board. They certainly also supported distributing the Word of God, but not through organizations

where a man's authority was determined because of his social connections and not his place in the church.[177] But Sunday schools they opposed in any form — not because they did not want to bring up their children in the faith, but because these Baptists were convinced that "giddy, unregenerated young persons" who confirmed a child's "natural notions of their own goodness" were no substitute for godly parents.[178]

Firm in purpose and conviction, Old School Baptists deliberately stayed out of the "mainstream" movements. In addition, their insistence on certain particulars, like no musical instruments in worship — since they were not directly instructed in the New Testament — made them seem austere. To some, they earned the name "hard shell" quite fairly.

Joseph Coffman, for one, was growing thin toward the hard-shell ways. He had seen the numbers dwindle at the Salem congregation noticeably since the great revival, and he was ready for change. In 1845, Coffman paid a visit to a New School or Missionary Baptist association meeting in Frederick County. It was there he met John Massey, a 26-year-old lawyer turned Baptist preacher.

To say the least, Massey was not exactly what Coffman had in mind. He was far too young and inexperienced. How would such a recent addition to the Baptists be able to stand up to the tough-minded Old Schoolers in Rockingham? Still, this fellow seemed to be his only option, so setting aside his misgivings, Coffman invited Massey to come to Rockingham and preach what he believed.[179]

The Sunday Massey visited the Coffmans, he was scheduled to preach at two places. Massey rode twenty-two miles to his first appointment in the morning. That afternoon, it was another six-mile jaunt to his second appointment.[180] As Massey approached the meeting place on his horse, one of the older members of that congregation had mixed feelings. "I feared that you *would* not come," he later told Massey, "and when you rode up, I wished you *had* not come — a mere boy instead of the man I expected."[181]

Instead of allowing his youthfulness to become a liability, Massey turned it into an asset, from that time on riding a 120-mile stretch between Morgantown, Virginia across the Allegheny Mountains, and down to the Augusta County line. And he preached anywhere and everywhere — churches, schoolhouses, private homes, groves, even once in the upper story of a distillery above the rising smells of fermenting grains. By that fall, Rockingham's first Missionary Baptist church was organized with twelve people. Salem was its name — the same as the nearby Old School church — and the word, ironically, meant peace.[182]

Though just the presence of a New School preacher had been enough of a curiosity to bring out a good crowd in the beginning, Massey must have seen the problem with the Linville Creek meeting house at once. It was in the wrong place. Once on the main thoroughfare from Wheeling through Brock's Gap and on to points east of the Blue Ridge,[183] the building now sat upon an out-of-the-way hill. It was a beautiful view from that spot, and there had been much history there, but to Massey it seemed there was little future. Here was the oldest Baptist meeting house in all Rockingham, not set upon a hill, but *stuck* upon it.

With limited resources and an eagerness to be useful, he moved it — first west on the old Williamsburg Road, then north, along a much-travelled route running north from

Greenmount where the Bowmans lived. All in all, they carried the church about a mile or more, to where the road bent sharply to the right, and there they set it down.[184]

At least one of the old trustees decided to take Massey to court. At issue was the question of ownership. Both Old and New School Baptists traced their heritage to the Linville Creek group. Trained as a lawyer, Massey argued on his own behalf and readily agreed with his accuser. "But," he added, "I beg to state that I placed it in a more convenient place, where more people can and will attend services." Who knows whether or not the judge had "New School" leanings of his own, but the argument made sense, and Massey was acquitted.[185]

By the 1840s, Lutherans, Presbyterians, and Baptists had all split over the new methods and practices. Mennonites had struggled with these same issues in the case of Frederick Rhodes, while Dunkers remained essentially unified in their support of primitive Christianity.[186]

Of course, among those who largely avoided the split over missions and Sunday schools were the Methodists.[187] After all, they were the "culprits" in much of those endeav-ors. It would seem that they might be able to avoid the next hurdle as well, but it would prove to be a stumblingblock over which they and the entire nation would fall.

CATARACTS

1850 - CONCLUSION

A cataract signals a marked change in the river's progress. The channel drops violently away, spurning attempts to navigate it, forcing a decision. So it was when our nation divided. Some were lost within its thunder; others felt the falling mists on calmer waters below.

HARMONY AND DISCORD

More than a thousand horses stood on the broad plain at the headwaters of Linville Creek. Tied to each other or to the nearest fence post or rail, some were restless, stamping their feet with an eagerness to get away from this strange gathering. Others, still in full harness connected to a carriage or buggy, stood with defined resignation.

Nearby sat a little brick chapel, hopelessly dwarfed by the 1,500 people collected here this Saturday morning in June. To accommodate the crowd, a stand had been erected in the field. All that was missing now was the appointed speaker, watched for eagerly up the long Greenmount Road.[1]

Isaac N. Walter had been making visits to

OPEN FIELD
near Antioch Church

Rockingham county on and off for the last fourteen years now, but needless to say, when the travelling minister from Ohio arrived a little later that day, he could easily determine this was "the largest congregation assembled that I ever saw in that place."

Walter represented a new denomination in the county, the Disciples of Christ. On his first visit here in 1828, fourteen people had joined with "the despised people called *Christians*," as members of the new group were more generally known.[2] The young preacher was especially befriended by Martin Burkholder, a wealthy Rockingham resident who allowed him to hold meetings in his home.[3] In October of 1832, at his second appointment at Mr. Burkholder's, Walter was encouraged that "eleven respectable members united with the church."[4] By June the following year, he was dedicating a new brick chapel near the Burkholder property along the Greenmount Road.[5]

The Disciples of Christ had been ignited in part by the ecumenical fervor then sweeping the nation and spread by the determined preaching of Alexander Campbell.[6] Like many others before them, the Campbellites (as they were sometimes called) longed for a simpler conception of Christianity, free from denominational creeds and regulations.

In his dedication sermon, Walter explained that the new "Christians" held that the Word of God — the Bible — was the only rule of faith and practice, and that Christian character was the only test of fellowship. Since the name "Christian" was first used in the ancient city of Antioch, the new brick chapel in Rockingham would be known as Antioch Chapel.[7]

In keeping with the tenor of the Protestant reformation, the Christians also argued for the right to use personal judgment in matters of theology. But there was an enormous gulf between personal judgment and individual speculation. Confusing the two had led Walter down the thorny path he was now taking to the waiting throngs that June day in 1842.

Among those attending was Benjamin Bowman, the second of that family in Rockingham. Like his father before him, he was a leader among the Dunkers, the Brethren of "German Baptists," but it hadn't always been clear he would follow in his father's footsteps.

It is often in dying that the true character of an individual becomes clear, as if the process somehow begins to wipe away the grime and smudge from an old mirror to see more clearly what it was reflecting. Joseph Travis saw this in a schoolmate of his, William Steward, a boy of about sixteen who became deathly ill. Though described as a "moral, upright, modest, and high-minded youth," during his sickness, William "become convinced of the necessity of a radical change of heart." He gave his life, what little breath was left, into the care of Jesus, seeking and finding the forgiveness of sin, and receiving the gift of eternal life. Joseph, only a couple of years younger than William, visited the young man on the night of his death.

He had not turned himself in bed for four days, and was speechless. The physician, who, by the way, was a Methodist preacher, concluded to have prayer in the room where Mr. Steward lay: not, as he thought, for his sake, whom he viewed already unconscious of any about him, but for the sake of the company present. But whilst at prayer, Mr. Steward rose up in the bed, with the death-rattle on him, and shouted aloud,—Glory!

glory! glory to God! I am going safe home to heaven!—meanwhile clapping his pulseless hands together, and raising them in token of complete victory over death, hell, and the grave. He gently laid his head on his dying-pillow, and in a short time breathed his last, without a sigh or groan, and winged his happy flight to the regions of endless bliss. The language of my heart was, "Let me die the death of the righteous, and let my last end be like his." I went home, but did not enter the house. I sought a fence-corner in the darkness of the night, and there, upon my bended knees, I covenanted with my heavenly Father, if he would but give me the religion of William Steward, I would serve him all my days.

Joseph Travis referred to this sort of evidence as "stubborn facts," and the comparison of William's death to that of another schoolmate who died miserably without Christ led Travis to determine "to serve the true and living God, and to seek of genuine and experimental godliness."

At the other end of life, in the year 1848, German Reformed minister Johannes Braun also took ill. For this devoted servant, so used to covering a wide territory in

Young Benjamin had been known as a sort of wild spirit in his early days. One evening while at home, he happened to overhear the voices of his parents. Night after night, they had faithfully prayed for their son to turn away from his own plans and come to Christ. Benjamin stopped to listen that night, and as he listened, he was touched by their love and the love God was showing to him. Soon afterward, he committed himself to serve his Savior, and eventually found his way into the ministry of the Dunker church. For the last five years now, he had been an elder in the Greenmount congregation whose own meetings were held in this very neighborhood.[8]

The Dunkers shared a common principle with the Disciples of Christ: both sought a renewed practice of "primitive" Christianity. Perhaps Bowman was intrigued by the connection, or, perhaps like most of the others, he was curious as to how this preacher from Ohio could be so certain of knowing the time of Christ's return.[9]

A little over a week before Walter's scheduled appointment, the Dunkers had held a council meeting at the old Garber meeting house. The subject was marriage,

but the sentiment was familiar. The enemy of souls — Satan — was out to destroy and "Nothing but the flaming sword of God's Word and Spirit can keep him out of the church."[10] In announcing his appointment, Walter had said he would back up his prediction with Scriptures. Bowman was sure to be all ears.

The sermon, Bowman reported later, was nothing short of eloquent. Known for his friendly, sociable nature by which he carried great influence, Walter could be a very convincing speaker. Yet, his explanation of how he could determine a point in time that Jesus Himself did not know was apparently not very persuasive, at least "to the thoughtful."[11]

Benjamin Bowman was certainly among "the thoughtful." Though an effective preacher, Bowman was not known to be a big talker. A friend once described him as "very considerate in forming an opinion, and exceedingly careful in reaching a conclusion." If he ever disagreed with someone, Bowman would typically not bring it up right away. Instead, he would mull it over, thinking through a clear response, which he would present with "arguments not to be refuted."[12]

Some time later, after the day of Walter's predictions had come and gone, he and Bowman met on the road. Embarrassed, but in keeping with his frank, gentlemanly manner, Walter spoke first.

"Well, Brother Bowman, I was mistaken."

"Yes," Bowman returned, "but I had discovered that before you told me."[13]

————

Despite their goal to renew traditional Christianity, the Campbellites had a sticking point with other denominations in their understanding of the Trinity — the belief that God is one God yet three persons: God, the Father; God, the Son (Jesus Christ); and God, the Holy Spirit. Walter's own beliefs led him to debate the issue with J. C. Lyon, a Methodist minister in Harrisonburg.[14] For Rockingham Methodists, though, this would only be a small part of their troubles.

The year after the big meeting at Antioch, Rockingham native and Methodist preacher Layton J. Hansberger came under fire for owning slaves. Officially, the Baltimore Conference of the Methodist Episcopal Church favored a gradual and ultimate emancipation of enslaved Africans, but practically they had a tight rope to walk. Since their territory included both slave-holding and non-slaveholding states, Baltimore Conference Methodists had attempted to navigate between abolitionism on one hand and voluntary slaveholding on the other.[15] Though a local preacher in Virginia might be allowed to hold slaves, for a travelling preacher the rules had to be different. It was a known fact that slaveholders "would not be kindly received" in most of the territory served by the conference.[16]

The discipline of the Methodist church supported this ruling, yet the Baltimore Conference still was delicate in their resolution. They informed Hansberger and several others that they were "most affectionately and earnestly urged, and required…to free, and rid themselves, of the relation of master to their slaves."[17]

In his own words, Hansberger "was unwittingly drawn" into his connection with slavery through a marriage contract, yet his ordination as elder depended upon him ending that connection.[18] Despite the preacher's intentions, this was no easy task. New laws

his younger days and continually eager to do good, the illness was confining and frustrating. Many times he asked why he had lingered so long when his heart's desire was to be with his Lord in heaven. One day after he had shared a few thoughts with those in his sick room, he saw tears and smiles on their face. "This must be why I am still here," he realized.

But Braun, with his long, silvery hair giving him the appearance of the venerable patriarch he had been, was ever eager for the beginning of a new life. He had run his course. He was now ready to go home. It reminded him of another time he had almost met death, as a young man during his voyage to America more than fifty years ago. One day, he told the story to a visitor.

After having encountered many severe gales and storms, we came at length into Chesapeake Bay. Here again we met with strong, contrary winds and fierce storms, so that we wrought for nine days in sight of the port. Every now and then our old bark would screech and groan as if all were going to pieces, and we should perish in sight of land. But at length the storm abated; there was a pleasant breeze in the right direction, and we just went right in! Just so

153

written some years ago following the bloody insurrection of slaves in Southampton County made emancipation in Virginia almost impossible.[19] There were now five slaves in his household, a father about 60 years old, a mother of 53, two girls about 19 and 12, and a boy of 15. Though the parents were, as Harnsberger noted, "beyond the age when it is supposed proper to set them free," the following year the Baltimore Conference still required that he give definite assurance that the freedom of the three younger slaves was secured before his ordination as elder could proceed.[20]

Hansberger's cooperation with the existing Discipline would be eclipsed that year by a higher ecclesiastical authority. Bishop Andrews, one of the several men holding the highest office in the Methodist Episcopal church, had also inherited slaves through marriage. When called upon to relinquish them, he refused.[21] What the Baltimore Conference required of their travelling preachers, the Bishop himself would not do. Andrews' action solidified the ideological split in the Methodist church over slavery. Now there would be two churches, North and South.[22]

In Virginia, most churches east of the Blue Ridge were part of the Virginia Conference, now aligned with the Methodist Episcopal Church, South. West of the Ridge, Methodist churches were part of the Baltimore Conference, still part of the "Northern" church as long as the northern group would not condemn slaveholding as a sin or refuse admission to slaveholders.[23] Yet the plan of separation had an important proviso: not just Conferences, but individual congregations bordering on the line of division would be left free to determine whether they would affiliate with the Northern church or the new Methodist Episcopal Church, South.[24]

Almost immediately, emissaries from the Virginia Conference began their campaign in Rockingham. The rights of Virginia citizens — especially of slaveholders — were neither "regarded nor protected" by the Baltimore Conference, they argued. The only choice was to join the Virginia Conference, for "then only, and not till then…[will] the owners of Slaves be enabled to be at rest."[25]

In Harrisonburg, the congregation had already split, the majority joining the Southern church, and a number of other congregations had divided loyalties. Members of the Baltimore Conference were incensed at what they saw as a territorial breach, but the Virginia Conference felt otherwise. Methodists at Elk Run, Keezletown, Bridgewater, and elsewhere ran to the Southern ranks.[26]

By 1846, a flurry of petitions reached the Baltimore Conference from Rockingham. Some, like Mt. Crawford and Bridgewater, wanted to stay in connection with the Northern church, and strongly objected to the "uncalled for attacks of the Divisionists of the South." Those from Wesley Chapel and Fellowship Schoolhouse not far from Lacy Springs were concerned that their rights as slaveholders be upheld. The entire East Rockingham circuit proposed that the Baltimore Conference be divided to include only slaveholding territory.[27]

The North-South issue was not the only source of division among the Methodists in Rockingham. The same year the North-South split took place, a local preacher by the name of Benjamin Denton left the Methodist ranks having "taken some exceptions to the proceedings of some of the preachers and people." Though the slaveholding issue was at the forefront of public debate, this was not Denton's first conflict with the Methodist church. About eight years earlier, the preachers of the Rockingham Circuit had deprived Denton of his credentials for "an alleged want of gifts and usefulness."[28] Denton appealed to the Baltimore Conference and was reinstated, but perhaps a few old issues still lingered.

Denton's connections with the Methodists went back thirty years or more. He had been preaching at least since 1815, and in 1820 had donated a lot for a Methodist meeting house adjacent to his own property near Dry River in the western part of the county. For some time now, John Blakemore, a member of Mt. Solon Lutheran church in Augusta, had been ministering at the meeting house there known as Friendship as well as in other nearby congregations. Though not an ordained preacher himself, Blakemore was working under the auspices of Lutheran minister Peter Shickel.[29] In May of 1845, Denton tried to persuade the budding evangelist to leave the Lutheran church, but Blakemore refused, hoping instead to be ordained by the Virginia Lutheran Synod.[30] By the following year the Methodist classes at Briery Branch and Dry River had "all joined Blakemore."[31]

with Denton and a few others, formed the Arminian Union Church, a unique and origi-

D R Y   R I V E R

In May of 1847, after two years of unsuccessfully seeking Lutheran ordination, Blakemore cut his ties with the denomination. Shickel was saddened by the turn of events, but there was nothing more to be done. Now on his own, Blakemore, along

nal denomination.

The very next year when they met, Denton found it difficult to conduct business since, as he put it, he had "been grossly insulted upon my post by one of the members."[32] The issue worsened with time, and by 1849 Denton had left Blakemore and started a new group, the *Separate* Arminian Union Church.

Despite the name "Arminian," emphasizing man's ability to choose his eternal destiny, it seems this new group held to a somewhat unique blend of Arminian and Calvinist doctrine. While they acknowledged that "true faith cannot proceed...from the force and operation of free will," the Separate Arminian church also recognized that God gave to those "who are regenerated by his grace, the means of preserving themselves in this state." In other words, while people can't choose God's way simply by applying their own effort, their own effort had a lot to do with making that choice stick. The preachers of this new denomination were also cautioned to let their "whole deportment be serious and solemn."[33]

FUNK'S PRINT SHOP

Though Denton published a little volume detailing their doctrines and justifying the history of the group, by 1851 Denton and twenty-four others had rejoined the Methodist Church, establishing again the class at Friendship. The Separate Arminian Union Church was no more.[34]

The publisher of Denton's book was Joseph Funk, another resident of western Rockingham in nearby Mountain Valley, some twelve miles west of Harrisonburg at the foot of North Mountain.[35] Just two years earlier, Funk had opened his own print shop beside his home. Though his 1816 German-language songbook had not necessarily been a big seller, since then he had developed a popular reputation as a music publisher. It began in 1832 with *Genuine Church Music,* his first English-language production.[36]

In 1847, Funk published *A Selection of Psalms, Hymns, and Spiritual Songs,* the first English hymnbook used by the Mennonite church and the first printed at his new shop beside his home. Though the Mennonite church was open to using English in their services, the book would

patterns. Instead, users of the book were directed to the tunes in *Genuine Church Music,* by now in its fourth edition.[37]

The explanation of music theory at the beginning of *Genuine Church Music* — later called the *Harmonia Sacra* — was simple and clear. Funk directed his instruction not to music professionals, but to everyday men, women, and children. In addition to notes printed on the scale, each also had a

SHAPE-NOTES
from Psalm 100, appearing in Funk's 1832 Genuine Church Music

contain no written music, something they still considered to be a nod toward worldly

distinctive shape, making it more easily recognizable for students just learning to read music.[38]

Funk and his sons, Solomon and Timothy, also helped pioneer singing schools throughout the state. They would come into an area for a period of two weeks or so, and teach those interested in learning to sing and read music. The Funks suggested that probably the highest goal of any education was "to develop the natural resources of *the mind;* to bring out and develop its faculties and powers, *socially* and *morally,* as well as intellectually."[39]

Music, in particular, was worthy not only to study as a science, but as the language of sentiment and feeling "it deadens the feelings of hate, and… enkindles the flame of devotion on the altar of the Christian's heart…" To learn to sing and enjoy this great blessing, they felt, should be the privilege of all.[40]

> *"My highest conception of patriotism is found in the man who loves the Lord his God with all his heart and his neighbor as himself. Out of these affections spring the subordinate love for one's country; love truly virtuous for one's companion and children, relatives and friends; and in its most comprehensive sense takes in the whole human family. Were this love universal, the word patriotism, in its specific sense, meaning such a love for one's country as makes its possessors ready and willing to take up arms in its defense, might be appropriately expunged from every national vocabulary."*
> — *John Kline, 1849*

But despite this high praise coming from the Funks, singing schools — like written music on a page — were not acceptable for Mennonites. Musical instruments too, were disdained as an imitation of the formal churches. Once, it seems, Funk attempted to entertain several Mennonite ministers by asking his sons to accompany a song on their instruments. The leaders were not amused.[41]

In spite of the opposition, Funk's conviction that singing should be for *everyone* in the church — not set apart for a select choir — would be ample momentum for a long and rich musical heritage for the Shenandoah Valley and elsewhere. Mennonites themselves would find their own traditions strengthened by it.[42]

159

The Virginia Mennonite's switch from German to English and their acceptance of singing schools were both pushed forward by Bishop Martin Burkholder. Like his father, Peter, who had played a pivotal role in the construction of Mennonite meeting houses a quarter of a century earlier, Martin was aware of a need for ordered change in the church.[43] Funk's *Selection of Psalms,* *Hymns, and Spiritual Songs* had appeared in print about the time Martin received his orders as a bishop.

It helped that Burkholder was not simply bilingual, but also one who was said to have preached the Word of God with great effect. Through his leadership, Funk was encouraged to translate other works from German into English for the use of the

JOESEPH FUNK'S HOUSE
as it appears today in Singer's Glen,
formerly Mountain Valley

160

Mennonite church.[44]

In response, Funk chose a classic German text written by his own grandfather, Bishop Henry Funk, and first published in Philadelphia a century earlier. *A Mirror of Baptism* was the English translation of the title, but for one influential reader, it would cast an altogether different reflection.[45]

John Kline had been a preacher in the Dunker church for several years when *A Mirror of Baptism* appeared. He was immensely useful in the Dunker church, and served many not only with his ministerial skills, but also with his abilities as a self-taught physician.

But Kline, a close associate of Benjamin Bowman, Jr., shared the Dunker insistence on correct form and practice based on their understanding of the New Testament. Revisiting the old dispute of Mennonite Peter Burkholder and Dunker Peter Bowman during the early part of the century, Kline penned a strongly-worded review of Funk's translation, one which apparently took the Mennonite music publisher completely off-guard.

Kline was not one to mince his words, and charged both the author as well as the translator with "wilful dishonesty…as also with prejudice, ridiculous and weak ideas, and errors of different kinds."[46] To Joseph Funk, the review was not the work of a self-denying Christian, but had the marks of pride throughout. Kline had not only chosen the injustice of picking an argument with a man who could no longer speak for himself — the long-deceased Henry Funk — but had also "pointed his keenest quaver" at the translator.[47]

Like others who had entered this fray in the past, Joseph Funk disclaimed any love for controversies. But Funk had something else to commend him beside his words. For years he had "been striving — with the help of the Lord — to divest myself of all party spirit in religious matters." Outward forms, he grieved, had grown more important than "inward purity of heart, Christian love, humbleness of mind, and forbearance," clearly a disorder of priorities.[48]

Now nearing eighty and a faithful member of the Mennonite church, Funk had

161

repeatedly demonstrated his focus on the more central issues of faith. His son, Solomon, had first joined the Methodist out of the four — Timothy, Solomon, and Benjamin — would become ministers.[49]

For Funk, the basic question was "Who

RITCHEY'S SCHOOL HOUSE

church in Harrisonburg; another, Jonathan, the Presbyterian church at Turleytown. Later, the two boys, along with their brothers Timothy and John, became Baptists. Three are members of Christ's Church which he has purchased with His own blood?" He had been closely acquainted with very many members of different churches — Dunkers,

Mennonites, Baptists, Lutherans, Presbyterians, German Reformed, Methodists, United Brethren, Episcopalians and Campbellites — had even known their fathers and grandfathers in some instances. Among them he had found many who were "more pious, devoted, and zealous Christians than himself."[50]

In Funk's estimation, the central core of the Christian faith was to "believe in One God, Father, Son, and Holy Spirit…the Creator and Upholder of all things visible and invisible, and the Saviour of mankind and Comforter of His people."[51]

Nonetheless, Funk proceeded to defend the positions taken in *A Mirror of Baptism* in a lengthy work called *The Reviewer Reviewed*. A year later, Kline followed up with *Strictures and Reply*, which proved to be the last printed volley from either side.[52]

Though the debate occupied center stage for a time, it was by no means the defining moment for Funk or Kline. John Kline had a long and useful service as a minister in the Dunker church, making many trips west into Brock's Gap and beyond. Here, he saw, there was an eagerness to hear the Word of God preached.[53]

He was especially devoted to the young people in the congregations. One of his frequent stops was at the schoolhouse belonging to Philip Ritchey, along Little Dry River up in the Gap.[54] Philip's daughter, Catherine, recalled that of the many times Kline visited, she could not remember seeing him leave without first taking the hand of every young person within reach and quietly saying something to each. "I do not know what he said to others," she remembered, "but I know, as if but yesterday, what he whispered to me. It was this: 'Do not neglect the salvation of your soul: *it is the* ONE THING *needful.*'"[55]

Despite Funk's perception of pride in Kline's written review, the Dunker preacher was deeply aware of his own need before God. "Of one thing I am sure," he wrote several years before his published debate with Joseph Funk. "No one will ever have a just right to boast of his own goodness, or lay claim to preferment on the score of his own obedience."[56] Though he disagreed sometimes sharply over doctrinal points with other denominations, he remained on friendly terms with several of their ministers, including Presbyterian Henry Brown of Harrisonburg.

Besides Rockingham, Kline boldly travelled east of the Blue Ridge with the Dunker message. At a Methodist church in Albemarle County, he was present when Benjamin Bowman baptized Henry Coverston and his wife, perhaps the first Dunker baptisms in eastern Virginia.

The mountains were not the obstacle here. It was slavery. In Albemarle, Dunkers could preach to the poor, but not to the rich. Anyone who wanted to be baptized into the Dunker church[57] must agree to relinquish their slaves as property. Yet the church understood that it would be a raw and unjust freedom to "turn them off houseless and homeless." Since Virginia law did not allow for emancipation, members were allowed to continue to care for the needs of their former slaves "until suitable and lawful provision can be made for their complete emancipation."[58]

Like the Methodists of the Baltimore Conference, the Dunker church was aware they were walking a fine line here. Public feeling ran high on this issue, and while the Dunkers were reluctant to irritate it, they remained true to what they held "sacred as their line of Christian duty" before God.[59]

Thankfully, they were not alone.

———

John Kline had some misgivings about the United Brethren. To him, their focus on gaining converts seemed to be at the expense of helping people grow in Christ through discipleship.[60] Yet, generally, there were still plenty of points for agreement. At the heart of it all, both insisted on the need to trust Christ alone for salvation. That was the good news of the Gospel. But United Brethren stood solidly with the Dunkers on another issue of justice — they were opposed to slavery.

Like their Methodist cousins, United Brethren had issued an early proclamation against human bondage, but they went farther, demanding that "all slavery, in every sense of the word, be totally prohibited and in no way tolerated in our community." In this area at least, they had remained distinct from the Methodists.[61]

Nor had they gained the social prestige of Methodists or Presbyterians. When their ministers met at the annual conference of

1855, they were viewed by some as just a bunch of "fanatics, or fit subjects for a hospital for the insane."[62] Perhaps that spared them the necessity of being overly concerned with the opinions of men. Or perhaps it was their refusal to submit to those opinions that left them free to pursue the call of God.

Like the Mennonites and Dunkers, their strong stance against slavery made preaching on the eastern side of the Ridge almost impossible. They had stayed true at least to that part of their inheritance from the peace-loving churches. On the other side of the coin, United Brethren were not at all wedded to the pacifist leanings of Anabaptism. That, at least, was evident in the person of George Rimel.

TURLEYTOWN CHURCH

Rimel was neither an impressive scholar nor a man of words. In fact, his bulky, "beefeating" appearance gave him the rugged look of a farmer — which in fact he was. Once, while serving on the Rockingham circuit, Rimel was staying with Andrew Horn not too far from Turleytown. There was a free church there, Rimel discovered, which sat largely unused. A group of ruffians had seen to that. Preaching did not suit their style, and they had opposed every minister that had come there.

Rimel took this as a challenge. For the immediate future, he would be on a tour through Brock's Gap and further west, but upon his return, Rimel wanted an appointment to preach at the empty church of

Turleytown.

If for no other reason than curiosity, people must have filled the meeting house to see what would happen when George

just what they were after. He called out to someone for their names. Unintimidated, the bullies called out their own names, which Rimel wrote down on a slip of paper.

WITTENBERG CHAPEL

First a Lutheran building, later sold to the Dunker church (from a postcard print)

Rimel, the rough-hewn preacher for the United Brethren, took the Turleytown pulpit. About halfway through his sermon, the rowdies began their show. Politely, Rimel asked them to quiet down, but the attention was

"Tomorrow," he informed them, "I shall see the proper officers of the law and have you arrested and presented for your unruly conduct here tonight."

For some reason, that seemed to end the

disturbance that evening, but the next morning while riding through the town, Rimel met up with the group of troublemakers again.

Grabbing the reins of Rimel's horse, the leader demanded the list of names Rimel had written down the night before. Rimel refused. There was a sudden movement as the leader grabbed the hefty Rimel and tried to pull him off his horse.

"Hold on," Rimel said unruffled, "I can get off myself." Dismounting, Rimel quietly slipped off his coat. Now it was his turn to present a challenge.

"I am not afraid of all the people in Turleytown," Rimel began, "and I can whip them all if they will fight fair."

Chest to chest with his accusers, the rowdies must have seen for the first time what a large man the preacher was. This was no small talk.

"I can whip the whole pack of you. I shall only need to get in one or two licks on a man, and every man I hit will never know what hurt him."

At that, Rimel pulled back his arm and took a tremendous swing at the ruffians' leader. Only a fool would stand in the way of that fist, and the bully took off running. Seeing no one else interested in making good on his offer, Rimel got back on his horse and rode away.

Just then, one of the rowdies came up to him, this time with a much changed outlook. It seemed that they had a great deal of respect for a "brave man." Now, they promised, they would protect him from any further disturbance whenever he preached.

After that, as the story goes, "Turleytown was a reformed place."[63]

Rimel's encounter was no doubt repeated as a great joke many times over, but the difficulties facing the nation over slavery could not be lightheartedly dismissed. Trouble was coming, and the signs were everywhere.

One Sunday evening in the summer of 1859, the sky over Rockingham appeared to be illuminated with a scarlet red hue almost the entire night.

"What it may portend I know not," wrote John Kline in his journal the following day. "People may brand me superstitious, but I can not resist the impression that this, with other signs, betokens the shedding of blood in our land."[64]

BATTLE LINES

When he left Harrisonburg in 1854, John Massey accepted the call of three Baptist churches on the east side of the Ridge in Albemarle and Nelson counties. The first two years, he and his family boarded at a house near the line between those counties, and for several days they had a particular visitor, a man who introduced himself as Dr. McLane.

In Massey's opinion, Dr. McLane was both well-informed and intelligent, with very agreeable manners. The doctor's mission, it seemed, was to travel around and treat conditions of hernia. In evidence of his calling, the light wagon he drove was filled with trusses. Few people realized, said the doctor, how frequent this condition was among the Negroes, which is why he stayed among them whenever he had the opportunity.

On top of his medical training, Dr. McLane appeared to have religious leanings as well. As Massey later recalled, he "affected great piety, and seemed familiar with the Bible. He wished me to make an appointment for him to preach."[65]

All the same, Massey had an uneasiness about this stranger, "an instinctive feeling that he was not what he professed to be." McLane's request to preach was declined, but a few years later, he had found his own platform: the gallows in Charlestown.

It was less than two months after John Kline had watched the strangely red sky over Rockingham when John Brown and his twenty-one accomplices made their raid on Harper's Ferry in October of 1859. Brown's goal was to rapidly arm African slaves and white sympathizers who sought an end to slavery through violent force. A detachment of Federal troops under the command of Colonel Robert E. Lee quickly brought an end to the rebellion, but the real issues would not be contained so easily.

Like Nat Turner, who almost thirty years earlier had led a bloody uprising in Virginia, which killed more than fifty people, Brown used Biblical language as a foil for his violence. But there was one particular distinction between Brown and Turner, a distinction that would place Brown's arguments even more dramatically before the whole nation. His skin was not dark.

Papers and pulpits in the Valley of Virginia were quick to reprehend Brown's raid, and took particular note of the reaction from ministers in the North, as quoted by the *New York Observer*: "Of the five hundred preachers in this city we have heard of but TWO, who ventured to give the sanction of their pulpits to the support of the highest crime perpetrated in this country since the treason of Benedict Arnold."[66]

As Brown's much-anticipated trial drew the attention of both North and South, his prison cell was visited by many, including John E. Massey. Likely he had seen a picture in one of the papers, but when Massey saw the prisoner he knew for certain. The man who had become the focus of national debate was none other than the boarding house stranger, Dr. McLane.

The year after Brown's execution, Methodist leaders assembled for their General Conference at Buffalo, New York. Ever since the church had split North and South over the slavery issue, most of the Rockingham Methodists had stayed with the Baltimore Conference and the Northern church. But by 1860, weary of the "odious" sentiments of the North, East Rockingham and other circuits in the Rockingham district were urging the Baltimore Conference to make a clean break with the Northern church, whose principles were in direct conflict with her Virginian constituents.[67]

But the conference of 1860 was firm. Slaveholding in any form was no longer acceptable in the Methodist Episcopal church of the North. Plainly and simply, they said, "the buying, selling, or *holding* of human beings, to be used as chattels" violated Jesus' teaching to "Do unto others as you would have them do unto you."[68]

Churches in Rockingham and throughout the Valley saw this as a surrender to politics in the pulpit, as a "new chapter" in the Methodist Discipline. The next year, at the annual conference held in Staunton, emotions ran high as question after question over the slavery issue came before the chair. On March 23, 1861, over a sharply divided vote, the majority decided to withdraw the Baltimore Conference from the Northern church.[69]

The Methodists in the Valley had claimed several reasons why the "new chapter" was not acceptable. The laws of Virginia, for one, prohibited the emancipation of slaves. Even without legal obstacles, the loss of slaves would present an entire change of life for the masters, in addition to a loss of valuable "property." But perhaps the most intriguing was their appeal to history, to "the education of the southern conscience through generations of civil and religious recognition of the slavery institution."[70] The issue of slavery had already split the Baptists and the Presbyterians, even the German Reformed.[71]

In the face of a number of southern states that had already withdrawn from the Union, Virginia still remained. A convention earlier that year was perhaps the first indication that she might secede as well, but at least one delegate from Rockingham had promised the voters he would *never* under any circumstances vote for secession.[72]

John F. Lewis, a great-great-great grandson of Thomas Lewis, though part of a political minority in Rockingham, found himself a member of the 1861 Virginia convention.[73] In the first ballot on secession, the vote was strongly against leaving the Union, but when newly elected President Abraham Lincoln called for volunteers to bring the seceded states back into the Union, the Virginia convention reversed its decision thirteen days later on April 17, 1861, voting eighty-eight to fifty-five to recommend that the state secede.[74] True to his word, Lewis refused to sign the secession ordinance. At that convention, he was the only man east of the Alleghenies to remain true to the Union.[75]

Throughout the war, Lewis would stick by his principles and to the old home at Lewiston. Though he remained a non-combatant, Lewis managed to stay on the good side of his neighbors and the government by operating the nearby Mt. Vernon Forge, reserving much of the iron it produced for the Confederate cause.[76] But there was at least one pro-Union man who thought it wise to leave. In nearby Port Republic, Methodist minister Thomas Wysong, not fully sympathetic to the South's intentions, quietly slipped away without telling anyone of his plans.[77]

The Sunday after the vote, churches everywhere were abuzz with the talk of war and secession. "There is great commotion everywhere in the realm of thought and sentiment," wrote Dunker leader John Kline, "men's hearts failing them for fear, the sea and the waves of human passion roaring."[78] Many throughout the Valley sought refuge in the bottle. Temperance — or more accurately, abstinence from alcoholic beverages —

had for decades been a moral position for many church groups. With the prospect of war, drinking was reported to have increased five-fold, and many saw legislated prohibition as the only effective solution.[79]

In May, the Annual Meeting of the Dunker Brethren at Beaver Creek meeting house brought together people from both

SOLOMON FUNK'S STONE HOUSE

Mennonites and Dunkers were not the only denominations who held to non-resistance during the Civil War. Solomon Funk, a member of the Turleytown Baptist Church, lived more or less in confinement at his house near Singers Glen for two years, eight and one-half months. A small man, Funk climbed through the false top of a cabinet and secluded himself in the attic in order to avoid the Confederate draft. He would not venture beyond his own property until after the war was over.

effort to prevent the war. So on the Fourth of July they appointed a time for a delegation from the South and one from the North to get together to see if they could not come to an agreement. When that day came, we saw something we never saw before. The sky was overcast but was not cloudy. It was so dark the sun scarcely shone through. There was, however, a straight line from east to west over the Mason and Dixon line, north of which it was clear as crystal. The southern sky was gloomy.

At that time there was a comet north from us, the largest I ever saw, and we noticed all day long the peculiar atmosphere and dim shining of the sun and how the sky was overcast but did not seem to be cloudy. We were thinning corn and we thinned until about dusk. As my father, three sisters, and myself in the evening were coming out of the cornfield, we looked up to see the comet. That comet was just on the hazy side of the line. We could barely see the comet, but while we were looking up, a fiery ball started as though from the tail of the comet and looked as big as a bushel basket. When it appeared to be halfway to the earth, it exploded and re-exploded. Little pieces would explode and re-explode.

It was one of the most awful sights I ever witnessed at the time of the war. When

North and South perhaps for the last time in the foreseeable future. Both Dunkers and Mennonites knew the cost to obey God rather than man. To wage war would be a violation of their conscience and the law of Christ. When those attending Annual Meeting left, they went with heavy hearts.[80]

Kline wrote several letters to Governor Letcher of Virginia and others in authority, explaining the position of the German Baptist Brethren. "I feel sure that if we can be rightly understood as to our faith and life, there will be some way provided for their exemption," Kline believed. "Many have already expressed to me their determination to flee from their homes rather than disobey God."[81]

Meanwhile, hundreds of volunteers from Rockingham joined in the war effort on behalf of the Confederacy, most forming a part of the Tenth Virginia Regiment. Unbelievably, despite a desperate lack of ammunition and up-to-date fire arms, the Confederate army was successful on many occasions.[82] "We are victorious so far," wrote one Rockingham soldier to his wife on day of the Battle of Manassas, the first major battle in the war. Hearing reports of the battle

from his encampment several miles to the west at the Winchester Fair Grounds, he noted, "It is the pivot on which our struggle is to turn." War in Rockingham was not immediate, but it seemed quite close at hand. "If anything of that sort should happen," he warned his wife, "Uncle must drive our stock away. And not be caught as were many of the farmers in Berkley, who lost every thing, stock, negroes & all."[83]

For some this war would be about getting caught. For others, it would be about getting free.[84]

———

Though the people of Rockingham had yet to see the Union blue on their soil, the fearful prospect of war was sometimes threatening enough. One Sunday afternoon, a report that African slaves were "breaking out and committing fearful outrages flew as on the wings of the wind."[85] Rockingham had far fewer slaves than most counties in Virginia, but the thought of open rebellion was still a terror. In the end, the story proved to be only a rumor.[86]

Even before the war began in earnest, there was drilling at regular musters. One drill field was at New Erection, the meeting place of the New School Presbyterians.[87] That denomination had divided twice now, once over the "new evangelism," and again in 1858, over slavery.

In June of 1861, a Confederate captain appeared at Weaver's Mennonite church with an announcement: all males between 18 and 45 must report for military duty the following week. Peter Hartman, not yet fifteen years old, later remarked, "I never want to see another day like that — a whole congregation in tears."[88]

When the order came to report, most Mennonites complied. One who refused, Michael Shank, was taken out of his house and down the Valley north of Winchester. There was no choice in the matter. Shank would serve whether he liked it or not.

Yet even though forced into battle, Mennonites and Dunkers still held to their convictions. Many took a "no-shoot pledge," as did Mennonite Christian Good.

After one battle, Good's captain approached him questioningly, "Did you shoot?"

"No," replied Christian, "I didn't see anything to shoot at."

Incredulous, the captain fired back, "Why, didn't you see all those Yankees over there?"

"They're people," came Christian's straightforward answer. "We don't shoot people."[89]

General Thomas Jackson, himself a devout Christian and member of the Presbyterian church in Lexington, knew the resiliency of the pacifist groups. "They can be made to fire," he wrote to the Governor's aide, "but they can very easily take bad aim." Jackson had hoped to organize Mennonites and Dunkers into groups of one hundred men each, to drive wagons and take care of the teams. He had pledged that to the best of his ability, he would use them in ways other than fighting.[90]

That solution was not suitable to many Dunkers and Mennonites. In March of 1862, two separate groups, one of seventy-two men, the other numbering eighteen, headed west. For the most part they were members of the Dunker and Mennonite churches, though others had tagged along.[91] They intended to pass through Union lines and

that roaring stopped, I could hear my heart beat. When my father turned around he said, "That means war." We did not need to wait to hear from Washington. Soon after, it was learned that the special agents of the sections could not decide the case. The armies were in the field ready for war. Side 11

onto freedom, much like the slaves who travelled the Underground Railroad. Somewhere near Petersburg, West Virginia, the largest group was stopped by a handful of men, Confederate soldiers who had been paroled by the North and were under oath not to harm the interests of the United States until properly exchanged.

"Give up your arms!" the Confederates demanded, ignoring their promise.

"O, brethren," Joe Heatwole encouraged his friends, "pray mightily to God. He will deliver us!"

The fleeing band pulled out their weapons — the Bible and their New Testaments — but the soldiers did not take them. Peacefully, the Confederates marched the quiet group back through the mountains toward Rockingham. Though there was plenty of opportunity to slip away through the woods and darkness, the non-resisting Brethren stayed together. No one really wanted to make additional trouble for those men who would be left behind under Confederate guard. Before the long journey was over, only two had escaped to tell those at home what had happened. After a short stop at Staunton, the rest were taken by train to Richmond's Libby Prison.[92]

At Richmond the prisoners were examined by the War Department's Sydney S. Baxter. Thoroughly convinced these men were committed to non-resistance, Baxter gave those he interrogated the following instructions: "Gentlemen, I will ask you a good many questions, and if I ask any that you cannot answer, you need not say anything." In the end, there was only one question the group did not answer.

"Would you feed the enemy," Baxter inquired, meaning the Union soldiers, "should he come to your house?" A "yes" to this question would mean trouble, for the non-resistors would be easily accused of aiding and abetting the Union cause. Knowing their dilemma, Baxter answered the question for them, "We are commanded to feed our enemies."

In his official report, Baxter noted that not only was there no intention to aid and abet the enemy, but several had done much to support the families of volunteers. Some had furnished horses to the cavalry. All of them are friendly to the South and they express a willingness to contribute all their property if necessary to establish our liberties.[93]

During their internment, the Virginia legislature passed a law exempting non-resistant persons who were members of the peace-loving sects after they had paid a $500 fine plus two percent of the assessed value of their property. Peter Hartman's father was one of those who helped solicit the funds to get the prisoners back to their friends and families. Thousands of dollars were quickly and easily collected from Dunkers and Mennonites eager to help. The prisoners were home within six weeks.[94]

But the trials for Mennonites and Dunkers were not over. On Saturday, April 5, 1862, authorities arrested John Kline at his home near Bowman's Mill and took him to the Court House at Harrisonburg.[95] Kline, now about two months away from his sixty-fifth birthday was twenty years past the eligible draft age, but he was a known leader among the Dunkers, and rumors intimated he might be guilty of treason and conspiring with the enemy.[96]

Kline and his fellow prisoners, including seventy-two-year-old Mennonite leader Gabriel Heatwole, were kept in the large jury room for about a week and a half. On April 16, a Wednesday, it was decided to move the group north to New Market. Heading along the hard-packed surface of the Valley Pike, they travelled about nine or ten miles the first day. By evening, they had reached Bethlehem Church, their temporary guardhouse for the night. The next morning, back out on the Valley Pike, the group travelled about two miles farther when they heard a distant rumble — Federal cannons at Mt. Jackson.[97]

With little delay, the prisoners were given an about face and hastily returned to Harrisonburg. The next day, April 18, there was "great excitement and confusion in town," wrote Kline in his diary. General Jackson and his troops passed through the Rockingham capital, retreating from the advancing Union forces, and "the Federal troops are hourly looked for."[98]

War had come to Rockingham.[99]

———

"We were constantly on the move," wrote a former private in the Rockbridge Artillery of the months of April and May,

BETHLEHEM CHURCH

advance, even give the impression that he was on his way to Washington, Jackson could help save the Confederate capital.

The army of the Valley marched so far and fast the spring of 1862, they would earn the nickname of "Jackson's Foot Cavalry."[101] Always anxious for the spiritual condition of his men, Jackson insisted on chaplains taking advantage of Sunday, even when the enemy was close at hand and likely to attack.

"I remember several times when our service was disturbed by shells flying over us and breaking up our meeting," the artillery private recalled.[102]

Jackson had urged that every Christian denomination should send into the army "some of its most prominent ministers who

1862, "so that we had but very few opportunities for holding religious services, even on Sabbath."[100]

Jackson had brought his army into the Valley of Virginia as a ruse to keep the heat off Richmond. If he could detain the Union

are distinguished for their piety, talents and zeal." As far as the Confederate general was concerned, denominationalism should be left out of the picture altogether. The primary question asked about any minister should be, "Does he preach the Gospel?"[103]

Strange as it may seem, chaplains did not use their opportunity to expand upon the rights of southern secession, but instead focused upon the plain and simple Gospel of Christ. Even a sermon based on the text "Be ye men of good courage" was described as "no war philippic, but an earnest, heartfelt, Christian discourse." Confronted often with the prospect of death, many soldiers drew closer to God than ever before in their lives, and there was an eagerness to hear the Gospel of Christ, to pray, and sing the songs of faith, no matter what the hour.[104]

When Sundays would not suit, the rest of the week would have to do. On various days "at irregular hours," there would be a notice of preaching or a prayer meeting, each of which would be well attended. As one remembered, "every notice of such an appointment was always hailed with joy by the men."[105] Of course, not everybody felt that way!

Each day, the army was up early, marching day after day to near exhaustion. "It rained every day and every night," recalled William Oates, captain of the Fifteenth Alabama, recalling Jackson's southern march toward Harrisonburg at the beginning of June. "The road was shoe-mouth deep in mud. My feet were blistered all over, on top as well as the bottom. I never was so tired and sleepy."[106] Oates fell asleep even while marching at the head of his column, and would have to be shaken awake by his orderly sergeant. Those without an iron man to keep them going fell so far behind that they were easily captured by the closely pursuing enemy.[107]

When they did finally reach camp, Jackson's army was "tired, hungry, worn-out, besides having our rations to cook." Yet William Jones, chaplain of the Thirteenth Virginia, recalled that "on that whole campaign I never found the men too weary to assemble promptly for the evening service."[108]

The long marches were a challenge to the chaplains as well, since they had to compose their sermons on the run. On one march, Jackson pushed his army nearly thirty-six miles in twenty-four hours, setting up camp on a Sunday. "I doubt if we ever made better sermons," reflected Rev. Jones twenty-five years later, "than under the inspiration of which many of those brave fellows would ever hear."[109]

By Friday, June 6, Jackson was southeast of Harrisonburg, his army stretched out for

UNION SOLDIERS
marching into Harrisonburg

the circumstances which surrounded us and the consciousness that we were preparing to deliver the last message of salvation some five miles from Union Church at Cross Keys to Port Republic. He had come here to neutralize the two Union armies in hot pur-

suit. Frémont had been following Jackson along the west side of the Massanutten, with Shields trying to connect from the east. If trapped, Jackson figured he had an escape route over the Blue Ridge through Brown's Gap. Now confident that his mission was complete, the Confederate commander reported to headquarters that his present position would prevent the Union generals from joining their armies. "At present I do not see that I can do much more than rest my command and devote its time to drilling."[110]

But Frémont and Shields were not quite so neutralized as Jackson had supposed. Engagements with Frémont's forces southeast of Harrisonburg later that day brought bleak news to Jackson — Major-General Turner Ashby, the able and trusted leader of his cavalry had been killed. Perhaps Jackson then realized that more conflict was likely ahead.

Sunday morning, June 8, dawned with

An African minister who was a slave once asked Dunker elder Jonas Graybill what he thought of the war. "It is an awful thing for a Christian nation to be engaged in," replied the pacifist-minded Graybill. "This is true," the slave agreed, "but there are thousands of us poor slaves who are praying that the Lord will so overrule this war that we may be free."

---

the hope of the first restful Sabbath in three weeks or more, but chaplain George B. Taylor, feeling that a battle was imminent during the day, decided to get a sermon in while he still could. That morning, a large part of Elzey's Brigade assembled to hear the chaplain of the Twenty-fifth Virginia.[111]

As the sun began to climb over the warming fields of wheat that flowed across the open land, Frémont's forces engaged the Fifteenth Alabama, who had been positioned on picket at the Union church. Still Taylor kept on, no doubt urging his listeners to follow Christ for their eternal hope, and with the enemy lines growing closer, the men continued to listen. Within the hour, the Fifteenth Alabama had been driven back, running for their lives a full mile through fields and over fences, and finally to the safety of Confederate artillery.[112]

As Taylor was about to make his third

A SERVICE INTERRUPTED

point in the sermon, the colonel of his regiment rode up with the news.

We have orders to fall in. Close as soon as you can, Mr. Taylor.

Quickly the Twenty-fifth Virginia was rushed up to reinforce those preparing to face the brunt of the Federal attack.[113] Within moments, "the shock of battle succeeded the invitations of the Gospel, and men were

As the moon rose upon the field that night, the mangled bodies of men and boys lay scattered over the ground.[115] The Federals

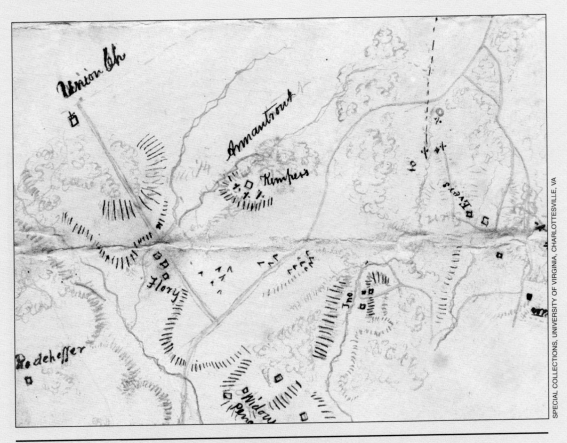

BATTLEFIELD MAP
Jed Hotchkiss, mapmaker for Stonewall Jackson, drew this map near the time of the Cross Keys - Port Republic battles

summoned from that season of worship in to the presence of their Judge."[114] It would be a long and costly Sunday.

had retreated that hotly-contested mile back to positions around Union church. The little building, nestled among a grove of oaks, now "showed many scars of heavy shot and shell." Frémont would of necessity use the building as a hospital for the wounded and dying. As at least one correspondent for the *Rockingham Register* walked the battlefield under the mild light of the moon that evening, he too saw "how dreadful had been the carnage."[116]

The next day, burning the North River bridge between himself and Frémont's men, Jackson would fight Shields near Port Republic. It would produce another victory, but again at a bloody price.

The battles of Cross Keys and Port Republic were a final blow to the Union armies arrayed against Jackson, and at least

JOHN KLINE'S HOUSE

182

for the time being they would leave the Valley in peace. More importantly, Jackson had accomplished his primary mission to dis-

KLINE'S
SADDLEBAGS

tract the forces advancing against Richmond. "We have fought on three Sundays in succession, which will do pretty well for a religious Gen[era]l," wrote one of Jackson's colonels.[117] But this was only the beginning.

War did more than stain the soil of Rockingham, it brokered mortality into the hearts and minds of its citizens. For Mennonites and Dunkers, whose public squabbles over theological issues had used

its share of printer's ink, the war would be a forceful reminder of their shared heritage — not only in Christ, but also in their commitment to respect the life of another human being.

John Kline had been released in April from his interment in Harrisonburg's court house, but it wasn't until October that he finally paid a visit to his "old friend, Joseph Funk." The venerated music publisher was in failing health. Softened by his condition, in gentle understatement Kline recalled that the elder Funk "had been somewhat ruffled in his feelings by my *Strictures and Reply* to his published writings on baptism and feet-washing."[118]

JOHN KLINE'S
HAT

The two men were reconciled that day. Given their own conflict and the recent maelstrom of war that had torn through the Valley, they could easily have been reminded

There is a calm, a sure retreat
'Tis found before the mercy seat.[119]

Eleven weeks later on Christmas Eve,

HEADING NORTH
Dunkers obtain their official passes

of the words of a song found in the *Harmonia Sacra* :

From every stormy wind that blows
From every swelling tide of woes

the father of song in the Shenandoah Valley left to enjoy his final place of retreat. He was eighty-five years old.

Kline continued to go back and forth across the Union lines to attend the

Dunker's Annual Meeting in the North. Other Dunkers and Mennonites found similar passages out of the turbulent South, for different reasons. Their exemptions, it seemed, were temporary, good only from furlough to furlough. Mennonite Philip H. Parret had been drafted in 1862 and assigned to Jackson's army as part of Colonel Allen's Second Virginia Regiment. His first and only opportunity to leave the army came in the spring of 1864. Given a fifteen day furlough, Parret showed up at his home on Easter morning, while his family was at breakfast. A few days later, he and other "Union men" took off through the mountains for the North and freedom.[120]

One night at about eleven o'clock, a group of men left from Abraham Funk's, about two miles west of John Kline's house, and headed west for one of the many mountain gaps and safety in Union territory. As they reached the steep bank along the North Fork of the Shenandoah, rebel scouts were spotted, and the entire group scrambled a hundred feet down the bluff to the edge of the river and safety. All were safe except one. George Sellers broke his leg on the mad dash down to the water's edge. Friends took him back to Funk's home. For the next several weeks, Kline, a doctor by his own training and reading, treated Sellers secretly.[121]

Besides "official" trouble with the Confederate army and government, there were other difficulties for non-resistors in Rockingham during the war. Even though they supported the families of volunteers — sometimes selling their own produce at a loss to help out their neighbors — their stance against slavery, the draft, and the Southern cause made them enemies of many.[122] Samuel Coffman, a bishop ordained by the Mennonites just after the war had begun, had spoken out very heartily from his pulpit against the draft. Though he had received an exemption from military duty, that refuge was threatened by a Confederate general camped near the Coffman home who reportedly pledged to make Coffman and all his followers fight. Another opponent reportedly said, "Coffman ought to be hung on the highest tree in the state of Virginia." Coffman planned to take his entire family north for a while, but after they had packed up their belongings, he changed his mind and left the county alone, returning after things cooled down.[123]

Abram Good, another Mennonite, piloted many groups like the one leaving from Funk's house to safety across the mountains, into Ohio or Pennsylvania. Confederate scouts had been told to shoot him on sight. But Good had his hiding places, perhaps up in the mountains or through a trap door in his home or barn. Once, the scouts found him at home and planned to execute him. Calmly, Good asked permission to send for help in writing his will. In the meantime it was discovered that he and the captain of the scouting party had been childhood friends. Happily, he was allowed to go free.[124]

Kline himself had been arrested more than once, but each time he had been released. Still, he was not a popular man among many in Rockingham. Doubtless some suspected his constant goings and comings across enemy lines entailed something more than "religious" purposes.

In June of 1864, Union General Hunter occupied much of the Valley of Virginia, including the area around Harrisonburg. Hunter's men burned mills and factories, broke open stores and destroyed at least one newspaper office. But the worst of their acts were personal. By direct orders from the General, soldiers robbed each family of all their provisions, leaving them with enough food for only three days. The *Rockingham Register* reported that some Valley citizens had taken the oath of allegiance to the United States during the occupation. Suspicion and anger were running high.[125]

On June 15, 1864, Kline was returning home after having his faithful horse, Nell, outfitted with new shoes. Somewhere within the cowardly protection of a ridge of trees, shots were heard. John Kline was dead. His body had been cut through by several bullets, "but a smile rested on his face."[126] The gift of his life would be remembered by many for years and years to come.

Only two months after Kline's death, thirty-three year old Union General Philip Sheridan entered the Valley. Ulysses S. Grant, now in charge of the entire Union army, had given Sheridan orders to leave the Valley of Virginia a wasteland. Nothing was to be left to furnish supplies for the Confederates.[127]

Days later many others in Rockingham would seek mercy but find it wanting. Even those who supported the Union would find no quarter. As Sheridan withdrew north, down the Valley to Winchester, he set fire to barns and mills, fields and crops. Instead of the crisp blue of October skies, a solemn haze clung desperately to the charred ground.[128] The harvest month — usually a time for corn-shucking bees and other joyful gatherings — would leave many families with nothing.

Sheridan offered any who wished to go back North a free passage with his wagon train. With the Confederacy now desperate for any and all recruits to salvage their struggling war effort, the last exemptions for the draft had been removed. By the scores, Mennonites and Dunkers went to the Union commander and obtained their passes.[129]

For now, it was time to leave. Before long, it would be time to rebuild.

By war's end, the Valley of Virginia was in ruin. "Everything has been destroyed that would destroy," wrote traveller James Black in June of 1865.[130] In Rockingham alone, an estimated $25,500,000 in physical property had been lost. Besides 150,000 bushels of corn and wheat, some 450 barns and 37 mills were gone.[131]

Personally, the losses were felt deeply. The family of Mennonite preacher Samuel Shank, who lived two miles south of Broadway, lost both their house and barn despite initial assurances that nothing on their property would be harmed.[132] Dunkers appealed for help to their friends in the North on behalf of one of their elders, Peter

THE SHANK HOUSE
After Union soldiers set the Shanks' barn on fire, wind blew the flames toward the house where sawdust insulation offered quick kindling for the frame structure. With the help of their neighbors, the Shanks built this fine, three-storied brick home.

Crumpacker, who had lost $3000 "getting his brethren out of prison, and by being robbed by the rebels." A collection on his behalf was recommended by the Annual Meeting.[133]

Despite the devastation, recovery in Rockingham moved quickly. Within one six-month period, Henry Rhodes and David Weaver, described by the *Register* as "plain Rockingham 'dutch' mechanics," built eight large Swiss-style barns. "These are the men to 'reconstruct' the country," the paper proclaimed, alluding to the Federal program of reshaping the South into a more compatible part of the Union.[134]

BISHOP J.J. GLOSSBRENNER

But hard work was not enough in post-war Rockingham, nor were all "dutch mechanics" equally appreciated. "By the way," the short notice concluded, "these gentlemen are opposed to the radical, negro-loving tribe, some few of whom, we are sorry to say, disgrace noble old Rockingham." For some, bitterness against Mennonites and Dunkers who refused to take part in the Confederate war effort would linger for decades.[135] But the sharpest attacks were not directed toward the non-resisting "dutch," but toward the bold and public statements of a group with historical ties to both, the United Brethren in Christ.[136]

Throughout the war, there had been strong feelings against United Brethren in

OLD SALEM CHURCH

Only one church bulding for the United Brethren was erected in the Confederacy during the War, and that was this building, close to Singers Glen and known as Salem. Actually, the building was only moved from nearby Green Hill, having served both Methodists and Lutherans. Glossbrenner crossed the lines into West Virginia in order to get the glass.

the Valley of Virginia. Most of the denomination lived in free states, and the church not only continued to hold slave-owning as a barrier to membership, they also embraced abolitionism.[137] Some Southerners insisted that the group would have to be banished from Virginia if the Confederacy was established. Others had a more permanent solution: they were for hanging them.[138]

At their first national meeting following Lee's surrender, the United Brethren had spoken immediately "in favor of placing every inhabitant of the land, black and white, on an equality before the law."[139] Among other things, that meant one man, one vote for freed slaves throughout the former Confederate states. Such words rang bitterly for many in Virginia, who considered "Negro enfranchisement" a final blow to

Southern dignity and pride, even a provocation that could incite renewed violence.[140]

In the Staunton paper, a bitter debate raged for months between United Brethren Bishop J. J. Glossbrenner and prominent Augusta county citizen, Major McCue. With his conciliatory manner, Glossbrenner had managed to remain in Augusta throughout the war years, but the reported hostility of the United Brethren toward things southern had fanned the flames of this old opponent.[141]

Glossbrenner stood strong in his advocacy of legal rights for African Americans, but on this he was opposed by even those of his own denomination in Rockingham. In a letter dated October 1, a "former member" of the United Brethren in Keezletown urged the Virginia Annual Conference to repudiate the resolutions on equality, otherwise he warned, "very many of the church members will seek connection in other branches of the Christian Church."[142]

That same month, African Americans were taking matters into their own hands. At least since 1819, it had been illegal in Virginia for slaves or free blacks to assemble together for public worship unless a "white" person was in charge of the services.[143] Now things would be different. Several former slaves met at the home of Daniel and Maria Brown on the corner of Rock and German Streets to discuss organizing a church. They would align themselves with the Methodists, who as a denomination had been supporting independent African churches since the last century.[144]

By the following summer, the group was ready to build the first African American church building in Harrisonburg. A committee of invitation composed of Andrew Edmundson, the preacher in charge, along with George Gwinn, Joseph T. Williams, Benjamin Rice and Robert Vickers wrote a letter to several local ministers inviting them to a fund raising dinner at the Court House on Friday, July 27, 1866.

The dinner was held, speeches were made, and $100 raised for the venture. But underlying the entire event was a question held precariously in the minds of many Rockingham residents: what would this change mean? Would independent African American churches pave the way for social equality, a mixing of the "races?"[145] The *Rockingham Register* was pleased to report

Over the years there had been a number of behaviors that various denominations decided were wrong. Some of these issues had strong biblical backing; others were less clear. But one that seemed to have longevity as well as broad support was "temperance." Though the origin and usual use of that word meant self-restraint or moderation, in this application it was used to mean abstinence — in particular, total abstinence from any alcoholic beverages.

Historically, not every denomination or sincere Christian agreed with abstinence. As part of his arrangement for his care, Adam Mueller stipulated that his son-in-law must provide him with thirty-three gallons of whiskey annually. And in 1794, when the Virginia Synod met in Harrisonburg, it was the Presbyterians who had stood to support the "Whiskey Boys" of western Pennsylvania, in spite of the gathered militia headed north to suppress that insurrection.

During the 1800s, support for temperance gradually grew under the wing of social reform some thought would usher in the millennial reign of Christ foretold in the Bible. But what sometimes made the temperance cause a particularly thorny issue for churches was its link with other groups and agendas. In 1835, when a meeting of the Temperance

that, as far as they could tell, there seemed to be no change at all. The segregated dinner was served to all by their hosts, not one of whom was "indicating the slightest approach of undue familiarity with their white friends." Then, waxing warm on an old bit of slavery theology, the editor noted that "our colored people…have a more correct and appreciative conception of their social status than the foreign and heartless philanthropists who would teach them that ineffaceable distinctions which God has made can be broken down at pleasure by the will of men."[146]

The editor's irritation was crystallized by current events. About this same time in Court Square, there was preaching by Reverend E. W. Pierce, sent by the Baltimore Conference of the Northern Methodist church. A small group of African Americans and some rowdy white boys made up his audience. Pierce was not given leave to preach in any church in Rockingham, so he went wherever he was invited. At Port Republic, there was preaching to African Americans in Down's Tanyard, near the river.[147]

The first Sunday in September, Pierce

was offered the home of Mrs. Bamber in the north end of town, but when her son wouldn't let him in the door, the Northern minister began preaching in the street. Some African American women were present, and they joined in when Pierce began a hymn. Not liking this chain of events, the rowdies who had assembled began to get loud. Turning to one of them, an African American woman spoke up and in return "received pretty rough handling." The end of the matter saw Pierce arrested and made to post bond to keep the peace during the next year. The "meddling Northerners" would be kept out one way or the other.[148]

As it neared completion, the new church building for African Americans was put forth by the *Register* as "one of the best evidences in the world that a kind feeling exists here between former master and servant." Its dedication on Sunday, November 25, 1866, was attended by a large number of citizens. An article in Harrisonburg's other paper, *The Old Commonwealth*, candidly described the ceremony as "well calculated to impress the minds of the colored people that the only friends they have on earth upon whom they can rely are their former owners and masters."[149]

Regardless of the published views of Harrisonburg's press, African Americans continued to take the initiative to become established as a free people. While those in town were busy getting a building completed, "freedmen" north of town were seeking another important course.

There was already a sizable community of African Americans in the area around Lacey Springs and Mt. Tabor, about four to five miles north of Harrisonburg on the Valley Pike. Some of them approached American Tract Society representative George W. Stanley about starting a Sunday School for them, complete with its own library.[150]

Stanley had just done that for a small group at Mt. Tabor, and agreed to do the same for African Americans. Working along with Stanley was United Brethren minister J. W. Howe. Soon, African Americans in the area had established a congregation worshipping as a part of the United Brethren in Christ. By 1869, they had been deeded land for a chapel of their own. The African American community around it was known as Athens, and the chapel would take its name, too. But the name by which the little building would be best known would be Long Chapel, after its builder, Jacob Long. In time the community would be known as Zenda, after a nearby post office.[151]

The next year, 1870, the Virginia Conference of the United Brethren organized the Virginia Freedmen's Mission, appointing Reverend J. Brown to oversee it.[152] Coming when it did, the effort was likely generated in response to African American initiative. The key to longevity, however, would lie in developing leadership. And as local leadership was being developed, help would have to come from the outside. Laws had been in place for decades forbidding anyone in Virginia to teach any African — slave or free — how to read and write. To overcome those obstacles would take time, patience and determination.[153]

Notwithstanding opposition to "negro equality" within its own ranks, the denomination which had sixty-five years ago begun in response to a revival among German-speaking people would soon become the denomination of choice for many Africans seeking church affiliation in Rockingham.[154]

In addition to seeing the Virginia

Society was scheduled to meet at the old stone Presbyterian church in Harrisonburg, the Virginia Lutheran Synod was expressing serious misgivings about the temperance reformation, objecting especially to the abolitionist rhetoric circulating "through the medium of temperance papers." Not only did this cause an association between the two movements, the Lutherans believed it was unwise for ministers to sign on to such "ultra measure resolutions on subjects foreign to their calling, or in which, at best, they are not otherwise concerned than as individuals." As an example of the extremism they saw, the noted that some temperance reformers had gone so far as to suggest that wine should not be used for the communion meal.

Within another handful of years, the Virginia Synod was not only supporting temperance, it was instructing their ministers to organize temperance societies right along with prayer meetings and to make a regular report of their progress. As with the Lutherans, many denominations eagerly adopted the temperance cause as their own.

Among these was the United Brethren, who had supported abstinence from alcoholic beverages even before the rise of temperance societies. Along with other denominations, they had also opposed "secret societies," groups whose membership involved them in secret rites, initiation ceremonies and the like, aspects considered incompatible with the spirit of openness and truth the gospel enjoined.

That commitment was tested, however, with the rise of the Sons of Temperance, a secret society that promoted the very object so many churches had supported. In secret societies and the use of alcoholic beverages, the churches stood against two established pillars of old Virginia society. After a lively debate, the United Brethren ministers went on record as opposing all secret societies, whatever their public goal.

The rule stood until 1861, when a new discipline was adopted. During the next year, as the country dove into one of its gloomiest periods, the production of distilled spirits increased more than five hundred percent. It seemed the message of temperance was now more important than ever, and much of the general public feeling against secret societies had subsided.

After the war was over, the Dunkers faced the same issues. In 1867, the question was brought before their Annual Meeting.

Inasmuch as the church of the brethren has always endeavored to maintain the principle of temperance, will the brethren composing this Annual Meeting admit that members may join a

Freedmen's Mission of the United Brethren get underway, the year 1870 would also see the various state conferences of African American Methodists set apart as a distinct denomination — the Colored Methodist Episcopal Church.[155] Because of its close ties with their former masters, older African American groups berated it as "the Rebel church," "the old slavery Church," or "the kitchen church." In Rockingham, the last name had a sting of reality. In Port Republic before the war, one congregation of blacks had held their meetings in the kitchen of a local boarding house.[156]

LONG'S CHAPEL

On that side of the valley which Adam Mueller had called home a hundred years ago, most of the former slaves had taken their right to freedom and left, but there were still some few who had stayed on.[157] Several found jobs at the old iron furnace up on Naked Creek near the Page County line. The operation was under new management — two Northerners by the names of Milnes and Johns — but business was so successful that no complaints were heard about the Pennsylvania owners. It was a source of employment for three hundred men, and a strength of financial rejuvenation for the entire county.

Interestingly, the owners built a chapel on the premises for the workers, and supplied two Methodist ministers. Since the employees at the furnace were both "white" and "black," this little house of worship was perhaps the only one in the entire county used generally by people regardless of color. As a chapel, it was sure to have no gallery, no barrier of distance between those of different skin tones. Yet, perhaps to preserve the peace in reconstructing Rockingham, so-called "whites" and "blacks" apparently were not permitted to share the same benches "upon terms of equality."[158] At least coming down from the gallery was a move in the right direction.

Owning their own church buildings and organizations was only a part of growing in freedom for African Americans. Among other things, they wanted the freedom of a fair wage for a good day's work, the right to vote, and most essentially, a place to call their own.[159] In Rockingham, several African American communities would take root. Besides Harrisonburg and Athens, other communities were formed at The Peak near Singer's Glen, at Greenwood against the Massanutten Mountain just west of Elkton, and near Pleasant Valley not far from the old Whitesel's church.

In each of these communities, churches were a central feature of community life, a place of independence and new-found dignity. In other Rockingham communities, there would be similar accomplishments.

———

At its outset as an official Anglican enterprise in the seventeenth century, the

temperance society, in the present form such societies take, outside of the church?

The Dunker church had ruled against the Sons of Temperance twenty years earlier, but now the issue was a more open-ended one. Temperance societies could apparently take on the form of a collective moral crusade, with or without secret meetings. Would this be acceptable to the church?

Answer: As our brotherhood has, again and again, taken decided ground against intoxicating drinks as a beverage, and recommended to the brethren to abstain from their use as such, we see no necessity of joining ourselves to any other organization; and, therefore, we can not allow brethren the privilege of doing so, but renew our solemn protestation against the use of intoxicating drinks as a beverage, and consider it the duty of every member of the church to use his influence against them.

Separate societies — even if they were not secret — wouldn't be needed to advance the moral causes of the denomination, the leadership decided. Even temperance required some moderation of its own.[Side 12]

government of Virginia had given almost no quarter to persons adhering to the Roman Catholic tradition. There were, of course, those of the Roman faith scattered about the colony from earliest days. Stephen Schmidt, a resident of the Valley in the mid-1700s, showed kindness to the ostracized Moravian missionaries travelling through by letting them stay at his home. He, for one, understood what it was like to be refused religious freedom. At least two indentured servants in old Augusta County were described "Papists," but the privilege to worship in their own style and form was never a possibility.[160]

welcome change. The first Catholic bishop to America, John Carroll, travelled across the ocean with Rockingham native James Madison, who had just received his ordination in England as the first bishop of the Protestant Episcopal church of Virginia. Yet, prejudices continued to linger throughout the new nation. Even as late as the 1850s with a large number of Roman Catholics entering the United States, a vigorous opposition was rallied against them in many states.[161]

"It is all traceable to two great facts: first, the humble, peaceful, moral and charitable lives of the members; last, the simple and unperverted truths they teach. Without the first, the last would have made no impression on my heart."
— Addison Harper, on his commitment to Christ and membership in the Dunker church, circa 1866

Of course, the political climate had been far more hostile a hundred years or more ago. The Spanish inquisition and the hostility of French monarch Louis XIV to Protestant realms closely tied Papal authority with fears of insurrection and disloyalty. With the independence of the American colonies and a new Constitution, religious liberty was a

The Lanahans were one of the earliest Roman Catholic families in Harrisonburg. Just after his marriage with the widow Margaret Cravens, Denis Lanahan moved to Harrisonburg in 1782 where he eventually took up the proprietorship of Harrisonburg's hotel. Soon after he was joined by his brother Timothy and his family from Ireland. Timothy's son, John, was born in Harrisonburg in 1815. After his marriage, he joined the Methodist church like his wife, and within a few years was licensed as a Methodist preacher.[162]

By the end of the Civil War, there were perhaps fifty or more people in Rockingham who preferred to worship in the Roman Catholic tradition, but the only services to be hoped for came from a Jesuit priest in Augusta, Joseph Bixio.[163] Bixio was no stranger to the Catholic community here. Even before the war he had celebrated Mass once at Muhlenberg Lutheran church on North Main in Harrisonburg. Throughout the war, Bixio served as chaplain to both Confederate and Federal soldiers, crossing the lines so many times that General Sheridan considered him a spy. Almost certainly he kept up his visits with his friends in Rockingham.[164]

In December of 1865, Bixio invited "Reverend Father Maguire" from Georgetown to come preach in Augusta, Albemarle and Rockingham. As part of his tour, Maguire held meetings in Harrisonburg for four days, which according to one observer, "produced a great impression…especially among Protestants, who thronged every night to hear him."[165]

Rockingham Catholics had already rented a public hall, but the fifty-eight communicants were not yet numerous enough to build a church of their own.[166] The correspondent from Staunton assured the readers of the Baltimore *Catholic Mirror* that "Catholic emigration [to the Valley of Virginia] would meet here with a welcome that just now would be extended to no other class." Though the writer gave no particular reason for his optimism, he did note that land was cheap and that considerable (but well rewarded) labor would be needed to revive the Valley from the destruction it had suffered.[167]

In any case, Catholics did not flock to Rockingham in the succeeding years. In February of 1866, Bixio wrote from Staunton describing his own financial troubles, "owing to the improvements, indispensable ones, made in my school house." It would take time to establish roots and build a lasting congregation in Rockingham, despite being well-received by the community.[168]

In March of that year, Roman Catholics in Harrisonburg were still meeting in what was known as the Catholic Chapel, a small building once used as a schoolhouse. The paper announced two Masses scheduled one particular Sunday, one at ten o'clock in the morning, the other at 3:30 in the afternoon.[169] Six years later, as the local economy continued to recover, Catholics once again gathered interest in constructing their own church building, and by June of 1876 they had purchased the church building just across the railroad tracks on West Market, once occupied by the independent Baltimore Conference Methodists.[170]

About the same time, another group of people ostracized since colonial times was beginning to establish themselves in Rockingham. Though two Jewish merchants had operated a store in Port Republic during the early part of the century, it wasn't until a half century later that the beginnings of a Jewish community in Rockingham started to take shape. Sometime during the 1850s, the families of Leopold Weiss, Herman Heller, Samuel Loewner and Jonas Heller moved to the county from Bohemia, the home of fifteenth century reformer Jan Hus, and the place where the Thirty Years War began in 1618.[171] From the seventeenth century on,

Bohemia had been an imperial territory of the Austrian empire. Following the failed popular revolts in 1848 demanding democracy, many of the Jewish faith came to America. Typical of this older, more educated generation of Jewish immigrants, Samuel Loewner was a peddler, making combs from cow horns and selling them throughout the state. Once he moved to Harrisonburg, Loewner began a different type of carving, sculpting tombstones from local limestone, polishing and lettering each by hand.[172]

When the war began, Samuel's son, Emmanuel, along with Adolph and Albert Weiss all volunteered for service in the Confederate army. Jewish men from both sides of the Mason-Dixon line would serve in their respective armies. Perhaps it was a statement for the democracy they wanted so dearly.

After the war, a number of other Jewish families came to Rockingham, and soon the number was large enough to organize formal services. At first, they rented a small room on West Market. Samuel Loewner, Civil War veteran Adolph Weiss, and recent addition Simon Oestreicher conducted services according to the conservative Orthodox tradition beginning in 1867.[173]

As the group grew, they moved from one rented room to another. In 1869, a congregation was officially organized, and by 1877 it was incorporated as The Hebrew Friendship Congregation of Harrisonburg, Virginia. In another fourteen years, they would build a synagogue and call it Beth-El, "the house of God."[174]

―――――

It was perhaps appropriate that as newer groups to Rockingham were finding their way, a remnant of the "old church," never established when Rockingham was set off as a distinct county, would finally be revived.

Not long before the war began, attempts had been made to reorganize the old Rockingham Parish of the Episcopal church. For a time there were worship services held at Port Republic, not far from the boyhood home of James Madison, first bishop of the Protestant Episcopal Church in Virginia.[175]

But it was John F. Lewis, the pro-Union man who would be twice elected as Virginia's lieutenant governor and once as its Senator during the years of Reconstruction, who played a central role in seeing the old church begin on solid footing. Lewis's sister, Elizabeth, had married James Clifton Wheat, an Episcopal minister and Vice Principle of the Virginia Female Institute in Staunton. Wheat took time out of his busy schedule to make occasional trips to Rockingham to conduct services. After the war he came again to Port Republic, near his wife's family home of Lewiston, where the parish was reorganized in 1865.[176]

In late winter of 1866, Lewis convened a meeting of several people in Harrisonburg. There, a vestry of twelve was elected and two churchwardens were chosen, John F. Lewis and Andrew Lewis.[177] For a while, the new rector Henry A. Wise, son of a Virginia governor, held services alternately in Harrisonburg and Port Republic. In Harrisonburg, the group met in the upper story of Samuel Shacklett's Main Street warehouse, a place then known as Shacklett's Hall.[178] By 1869, they were occupying their new building on the northeast corner of Main and Bruce.[179]

Like the Episcopalians, Baptists in the

Valley had had their struggles. As one Baptist resident west of the Blue Ridge put it, "There are two things that this magnificent region will not produce — *sweet potatoes and Baptists.*"[180] Old School Baptists were still meeting in Brock's Gap, and once a month in Harrisonburg at Shacklett's Hall where the Episcopalians met temporarily.[181]

Early in 1866, there was only one "missionary" or "regular" Baptist church building in the entire county, the one at the north end of Mt. Crawford along the Valley Pike.[182] In fact, in the entire Valley from Lexington to Winchester there were but three regular Baptist churches "simply because the Baptists have not put forth proper efforts to 'possess the land,'" according to former Civil War chaplain John William Jones. There had been few enough Baptist ministers in the Valley, an area dominated by "Pedobaptist brethren," and those few had not stayed long.

The same year Jones penned his hope of brighter prospects for Valley Baptists, another former Civil War chaplain serving in Rockingham was seeing it happen before his eyes. A. B. Woodfin, who had travelled with the 61st Georgia, was now serving the

Baptist church at Mt. Crawford. During the early part of 1864, Woodfin had seen revival sweep throughout an entire brigade, with scores of men "nightly inquiring the way of life." It was his hope that these "Christ-loving" soldiers would go home and be "holy firebrands in our Churches!"[183]

With or without the influence of the soldiers' faith, the Mt. Crawford church, scattered and disorganized after the war years, began to undergo a remarkable transformation. Less than four months after his pastorate began, Woodfin and the church at Mt. Crawford began a protracted meeting. During three weeks in late August and early September of 1866, Woodfin reported that close to "sixty souls professed faith in Christ, and forty additions have already been made to the church. We are expecting more." Supported by frequent prayer meetings, by January of the next year, there were about eighty new members added to the Mt. Crawford Baptist church.[184] Three years later, as the Episcopalian house of worship took shape, not far away the regular Baptists were organizing their first church in Harrisonburg. Before long there would be additional congregations meeting at

Bridgewater and Singer's Glen, the new name for Joseph Funk's home of Mountain Valley.[185]

Three of Father Funk's sons — Benjamin, Timothy, and Solomon — had served the local Baptist churches as preachers.[186] One fall day in 1866, all three brothers were scheduled to speak at a picnic in Turleytown. This was a Sunday School picnic, but this was no small town affair. Three or four hundred people were in attendance representing four different Sunday Schools — Turleytown, Roudabush's Mill, Salem, and Linville Creek — all nearby neighbors.

The procession began at the church and proceeded to a nearby grove where the entire assembly ate "an elegant dinner…prepared by the good ladies of the neighborhood." Afterwards, the three Funk brothers and two others all gave speeches. This was followed by a presentation of beautiful music sung by the School, this under the direction of another Funk, "Thomas W." After a few more remarks the entire crowd formed a procession back to the church.[187]

Sunday Schools were a big item in Rockingham during the years of Reconstruction. Picnics abounded every-

where, and at least one revival was attributed to the activity of a Sunday School during the summer.[188] Once a bone of contention between "New Schoolers" and "Old Schoolers," Sunday Schools now seemed in many places to have the opposite effect, uniting members of various denominations in a common purpose to teach their children the basic truths of the Bible.[189]

The same was true of the efforts of the Rockingham Bible Society, which seems to have received a renewed vision after the war.[190] Several auxiliary societies were organized throughout the county at Fellowship, Mt. Crawford, Bridgewater, Port Republic, and Peale's Crossroads, the site of the reorganized Union church congregation of Presbyterians. The goal of the society was to give a Bible "to any family destitute of the Scriptures and not able to pay for a copy; [and] to any colored person able to read and deserving a bible or testament."[191] The last goal, though admirable, would require a willingness to give by teaching as well.

Cooperation among denominations was doubtless fueled in part by the non-sectarian spirit which had prevailed among chaplains throughout the war, when — at least in the army — there seemed to be "a truce to denominational bickerings." The interest among chaplains was to work together to "make men Christians," and then leave it up to the individual to decide which denomination they would choose.[192] Even Mennonites and Dunkers, drawn closer together through their time of common sufferings, began to build their own "union" church buildings throughout the county.

But those that had the most to gain — or potentially to lose — as a result of the war were African Americans. By 1875, they had begun to gather momentum in organizing their own new churches. On July 11 of that year they dedicated a Baptist church — Shiloh — on the corner of Federal and Wolfe Streets.[193] The Rockingham Freedman's Mission of the United Brethren also got their first consis-

tent leadership that year from Iowan S. T. Wells. The next year, he would organize a church in Harrisonburg, too. "Quite a number have already joined the new church," the *Register* reported, "and the probabilities are that quite a numerous church will be formed. It is contemplated to build a church for the use of the congregation at an early day."[194]

By way of distraction, there was also something of the sensational in the news from Rockingham in the year 1875. Its public focus was a man named William C. Thurman. A Northern man, Thurman had been associated with the Baptists, but in 1862 his very persuasive writing on non-resistance had won the very timely admiration of the Dunkers, then seeking relief from the Confederate draft. Admiration quickly turned into ordination, as Thurman was elected as a minister in the Greenmount church that same year.[195]

Thurman was both persuasive and well-educated, and his style must have charmed many. Shortly before the war ended, he published a treatise on the coming of Christ. Like the Millerites before him, he believed that through certain calculations he could determine the exact day of Christ's return to earth. The same year he published another work on *The Ordinance of Feet Washing as Instituted by Christ.*[196]

Initially, Thurman's ideas were well received by the Dunkers, including Benjamin Bowman. Even when his first prediction for Christ's return failed in September 27, 1868, Thurman still managed to keep about one hundred faithful followers, but these were not apparently all focused on his millennial predictions. Instead, they argued in a letter to the *Rockingham Register*, these members of the Greenmount congregation had sided with Thurman on his particular practice of foot-washing, for which he had been expelled from the church.[197]

But Thurman would not give up on his calculations. He set another day, April 19, 1875. A number of people assembled at the farm of Joseph Bowman, and quietly seated themselves at two long tables. There were fifteen men and eighteen women, some of whom had children in their arms. According to the figurings, Christ would return between 6 p.m. and midnight, but the congregants were dismissed around 9:30 that night with little hope that anything would happen in the next couple of hours.[198]

Like a dazed and beaten fighter still looking to land a knockout, Thurman predicted another day the following year, with equal results. Eventually, the group disbanded, with many re-joining the Dunker church, others dropping out of "religious" groups altogether. Thirty years after his third failed prediction, Thurman died in the Richmond poorhouse, forecasting the end of the world in 1917.

———

Eighteen seventy-six, the year of Thurman's third prediction, marked one hundred and fifty years since the coming of Adam Mueller and his family to the Valley of

Virginia. More than once his simple question to the Moravian missionaries must have echoed through here — "Are you sent from God?" The answer was required of everyone who lived and made their home between these mountains.

Divisions and anger, arrogance and doctrinaire bickering had often defined religious life here, like some errant stream tapping into a different source and trying to force its way to the sea. The fury and babble of those bitter waters had been nothing better than distractions, yet an unconscious traveller could soon find himself drowning beneath their thin surface.

And then, there was a deeper river, moving steadily, full of quiet, gentle strength. Its sound was not always heard above the prattle of daily business, but its waters had made this valley grow and flourish. It had not been lessened by tides of years pulling and pushing against its banks. Its source was sure and certain, constant through all generations. And those who drank from it knew its song well.

There is a river whose streams
make glad the city of God,
The holy place of
the tabernacle of the Most High.
God is in the midst of her,
she shall not be moved;
God shall help her, just at the break of
dawn.
The nations raged, the kingdoms were
moved;
He uttered His voice, the earth melted.
The LORD of hosts is with us;
The God of Jacob is our refuge.[199]

endnotes

GUIDE TO ABBREVIATIONS FOUND IN THE ENDNOTES

Archives & Special Collections

ABWC   Archives of the Baltimore-Washington Conference
Lovely Lane Museum
Baltimore, MD

AUMC   Asbury United Methodist Church
Harrisonburg, VA

BC   Alexander Mack Library
Bridgewater College
Bridgewater, VA

EMU   Menno Simons Historical Library
Eastern Mennonite University
Harrisonburg, VA

ERHS   Evangelical & Reformed Historical Society
Lancaster Theological Seminary
Lancaster, PA

EUB   Evangelical United Brethren Church Archives
Shenandoah University
Winchester, VA

HRHS   Harrisonburg-Rockingham Historical Society
Dayton, VA

HSP   Historical Society of Pennsylvania
Philadelphia, Pennsylvania

JMU   James Madison University
Special Collections, Carrier Library
Harrisonburg, VA

LTSG   A. R. Wentz Library
Lutheran Theological Seminary, Gettysburg
Gettysburg, PA

LV   Library of Virginia
Richmond, VA

MRL   Massanutten Regional Library
Harrisonburg, VA

PHS   Presbyterian Historical Society
Philadelphia, PA

PAM   Presbyterian Archives
Montreat, NC

RMC   Randolph-Macon College
McGraw-Page Library
Ashland, VA

UVA   Albert H. Small Special Collections
UVA-M   Microforms Room
Alderman Library
University of Virginia
Charlottesville, VA

VBHS   Virginia Baptist Historical Society
University of Richmond
Richmond, VA

VHS   Virginia Historical Society
Richmond, VA

VLS   Virginia Lutheran Synod Archives
Salem, VA

VMI   Virginia Military Institute Archives
Preston Library
Lexington, VA 24450

Frequently Used Sources

ACDB   Augusta County Deed Book

ACOB   Augusta County Order Book

ACWB   Augusta County Will Book

APVB   Augusta Parish Vestry Book

Hening   Hening's Statutes (Laws of Virginia)

JHB   Journal of the House of Burgesses

JHMM   Journal of Henry Melchior Muhlenberg

OCDB   Orange County Deed Book

OCOB   Orange County Order Book

OCWB   Orange County Will Book

OR   The War of the Rebellion: A Compilation of the
Official Records of the Union and Confederate
Armies

RCDB   Rockingham County Deed Book

RCMB   Rockingham County Minute Book

RCWB   Rockingham County Will Book

/Burnt   Rockingham County, Burnt Records

ENDNOTES FOR PAGES 3-10

VL	Virginia Lexington Presbytery Microfilm Copy located at Shenandoah Presbytery Harrisonburg, VA
VMHB	Virginia Magazine of History and Biography
f (or ff)	In a published citation, "f" refers to the page immediately following, e.g., 336f represents pages 336-337. Similarly, "ff" almost always indicates the next two pages, e.g., 12ff refers to pages 12-14.
	Virginia census information is available at a number of local and university libraries.

NOTES FOR CHAPTERS 1, 2, and 3 — HEADWATERS

[1]The earliest descriptions of Virginia landscape near the mountains note its openness and clear advantages as pasture land, though the topography and other evidence confirms it was not entirely treeless. John Lederer, *The Discoveries of John Lederer,* Charlottesville, VA: University of Virginia Press, 1958, p. 34f; see Robert D. Mitchell, et. al., "European Settlement and Land-Cover Change: The Shenandoah Valley of Virginia During the 18th Century," June 1993, pp. 24ff, 79f, 84f, JMU; Charles E. Kemper, ed. "Documents Relating to a Proposed Swiss & German Colony in the Western Part of Virginia," *VMHB* 29:287ff; *The Diary of Robert Rose,* Edited and annotated by Ralph Emmett Fall. n.p.:McClure Press, 1977, p. 105 (1 June 1751 — "In a word I think Providence designd this country for pasturage…"); Red deer and buffalo were present for decades after Mueller's arrival. ACOB 1:151 (18 February 1746: the penalty for killing red deer was a hefty £1 per animal); Lyman Chalkley, *Chronicles of the Scotch-Irish,* 2:77. A petition signed by Mueller and others places him in what is now called the Page Valley, near the Shenandoah's south fork. Family tradition specifies that the Muellers first settled on the Hawksbill River, an eastern tributary of the Shenandoah in present-day Page County. Harry M. Strickler, *Massanutten: Settled by the Pennsylvania Pilgrim, 1726,* Published by the author, 1924, pp. 26-28; Charles E. Kemper, "Adam Muller (Miller), First White Settler in the Valley of Virginia," *VMHB* 10:84f. Tradition also states that the Millers moved from this first location because some of their children died from malaria. The incidence of malaria in this valley during the 18th century is echoed in Harrison family tradition. J. Houston Harrison, *Settlers by the Long Grey Trail.* Baltimore: Genealogical Publishing Company, 1975, p. 10; Adam Mueller's naturalization certificate, dated 13 March 1741/2, states he had "settled and inhabited for fifteen years past in Shenandoah in this colony…" Harry M. Strickler, *A Short History of Page County Virginia.* Harrisonburg, VA: C.

J. Carrier Co., 1985 [Richmond, 1952], p. 49f; Charles E. Kemper, "Adam-Miller," *VMHB* 31:353.

[2]Karl Baedeker, *The Rhine from Rotterdam to Constance.* New York: Charles Scribner's Sons, 1906, pp. 255, 258. James Fenimore Cooper, *The Rhine.* Albany, NY: State University of New York Press, 1986, p. 136f. It is also interesting to note that an early name for the Hawksbill River, now in Page County, was "Lorraine Run." Lorraine is an area along the Rhine River. Patents 15:426 (27 January 1734).

[3]Paul MacKendrick, *Romans on the Rhine: Archaeology in Germany.* New York: Funk & Wagnalls, 1970, pp. 100f, 125ff.

[4]The Edict of Milan (A.D. 313) gave Christians toleration throughout the Empire. The *Cunctos populos* of Theodosius I in A.D. 380 codified the distinction between "Catholic Christians" and heretics. *Documents of the Christian Church,* selected and edited by Henry Bettenson. 2nd edition. London: Oxford University Press, 1963, pp. 22f, 31. Perhaps the most concise and readable history of the Christian faith is Kenneth Scott Latourette's *Christianity Through the Ages,* New York: Harper & Row, 1965. In this thin volume, the former Yale history professor manages to take large sweeps of history and present them to a wide audience.

[5]"For the true Christians have never persecuted the innocent, but were always persecuted themselves; and in the primitive church, even in the time of Constantine, when the bishops began to rise a little higher in the world, and were protected by the Emperor, it was considered an abomination to persecute any one; they, however, suffered persecution themselves. It was then deemed such a detestable thing, to put to death or persecute any one for heresy, that Bishop Ithacius was excommunicated and separated from the church, because he, through the tyrant Maximus, had brought about the death of Priscilian, the heretic; as the Roman cardinal, Cæsar Baronius, very plainly describes in his church history, for the year 385. He also states further, that it is utterly incompatible with the meekness of a pastor." Thieleman J. van Braght, *The Bloody Theater or Martyrs Mirror of the Defenseless Christians.* Scottdale, PA: Herald Press, 1975, p. 357.

[6]Ephesians 2:8, 9.

[7]The most thorough history of Schriesheim appears to be Hermann Brunn, *1200 Jahre Schriesheim.* Mannheim: Suedwestdeutsche Verlangsanstalt GmbH, 1964.

[8]The Donation of Constantine was proved to be a forgery some time later. Bettenson, *Documents,* 135.

[9]"Palatine" was an old Roman title. "Throughout its history the Palatinate changed continuously in size with the fortunes of war, but its geography, agriculture and commerce were always governed by the rivers which are both the chief lines of

demarcation between one region and another and the main highways — the Rhine and its tributaries, the Neckar and the Nahe." Henry J. Cohn, *The Government of the Rhine Palatinate in the Fifteenth Century.* London: Oxford University Press, 1965, p. 3.

[10]Johann Loserth, *Wiclif and Hus.* Translated by M. J. Evans. London: Hodder and Stoughton, 1884, p. 19. A notable and lasting contribution toward *personal* reformation is attributed to the pen of Roman Catholic monk Thomas à Kempis. Completed around 1427, *The Imitation,* or *Following of Christ,* reflected a determination to live a life of simple devotion to Christ. Since *The Imitation of Christ* did not connect this devotion to specific doctrines of the Roman church, it became an inspiration for Protestants as well. As early as 1733, an edition of Thomas à Kempis' popular book was abridged and translated into English by Protestant leader John Wesley. See *The Christian's Pattern; or A Treatise on the Imitation of Christ.* London: J. Mason, 1733.

[11]John Wesley, *Journal,* 1:124.

[12]"Ut novitatem, que ibidem de Wiclefistis exsurrexit, possimus eradicare." Translation courtesy of David Larrick. Letter from King Sigismund to Elector Lewis of the Palatinate, 11 July 1418, *Reichstagsacten,* vii, 349, quoted in Loserth, *Wiclif and Hus,* 84. For a brief overview of the history of these Wyclifites, including their survival after Hus's death, see www.moravian.org/history.

[13]Martin Luther to Pope Leo X (1518), in Spaeth, Reed, Jacobs, et. al. *Works of Martin Luther.* Philadelphia: A. J. Holman Company, 1915, 1:44ff. This and other writings of Luther can be found online at http://www.iclnet.org/pub/resources/text/wittenberg/wittenberg-luther.html.

[14]Martin Luther to Pope Leo X, in Spaeth et. al., *Luther,* 1:44ff.

[15]There were actually two Papal bulls excommunicating Luther. The first, given to Frederick, Elector of Saxony, to carry out in 1520 was never accomplished, and Luther burned the decree publicly. The second was issued 3 January 1521. Bettenson, *Documents,* 279f. Charles V was also directly opposed to Menno Simons and his followers, later known as Mennonites. *Martyrs Mirror,* 442f.

[16]Bettenson, *Documents,* 283f.

[17]"*Cuius regio, eius religio.*" Bettenson, *Documents,* 301f; Kidd, *Documents Illustrative of the Continental Reformation,* edited by B. J. Kidd. Oxford: Clarendon Press, 1911 [1967], pp. 362ff.

[18]The records of [St.] Peter's Lutheran church, just across the Shenandoah from Mueller's home at Green Meadows in pres-

ent-day Rockingham, began with just such a declaration. *Records of St. Peter's Church,* originals at VLS.

[19]Bettenson, *Documents,* 205f has an explanation of the development of this doctrine from the 9th to the 12th centuries, during which time it gained wider acceptance. He explains it as follows: "In its technical sense transubstantiation denotes a doctrine which is based on the Aristotelian philosophy as taught by the schoolmen, according to which a physical object consists of 'accidents,' the properties perceptible by the senses, and an underlying 'substance' in which the accidents inhere, and which gives to the object its essential nature. According to the doctrine of transubstantiation the accidents of bread and wine remain after consecration, but their substance is changed into that of the body and blood of Christ." The Lutheran view was that Christ's body and blood became mystically present in the bread and wine without changing their substance, a doctrine called *con*substantiation.

[20]I Peter 2:9.

[21]Calvin's contemporary biographer, Theodore Beza, supplies much first-hand information on the events of the day. The placard of 17-18 October 1534 decried the "pompeuse et orgueilleuse Messe Papale…quand en icelle nostre Seigneur est si outrageusement blasphemé…" Kidd, *Continental Reformation,* 528.

[22]Reformation among the Swiss was more easily accomplished politically, since the Confederation in existence at that time allowed for the maintenance of separate and distinct districts with "no central organized authority." "Switzerland," *Catholic Encyclopedia* at www.newadvent.org/cathen/14358a.htm.

[23]This distinction did not diminish over the years. Paul Henkel, an itinerant Lutheran minister in the Shenandoah Valley remarked that in a conversation he had with a Mrs. Stephan in 1782, she noted that the doctrine of the Holy Eucharist as taught by the Reformed Church "was not correct: that they teach that it is only a memorial, and not the true Body and Blood of Christ. Luther, however, taught correctly when he said it was the true Body and the true Blood; for Christ himself had taught this." "Paul Henkel's Tagebuch and Day Book," A Translation by Eugene Van Ness Goetchius. August 1, 1948. Masters Thesis, University of Virginia, pp. 30f.

[24]Heinz Schilling, "Between the Territorial State and Urban Liberty: Lutheranism and Calvinism in the County of Lippe," in *The German People and the Reformation,* edited by R. Po-chia Hsia. Ithaca, NY: Cornell University Press, 1988, pp. 270, 281; Brunn, *Schriesheim,* 240.

[25]Brunn, *Schriesheim,* 240.

[26]Zwingli wrote on 16 April 1522 that "if Christ by his death made us free from all sins and burdens; then we are also in

baptism — that is, in belief, freed from all Jewish or human ceremonies and chosen works." About three years later, Zwingli wrote, "For some time I myself was deceived by the error and I thought it better not to baptize children until they came to years of discretion." *Ulrich Zwingli Early Writings,* edited by Samuel Macauley Jackson. Durham, NC: The Labyrinth Press, 1987 [Originally published as volume one of *The Latin works and correspondence of Huldreich Zwingli.* New York: G.P. Putnam's Sons, 1912], p. 108; *The Sources of Swiss Anabaptism: The Grebel Letters and Related Documents,* Edited by Leland Harder. Scottdale, PA: Herald Press, 1985, p. 697, note 22. See also W.P. Stephens, *Zwingli: An Introduction to his Thought.* Oxford: Clarendon Press, 1992, p. 90f.

[27]John Calvin's first draft of his much-acclaimed *Institutes of the Christian Religion,* was an attempt to distinguish the French reformers from these anarchist re-baptizers, a confusion the French king was spreading throughout Europe in defense of his own ruthlessness against the Huguenots. Von Sittert's apologetic for the Mennonist faith written in 1664 was largely an attempt to distinguish the followers of Menno from this radical sect. As late as 1823, Rockingham County Dunker leader Benjamin Bowman recalled the wrong-minded attempt of the Muenster leaders in attempting to bring about Christ's kingdom on earth by human force, a charge he leveled at those attempting to organize a single Christian church. *T. T. van Sittert's Apology for the Anabaptist-Mennonite Tradition, 1664.* Translated and edited by J.C. Wenger. Privately printed, 1975, EMU; Benjamin Bowman, *A Simple Exhibition of the Word of God,* fragment translated in *The Gospel Visitor* 1862, pp. 49-52, BC.

Side 1 Preface to the Epistle of St. Paul to the Romans in *Luther's Works, Volume 35: Word and Sacrament I.* Edited by E. Theodore Bachmann, Philadelphia: Muhlenberg Press, 1960, pp. 370f.

[28]The bounty was placed by the authorities of Leeuwarden on 7 December 1542. *The Mennonite Encyclopedia,* Scottdale, PA: Mennonite Publishing House, 1957, 3:579f. "…this sect would doubtless be and remain extirpated," wrote Her Majesty's councillors in Friesland to the Queen, "were it not that a former priest Menno Symonsz who is one of the principal leaders of the aforesaid sect and about three or four years ago became fugitive, has roved about since that time once or twice a year in these parts and has misled many simple and innocent people." Letter written at Leeuwarden on 19 May 1541, quoted in *The Complete Writings of Menno Simons, c. 1496-1561.* Translated by Leonard Verduin. Scottsdale, PA: Herald Press, 1956, p. 17. Harry Brunk, in his *History of Virginia Mennonites,* notes that "Somewhere, somehow the Mennonites lost their pristine or early evangelical fervor and zeal." Harry A. Brunk, *History of Mennonites in Virginia,* Harrisonburg, VA: H.A. Brunk, 1959, Volume 1:360f.

[29]Interestingly, this first confession did not include material

specifically on baptism. *The Complete Writings of Menno Simons,* translated by Leonard Verduin, edited by John Wagner, biography by Harold S. Bender. Scottdale, PA: Herald Press, p. 20.

[30]Early names were Menists, also Menoists, later becoming Menonists. See *Menno Simons,* 20. The word Mennonist (with two "n's") appears in the English version of the 1727 Dordrecht Confession printed in Philadelphia by Andrew Bradford, and again in the 1810 reprinting by Ambrose Henkel at New Market. The word Mennonite is used as early as 1837, in the longer English confession translated by Joseph Funk, and printed at Winchester. For consistency, the spelling Mennonist will be used throughout their earlier history.

[31]Referencing the words of the psalmist, the Mennonists referred to themselves as "the quiet in the land" [*die Stillen im Lande*] — "For they do not speak peace, but they devise deceitful words against those who are quiet in the land." Psalm 35:20, *NASB.*

[32]Brunn, *Schriesheim,* 96f; All of the deaths during this time were not directly the result of combat or depradations by soldiers. For the three or four decades following 1528, about fourty-two Anabaptists — eight of whom were women — were put to death in Berne. *Martyrs' Mirror,* 703.

[33]"Generalizations about this 'pre-statistical' age are always risky.…With appropriate caution we can say that the loss in population was not made good in central Europe until the beginning of the eighteenth century." J. V. Polišenský, *War and Society in Europe, 1618-1648.* Cambridge: Cambridge University Press, 1978, p. 199.

[34]Günter Fillbrunn, Schriesheim historian, personal communication, 30 July 2000.

[35]Delbert L. Gratz, *Bernese Anabaptists and their American Descendants.* Goshen, IN: Mennonite Historical Society, 1953, p. 39; Charles E. Kemper, "Adam-Miller," *VMHB* 31:353.

[36]Brunn, *Schriesheim,* 240. In 1671, another 700 Anabaptists from Berne — many of them aged and infirm — "found themselves compelled to leave their abode, forsake their property, and, many of them, also their kindred, together with their earthly fatherland, and betake themselves with the others to the Palatinate, in hope that the Lord should so order it, that they might find a place of abode there." *Martyrs' Mirror,* 1126f.

[37]Brunn, *Schriesheim,* 106f.

[38]*A Huguenot Exile in Virginia, or Voyages of a Frenchman exiled for his Religion with a description of Virginia and Maryland.* From the Hague Edition of 1687. Introduction and notes by Gilbert Chinard. New York: the Press of the Pioneers,

1934, p. 106.

[39]See W. B. Chilton, "The Brent Family," *VMHB* 17:308ff; *Exile,* 41, 179f.

[40]The reference was to the *Accomplissement des Prophéties ou la Déliverance de l'Eglise by Monsieur de Jurieu pub-lished at Rotterdam in 1686. Exile,* 43, 162f, and note 1.

[41]"A True Account of the Barbarous Cruelties Committed by the French in the Palatinate, in January and February last." Faithfully translated from the High Dutch Copy. With Allowance. London: Printed by Randall Taylor, 1689, p. 2. Broadside, UVA-M; Brunn, *Schriesheim,* 112.

[42]"An Account of the Present Condition of the Protestants in the Palatinate," In Two Letters to an English Gentleman. [The last dated Heidelbergh, February 7, 1699.] London: Printed for Richard Parker, 1699, p. 2, UVA-M.

[43]Brunn, *Schriesheim,* 138.

[44]"Present Condition," 10.

[45]"Present Condition," 2.

[46]These included transubstantiation as well as the traditional Roman auricular (spoken) confessional before a priest. Bettenson, *Documents,* 328f; Blackstone 4:47 (31 Henry VIII c.14).

[47]One listing of these Thirty-Nine Articles of the Church of England is in the appendix to a book written by John Thomson, an early Presbyterian minister in the Valley of Virginia. See *An Explanation of the Shorter Catechism* [of the Presbyterian church]. Williamsburg, VA: Printed by W. Parks, 1749. Thomson included these so that both Anglicans and Presbyterians might understand that the doctrinal differences between the two were quite small. Thomson, *Catechism,* Appendix iii, iv, UVA (microfilm).

[48]Hening 1:68f. For these early laws relating to religious expres-sion in Virginia, see Virtual Jamestown at http://jefferson.vil-lage.virginia.edu/vcdh/jamestown. See also Brydon, *Mother Church,* 1:2.

[49]*Exile,* 85 note.

[50] The English statute referenced as I William & Mary st.1 c.18 was "for exempting their majesties' protestant subjects, dissent-ing from the church of England, from the penalties of certain laws." The lingering issue with "Papists" was intensely political, driven by issues of earthly allegiance and sovereignty. "[W]hile they acknowledge a foreign power [viz., the Pope], superior to the sovereignty of the kingdom, they cannot complain if the laws of that kingdom will not treat them upon the footing of

good subjects." William Blackstone, *Commentaries on the Laws of England.* London: A. Strahan, 1809, 4:52ff.

[51]A classic example of the "cavalier" attitude toward Virginia proclamations on the frontier was the Frederick county justice who requested an illegal itinerant missionary to perform a marriage: "…we do not pay any attention to the proclamation issued against you." Rev. William J. Hinke and Charles E. Kemper, eds., "Moravian Diaries of Travels through Virginia," *VMHB* 12:67. Another example would be the long-held parley Augusta county leaders kept up regarding the colonial Anglican "establishment" during the late colonial period.

[52]The British parliament assured this limited freedom of wor-ship by exempting dissenters from adherence to the 34th, 35th, and 36th, as well as part of both the 20th and 27th Articles of the Anglican Church. The document may be read online at http://members.rogers.com/jacobites/documents/1689tolera-tion.htm. The Virginia law enacted in 1699 essentially allowed protestant dissenters who attended their own house of wor-ship once every other month exemption from the fines imposed for not attending an Anglican church or chapel. Hening 3:171; In 1772, some in Virginia were claiming the Act of Toleration had no effect since it was not part of the original charter, or that they would keep it out of the colony as they did the Stamp Act. Morgan Edwards, "Materials Toward a History of the Baptists in the Provinces of Maryland, Virginia, North Carolina, South Carolina, and Georgia," unpublished manuscript (microfilm facsimile), 1772, p. 105f, UVA.

[53]*Documents, Chiefly Unpublished, Relating to the Huguenot Emigration to Virginia,* edited and compiled by R.A. Brock. Richmond, VA: Virginia Historical Society, 1886, New Series 5, p. 55; *Miscellaneous Papers 1672-1865, Collections of the Virginia Historical Society, 1672-1865.* Richmond, VA: The [Virginia Historical] Society, 1887, New Series 6, p. 64 (quote).

[54]*Calendar of Virginia State Papers.* Arranged and edited by William P. Palmer, Vol. I. Richmond, VA, 1875, p. 78.

[55]*The Official Letters of Alexander Spotswood.* With an intro-duction and notes by R.A. Brock. In two volumes. Richmond, VA: Virginia Historical Society, 1882, 1885, 1:167 (26 July 1712).

[56]The struggle between the Monocans, a native American peo-ple, and the English is summarized in James Lukin Bugg, "Manakin Town in Virginia," Masters Thesis, UVA, 1942, 11-21; "Report of the Journey of Francis Louis Michel," translated and edited by William J. Hinke, *VMHB* 24:29f; *New Series* 6:64.

[57]Hinke, "Report," *VMHB* 24:122.

[58]*New Series* 5:54f; *New Series* 6:64; Hening 3:478f.

[59]Hening 3:434f. According to his naturalization papers, this

1705 law was the basis for Adam Mueller's naturalization in March, 1741/2, although the 1740 law passed by Parliament for naturalization of aliens in the American colonies was also a factor, since it required a minimum seven-year residence prior to naturalization. Lizzie B. Miller, "First Settler in the Valley," *William and Mary Quarterly,* 9:132; "Virginia Naturalizations, 1657-1776," Research Notes No. 9, Library of Virginia at http://www.lva.lib.va.us/whatwehave/notes/rn9_natural1657.pdf.

[60]Kemper, "Swiss and German," *VMHB* 29:1ff. On 8 March 1710, fifty-six Anabaptists were put on board a ship at Berne. Thirty-two were freed at Mannheim on 28 March, and the rest were freed by the efforts of the Dutch government and the Holland Mennonites on 9 April. As early as 1699, the Bernese government was looking to send Anabaptists to an island in the East Indes so they would not be able to return. Gratz, *Bernese Anabaptists,* 56f.

[61]Spotswood, *Letters,* 1:152.

[62]Vincent H. Todd, *Christoph von Graffenried's Account of the Founding of New Bern,* Raleigh, [NC]: Edwards & Broughton Printing, 1920, p. 258; Spotswood, *Letters,* 2:66 (15 March 1713/4).

[63]Spotswood came under severe criticism for this and other actions. Spotswood, *Letters,* 1:26 (24 October 1710); 2:66, 70 (21 July 1714); 217f.

[64]"The Germans in Madison County, Virginia," translated and annotated by William J. Hinke, *VMHB* 14:136-170.

[65]Rev. W. P. Huddle, *History of the Hebron Lutheran Church Madison County, Virginia, 1717 to 1907....* Madison, VA: Hebron Lutheran Church, 1990, page 3 (note 2).

[66]Huddle, *Hebron,* 9; *Historical Collections Relating to the American Church.* Edited by William Stevens Perry, Vol. 1 — Virginia. Hartford, CT: Church Press Co., 1870, p. 247f.

[67]For the lawsuits against these Germans see "The Early Westward Movement of Virginia," edited and annotated by Charles E. Kemper, *VMHB* 13:364-367; Huddle, *Hebron,* 7, 12ff; Several suits were dismissed on 8 July 1724. Spottsylvania County Will Book A:87. In September 1735, someone was accused of insulting and abusing those engaged in divine worship at the German Chapel. The charge was later dismissed. Orange County Grand Jury proceedings noted in Ulysses P. Joyner, Jr., *The First Settlers of Orange County, Virginia.* Baltimore: Gateway Press, Inc., 1987, p. 143. Fairfax Grants K:155 to John Carpenter in 1760 mentions "where the German chapel stood." Hinke, "Madison County," *VMHB* 14:153f.

[68]Hinke, "Madison County," *VMHB* 14:143, 148 note 10, 153f.

[69]According to Huddle, this second colony was also joined by people coming south from Pennsylvania. Huddle, *Hebron,* 11.

[70]"I bless the Lord in obtaining it [Pennsylvania]…and desire that I may not be unworthy of His love, and do that which answers His kind providence, and serve His truth and people that an example may be set up to the nations, there may be room there, but not here for such a holy experiment." William Penn to James Harrison, 4 September 1681, quoted in Arthur Pond, *The Penns of Pennsylvania and England.* New York: The MacMillan Co., 1932, p. 167.

[71]*George Fox and the Children of Light,* Edited and with an introduction by Jonathan Fryer. London: Kyle Cathie Limited, 1991, (Journal) p. 55.

[72]*Fox,* (Journal) 48.

[73]*The Frame of the Government of the Province of Pennsylvania in America: Together with certain Laws Agreed upon in England by the Governour and Divers Free-Men of the aforeside Province....* Printed in the year 1682, p. 11, UVA.

[74]Johannes Mack was baptized 19 April 1703. *European Origins of the Brethren,* edited by Donald F. Durnbaugh, Elgin, IL: The Brethren Press, 1958, p. 53.

[75]*The Brethren in Colonial America,* edited by Donald F. Durnbaugh, Elgin, IL: The Brethren Press, 1967, p. 14.

[76]Like other radical pietists, the Tunkers were significantly influenced by the writings of Gottfried Arnold whose 1696 publication *Die erste Liebe (The First Love)* attempted to portray the life of the first century Christians, considered a benchmark for doctrine and worship. See the sidebar, "Pious Desires," beginning on page 25. *The Brethren Encyclopedia,* 1:57; 2:775ff; 2:1158. Schwarzenau was also a refuge for the Huguenots after 1685.

Side 2 Philip Jacob Spener, *Pia Desideria.* Translated, edited and with an introduction by Theodore G. Tappert. Philadelphia: Fortress Press, 1964, pp. 8ff, quotes 13, 57; *The Brethren Encyclopedia,* 1:57, 453, 614f. I John 3:18 (RSV) states: "Little children, let us not love in word or speech but in deed and in truth." Despite Spener's focus on the law of love, some pietists would develop legalistic behavioral codes. One included, "Guard yourself from unnecessary laughter. All laughter is forbidden." *Pietists: Selected Writings.* Edited and with an introduction by Peter C. Erb. New York: Paulist Press, 1983, p. 112. The Lutheran missionary Caspar Stoever, Sr., was in correspondence with Francke's son at Halle, and was bringing a copy of Spener's *Consilia* in three volumes back to Virginia the year that he died. OCWB 1:86.

[77]Durnbaugh, *Colonial America,* 86ff. The first Dunker Brethren, a group of about twenty families, had arrived in

America under the leadership of Peter Becker in 1719. Initially they spread out in the new colony of Pennsylvania, a condition which 18th century historian Morgan Edwards said "incapacitated them to meet for public worship; and therefore they soon began to grow lukewarm in religion." According to Edwards, this first group experienced a brief revival but again soon "settled on their lees" until the arrival of Mack and company. Morgan Edwards, *Materials Towards a History of the Baptists in Pennsylvania.* Volume 1. Philadelphia: Jos. Cruckshank and Isaac Collins, 1770, p. 64f, UVA.

[78]Letter from Christopher Saur dated 1 August 1725, in Durnbaugh, *Colonial America,* 35f. Not long afterward, the name of Christopher Saur would become known for printing numerous German-language publications, including the newspaper *Pennsylvanische Berichte.*

[79]*The Journals of Henry Melchior Muhlenberg, In Three Volumes.* Translated by Theodore G. Tappert and John W. Doberstein. Philadelphia: The Evangelical Lutheran Ministerium of Pennsylvania and Adjacent States and the Muhlenberg Press, 1945, Volume 1, p. 144 (May 1747), hereinafter cited as *JHMM.*

[80]See *Minutes of the Provincial Council of Pennsylvania,* Vol. 3, Harrisburg, [PA]: The State [of Pennsylvania], 1840, p. 282 (2 February 1726/7).

[81]According to family tradition, Mueller followed Spotswood's route from Williamsburg. Kemper, "Miller," *VMHB* 10:84.

[82]Spotsylvania began as a separate county on 1 May 1721. Hening 4:77.

[83]The Treaty of Albany, ratified in 1722, is printed in Hening 4:99-103.

[84]William Beverly to James Patton, *William & Mary Quarterly* 3:226f. While Beverly was satisfied with families from Ireland or Pennsylvania, William Byrd said he would "much rather have to do with the honest Switzers than the mixed people that come from Pennsylvania." William Byrd, *Natural History of Virginia.* Richmond, VA: Dietz Press, 1940, p. xxi.

[85]On 23 November 1738, Samuel Tscheffely from Berne requested 20,000A "on some of the main branches of James River next adjoining to the lands already granted for the settlement of divers families of Swiss and German Protestants which he proposes to import in or to make provision for a larger number." "Journals of the Council of Virginia in Executive Session, 1737-1763," *VMHB* 14:231.

[86]*Minutes of the Board of Property of the Province of Pennsylvania (1687-1732).* Edited by William Henry Egle. Harrisburg, PA: E. K. Meyers, 1893, p. 552; Kemper, "Swiss and German," *VMHB* 29:287ff.

[87]Kemper, "Swiss and German," *VMHB* 29:287ff.

[88]17 June 1730. *Executive Journal of the Council of Colonial Virginia.* Vol. IV. H.R. McIlwaine, Editor. Richmond, VA: Virginia State Library, 1930, p. 224.

[89]"…for ye northern men are fond of buying land there, because they can buy it, for six or seven pounds pr: hundred acres, cheaper than they can take up land in pensilvania and they don't care to go as far as Wmsburg." Palmer, *Calendar,* 1:218.

[90]Letter from Francis Thornton, 28 November 1733, Palmer, *Calendar,* 1:220.

[91]*Executive Journal,* 4:316. Patents 15:127ff, LV.

[92]These various groups were present by the summer of 1748. Inspirationists were those who believed that God could speak through his Holy Spirit directly to an individual believer. Hinke and Kemper, "Moravian Diaries," *VMHB* 11:229, 239 and note.

[93]Orange County Judgments 1736, abstracted in *Orange County, Virginia, Deed Books 3 & 4, 1738-1741, Judgments 1736.* Abstracted and compiled by John Frederick Dorman, Washington, DC, 1966, p. 60.

[94]A child born to he Seltzers' was baptized by Caspar Stoever, Jr. on 28 April 1734, about a week before the Stoevers' own child was born and later baptized in the church at Lebanon, Pennsylvania. Ludwig Stein and his wife, Maria Catarina, acted as sponsors for both baptisms. *Early Lutheran Baptisms and Marriages in Southeastern Pennsylvania, The Records of Rev. John Casper Stoever from 1730 to 1779,* with an index by Elizabeth P. Bentley. Baltimore: Genealogical Publishing Co., Inc., 1982, pp. 19, 32. The original record is at HSP.

[95]Their full names were both Johann Caspar Stöver (spelled generally Stoever after their arrival), but both went by Caspar. Orange County Court Records, Judgments 1735, abstract in *Orange County, Virginia, Deed Books 1 & 2, 1735-1738, Judgments 1735.* Abstracted and compiled by John Frederick Dorman, Washington, DC, 1961, p. 69; *The Correspondence of Heinrich Melchior Mühlenberg.* Vol. I, 1740-1747. Edited and translated by John W. Kleiner & Helmut T. Lehman. Camden, ME: Picton Press, 1986, 1993, p. 169; Ralph Beaver Strassburger, *German Pioneers: A Publication of the Original Lists of Arrivals in the Port of Philadelphia, From 1727 to 1808.* In two volumes. Edited by William J. Hinke. Baltimore: Genealogical Publishing Co., Inc., 1983 [originally published Norristown, PA, 1934], Volume 1, p. 22. Johann Caspar Stöver, Miss., and Johann Caspar Stöver, Ss.Theol. Stud. are included on lists 8A and 8B of "Palatines imported in the Ship James Goodwill, David Crockatt, Mr, from Rott[e]r[dam], but last from [Deal] as by clearance dated 11 September 1728." Eighteen days later, on 29 September, they landed in America. Stoever,

Baptisms & Marriages, 4.

[96]Caspar Stoever, Jr. was born 21 December 1707. Huddle, *Hebron,* 20; Stoever, *Baptisms & Marriages,* 3.

[97]Stoever, Sr. was with the Robinson River Lutherans at least by 28 February 1733. The financial records of the church for several months beginning in January 1733 are in OCWB 1:54ff. The church also provided land and a house for their new minister.

[98]Hinke, "Madison County," *VMHB* 14:149.

[99]A Christopher Zimmerman was a witness to a deed in the Massanutten area as early as 23 May 1739. OCDB 3:149ff (23-24 May 1739: Martin Coffman of Lancaster to Matthias Seltzer of Augusta). An obvious point of contact for the Massanutten and Robinson River German communities was Thornton's Mill, just east of the Ridge across Thornton's Gap, now traversed by Route 211. Thornton had a mill in operation at least by 1726. Spotsylvania County Order Book 1:129 (6 December 1726); OCOB 1:5 (18 February 1734).

[100]Michael Rheinhardt's children were baptized at this same time. Stoever, *Baptisms and Marriages,* 13 (1 May 1739).

[101]The will was probated 20 March 1738/9. OCWB 1:84ff. There is a revised translation in Hinke, "Madison County," *VMHB* 14:157-166; Stoever, *Baptisms and Marriages,* 19.

[102]Earle E. Cairns, *Christianity Through the Centuries.* Grand Rapids, MI: Zondervan Publishing House, 1954/1967, p. 346f.

[103]The letter from the synod was written on 28 May 1738. Gooch's reply was penned 4 November 1738. *Recrods of the Presbyterian Church in the United States of America, 1706-1788.* New York: Arno Press, 1969, pp. 138f, 142 (26 & 30 May 1738), 147 (28 May 1739), hereinafter cited as *Presbyterian Records.*

[104]"Governor Gooch, himself of Scotch origin and education" would later welcome a group of Virginians who identified themselves with the Presbyterians as "not only tolerated but acknowledged as part of the established church of the realm." William Henry Foote, *Sketches of Virginia,* Philadelphia: Wm. S. Martien, 1850, 1:124.

[105]Dissenters were exempted from subscribing to the 34th, 35th, 36th and part of the 20th [Anglican] Articles of Religion. Gooch's letter dated 29 August 1737 and the petition which requested Williams' license are transcribed in *Orange County, Virginia, Deed Books 3 & 4, 1738-1741, Judgments 1736.* Abstracted and compiled by John Frederick Dorman, Washington, DC, 1966, pp. 101, 107f.

[106]"William Williams a presbyterian Minister, Gent. having taken the oaths appointed by Act of parliament to be taken instead of the oaths of Allegiance and Supremacy and the oaths of abjuration, Subscribed the Test and likewise Subscribed a declaration of his approving of Such of the thirty nine Articles of Religion as is required & certified his intention of holding his meetings at his own plantation & on the plantation of Morgan Bryan — which is admitted to record." OCOB 1:213 (22 September 1737). Though all the land west of the Blue Ridge was Orange County at this date, Williams and Bryan were living in or near present-day Frederick County when Williams received his license to preach, as the petition from the "inhabitants of Opeckon and Shenandore" indicates. A Morgan Bryan did settle in the Linville Creek area in what is now Rockingham County, and a William Williams also eventually moved into the area south of the Peaked Mountain around Mill Creek in Rockingham. According to the Orange County Deed Index, deeds for William Williams do not begin until 28 April 1738. Whether or not this Rev. William Williams is the same as the Williams who settled in Rockingham is not certain, but the William Williams of Mill Creek was a Presbyterian who was sued to pay for his share of the meeting house as early as 1752. Charles E. Kemper, "The Early History of the Peaked Mountain Presbyterian Church, Rockingham County, Virginia," *Journal of the Presbyterian Historical Society* (1919), 10:23, footnote 14. See also OCOB 2:214 (26 June 1740: William Williams appointed constable in room of Samuel Scott). Children of Scott, Williams, and their neighbors were baptized by Presbyterian minister John Craig on 23 December 1740. John Craig, *A Record of the names of the Children Bap[tize]d by the Revd. John Craig...,* UVA (microfilm). The phrase "meeting house(s)" is used throughout this book since it appears to be a more common earlier spelling.

[107]For more on how this conflict between Anglicans and dissenting ministers materialized west of the Blue Ridge, see "The Wedding Game" in chapter five.

[108]In June of 1738, Williams brought suit in Orange County court against those who signed the paper. "Some of the defendants immediately begged to be excused, claiming they had been led into signing the document; others admitted they were sorry for what they had done but that they too had been 'overpersuaded.' The suit against some of the defendants was dismissed, while Mr. Williams pursued his charges against others for many successive terms of court." William H. B. Thomas, *"Faith of our Fathers!..." Religion and the Churches in Colonial Orange County,* Bicentennial Series No. 2, April 1975, Orange County Bicentennial Commission, 1975, p. 11.

[109]*Presbyterian Records*/Philadelphia Synod, 147 (28 May 1739).

[110]A famine in 1740-1741 spurred the Irish emigration to 10,000 in one season alone. See James G. Leyburn, *The Scotch-Irish: A Social History.* Chapel Hill, NC: UNC Press, 1962, 170ff.

[111] The phrase "Irish path" was used at least as early as 26 March 1739. Patents 18:252, LV. A petition dated 30 July 1742 mentions the Indians "road to ware [i.e., war]" and requests the governor to commission a militia. Palmer, *Calendar,* 1:235. The Irish path was used to describe that branch of the main north-south road that led to Staunton. The main road itself was east of today's Interstate 81, leaving Route 11 near Tenth Legion, running through present-day Keezeltown, Cross Keys, and crossing the North River at Beard's Ford, west of Port Republic. From there, its southward course took it on to the Tinkling Springs Presbyterian meeting house [first used 14 April 1745 when half built]. The court order read for the road to begin at Thom's Brook on the original Frederick County line, to Benjamin Allen's Ford and Robert Colwell's path. For the next ten miles, John and Daniel Harrison were to oversee its construction. From there to Stevenson's Spring, Robert Craven and Samuel Stewart were overseers, and from Stevenson's Spring across Beard's Ford to Alexander Thompson's ford on the Middle River in Augusta, it was under the oversight of William and John Stevenson. OCOB 4:331, 430f, 441 (24 May; 27, 28 September 1745). Note that there was also a Stevens's/Stephenson's Spring by the Lower Meeting House (later Augusta Stone [Presbyterian] Meeting House). OCOB 4:172 (26 July 1744: to the Lower meeting House on Steven's Spring; Augusta County Land Entry Book, p. 2 (16 May 1746: "200 acres for ye Meeting house of ye Lower Congregation where it is now Built including a spring joyining Thomas Stephensons land"); Harrison, *Grey Trail,* 150; Craig, Baptisms, 14 April 1745 (half built), UVA (microfilm).

[112] Undated Petition, Palmer, *Calendar,* 1:220; The Robinson River Lutherans met Native Americans occasionally while hunting and invited them into their homes where the Germans "showed them much kindness. Hence, the report had spread among the Indians that they were kinder people than the English and Spanish." This is based on Stoever, Sr.'s report as understood by Councillor Koehler and related in a letter dated 11 May 1736. Hinke, "Madison County," *VMHB* 14:146.

[113] John Craig, "Autobiography," 26. Microfilm of original manuscript in *Records of the Lexington Presbytery,* UVA (microfilm). Even along the Wagon Road relations between Native Americans and settlers could be positive.

[114] *Legislative Journals of the Council of Colonial Virginia,* 2:864 (4 November 1738). Though the specifics of these petitions are not mentioned, their progress is minimally chronicled from 8-20 November in the *Journals of the House of Burgesses of Virginia, 1727-1734, 1736-1740,* Edited by H. R. McIlwaine. Richmond, VA: Virginia State Library, 1910, pp. 330ff. The petition of 30 July 1742 indicates the Governor was dragging his feet on those commissions, much to the chagrin of the frontier inhabitants. That year a large number of people were killed by the Indians. Augusta Court Judgments May 1750(A), McDowell v. Borden, 25 August 1747, noted in Chalkley, *Chronicles,* 1:302; Palmer, *Calendar,* 1:235. Hening

5:80, re: formation of Augusta and Frederick.

[115] Craig, Autobiography, 25. Assigned to itinerate in Virginia for the first time in the fall of 1739, Craig was ordained 3 September 1740 and licensed for Orange County on 26 February 1740/1. *Minutes of Donegal Presbytery,* 1:189, 191, 196, UVA (microfilm; originals at PHS); OCOB 2:311 (26 February 1740/1: "John Craigg a presbyterian Minister in open court took the oaths appointed by Act of Parliament to be taken, instead of the Oaths of Allegiance and Supremacy & the oath of Abjuration & Subscribed the Test wch is ordered to be certified.")

[116] Craig, Baptisms, UVA (microfilm); Though most Presbyterian baptisms were for those just coming into the world, Craig may have baptized one person about to take leave of it — Jacob Stauber, "an adult person," in March of 1741. Stauber had a son by the same name, but the elder Swiss whose Peaked Mountain cabin was at the northern end of Craig's regular congregations died that same month. Craig, Baptisms, 14 March 1741; OCWB 1:140f, 150f, 154f, 202ff. Stauber, Sr.'s will was probated 26 March 1741. Craig's baptismal records indicate he served many who lived in what is now southern Rockingham. Craig was joined in Virginia not long afterward by John Thomson, also a member of Donegal Presbytery. See Minutes of Donegal Presbytery, as well as John Goodwin Herndon, *John Thomson,* privately printed, 1943, UVA (microfilm).

[117] The pledge required by the Test Act of 1673 read, "I., *A. B.,* do declare that I do believe that there is not any transubstantiation in the sacrament of the Lord's Supper, or in the elements of bread and wine, at or after the consecration thereof by any person whatsoever." It was entitled "For preventing the dangers which may happen from popish recusants [persons who refuse to comply]…" Bettenson, *Documents,* 418ff (quote 420).

[118] Foote, *Sketches,* 1:109ff. New Side Presbyterian minister John Todd was in the Valley in the fall of 1750. ACOB 2:501 (29 November 1750). Other Presbyterian ministers who were licensed by the Augusta Court during this period included Samuel Black and Alexander Cummings. ACOB 1:202 (22 May 1747); ACOB 2:76 (16 February 1748/9).

[119] On 9 April 1741, though the presbytery had been pleased with Hindman's sermons on trial, after hearing the contents of a letter and reflecting on his behavior, they judged that his "imprudence & childish Simplicity" made it "dangerous to admitt him into Such a weighty and difficult office" as that of a minister and suggested he "desist his pursuit" of ordination. On 1 June, since Hindman had received their news with a "Christian and agreeable carriage," they decided to give him another chance. *Minutes of Donegal Presbytery,* 1:212, 216f, 226 (7 & 9 April, 1 June 1741), UVA (microfilm).

[120]Hindman was assigned to itinerate in the Valley of Virginia as late as July-October 1744, from "Opickin" to Cub Creek on Round-oak and back again. *Donegal Presbytery,* 1:228 (13 June 1744). Hindman appears elsewhere in the Donegal minutes on 9 December 1740; 16 June, 2 July, 10 & 11 November 1742 ("supply in the back parts of Virginia in a circular itinorant mannor as before until our next meeting" *Donegal,* 1:249); 5 April, 30 May, 21 June 1743; 12 June 1744; 26 March, 11 June 1745.

[121]Craig, Autobiography, 27f.

[122]Gooch's testimony before the Grand Jury found in the *American Weekly Mercury,* Philadelphia, August 1745, printing Gooch's statement of 18 April 1745), the Synod of Philadelphia's response of 28 May, and Gooch's reply of 20 June are all in *Minutes of the Philadelphia Synod,* 182ff. The Philadelphia synod's letter was written by John Thomson, a member of Donegal Presbytery who had begun preaching in Virginia. During this same session of Synod, the Philadelphia group allowed creation of the New York Synod, which was composed of the "New Light" ministers. Minutes of Donegal Presbytery; Herndon, *Thomson,* 48f; *Presbyterian Records,* 181. Thomson also wrote *An Explication of the Shorter Catechism,* published in Williamsburg in 1747, UVA (microfilm).

That fall another threat arose: James II's grandson, Charles Edward Stuart, "a popish pretender of the house of Stuart" whom France was apparently hoping to place on the English throne. Virginia quickly pledged their support to the house of Hanover, and when things looked bleak, a fast day was called for 26 February 1746, a fast kept also by the young Presbyterian in the Valley, John Craig. This was significant, since some Virginians anticipated support for the Scottish prince among Presbyterian dissenters. Since France was a Roman Catholic power, fears from that quarter were a concern as well. "A proclamation was also issued against Romish priests, sent, it was alleged, as emissaries from Maryland, to seduce the people of Virginia from their allegiance." Bonnie Prince Charlie, as he was popularly known, was defeated finally at Culloden, 16 April 1746, but not before he had posed a serious threat to London. Charles Campbell. *History of the Colony and Ancient Dominion of Virginia.* Philadelphia: J.B. Lippincott & Co., 1860, p. 436f; Dan M. Hockman, "Commissary William Dawson and the Anglican Church in Virginia, 1743-1752," *Historical Magazine of the Protestant Episcopal Church* 54 (1985):134f; Craig, Baptisms, 17? (14 March 1741).

[123]The governor's speech to the House of Burgesses was on 30 March, 1747, and the proclamation was issued 3 April 1747. VCRP, NS706 C.O.5/1326, Reel 43, UVA. The Capitol had burned exactly two months earlier on 30 January 1746/7.

[124]Craig, Baptisms, (5 April 1747: "This day John Hindman attend having turn'd his Coat & now appears in the quality of

a Church of England parson.")

[125]The first meeting of the Augusta vestry was on 6 April 1747, sixteen months after the first county court. ACOB 1:1 (9 December 1745); APVB 1 (6 April 1747).

[126]Hindman "not having freedom to give an answer" declined the call of two Presbyterian churches, Rockfish and Mountain Plains, on 11 June 1745. *Donegal,* 1:300. It is not out of the question that he had already been approached by Colonel John Patton and others about the position of parish priest. Hindman was licensed for Virginia on 22 September 1746, but served Augusta Parish for less than two years. ACWB 1:101f (15 February 1748/9: John Stephenson to administer Hindman's estate); Edward Goodwin, *The Colonial Church in Virginia,* Milwaukee, WI: Morehouse Publishing Company, 1927, p. 278. In addition to fifteen books of sermons and two ministers gowns, Hindman owned twenty-seven horses and a jockey coat and cap. ACWB 1:198f (29 November 1749). He had borrowed at least part of the money for his ordination trip to England from John Stephenson, near whose home there is said to have been an old race track. ACOB 2:333 (2 March 1749/50), and Kemper, "Peaked Mountain Presbyterian Church," *Journal of the Presbyterian Historical Society* 10:20. Kemper footnotes Court Papers 1751 to 1753 re: the 1751 chancery suit brought by Hindman's brother-in-law, John Fletcher, against John Stephenson.

[127]The next May, the chinking in the Staunton courthouse showed cracks four to five inches wide and several feet long, and there was still no glass in the two windows. ACOB 1:316 (18 September 1747); ACOB 2:34 (21 May 1748). That same May court, three new Presbyterian meeting houses were recognized, and another dissenting minister, Andrew McKay, was licensed. ACOB 2:20 (20 May 1748).

[128]APVB 2 (6 April 1747). The parish delayed "Building a Glebe and such other necessaries as are Prescribed by Law for the space of Two Years untill the Parish be more able to Bear such Charges." They made no promises for a church building. Though land was given for such a structure by 1750, the vestry did not agree on building it until the spring of 1760. APVB 318 (20 May 1760). As a concession, the vestry allowed interested parties to build a chapel of ease — a house of worship usually built to serve those unable to reach the parish church — on Daniel Harrison's plantation. Though Harrison had patented most of his land on the Dry Fork of Smith's Creek, by 1746 he had obtained a 215A parcel "on the West fork of Naked Creek" where he located his stone house, familiarly known as Fort Harrison. He purchased additional land here in 1749 from Samuel Wilkins, and obtained another 65A patent in 1755. These three plots were willed to his son Benjamin who inherited the stone house property. Patents 19:1131f (20 August 1741); Patents 21:542ff (30 August 1743: William Skillirn, 343A "on the Head of a Draft of Linnvells Creek and on both Sides of the Irish Road...Beginning at two

White Oaks on the East Side of Daniel Harrison's Path");
Patents 24:424 (25 September 1746); Patents 31:645 (10
September 1755:"65A adjoining the land he lives on and cross-
ing his mill pond"); APVB 3f (20 April 1747:"On the motion of
John Smith Gent and others its Agreed that they have leave to
Build a Chappel of Ease on Daniel Harrisons Plantation
Provided it doth not affect the Parish now or hereafter nor
Exempt them from their Proportion of the Parish levy.");
Harrison, *Grey Trail,* 196f; ACDB 2:582, 586 (28 February
1749); APVB 9 (3 September 1747: Daniel Harrison and
Morgan Bryan appointed to procession land from Samuel
Wilkins to the Great Plain and Lord Fairfax's line); APVB 20
(includes a 215A parcel for Daniel Harrison in this return);
Chalkley, *Chronicles,* 1:482 (12 September 1801: Rockingham
County court survey for Benjamin Harrison). A second "chapel
of ease" in what is now Rockingham county was remembered
by General S. H. Lewis as being about five miles from Port
Republic on the road to Harrisonburg. This very well may have
been the building used by the Peaked Mountain Presbyterian
church.

[129]APVB 12 (21 September 1747). Hindman's annual salary of
£50 was the equivalent of 16,000 pounds of tobacco at three
farthings per pound, the rate established for the new counties
of Augusta and Frederick in 1738. Still, at least to one vestryman, it seemed insufficient. A petition was generated for the
next minister and certified to the colonial legislature who
decided to double it. Later there was a court case over the
issue. ACOB 3:241 (19 February 1751/2); Hening 5:80; APVB
400 (21 October 1765), 413 (22 November 1766), 421(letters
of 3 April 1766).

[130]OCOB 3:107 (26 February 1741/2). The fine at this time was
5 shillings or 50 pounds of tobacco for each month absented.

[131]ACOB 2:60 (20 August 1748:"A proposition from Sundry the
Inhabitants of this County for having the Dissenters turned
out from being Vestryman *[sic]* was recorded & ordered to be
certified to ye General Assembly for Allowance.") *Journals of
the House of Burgesses of Virginia,* 1742-1747, 1748-1749. H.
R. McIlwaine, Editor. Richmond, VA, 1909, 4:310 (30 November
1748). See also Commissary Dawson's letter to Bishop of
London 16 August 1751 in Perry, *Collections,* 1:380.

[132]Perry, *Collections,* 1:360f. The North and South Rivers that
Gavin forded were most likely the North (now Maury) and
South Rivers of the James. Just how far he may have come
down the Valley into the area to be embraced by Augusta and
Rockingham is not easy to determine.

[133]Gavin's first trip took place in the spring of 1736, soon after
he arrived in the frontier parish of St. James, Goochland
County, which at that time embraced all of present-day
Albemarle, just across the ridge from the future county of
Augusta and today's southern Rockingham. When Albemarle
was formed some eight years later, the statute noted that

Gavin's glebe was north of the James River and within
Goochland's new parish of St. James Northam. Henings 5:266-
269, esp. 268.

[134]Perry, *Collections,* 1:360f; Anthony Gavin to Bishop of
London, 20 October 1735, VCRP, Reel 591, p. 5, UVA; see also
Antonio D. Gavin, *A Master Key to Popery in Five Parts.* 3rd
edition. London, reprinted Newport, R.I., Solomon Southwick,
1773, UVA-M.

[135]The slaves were purchased with the monies collected by
Stoever, Sr. in Europe. With twelve slaves, he intended "to clear
enough land so that he together with another minister could
live on it without being a burden to the congregation." The
plan seems to have worked, for in 1749 the Lutheran leader
Muhlenberg noted, "From this land and slaves the minister
derives an ample income, so that he is not in the least burden-
some to his congregation on account of his support." Hinke,
"Madison County," *VMHB* 14:145, 170. There were seven slaves
working the several hundred acre glebe land in 1748. Hinke
and Kemper, "Moravian Diaries," *VMHB* 11:230. That Klug visited the Massanutten and other Lutheran congregations from
time to time is confirmed not only by the Moravian diaries, but
also that Mt. Calvary Lutheran Church in present-day Page has
a pewter communion cup dated 1727 and given by Thomas
Giffin, who gave the Robinson River Lutherans many similar
pewter items. Hinke and Kemper, "Moravian Diaries," *VMHB*
12:60f, note 15; Huddle, *Hebron,* 17. Giffin cup at VSL.

[136]Klug was apparently lonely in this remote outpost 300+
miles away from Philadelphia. Before long, "because he was
not careful about observing the proper *balance* with respect
to adiaphora and probably went to extremes, he fell out with
his congregation, but not with the established clergy." *JHMM*
2:374; Hinke, "Madison County," *VMHB* 14:169f. The Moravians
believed he had "great influence with the Governor," and were
told that he had warned the people about the Moravians.
Hinke and Kemper, "Moravian Diaries," *VMHB* 11:129; *VMHB*
12:60f, note 15.

[137]Details of this ecumenical attempt can be found in *The Life
and Letters of the Rev. John Philip Boehm,* edited by William
J. Hinke. NY: Arno Press, 1972 [reprint], pp. 89ff.

[138]Hinke and Kemper, "Moravian Diaries," *VMHB* 12:69.

Side 3 *The Letters of the Rev. John Wesley, A.M.* Edited by John
Telford. Vol. I. London: The Epworth Press, 1931, pp. 227, 230,
344ff. (8 August 1740); *The Journal of the Rev. John Wesley,
A.M.* in four volumes. New York: E.P. Dutton & Co., 1913, pp.
20ff, 90f, 99f, 124ff, 233; "Moravian Travels Through Virginia,"
VMHB 12:71; Frank Baker, *From Wesley to Asbury.* Durham:
Duke University Press, 1976, p. 190f; Letter of George
Whitefield to John Wesley, 24 December 1740 at
www.reformednet.org/refnet/lib/docs/reply.htm. Whitefield
and the Wesleys eventually settled their differences, as evi-

denced in a poem by Charles Wesley in 1755 which begins "COME on, my WHITEFIELD! (since the strife is past,/And friends at first are friends again at last)…" Lee, *Methodists,* 17ff; Hinke, *Boehm,* 89ff; Bishop of London to William Dawson, 6 March 1743/4, 6 September 1744, 28 July 1745, Dawson Papers. Library of Congress, 298, 301, 314. An original copy of the proclamation of Parliament with regard to the Moravians can be found at the Historical Society of Pennsylvania in Philadelphia.

[139]Hinke and Kemper, "Moravian Diaries," *VMHB* 11:229; 12:69f (25 March 1748); More than two years after the Moravians visit, Seltzer was appointed as an Augusta county magistrate by a commission dated 11 June 1751. His threat of imprisonment then was perhaps no more than a citizen's threat, but within the directives of the Governor's proclamation. As an influential citizen within his area, his words were probably not taken lightly by the Moravians. ACOB 3:176; Chalkley, *Chronicles,* 1:45f.

[140]The property, located in present day Rockingham county, contained 820A and was purchased from Joseph Bloodworth who had purchased it from Jacob Stauber. OCDB 5:199ff (27 May 1742). Mueller's homes can still be seen on the western side of Route 340 just north of Elkton. A historical marker is nearby. Mueller had been appointed as a constable for his home area as early as the winter of 1743 and again in 1744 and 1746. It is not clear whether or not he was acting in any official capacity when the Moravians arrived in 1749. OCOB 3:348 (24 February 1742/3); OCOB 4:198 (23 August 1744); ACOB 1:44, 48 (12 May, 18 June 1746).

[141]Mueller's question was a direct reference to a quote from the Apostle Paul, "Unlike so many, we do not peddle the word of God for profit. On the contrary, in Christ we speak before God with sincerity, like men sent from God." 2 Corinthians 2:17, *New International Version.* Mueller's comments also reflected the beliefs of "pietists" as well as his Mennonist neighbors at his earlier home. In the *Brief and Clear Confession* (1544), Menno Simons had addressed only two topics, the incarnation of Christ and the calling of ministers. Regarding the latter he wrote, "First, I would adduce this Scripture concerning the preachers: As my Father hath sent me, even so send I you. John 20:21. This Scripture remains unchangeable in the church of God. It means that all true teachers and preachers are sent of Christ Jesus, as He is sent of the Father, therefore we should consider who and what this Christ Jesus was, how and what He taught when the Father had sent Him." *Menno Simons,* 440f. Mueller was also no doubt drawing on the teaching from the Apostle John, "Beloved, do not believe every spirit, but test the spirits, whether they are of God; because many false prophets have gone out into the world." (I John 4:1, *New King James Version*). His "testing" the spirit of the Moravians does not really appear in their journals. Perhaps he trusted the opinion of his neighbors, the Schaub's, at whose home the Moravians

were welcomed anytime they were in the area. Another Virginia host of the Moravians declared "we have never heard anything wrong from these people in their sermons." It is likely that the Moravians kept to the basic message of the Gospel during their evangelistic tours and avoided any potentially controversial topics. Hinke and Kemper, "Moravian Diaries," *VMHB* 11:119, 126f.

[142]Hinke and Kemper, "Moravian Diaries," *VMHB* 11:127.

NOTES FOR CHAPTERS 4, 5, and 6 — CONFLUENCE

[1]In 1753, Staunton was reported to have about twenty houses. Hinke and Kemper, "Moravian Diaries," *VMHB* 12:146.

[2]John Harrison, Sr. reported he was 64 years old sometime during the early 1750s when he filed a petition for relief from the county and parish taxes since he was "not able to perform work according to ye Course of Nature to do more than to maintain my self and family." Undated petition, Augusta County Executive Papers, 1745-1776, Part 1 (VI.6), ACOB 4:4 (25 August 1753); Harrison, *Grey Trail,* 12ff, 171.

[3]John Alderson was a former member of the church from New Britain in Bucks County, Pennsylvania. Earlier they had split over a theological dispute regarding the sonship of Christ. Edwards, *Pennsylvania,* p. 50; Frederick County Deed Book 4:113ff (24-25 May 1756) in Amelia C. Gilreath, *Frederick County, Virginia Deed Book Series, Volume 1.* November, 1989, p. 144; Minutes of the Linville Creek Baptist Church, p. 8, HSP.

Originals of the Linville Creek Baptist Church minutes from 1756 to 1818 are at the Historical Society of Pennsylvania, in Philadelphia. Included in this record book are the first minutes of the Brocks Gap Old School (Primitive) Baptist Church near Runions Creek beginning in 1842, a congregation which had begun at least eighteen years earlier as an offshoot of the original Linville Creek group, but perhaps first officially organized as a separate congregation on 18 February 1843. Minutes of the Linville Creek Baptist Church, p. 97 (21 September 1816), 103ff, HSP; *Minutes of the Shiloh Association,* 1824, VBHS.

[4]Minutes of the Linville Creek Baptist Church, p. 9, HSP. The traditional location for the first meeting house is along the old Williamsburg Road, described in early records as "the road that goes from South Branch [now West Virginia] to Swift Run Gap, on land once owned by Thomas Bryan." Augusta County

Executive Papers, 1745-1776, Part 2 (IX.46, undated petition). Travelling in September 1784 on his way to Thomas Lewis's, George Washington rode through Brock's Gap, "[t]hen bearing more westerly by one Bryan's," then by the Widow Smith's and to Felix Gilbert's before he reached Lynnwood. *The Diaries of George Washington.* Volume IV. 1784 - June 1786. Donald Jackson and Dorothy Twohig, Editors. Charlottesville, VA: University Press of Virginia, 1978, p. 53f. Wayland reported that records indicated the building was there prior to 1756 and conjectured that it was originally built for Quaker services. John Wayland, *The Lincolns in Virginia.* Harrisonburg, VA: C.J. Carrier, Co., 1987 [1946], p. 48. Thomas Bryan's will of 23 January 1793 (proved 25 February 1793) reserved "two Acres wheron the Meetinghouse and grave yard Stands." Photocopy of original will, Private Collection; RCMB 2:126 (25 February 1793). Though the land was once owned by Robert McKay, a Quaker, he apparently lived for a time in the Massanutten area, a part of Augusta County until 1753 when the Frederick-Augusta line was redrawn. OCOB 1:159 (23 April 1737: south side River Sharendoe below Robert McCoys); OCOB 3:463 (23 June 1743: Robert Mckays old place upon South river); OCOB 4:324 (23 May 1745: road from Massanutten to Thornton's Mill, Robert McKay one of overseers) cited in Ann Brush Miller, *Orange County Road Orders, 1734-1749.* Charlottesville, VA: Virginia Highway and Transportation Research Council, 1984, pp. 22f, 87, 107; ACOB3:312 (19 August 1752: Robert and Moses McKay "being of the sect commonly called Quakers having solemned *(sic)* affirmed…"); Augusta County Fee Book 1762:4 (John Miller, a Quaker). Solomon Matthews, who operated iron furnaces in present-day Rockingham in the 1770s was also a Quaker. Harrison, *Grey Trail,* 336f. Matthews "affirmed" a deed from Abraham Lincoln (grandfather of the future president) who was about to move from Rockingham County to Kentucky. RCDB/Burnt 0:92 (26 June 1780).

[5]For the Presbyterians, baptism was not a definite affirmation of a new life in Christ, as it was for the Baptists. The Westminster Confession of Faith, the credal statement of Presbyterians written in 1643, states that "Not only those that do actually profess faith and obedience unto Christ, but also the infants of one or both believing parents, are to be baptized.…Grace and salvation are not so inseparably annexed to it, as that…all that are baptized are undoubtedly regenerated.…" Bettenson, *Documents,* 348. As an apparent concession, by 1773 the Linville Creek Church decided to allow its members to "have their children brought before the Church and the Minister, to take them in his Arms, and beg a blessing for them." Minutes of the Linville Creek Baptist Church, p. 20 (11 [2nd Saturday in] September 1773), HSP. Eighteenth-century Baptist minister and historian John Leland noted this practice among the Baptists was sometimes satirically called "dry christening." John Leland, *The Virginia Chronicle,* Fredericksburg, VA: T. Green, 1790, p. 42, UVA-M.

[6]Minutes of Linville Creek Baptist Church, p. 11, HSP.

[7]In 1744, the Treaty of Lancaster stipulated that the Native Americans could not take or kill anything belonging to any of the people in Virginia without their permission, "but behave themselves peaceably like Brethren." They could apply to a justice of the peace, militia captain, or similar person along the road for provisions to the next justice & c. It also limited their travel through Virginia to the "present Waggon Road." The Treaty Held with the Indians of the Six Nations, at Lancaster, in Pennsylvania, in June, 1744. Williamsburg: Printed and Sold by William Parks, [n.d., 1744], p. 75f, VCRP, 789 C.O.5/1326, NS706, UVA.

[8]Draper Manuscripts, Series D, Volume 1, "Border Forts," JMU-Microfilm. Referring to the Rangers or "professional" soldiers, Washington remarked: "…I believe they are more encompassd by fear than by the Enemy…" As for raising a local militia, Washington was told "that it was impossible to get above 20 or 25 Men, they having absolutely refus'd to stir, choosing as they say to die with their Wives and Family's…" George Washington's letter to Governor Dinwiddie, 11 October 1755, in *The Papers of George Washington, Colonial Series,* Volume 2 (August 1755–April 1756), W. W. Abbot, editor. Charlottesville, VA: University of Virginia Press, 1983, p.101.

[9]"The Wednesday following this riotous Action, it pleased God to permit the Heathen to fall on our Settlements, and disordered the whole worse than they had done themselves, the Week before." Miller had taken the pulpit on Wednesday, 21 September 1757. The Indian attacks began on 28 September. Minutes of Linville Creek Baptist Church, p. 11, HSP. John Craig, Autobiography, UVA (microfilm); William Henry Foote, *Sketches of Virginia,* Second Series, Philadelphia: J. B. Lippincott & Co., 1855, 2:32f.

[10]Shortly after Braddock's defeat, Augusta's Anglican priest John Jones was directed to preach, among other places, "at Capt Daniel Harrisons and at any Place Contiguous to Mr Madisons, at such times as said Jones shall think proper." APVB 166 (27 November 1755). Harrison's stone house, sometimes called Fort Harrison, was standing by the winter of 1749. ACDB 2:582, 586 (28 February 1749). "Contiguous to Mr. Madison's" may have been Madison's own fort, which he was in the process of building by the summer of 1753. Madison thanked his friends on the eastern side of the Ridge for sending guns, and though he was invited to come east for safety, he refused, resolving instead to complete the fort he was then building. Letter from John Madison, 19 August 1753, in William C. Rives, *History of the Life and Times of James Madison.* Volume I. Boston: Little, Brown & Co., 1859, pp. 5ff. Many older houses in the Shenandoah Valley have above ground slots in the walls of their stonework basements. Once thought to be "gun holes" for the forts, they are actually an archetectural feature of homes throughout the Rhine, incorporated to provide ventilation and light. Edward A. Chappell, "Acculturation in the Shenandoah Valley: Rhenish Houses of the Massanutten Settlement," *Proceedings of the American Philosophical*

Society, 124:60. Daniel Harrison's stone house may have had slots as well, though the renovation process would have obscured them.

[11]Foote, *Sketches,* [1856] 2:25 note; Another of these forts in present-day Rockingham was noted by Charles Kemper in 1930 as once located "On the east of a hill on the Van Lear place, about one mile south of Cross Keys…" Wayland, et. al. *Virginia Valley Records,* 302. During this same period, the Presbyterians of Virginia were sending missionaries to the Overhill Cherokees in present-day Tennessee. A. Mark Conard, "The Cherokee Mission of Virginia Presbyterians," *Journal of Presbyterian History* 58:35-48.

[12]In 1754, Augusta recorded 2,663 tithables. By 21 November 1758, there were only 1,386. In terms of population, this was a drop from about 10,000 to 5,000. APVB 142, 235. The massacre at Fort Seybert, just west of the current Rockingham border, took place on 28 April 1758. Richard K. McMaster, et. al., *Conscience in Crisis: Mennonites and Other Peace Churches in America, 1739-1789, Interpretation and Documents.* Scottsdale, PA: Herald Press, 1979, p. 127f. Mennonist letter dated 7 September 1758. Minutes of Linville Creek Baptist Church, p. 11, HSP. Both the Linville Creek Baptists and the Presbyterian congregations under Alexander Miller's charge had a difficult go of things after the raids had subsided. As the Baptists wrote, "by Reason of the Length of the Way, the Difficulty of Winter, the troubles of removing back from our Flights, caused by the Enemy, and great Affliction of the Small-Pox raging in the Land, we had not an Opportunity to meet in Church Order, nor hold Communion till the 10th of August 1760." Miller wished to be dismissed from his congregations since they could not pay his salary, and the Peaked Mountain church tried to include some members of John Craig's Augusta Stone congregation within their bounds, in order to have a broader base of financial support. Despite their lack of success in changing the boundary, Miller's congregations agreed to pay his salary, and he stayed on at least for the time being. Financial difficulties continued, however, and the pastoral relation was mutually dissolved by the Spring of 1765. Hanover Presbytery Minutes, 1:25 (5 October 1759: "A Petition from the Peeked Mountain Congregation was read; desiring a Centre between the Stone Meeting House and Cook's Creek M. House: or they will be deprived of Mr Miller's Labours."); 30f (1760, 30: "A Petition was presented to ye Pby from Peeked Mountain requesting a central Line between them and Stone Meeting House…"); 34 (24 September 1760); 70 (2-3 May 1764); 73 (3 October 1764); 76 (1 May 1765); See also the Cook's Creek Minutes, PAM.

Side 4 The German word *tunken* means "to put a morsel into sauce." The name Tunker or Dunker, as they became known in the Valley, resulted from the German pronunciation of the letter "T," which sounded to English ears more like "D." They sometimes identified themselves as the Dutch Baptist Society or the German Baptist Brethren. Linville Creek Baptist Church

Minutes, p. 81 (14 April 1810: still calling itself the Church of Christ), HSP; George Whitefield, *Journal,* London: Banner of Truth Trust, 1960, p. 370 (12 December 1739); Edwards, *Pennsylvania,* i, 50f, 64; Latourette, *Christianity,* [Smyth and Baptists]; RCMB 1:92 (28 May 1781: "Anderson Moffet an Anabaptist minister having satisfied the Court by a certificate from the elders of his sect that he is duly qualified to administer the sacraments, is licensed to perform the function of marrying by banns or license in this county."), in *Rockingham County, Virginia Minute Book, 1778-1792, Part 1.* Abstracted and compiled by Constance A. and Louise C. Levinson, Harrisonburg, VA: Greystone Publishers, 1985, p. 85. The Smith's Creek Baptists were organized into a distinct congregation from the Linville Creek group in 1774, but Moffett was serving the Linville Creek Baptists as early as 1787. Robert B. Semple, *A History of the Rise and Progress of the Baptists in Virginia.* Revised and extended by G. W. Beale. Richmond, VA: Pitt and Dickinson, 1894 [1810], pp. 230, 252, hereinafter cited as [Beale's] Semple, *Baptists in Virginia;* Wayland, *Virginia Valley Records,* 58.

[13]Interestingly, about 1752 a group of Dunkers associated with the Ephrata community settled on the Shenandoah River. They, too, must have been exposed to the Indian attacks. See Edwards, "Virginia," p. 104.

[14]Gerald C. Studer, "A History of the Martyrs' Mirror," *Mennonite Quarterly Review* 22:173-176. To appeal to the Dunker communities, some copies of the first edition included an engraved copper frontispiece showing the first Christian martyr, John the Baptist, immersing Christ in the Jordan River. The scene annoyed the Mennonists who baptized only by sprinkling. "Blutige Shau-Platz" and "John Peter Miller" in *The Brethren Encyclopedia* 1:154, 2:840. The full title of the book was *Der Blutige Shau-Platz oder Martyrer Spiegel der Tauffs Gesinnten,* translated *The Bloody Theater or Martyrs' Mirror of the Baptist-Minded.*

[15]*Martyrs Mirror,* 1141. "A great Martyr Book" was part of the inventory of Martin Kaufman. ACWB 1:197 (16 June 1749).

[16]These stories are recounted in Samuel Kercheval, *A History of the Valley of Virginia.* Fourth Edition. Strasburg, VA: Shenandoah Publishing House, 1925, pp. 84f.

[17]The plea was on 7 September 1758, and the reply from Amsterdam was dated 27 December. McMaster, et. al., *Conscience in Crisis,* 127ff.

[18]The Presbyterian minister Alexander Miller performed the wedding ceremony of Michael Carn and Elizabeth Persinger on 13 March 1759 "at the Dutch meeting." Minutes of Cook's Creek Presbyterian Church, PAM.

[19]These congregations are named in Schlatter's letter of 25 June 1751, but all except Massanutten are mentioned earlier in

the Coetus Records of 1747. The "Shenandoah" congregation appears to have been located along the North Fork, in the Strasburg/Woodstock (Mullerstadt) area. Schlatter's journal notes a call from Virginia on 30 January 1749. Rev. H. Harbaugh, *The Life of the Reverend Michael Schlatter*. Philadelphia: Lindsay and Blakiston, 1857, pp. 173ff., 189, 204. *Minutes and Letters of the German Reformed Congregations in Pennsylvania, 1747-1792*. Philadelphia: Reformed Church Publication Board, 1903, p. 37, hereinafter cited as *Coetus Records*. See also J. Silor Garrison, *The History of the Reformed Church in Virginia, 1714-1940*. Winston-Salem, NC: The Clay Printing Co., 1948, p. 29f. which includes John Wayland's analysis of Schlatter's Virginia journey.

[20]*Pennsylvanische Berichte* March 16, April 1, July 1, September 1, 1755, referenced in Aaron Fogleman, *Hopeful Journeys: German Immigration, Settlement, & Political Culture in Colonial America, 1717-1775*. Philadelphia: University of Pennsylvania Press, 1996, p. 141, 213 (note 29). In 1747, the Lutheran leader Henry Muhlenberg, noted that in the five years or so since his arrival, "scarcely half of the original members of the country congregations are left," most having moved to the south and west for cheaper, more available land. *JHMM*, 1:141-2.

[21]ACOB 1:168 (18 March 1746/7: road order); ACWB 3:337ff (18 September 1761, Will of Jacob Harmon: "I do hereby give to the use of the Church near the Meeting house now built two acres of Land for ever."); ACWB 3:384 (23 February 1764); Peaked Mountain Lutheran/Reformed Church records, p. 7 (27 February 1762: first baptisms by vanGemuenden), MRL Vault. Harmon was naturalized in 1758 and received the sacrament from "Reverand H? Wortman," presumably an early Lutheran or Reformed minister in that area. ACOB 6:180 (16 August 1758).

[22]Harbaugh, *Schlatter*, 344.

[23]Adam Röder had moved into this area sometime before 26 July 1748, when his presence was noted by the Moravian missionaries. Hinke and Kemper, "Moravian Diaries," *VMHB* 11:239.

[24]ACWB 3:384 (23 February 1764, proved 19 March 1765). Capt. Peter Schowll appears on a 1742 list of the Augusta militia. "Militia Companies in Augusta County, 1742," *VMHB* 8:280; OCOB 1743-1746:49, 108. Scholl was also one of the first justices in Augusta. ACOB 1:1 (9 December 1745). The deed for Röder's church from the Röders and Benders was to Peter Scholl on behalf of the Presbyterian [viz., German Reformed] church, and to Michael Neice (Nease) in behalf of the Lutheran church. ACDB 19:227f (20 May 1765: a meeting house was standing on the lot at this time). Paul Henkel mentions a Michael *Nebs* of the Pine Church, just north of the Rockingham county line. Henkel, Tagebuch, 59.

[25]*JHMM* 2:306ff; Huddle, *Hebron*, 37f. This belief about baptism

was expressed by Luther, "Baptism…brings and gives faith, where a man desires it." Articles of Schwabach, No. 10, 16 October 1529; also Kidd, *Continental*, 255 re: 15th article of Marburg Colloquy.

[26]*JHMM* 2:306.

[27]The two letters from Fort Run were dated 9 February and 17 May 1766, and the two from Culpeper 20 December 1765. *JHMM* 2:306f, 311.

[28]*JHMM* 1:145, 2:306ff, 2:310. Schwarbach was ordained 10 June 1766.

[29]Henkel, "A Short History of the German Evangelical Lutheran Congregations and their Pastors in the State of Virginia," typescript, p. 2, LTSG.

[30]*Coetus Records*, 157 (9 November 1757); *JHMM* 1:145 (1747); *Documentary History of the Evangelical Lutheran Ministerium, 1748 to 1821*. Philadelphia: Board of Publications of the General Council of the Evangelical Lutheran Church in North America, 1898, p. 438.

[31]See Frederick George Livingood, *Eighteenth Century Reformed Church Schools*. Norristown, PA, 1930, pp. 226ff; Schlatter had 1000 copies of an ABC book printed around 1752 and gave copies to the school children. *Coetus Records*, 89 (1753).

[32]*Documentary History*, 51f (1760).

[33]*JHMM* 2:373 (2 September 1768). The congregations he served perhaps included Culpeper, Fort Run [Röder's], Peaked Mountain, Lower Peaked Mountain, Massanutten (perhaps the early "Flatwoods" congregation sometimes noted), and probably Mullerstadt (Woodstock) and Strasburg, but Schwarbach's ministry extended far beyond the Valley, to the South Branch of the Potomac across the Alleghenies. Interestingly, at the end of his strength, he confirmed a young boy who would be an energetic itinerant for the Lutherans far west of the Ridge. Schwarbach confirmed Paul Henkel, then 13 years old, in the year 1768. Paul Henkel remembered that "every month he [Schwarbach] travelled through the communities and performed the duties of his office. I was sent to him with several others for instruction in the catechism and confirmed. Although this experience seemed lost on me as on many others, nevertheless I know from experience that it had its effect.…At all times I liked to hear him talk. I also liked to hear the public sermons, especially when they were delivered with earnestness and impressiveness." Schwarbach's visits were apparently both frequent and memorable. Henkel, "Short History," 1f; Henkel, Tagebuch, 5.

[34]Culpeper County Deed Book E:138ff.

[35]Around 1754 Daniel Marshall, a Presbyterian influenced by the preaching of "new light" George Whitefield, came into the Opequon (Frederick County) area. Marshall was soon convinced of the need for "believer's baptism" and joined with the Baptists there. Shortly afterward, Marshall moved to North Carolina, but others apparently preached a similar message in the Frederick county area with the same enthusiasm. It was here that the Pennsylvania German Mennonite Martin Boehm "obtained new light" as well during his 1761 visit. "Notices of the Life and Labours of Martin Boehm and William Otterbein; and Other Minsters [sic] of the Gospel Among the United German Brethren," *The Methodist Magazine* (1823) 6:210-214, 249-256. James B. Taylor, *Virginia Baptist Ministers.* Philadelphia: J. B. Lippincott & Co., 1859, 1:19.

[36]Henry G. Spayth, *History of the Church of the United Brethren in Christ.* Circleville, OH: Conference Office of the United Brethren in Christ, 1851, pp. 32ff, quote 34, UVA; Baptists called for a preacher from the Philadelphia Association, and were sent Elder Benjamin Miller. "When he came he was highly delighted with the exercises, joined them cordially, and said if he had such warm-hearted Christians in his church he would not give gold for them. He charged those who had complained, rather to nourish than complain of such gifts. The work of God revived among them, and considerable additions were made to the church." [Beale's] Semple, *Baptists in Virginia,* 376.

[37]Spayth, *United Brethren,* 29; Boehm reported that his "ministerial labours began about the year 1756. Three years afterwards by nomination of the *lot,* I received full pastoral orders." *Methodist Magazine* 6:211.

[38]Boehm, *Reminiscences,* 225. Boehm described his own conversion experience as a process: "By deep meditations upon the doctrines which I myself preached of the fall of man, his sinful state and utter helplessness, I discovered and felt the want of Christ within." In Virginia around the year 1761, Boehm "saw many gracious souls who could give a rational and scriptural account of their experience and acceptance with God; these assurances roused me to greater efforts to obtain the blessing." *Methodist Magazine* 6:211.

[39]Spayth, *United Brethren,* 41.

[40]*Coetus Records,* 240 (17 October 1765).

[41]Lange was one of three Reformed ministers presented to the Holland fathers for the Pennsylvania service in May 1766. He was ordained on 27 May and arrived in New York on 10 September 1766. Glatfelter, *Pastors and People,* 1:78; William J. Hinke, *Ministers of the German Reformed Congregations in Pennsylvania and Other Colonies in the Eighteenth Century,* edited by George W. Richards, Lancaster, PA: Historical Commission of the Evangelical and Reformed Church, 1951, pp. 135-138; *Coetus Records,* 254 (16-17 September 1767).

[42]*Coetus Records,* 255 (16-17 September 1767). They further directed "That Do[mine]. Lange as soon as possible be removed to another congregation," and that "he make a confession of the error he committed; which he has also done."

[43]Lange's visit to the Peaked Mountain "lower church" (clearly indicated as such in Lange's records), was on 22 October 1767, about a month after the meeting of the Coetus. Lange's list of names is the only known record of membership for this congregation by that name. They appear in the records of the Evangelical Reformed Church of Frederick, Maryland, in Lange's carefully written German script. Maryland State Archives, Annapolis, MD, Acquisition #MSA SC 334 (microfilm).

[44]This probably refers to the examination of personal conduct prior to taking the communion, spoken of in I Corinthians 11:23ff. Also, at annual sessions of the Coetus, the Reformed ministers practiced something called the "Censura Morum," an investigation into the conduct of the ministers. David Miller, *Early History of the Reformed Church in Pennsylvania,* Reading, PA: David Miller, 1906, p. 100f.

[45]*Coetus Records,* 286, 20-21 September 1769. Lange was in debt to James Johnson for £45, just £5 short of the original salary of the Anglican parish priest. The Reformed Coetus decided that a minister should expect 7 shillings 6 pence for marriages and 5 shillings for a funeral, but in Virginia both of these functions were officially the province of the Anglican priest. Lange's other potential sources of extra income were confirmations, communion, and baptisms. Baptisms, however, the Coetus had directed, were to be performed without any remuneration. Miller, *Reformed Church,* 123 referencing the *Coetus Records,* 1748. Augusta County Chancery Causes, November 1770(A) referenced in Chalkley, *Chronicles,* 1:361. The bond is dated 21 October 1768, likely about the time Lange moved into the area now embraced by Rockingham.

[46]Peaked Mountain Records, pp. 2ff (31 October 1769), MRL Vault. A combined German Reformed and Lutheran congregation had existed prior to this time. Officially, the burial service of dissenters was not considered an "act of religious worship." The King vs. Henry Murray, August 1749(B) referenced in Chalkley, *Chronicles,* 1:302. Presbyterians, and probably other dissenters in the Valley, were performing their own burial services by this time.

[47]ACDB 18:158 (22 October 1771: sheriff had sold Lange's 320A on head of Fort Run). Notes on Land Records and Misc. Subjects, Vol. IV, "Deed(s) from Miss Ruth Conn," p. 1: "20 October 1801, Christopher Whetsel and Ursilla [to] Mary Eve Conrad [for] $60 [on] Stony Run, 3 3/4 acres part of 248 acres granted to Charles Long by Peter Miller and Mary, 14 and 15 March 1769, Charles Long being gone so long he is presumed dead...before name(d) Ursilla Whetsel being his daughter and only child....," HRHS.

[48]"History of McGaheysville," in *The Rockingham Register* 13 May 1898, BC/Microfilm. Though this was written long after the fact by the students of the McGaheysville school, Mrs. Lange's grandson, John C. Wetzel was still "well and hearty" and doubtless a source for the article.

[49]Koontz was born on 26 March 1739. Stoever, *Marriage & Baptisms,* 13; Hinke, "Madison County," *VMHB* 14:157-166 (Stoever, Sr.'s will); [Beale's] Semple, *Baptists in Virginia,* 242; Taylor, *Baptist Ministers,* 1:100. See also Lowell Koontz, *History of the Descendants of John Koontz,* Parsons, WV: McClain Printing Co., 1979.

[50]Ireland said he "preached stately" at the Whitehouse and was instrumental in planting the "Menonist Baptist Church." James Ireland, *The Life of the Reverend James Ireland.* Winchester, VA: Printed by J. Foster, 1819, p. 189.

[51][Beale's] Semple, *Baptists in Virginia,* 246. "Whitehouse" is Morgan Edwards' spelling. Edwards, "Virginia," 118.

[52]Martin Boehm apparently was not one of those who arrived, since based on his actions in Frederick county, the results would have been very different. Boehm was a bishop until sometime perhaps between 1775 and 1780. See John Funk, *The Mennonite Church and Her Accusers.* Elkhart, IN: Mennonite Publishing Company, 1878, pp. 42-56. Martin Boehm notes that he, Otterbein, "and several other ministers, who about this time, had been ejected from their churches as I had been from mine because of their zeal, which was looked upon as an irregularity." *Methodist Magazine* 6:212; Boehm, *Reminiscences,* 379ff. Otterbein, though he may have been considered unorthodox in some points by his cohorts, retained his connections with the German Reformed church.

[53][Beale's] Semple, *Baptists in Virginia,* 246. It is interesting that the first English Baptists began as Separatists who fled England for Amsterdam, where they found themselves among the Dutch Mennonites. Deeply influenced by this group, they were "re-baptized" and several joined the Mennonite church. Later, divisions developed over Calvinistic and Arminian beliefs. See Cairns, *Christianity,* 367. Semple's picture of this community corresponds with the evaluation of the Moravian missionaries who visited Massanutten in the spring of 1748: "Most of them are 'Mennisten' who are in a bad condition. Nearly all religious earnestness and zeal is extinguished among them." Hinke and Kemper, "Moravian Diaries," *VMHB* 11:229.

[54][Beale's] Semple, *Baptists in Virginia,* 244.

[55]Ireland, *Life,* 184. This at least was one perspective. Paul Henkel, a Lutheran who was practically one of Ireland's neighbors, recalled, "Our localities had none of the so-called Church [Anglican] teachers. As far as the others were concerned, they were doubtless zealous teachers to me, who gave themselves much trouble to preach their doctrine to the people. But it seemed to me that it meant more to them to lead one person to their own party than to lead hundreds to Jesus, the Friend of sinners. I had more arguments with the teachers of the various denominations than was pleasant. What I remember most clearly about the various sects is that I had arguments with them." Henkel, Tagebuch, 17.

[56]Ireland, *Life,* 159ff; Lewis Peyton Little, *Imprisoned Preachers and Religious Liberty in Virginia.* Lynchburg, VA: J.P. Bell, 1938, pp. 428ff. The issue of whether or not to seek a license from the state was a dividing point between the Separate and Regular Baptists, though even those distinctions could be blurred. Ireland, a Separate Baptist who later joined the Regulars, went to prison for preaching without a license, but upon his release obtained a license and permission for the first Baptist meeting house in Culpeper county. After his release, the question of licensing was raised on 13 May 1771 in an associational meeting of Separate Baptists: "Whether it is lawful and expedient for our ministers to obtain license from the civil law, for only one or more meeting-places, and so be restricted from general license given them by King Jesus— Mark xvith chapter, 15th and 16th verses, etc.?" Though Baptists in the Valley were initially associated with the Regular Baptists, the two groups united on 10 August 1787 when licensing was no longer an issue. [Beale's] Semple, *Baptists in Virginia,* 73, 99.

[57]The title of the act was "A bill for extending the benefit of the several acts of toleration to his majesty's protestant subjects in this colony, dissenting from the church of England," published in the *Virginia Gazette,* 26 March 1772, and quoted in Edwards, "Virginia," 106ff. See also, Rhys Isaac, *Transformation in Virginia,* 184ff for remarks on the particulars of this time in Williamsburg.

[58]The sisters were all daughters of William Strother, whose home was "Ferry Farm" near Fredericksburg. The Strother sisters grew up there until 1738 when their mother, then a widow, sold it to Augustine Washington who moved in with his family, including his six-year-old son, George. George H. S. King, "Washington's Boyhood Home," *William and Mary Quarterly* Series 2 (1937), 17:265-281; APVB 2 (6 April 1747), ACOB 1:2 (9 December 1745: Madison first clerk of Augusta). Madison purchased his acreage in April 1751, with Lewis and Jones following that August. Though all three may have moved into the area at about the same time, Jones was still serving as a vestryman in Frederick Parish as late as 1752. Both his family and the family of Thomas Lewis were added to the tithables in Augusta on 17 November 1757, just after the Indian raids in the Linville Creek area. ACDB 3:214 (3 April 1751: Madison), Augusta County Land Entry Book 1:10 (5 April 1751); ACDB 4:59ff (29 August 1751: Lewis); ACDB 4:70 (29 August 1751:Jones); ACOB 6:42 (17 November 1757); Frederick County Order Book 4:264 (7 August 1752: Gabriel Jones sworn in as a vestryman of Frederick Parish); Bishop [William] Meade, *Old Churches, Ministers and Families of Virginia.* In

two volumes. Philadelphia: J.B. Lippincott, 1857, Volume 2, p. 324f.

[59]James Madison, "An Oration, in Commemoration of the Founders of William and Mary College," August 15, 1772, by J. Madison, Student. Williamsburg: William Rind, 1772, p. 6, UVA-M.

[60]Drawing upon the notion of a social compact, Madison suggested "There may be a Profession of Faith purely Social, the Tenets of which, it is the Province of the Legislature to determine. These, however, are to be considered, not as Articles of Religion, but, as Sentiments which the good Order of Society requires." Madison, Oration, 9ff (quote 11). On a slightly different tack, the Baptist petition came after the war in response to the Bill for General Assessment, which would have created a tax base to support members of any Protestant denomination. Fearful that this would just create another way for the state to become involved in the particulars of personal faith, they suggested the Assembly restrict itself to "supporting those Laws of Morality, which are necessary for Private and Public Happiness." 13 August 1785 in Religious Petitions Presented to the General Assembly, 1774-1802, Reel 425, LV.

[61]Though the new county of Boutetourt had been taken from Augusta during the 1769 session, requiring the election of a new vestry all the same, this was a separate act because "a majority of the vestry of the parish of Augusta…are dissenters from the church of England." Hening 8:432f. After the second act of the legislature, the citizens of Augusta managed to elect a vestry of nine, three short of the usual twelve, but at least nine willing to assent they were "Conformable to the doctrine and discipline of the church of England." ACOB 14:102 (15 May 1770), 337 (20 March 1772), 409 (20 August 1772); APVB 413 (22 November 1766), 486 (22 November 1771); Hening 8:504; Dissenters on vestries were nothing new, nor had they been unique to Augusta. See Commissary Dawson's letter to Bishop of London 16 August 1751 in Perry, Collections, 1:380. A 1752 act required a majority of the vestry to be Anglicans. Hening 7:302f.

[62]Muhlenberg, Correspondence, 110; William Eisenberg, The Lutheran Church in Virginia, 1717-1962. Roanoke, VA: Trustees of the Virginia Synod, Lutheran Church in America, 1967, pp. 58ff; Documentary History, 136f (25-27 September 1772); Meade, Old Churches, 2:313f. Meade quotes extensively from a biographer who had Muhlenberg's daily journal of his trip to London. He sailed from Philadelphia on 2 March and landed in Dover on 10 April 1772.

[63]Documentary History, 136f.

[64]APVB 490 (19 November 1772). This was very likely the Peaked Mountain "upper church" near Harmon's mill. Interestingly, a pewter baptismal bowl belonging to this church dates between 1771-1773. Bowl at HRHS.

[65]The pattern of sending Scotsmen to serve as Anglican clergy in Virginia was well established by the late 1600s, a fact which evidently caused no little stir in the colony. Perry, Collections, 1:30, 37ff, 119. Another curate —Adam Smith — served for five months from March to August 1773, shortly before Balmaine's arrival. APVB 494 (20 August 1773).

[66]The other was the parish church in Staunton, completed by 1763. This 1773-74 chapel could have been an enlargement of an earlier building on Harrison's plantation, or it may have been an entirely new structure at a different location. In any case, its planned dimensions were increased apparently before construction began. APVB 493 (16 March 1774: makes reference to earlier order of 18 November 1773). On 23 May 1774, the Virginia legislature received a petition from Augusta to divide their 7,200 square mile parish, which had but one church and 3,000 – 4,000 tithables. Journals of the House of Burgesses, 1773-1776, John Pendleton Kennedy, Ed., Richmond, VA: [n.p.], 1905, p. 121 ("upwards of ninety Miles long, and near eighty Miles wide"); The second "chapel of ease" in Rockingham associated with Balmaine's ministry and recalled by General Samuel Hance Lewis in his correspondence with Bishop Meade in the mid-19th century was located "about five miles north of Port Republic, on the road from that place to Harrisonburg. General Lewis was the grandson of Thomas Lewis, a strong Presbyterian who was a member of the Peaked Mountain Presbyterian church near present day Cross Keys. In 1770, Thomas Lewis offered a solution to the problem of sharing a single minister among Rockingham County's three Presbyterian churches — Peaked Mountain, Cook's Creek, and Linville Creek. Though not a communicant in the Anglican church himself, Thomas Lewis had married a staunch Anglican and supported the church's efforts. Even before Balmaine's arrival, the Peaked Mountain Presbyterian church building was a likely — and very available — meeting-place for Anglicans from this part of the county. Meade, Old Churches, 2:324, 440; Peyton, Augusta, 334. Minutes of Hanover Presbytery, 2:12ff (26-27 April 1770), UVA (microfilm).

[67]Muhlenberg had already represented Dunmore in the House of Burgesses as early as 1774, and in 1775 was elected Colonel of the Eighth Regiment, the "first regiment completed on the field." Meade, Old Churches, 2:314.

[68]Meade, Old Churches, 2:285f, 314f, 319f; Balmaine was one of several Anglican ministers who took leadership in the colonial cause. Another was Samuel Klug — the son of the early minister of the Robinson River Lutherans east of the Ridge — who had been schooled in England and was the parish priest at Middlesex. Goodwin, Colonial Church, 285; JHMM 2:374 (6 November 1768). It is from Bishop Meade, who knew Balmaine personally from their service together in the Frederick County parish, that we hear that Balmaine was chairman. Yet it was Silas Hart, who had been a part of the Linville Creek Baptist church, who was serving as Augusta's chairman on 3 October 1775. Perhaps both men held the position at dif-

ferent times. Peter Force, *American Archives,* Fourth Series, Volume III. Washington, D.C.: M. St. Clair Clarke and Peter Force, 1840, p. 940.

[69]Letter from Alexander Balmain to John Balmain, 18 October 1775, in Alexander Balmain. Ledger, 1775, 1782-1821, p. 25. Accession 20562. Personal papers collection, LV.

[70]"One-fifth of the population" from Presbyterian petition of 1776 in James H. Smylie, "Jefferson's Statute for Religious Freedom: The Hanover Presbytery Memorials, 1776-1786," *American Presbyterians* 64:361; Early Virginia Religious Petitions, (Augusta County) 9 November 1776. Lewis, who had served as a delegate from Augusta to the Virginia Conventions since March 1775, was a member of the Peaked Mountain Presbyterian church. *The General Assembly of Virginia, A Bicentennial Register of Members.* Compiled by Cynthia Miller Leonard. Richmond: Virginia State Library, 1978, pp. 112ff; Peyton, *Augusta,* 334. Minutes of the Hanover Presbytery, 2:12ff, UVA (microfilm).

[71]Hening 9:165.

[72][Beale's] Semple, *Baptists in Virginia,* 492ff (14 August 1775 petition of the Baptist Association, and Journal of the 1775 convention). See also Force, *American Archives,* Fourth Series, 3:383. The Baptists had requested their ministers be allowed to preach "without molestation or abuse," and the legislature granted that permission "for the ease of such scrupulous consciences as may not choose to attend divine service as clebrated by the Chaplain."

[73][Beale's] Semple, *Baptists in Virginia,* 247f. Years earlier, in 1761, 1769, and 1772, Virginia Mennonists had petitioned for exemption from militia duty on religious grounds. MacMaster, *Conscience in Crisis,* 156.

[74]Leonard, *The General Assembly of Virginia,* 125. The first session ran from May 5-June 28, 1777. Poage and the other delegates passed a law requiring all males over 16 to renounce allegiance to King George III and take an oath to the new Commonwealth of Virginia. It also enjoined those aware of any opposition to the Revolution to report it. It began rather pointedly, "Whereas allegiance and protection are reciprocal, and those who will not bear the former are not entitled to the benefits of the latter..." Hening 9:281; see also McMaster, *Conscience in Crisis,* chapter 6.

[75]Miller had been deposed as a Presbyterian minister by Hanover Presbytery more than ten years earlier. Foote, *Sketches* 2:73f. A detailed account of these proceedings, including Miller's letter, can be found in Chalkley, *Chronicles,* 1:504ff.

[76]Augusta County Court Martial Records, 1756-1796, 1807-1812, pp. 77ff (1777). Captain "Linkhorn's" [Lincoln's] compa-

ny also reported John Miller, Sr. and Jr. for missing six musters each that year. Michael Krouse/Crouse came to Virginia from Frederick County, Maryland where he had been fined for "non-association" with the patriot cause. There were also several Garvers [Garbers] in that part of Frederick who were were fined: John Sr. and Jr., Martin, Martin (son of John), and Samuel. John Gar[b]er, Senior's fine was remitted on 18 June 1776 because he was a minister [in the Dunker church]. The Garber family later settled in southern Shenandoah and Rockingham counties where they were instrumental in beginning the Flat Rock and Cook's Creek congregations. "Journal of the Committee of Observation of the Middle District of Frederick County, Maryland. September 12, 1775—October 24, 1776," *Maryland Historical Magazine* (December 1916), 11:252, 316, UVA; Emmert Bittinger, "The Jacob and Verena Bowman Family," *Mennonite Family History* (October 1997), p. 158.

[77]Early Virginia Religious Petitions, 19 June 1776, Frederick County. Entry from Virginia Journal of Convention, 1775-1776. Online versions of many early Virginia religious petitions can be found at http://memory.loc.gov/ammem/repehtml/repe-home.html.

[78]The original records for Miller's trials were at one time listed under Petitions, October Court, 1778. There were at least two cases, one from July 1776, the other from August 1777, each with different groups of witnesses. There is no mention of the 1776 case in ACOB 16:110. There is however, an artifact from the *American Archives* which indicates Miller was brought before the Committee of Safety in October 1775, accused of holding forth that "the opposition made to the unjust, despotick and tyrannical acts of the Parliament of *Great Britain,* relative to *America,* is rebellion." In this case, the court recommended that "the good people of this County and Colony have no further dealings [with him]...until he, by his future behaviour, convinces his countrymen of his sincere repentance for his past folly." *American Archives,* Fourth Series, 3:939f (3 October 1775). For the 1777 incident, Miller was fined £100 and sentenced to two years imprisonment. ACOB 16:231 (17 September 1777). Yet, his lawyers apparently raised objection to the court's decision. See ACOB 16:233f (Commonwealth vs. Martin Cryder: "...do assess a fine of Fifty Pounds and three years imprisonment to which the same objection was made as to Miller's"), and ACOB 16:234ff.

[79]*Documentary History,* 117 (27 June 1769).

[80]Franck's journal, which notes his letter to Muhlenberg of 30 September 1776, according to Lutheran historian William Eisenberg, was in Krauth Memorial Library at the Lutheran Theological Seminary of Philadelphia. However, it cannot be located. It is perhaps the only documentary record of the Lutheran congregation at Lower Peaked Mountain church before its division. Eisenberg, *Lutheran Church,* 49 and note. On 8 and 9 October 1776, Franck conducted baptisms at the Peaked Mountain, upper church, which indicates he must have

investigated the situation at the lower church firsthand. Peaked Mountain Church Records, MRL Vault.

[81]Records of Peter's Church, originals at VLS.

[Side 5] *The Diary of Robert Rose,* Edited and annotated by Ralph Emmett Fall. McClure Press, 1977, p. 23 (entry 21 December 1747). According to a letter written by Charles Kemper on 10 November 1918, James Young and Sarah McMurtry's marriage contract in 1751 stipulated that their marriage was to be solemnized "According to the rules and Discipline of the Church of Scotland." ACDB 7:252 (7 May 1751). Marriage Register & Journal of John Alderson, 1776-1798, S.O. File 1, A-1, VBHS; Miller, *Reformed Church,* 123; *Coetus Records,* 286 (1769); *JHMM* 2:373ff; Craig, Autobiography, 27; Hening 2:49; also 1748 act 6:81ff (1748 — "...and every minister shall have the benefit of the fees arising within his parish for marriages, and also for funeral sermons;"), 10:361ff (1780 — in force 1 January 1781), and 11:503f (1784 which allowed Quakers, Mennonists, and any other Christian society to solemnize marriages "in the manner and agreeable to the regulations that have heretofore been practiced in the respective societies."); Minutes of Cook's Creek and Peaked Mountain Presbyterian Church, PAM; Peaked Mountain Lutheran & Reformed Church, p. 40 (2 March - 7 December 1762), MRL Vault; *Old Tenth Legion Marriages in Rockingham County, Virginia...* Compiled by Harry M. Strickler. Dayton, VA: Joseph K. Ruebush Co., 1928, pp. 8ff; [Beale's] Semple, *Baptists,* 95, 496ff.

[82]Hening 9:420.

[83]Now relegated to civil authority only, the new oath of the vestry was probably identical to that required of the new justices: "I A. B. do solemnly swear, that I will be faithful and true to the commonwealth of Virginia: that I will, to the utmost of my power, support, maintain, and defend, the constitution and government thereof, as settled by the general convention; and that I will faithfully execute the office of —— for the county of —— and do equal right and justice to all men, to the best of my judgment, and according to law;" Hening 9:126f; 9:164ff.

[84]Allowing for a 15-20 percent growth rate exhibited in Augusta and Rockingham between 1778 and 1780, at the time of division 1,000 tithables were in Rockingham, compared to about 1,600 for Augusta. APVB 803 (1 February 1777: 2,643 tithables), 808 (21 May 1778: 1,800 tithables), 812; RCMB 1:402 (1779: 1,379 tithables), 1:82 (28 November 1780: 1,459 tithables), in Levinson, *Minute Book,* 1:77, 268. [Note that pages 401-402, recorded when Peter Hogg was clerk in 1779, are apparently out of place.] Using a multiplier of four, the population of newly formed Rockingham was about 4,000.

[85]Early Virginia Religious Petitions, 20 October 1778, entry taken from Virginia Journal of the House of Delegates.

[86]In January 1802 the Assembly declared all former glebe lands

belonged to the citizens of the Commonwealth, and the overseers of the poor in each parish were ordered to sell the glebe when it became vacant. Samuel Shepherd, Ed., *The Statutes at Large of Virginia, From October Session 1792 to December Session 1806, Inclusive, Being a Continuation of Hening.* Volumes I-III. Richmond, Va., 1835-1836, 2:314ff.

[87]RCMB 1:78 (23 October 1780: John Lauderbach, David Lauderbach, Nicolas Perry, John Kite, John Oker, George Holby, George Speers, John Fairbairn, John Slyker, James Grace, John Cleck, Peter Shoemaker, Jacob Bowman, John Leman, Jacob Ramboe), 88 (27 March 1781: Jacob Ramboe, Lewis Baker, Henry Swadly, Jacob Harper, Robert Stephenson, Henry Gregg, George Hamner, David Munger, Jacob Eversole), in Levinson, *Minute Book,* 1:73, 82. The fact that Tories also refused to report their taxable property did not help the cause of the peace churches.

[88]McMaster, *Conscience in Crisis,* 356f.; See also Durnbaugh, *Colonial America,* 353f. Even the Virginia legislature acknowledged the close bonds of community among the peace groups, dividing an individual's fine among "all the members of their respective societies." Hening 10:261, 334, referring to Mennonists and Quakers.

[89]Peter Brock, *Pacifism in the United States.* Princeton, NJ: Princeton University Press, 1968, p. 263; C. Henry Smith, *The Mennonite Immigration to Pennsylvania in the 18th Century,* Norristown, PA: [Norristown Press], 1929, pp. 293-306, UVA. Pennsylvania laws forcing an oath of allegiance to the Colonial government by 1 June 1778 were particularly harsh. Penalties included loss of property, fines, taxation at twice the rate charged to supporters of the revolution, imprisonment, and banishment from the colony.

[90]It appears that the original sentence may have been commuted by the state legislature, but the defendant was nevertheless executed. See Emmert Bittinger, *Allegheny Passage,* Camden, ME: Penobscot Press, 1990, pp. 221ff. Methodists, too, suffered similar difficulties. "If a peron was disposed to persecute a Methodist preacher, it was only necessary to call him a *Tory,* and then they might treat him as cruelly as they pleased. For in many places existing laws were little regarded....Some of the Methodists were bound in conscience not to fight; and no threatenings could compel them to bear arms or hire a man to take their places. In consequence of this, some of them were *whipped,* some were fined, and some imprisoned; others were sent home, and many were much persecuted." Jesse Lee, *A Short History of the Methodists, in the United States of America...* Baltimore: Printed by Magill and Clime, 1810, pp. 74f, 77.

[91]According to Brethren historian Emmert Bittinger, Brethren leader Benjamin Bowman, Sr., was fined in Frederick County, Maryland on 2 July 1776 for non-association with the patriot cause. See Emmert Bittinger, "Bowman," *Mennonite Family*

History (October 1997).

[92]As many as 800 to 1,000 troops were estimated to have waited for Tarleton, who had been driven back by Lafayette prior to his attempt to cross the Blue Ridge. The Assembly first met at the Augusta parish church on 7 June 1781, and then returned for several days after Tarleton had been repulsed. Harrison, *Grey Trail,* 243f.

[93]Henkel, Tagebuch, 9. In a very real sense, the conflict with the Indians had taken only brief interludes since the early 1750s. A number of Augustans — including perhaps Adam Miller's son, Adam — were killed at the battle of Point Pleasant in October of 1764, only a year after a treaty had ended the French and Indian War. The colonies revolution against England brought a renewed excuse for battle.

[94]Among the many reimbursements for goods and produce, there is one to John Hopkins [a Cook's Creek Presbyterian name] for 4 head of cattle...for use of the militia ordered on duty to Carolina, October 3, 1780, and another for a wagon, three horses, etc. lost in the service of General Stevans in Carolina on September 27, 1780. RCMB 1:121 (26 March 1782: for Hopkins' cattle in October 1780), 1:144 (23 April 1782: for September 1780 loss), in Levinson, *Minute Book,* 1:104, 119. Other examples of duties assigned to the Rockingham militia were scouting and keeping guard. Colonel Samuel Lewis' regiment marched to Williamsburg and "Little York" where they assisted in the surrender of Cornwallis and guarded the prisoners to Winchester. *Virginia Revolutionary Pension Applications,* Abstracted and compiled by John Frederick Dorman, Washington, D.C., 1958, 2:82f.

[95]2 November 1784. The Rockingham petitioners were supported by another petition from the Mennonist church in Virginia. McMaster, et. al., *Conscience in Crisis,* 332ff. A 1792 law did re-establish exemption and the following year Martin Kaufman's Separate Independent Baptist Church, composed of many former Mennonists, requested protection under this law but were denied. The 1792 law was also opposed by petitions from the Valley — with many German signatures — objecting to a show of favoritism toward particular sects which "evidently tends to destroy the harmony which should subsist, in society." Virginia Religious Petitions, Shenandoah County, 23 October 1793 (Coffman/Kaufman), 11 November, 21 November 1796 (quote); Brunk, *Mennonites,* 1:38. By 1799, the Assembly had removed every trace of law exempting Mennonists and Quakers from militia duty. Dunkers had never been specifically exempted by name in any act of the Virginia legislature. Shepherd 2:143 (23 January 1799).

[96]17 November 1784. Virginia Religious Petitions. Among the signatories was Silas Hart, a member of the Linville Creek Baptist Church since 18 May 1766. He became one of the first justices of Rockingham, and was also the county's first sheriff. Silas Hart's will of 1790 (probated 1795) left a bequest to the

Philadelphia Baptist Association which created no small stir. His executors refused to disburse it since the association was not incorporated. This begged the larger question of incorporation and entanglement with the state. [Beale's] Semple, *Baptists in Virginia,* 252f.

[97]Solicitor's Office Report to the Governor for the year 1783, 17 February 1785, in Palmer, *Calendar* 4:9f: "Many of the largest and wealthiest counties are charged with the greatest amount of delinquency..."

[98]Rockingham County Legislative Petitions, 20 November 1784, Box 225, Folder 15, LV. The petition contained 99 signatures. Laws in 1776, 1778, and 1782 encouraged the building and maintenance of these warehouses and provided government funds for their construction.

[99]By 1770, Dunkers had built a meeting house in Germantown township at Beggarstown. Three other Dunker meeting houses noted by Edwards that year were part of the distinctive cloister at Ephrata, and not part of typical Dunker practice. Edwards, *Pennsylvania,* 64-98, quote 90. Edwards had difficulty in obtaining information from the Mennonists in Lancaster county in the late 1760s, "owing, I believe, to a suspicion that a knowledge of their state would some way or other be to their prejudice." Edwards, *Pennsylvania,* 97f. The Dunkers he reported in Virginia in 1772 had "been much harassed by reason of their [Virginia] militia law and their scrupling to take an oath." Edwards, "Virginia," 104. It is no wonder that Mennonist and Dunker origins in Virginia are sometimes difficult to trace.

[100]D. H. Zigler, *A History of the Brethren in Virginia,* Elgin, IL: Brethren Publishing House, 1908, pp. 43ff.

[101]*The Life of the Rev. Devereux Jarratt, Written by Himself,* 107f, quoted in George Brydon, *Virginia's Mother Church* (2 vols.) Philadelphia: Church History Society, 1947-1952, 2:221 n19.

[102]Early Virginia Religious Petitions, 2 October 1776.

[103]Lee, *Short History,* 72f; *Methodist Minutes,* 26; As noted above, the Virginia legislature reduced the role of the vestry to purely civil functions in 1776, effectively "temporarily" suspending the Anglican establishment. At war's end, the existence of an established church was on tenuous ground in the new republic, but the last vestiges of preferential treatment for the Anglican tradition would not be eliminated until the next century.

[104]Letter from John Wesley to Dr. Coke, Mr. Asbury, and our Brethren in North America, 10 September 1784, in *Minutes of the Methodist Conferences from 1773 to 1813,* pp. 49ff; The conference of preachers met in Baltimore that Christmas Eve, but no minutes of their meeting are extant. Francis Asbury, *The Journal and Letters of Francis Asbury In Three Volumes,*

Elmer T. Clark, Editor-in-Chief, Nashville: Abingdon Press, 1958, 1:473ff.

[105]Winchester had 1650 inhabitants in 1790; Staunton was about half that size. U.S. Bureau of the Census, 1790, 10 n34; Asbury, *Journal and Letters*, 1:443.

[106]The quote is from William Hill, a Presbyterian leader. Foote, *Sketches*, 1:412.

[107]Though the records of many churches are blank through these war years, it would be wrong to assume that there was no interest in meeting together or in the spiritual life of the church. The family of Paul Henkel — a young man who would become a Lutheran leader in the Shenandoah Valley and elsewhere — "made arrangements with several of our households so that we could come together in a house on Sundays. A man who was from old England read the prayers and the psalms which were appointed in the English Episcopal [Anglican] Church." Henkel, Tagebuch, 9.

[108]Foote, *Sketches of Virginia*, 1:412ff, 466f. In 1789, in response to a request from the Cook's Creek minister the year before, the Lexington Presbytery recognized the Presbyterians in Harrisonburg as a distinct church, but this probably had no connection to the revival. Minutes of the Lexington Presbytery, 1788, 15 April 1789, referenced in Wilson, *Lexington Presbytery*, 376.

[109]In March, 1789, Baptist minister John Leland reported, "Since the year 1785, there has been a great work of God in Virginia, nearly 6000 have been baptized." John Leland, *The Virginia Chronicle*, Fredericksburg, VA?: T. Green?, 1789, p. 7, photostat of only known copy, UVA. In this 1789 edition, Leland also reported that at the beginning of the war, more than half the people in Virginia were dissenters. Neither statistic is repeated in the expanded 1790 editions. John Leland, *The Virginia Chronicle*, in *The Writings of the Late Elder John Leland*. New York: G. W. Wood, 1845, pp. 114ff; Minutes of Linville Creek Baptist Church, p. 34 (Saturday before 2nd Sabbath in December 1789); and see also p. 48 (8 December 1792: when the church "agree'd to postpone the Appointment of such Meetings…"), HSP. Further evidence of Baptist growth in Rockingham and vicinity during this revival is the mention of a "North River Church" (p. 33, 2nd Sabbath in November 1789), and "certain Baptists living on and about the North and Dry Rivers of Shenandoah." The latter group eventually united with the Linville Creek Baptists and was in effect the genesis of the Salem Baptist church near Dayton, constituted in 1813. Minutes of Linville Creek Baptist Church, p. 40f (13 August 1791), 41 (10 September 1791), 42 (3 September 1791: reporting on earlier meeting), 44f (12 February, 3 March, 10 March 1792), HSP; *Minutes of the Shiloh Association*, 1813, VBHS. Note also that the Ketocton Association churches gave up their practice of laying on of hands after baptism as an essential part of that ordinance, another effect the revival tended to produce. [Beale's] Semple, *Baptists in Virginia*, 388f.

[Side 6] John Firth, *The Experience and Gospel Labour of the Rev. Benjamin Abbott*. Harrisonburg, VA: Printed by A. Davisson. For James A. Dillworth, Rockingham County, Virginia, 1820, pp. 101f. This book had been published previously in New York in 1809. Interestingly, Dillworth soon afterward entered into the bookbinding business. *Rockingham Weekly Register*, 17 May 1823; Spayth, *A History of the United Brethren in Christ*, 30; Asbury, *Journal and Letters*, 1:212f, 221. About the same time, Methodist Bishop Francis Asbury spoke of a meeting in which "The operations of the Holy Spirit were very powerful in the congregation; so that there was a general melting." The terms "melting" and "melting time," used often in connection with the love feast, perhaps attempted to express this sort of powerful encounter with God, the overpowering of his divine presence. Asbury, *Journal and Letters*, 1:245 (28 July 1777: "melted into tears and shook like a leaf"), 295 (2 February 1779: "The operations of the Holy Spirit were very powerful in the congregation; so that there was a general melting; and amongst the young people, there were outcries and deep distress."); Newcomer, *Journal*, 57.

[110]Smith's Creek Baptist Church Minutes, 7 February 1789, quoted in F. Edward Wright, *Early Church Records of Rockingham County, Virginia*, Westminster, MD: Family Line Publications, 1998, p. 69. Originals (1779-1805) at VBHS.

[111]Lee, *Short History*, 107.

[112]Though the prayer book was used for a season, some of the preachers used to praying extemporaneously were not willing to use it, "[b]eing fully satisfied that they could pray better, and with more devotion while their eyes were shut, than they could with their eyes open. After a few years the prayer book was laid aside…" Lee, *Methodists*, 107. Brydon notes that "Bishop Madison speaks of the thousands of men who in accepting deistic principles gave up belief in God as a power in human lives, and denied the usefulness of any form of organized religion. This school of thought became exceedingly strong in Virginia, and had its center at the College of William and Mary." Brydon, *Virginia's Mother Church*, 479f.

[113]The Baptists also had a congregational form of church government, with various churches joining together in loosely structured "associations." The Methodists were hierarchical in structure, which caused some trouble early on within the denomination in Virginia. For a discussion of the "Republican Methodists," see Brydon, *Virginia's Mother Church*, 2:219.

[114]The Linville Creek Baptists would even try to cooperate — unsuccessfully — with the Methodists in building a new meeting house in late 1802. The Baptists would not use their own new building until the summer of 1809, more than four years after they decided to draw up a subscription to pay for it. Minutes of the Linville Creek Baptist Church, 13 November

1802, 9 March 1805, 20 August 1809, HSP. The deed was made by Robert and Reuben Harrison to the Methodist Episcopal Church Trustees, David Horner, Jeremiah Ragan, Richard Ragan, John Hicks, James Mitchell, John Harrison, and Joseph Denny. It is likely the building was not completely furnished until 1795. RCDB/Burnt 0:391 (26 October 1789); Harrisonburg was not established as a town until 1780, but Thomas Harrison's had been the place where court was held since 22 November 1779. Hening 10:295 (May 1780: "Thomas Harrison of the county of Rockingham hath laid off 50 acres of his land, where the courthouse for the said county now stands…"); RCMB 1:49 (22 November 1779: Court adjourned to Thomas Harrison's on account of a "dangerous and malignant fever" at the Smiths'), in Levinson, *Minute Book*, 1:49.

[115]The twelve amendments collectively known as the Bill of Rights were approved by the U.S. Congress on 24-25 September 1789. Ten of these were later ratified by the requisite number of states. Interestingly, Vermont's ratification in November of 1789 left Virginia as the last state to act, a decision it managed to put off with the help of its anti-Federalist contingent until 15 December 1791. The first amendment's language barring establishment of religion was initially resisted by the Senate. Leonard W. Levy, *Origins of the Bill of Rights*, New Haven: Yale University Press, 1999, pp. 40ff.

[116]Hening 12:84-86 (19 January 1786).

[117]Hening 11:532ff, 12:266f.

[118]Brydon, *Virginia's Mother Church*, 2:608ff.

[119]Goodwin, *Colonial Church*, 130. On the same ship bringing Madison home from his London ordination as bishop of Virginia, was "the Right Rev. Doctor John Carroll, recently consecrated Bishop of the Catholic Church in the United States." *Pennsylvania Gazette*, 22 December 1790.

[120]There is a tradition that someone by the name of Chambers officiated at the Staunton church, but left for Kentucky in 1788. Waddell, *Annals*, 277. The first post-war service in the Staunton church about which we have any detailed information was in 1811. Interestingly enough, it was conducted by former Methodist William King who had received ordination as an Episcopal deacon. Meade, *Old Churches*, 2:322. Rockingham's Episcopal parish would not be finally re-organized until 1865 at Port Republic. There were, however, Episcopal services at Port Republic in the 1850s by James B. Goodwyn and John C. Wheat. Wayland, *Rockingham*, 252; Meade, *Old Churches*, 2:324.

[121]Meade, *Old Churches*, 2:324.

[122]John Wesley strongly disapproved of Asbury's use of the title of *Bishop*. "I shudder, I start at the very thought," he wrote to Asbury on 20 September 1788, "put a full end to this." Asbury, however, does not seem to have been caught up in the trappings of protocol. On his way from Harrisonburg and Rockingham in June 1793, Asbury "was met by an old German, who shook me by the hand, and said he wished he might be worthy to wash my feet. Yea, thought I, if you knew what a poor sinful creature I am, you would hardly look at one so unworthy; but Jesus lives — O precious Christ, thou art mine and I am thine!" Asbury, *Journal and Letters*, 1:648 (11-13 August 1790), 760; Brydon, *Virginia's Mother Church*, 2:214.

[123]There was one notable difference between Baker and Jones, however. Baker did not own any slaves. Michael Baker was appointed captain of a militia unit towards the end of the Revolutionary War. *The Personal Property Tax Lists for the Year 1787 for Rockingham County, Virginia*, edited by Netti Schreiner-Yantis and Florene Speakman Love. Springfield, VA: Genealogical Books in Print, 1987; Harry M. Strickler, *Tenth Legion Tithables*, Luray, VA: published by the author, 1930, p. 33; Landowner's List of 1789 in Wayland, *Rockingham*, 449. RCMB 1:95 (29 May 1781), in Levinson, *Minute Book*, 1:88. Inside the front cover of RCDB/Burnt 0 is a copy of a deed dated 24 August 1779 from John and Hannah Miller to Michael Baker for 398 acres on the north branch of "Shannandoe" in the Gap of the Mountains. The plat, also described as lying on the east side of Beaver Dam Run and adjacent to Paul Kester's land, was first granted to George Forbush by patent on 12 January 1746 and then by deed to the Millers on 5-6 August 1748. ACDB 2:5ff (6 August 1748).

[124]Asbury, *Journal and Letters*, 1:648 (11-15 August 1790).

[125]*Methodist Minutes*, 84 (1789: Rockingham circuit established, 79 "whites," 5 "colored"), 94 (1790: 287 "whites," 48 "colored"). The Rockingham circuit at that time embraced more than the county itself.

[126]Rev. L. Rosser, *Class Meetings: Embracing their Origin, Nature, Obligation, and Benefits*. Richmond, VA: published by the author, 1855, p. 45. Classes originated to help collect monies to relieve the debt of the Bristol, England chapel, and were similar in nature to the meetings of the Fetter-Lane Society of which Wesley had been a part in his associations with the Moravians and others. In May 1738, they met together once a week "to confess our faults one to another, and pray one for another, that we may be healed." Wesley, *Journal*, 1:90. See also James 5:14-16.

[127]Rosser, *Class Meetings*, 57f. "It was in Georgia that Wesley had first witnessed the Moravian love feast, and this soon became one of the most moving religious occasions in English Methodism…." Love feasts faded in most places with the rise of the camp meetings. Baker, *Wesley to Asbury*, 190f. See also Frank Baker, *Methodism and the Love-feast*. London: Epworth Press, 1957, pp. 9-31.

[128]"Love Feast," *The Brethren Encyclopedia*. Philadelphia: The

Brethren Encyclopedia, Inc., 1983, 2:762ff. The love feast of the early church concluded with a distribution of food for the poor.

[129]*Virginia Gazette and Weekly Advertiser,* 6, 13 August 1785.

[130]"It was no uncommon thing for the farmer, for several years after the commencement of the French Revolution [1794, as he dates it], to sell his crops of wheat from one to two, and sometimes at two and a half dollars per bushel, and his flour from ten to fourteen dollars per barrel in our seaport towns." Kercheval, *Valley,* 153.

[131]Bishop James Madison, Address to the People of the Church, *Journal Convention of 1799,* 78-83, quoted in Brydon, *Virginia's Mother Church,* 2:480. Deism was widely promulgated in Thomas Paine's *The Age of Reason,* published in 1794 and 1795, who placed "religion" in stark opposition to the atheism which propelled the French revolution. Thomas Paine, *An Oration…Delivered, July 17th, 1799.* Boston: Printed by John Russell, 1799, pp. 5ff, UVA-M.

[132]Goodwin, *Colonial Church,* 132.

[133]Asbury, *Journal and Letters,* 1:644 (30 June 1790: in Virginia).

[134]Asbury had requested Otterbein to be one of those who "laid hands" upon him as part of his ordination as the Methodist bishop. Lee, *Methodists,* 91; Christian Newcomer, *The Life and Journal of the Rev'd Christian Newcomer.* Transcribed, corrected, and translated by John Hildt, Hagerstown, MD: FGW Kapp, 1834. [Facsimile reprint, Abram Sangrey, Editor. Lancaster, PA:…United Methodist Church, 1996], pp. 13f, quote p. 13; Henry Boehm, *The Patriarch of One Hundred Years…Reminiscences.* Rev. J. B. Wakely, [Editor]. Lancaster PA: Abram Sangrey, 1982 [Facsimile reprint of NY: Nelson & Phillips, 1875], p. 387. The United Brethren were also known by the following: the Brethren, the Unsectarian, the Liberty People, New Reformed, New Mennonites, and Otterbein's or Boehm's People, among other names. A.P. Funkhouser, *History of the Church of the United Brethren in Christ, Virginia Conference.* Dayton, VA: Reubush-Kieffer Co., 1921, p. 40f.

[135]George Adam Geeting [Güting], William Otterbein and Martin Boehm, have been described as the "clover leaf" of the early United Brethren church, and Henry Boehm considered Geeting the most gifted speaker among their preachers. Funkhouser, *Virginia Conference,* 43, 48. His name is spelled Meyer[s] in Newcomer's journal, but Moyers elsewhere. Bockett's stages, which ran in the early 19th century, took three days to make the trip from Staunton to Winchester. Carr, *Rocktown,* 5; Wayland, *Harrisonburg,* 342 (transcription of "Harrisonburg Fifty Years Ago," *Rockingham Register,* 5 October 1876).

[136]Newcomer, *Journal,* 30f.

[137]"Being convinced of the necessity of order and discipline in the Church of God, and having no wish to be at the head of a separate body, I advised serious persons to join the Methodists…" Martin Boehm quoted by his son, Henry Boehm, in *Reminiscences,* 374. Probably one of the main reasons for Boehm's advice was the Methodist organization of class meetings, a way of helping individual believers grow and remain accountable to God and one another. Even later, class meetings, held as necessary for membership in the Methodist society, were only suggested by United Brethren where it was "practicable" or "where the majority of the members regard it as profitable." *Disciplines of the United Brethren in Christ.* Translated and reprinted from the originals, edited by A.W. Drury. Dayton, OH: United Brethren Publishing House, 1895, pp. 21 (1815), 37 (1817). At their 1813 meeting, though, the United Brethren resolved that their statement of faith and formal discipline should be printed, they had not worked out the specifics of its contents. *Minutes of the Annual and General Conferences of the Church of the United Brethren in Christ, 1800-1818.* Translated by A. W. Drury. Dayton, OH: United Brethren Historical Society, 1897, p. 31 (6 May 1813), EMU; A. W. Drury, *History of the Church of the United Brethren in Christ.* Dayton, OH: United Brethren Publishing House, 1924 (1951), p. 819f, EMU.

[138]Records of Harrisonburg Methodist Church, AUMC.

[139]Asbury, *Journal and Letters,* 1:759f (1-5? June 1793), 2:49 (13-14 May 1795).

[140]The discord may also have been due to the Methodists' Arminian viewpoint vis-à-vis the strong Calvinism of the Baptists and Presbyterians. Asbury, *Journal and Letters,* 1:649. The Calvinism of the Baptists may be seen in the first two English Baptist confessions (1646, 1677) which stated, "God hath, before the foundation of the world, foreordained some men to eternal life through Jesus Christ, to the praise and glory of His grace: leaving the rest in their sin, to their just condemnation, to the praise of His justice…" Bettenson, *Documents,* 349, 351. Yet, Presbyterians, newly awakened as a denomination by a revival which included emotional expression, were attending Methodist meetings at this time.

[141]*Documentary History,* 187. Glatfelter, *Pastors and People,* 1:25-27. See also Eisenberg, *Lutheran,* 102f.

[142]The earliest known deed for Frieden's church is dated 8 October 1782, a facsimile of which can be seen in a local, unpublished history prepared by the congregation. A second deed is dated 4 September 1787. RCDB/Burnt 0:371f.

[143]*Documentary History,* 231f, 241, 287 (24 May 1796: Foltz); Glatfelter, *Pastors and People,* 1:15. Records of Upper Peaked Mountain Church, MRL; Eisenberg, *Lutheran,* 102f. John Foltz

spent several months with Lutheran minister Paul Henkel in the winter of 1788 "to learn German writing better" and later served as a teacher. Henkel, *Tagebuch*, 93; Johannes Foltz's brother, Sebastian, began preaching in Rockingham at this same time. Tradition holds that Sebastian donated some of his own land for the (Little) St. John's church at one time located near Singers Glen. *Documentary History*, 311 (June 1800), 337f (June 1803).

[144]His remarks referred to the Reformed congregation in Frederick, Maryland. Harbaugh, *Fathers of the Reformed Church*, 2:293ff, quote 294.

NOTES FOR CHAPTERS 7, 8, and 9 — RAPIDS

[1]Braun made his first trip to Virginia in October 1798 in the company of Carl Stock, his mentor who lived in Chambersburg, Pennsylvania. He was officially licensed by the Reformed Synod on 13 May 1800 at their meeting in York. *Acts and Proceedings of the Coestus and Synod of the German Reformed Church in the United States from 1791 to 1816 inclusive*. [Chambersburg, PA: M. Kieffer & Co., 1854], reprinted 1930 by instruction of the Eastern Synod; Garrison, *Reformed*, 63, referencing notes made by Braun in the 1841 Classis of Virginia records, ERHS. This particular trip likely originated from York, following his licensing by the Synod. Paul Henkel mentions that a travelling companion, Lutheran minister Johannes Volz, while on the road south of Staunton in December of 1788 "said he was afraid of robbers on the road, since it was reckoned to be twenty miles to the next house. My comfort was the fierce cold, because of which robbers would not stay outside." Henkel, *Tagebuch*, 93f. "After he [Braun] was licensed to preach the Gospel, he was told that he must go to Virginia, as a missionary to the German population then settled in Shenandoah and Rockingham counties; where he arrived, (as I am informed by an Old resident of Shenandoah, who says he remembers well when he came to his Father's house) Staff in hand, for it was not the good fortune of the early pioneers our Church, to be equiped *[sic]* after the order of the present day." J. C. Hensell, "Rev. John Brown D. D. of Rockingham County Va.," undated manuscript [1856?], ERHS. Hensell, a Reformed minister in the Valley, had known Braun for about sixteen years, from 1834 to 1850. The distance of 200 miles is an approximation from York to Braun's first residence in Rockingham, the former home of Reformed minister Daniel Hoffman who had died in June 1798. See the partial translation of Johannes Braun's memorandum book published as *Shenandoah Valley Family Data, 1799-1813*,

translated and annotated by Klaus Wust and edited in cooperation with Joseph H. Meyerhoeffer, Edinburg, VA: Shenandoah History, 1978, p. 8.

[2]Harbaugh, *Fathers*, 3:122ff.

[3]According to a later friend of Johannes Braun, "He once stated to me that when on Sea, he dreamed he was in Baltimore saw the city just as it was, & among other things the old Otterbine Church then standing on a hill in which he went & worshipped with the congregation. After he landed Baltimore instead of being a strange place was familiar to him every thing as he saw it in his dream & the church standing upon the hill, & when Sabbath came he went to that church & was greatly encouraged & profited." Letter of D[aniel]. Feete, 14 September 1856, Mt. Crawford, p. 2, ERHS. It was likely only after he arrived that he discovered the name of the pastor of the Evangelical Reformed Church on Howard's Hill was William Otterbein. Harbaugh, *Fathers*, 3:123 note; Drury, *United Brethren*, 114ff.

[4]Feete considered Braun's initial interview with Stock "accidental. He probably knew nothing of him untill he met him there & by that time fully came to the conclusion to study for the ministry," a conclusion Feete said was strengthened during his time under Otterbein's ministry. Feete, 14 September 1856, p. 2. John Philip Stock, Braun's mentor and a Reformed minister, should not be confused with Victor George Charles Stock (also Carl Stock, or V.G.C. Stochus), a licensed candidate to the Lutheran ministry who was at Peaked Mountain church on 6 March 1796. That year, Carl Stock reported both English and German schools in his charge. Peaked Mountain Church Records, MRL; *Documentary History*, 241, 283, 286, 290; Eisenberg, *Lutheran*, 90.

[5]"Father Brown," as his congregations called him, formally received a call from churches in Rockingham at the Coetus meeting on 12 May 1800. As was the custom, he was licensed for three consecutive one-year terms before being ordained, which took place on 10 May 1803. *Acts and Proceedings of the Coetus and Synod of the German Reformed Church, 1791-1816*. [Hereafter *Coetus Records* 2] Chambersburg, PA: Printed by M. Kieffer & Co., 1854 [reprinted 1930], pp. 26, 36. In Brown's own history of the Reformed Church in Virginia, he notes his service to Virginia began in October 1798. His second visit was the following February. Garrison, *Reformed*, 63, referencing the opening pages of the 1841 Classis of Virginia Minute Book. It was during his second visit in 1799 that Braun secured formal "calls" from three Rockingham churches (Friedens, 10 February; Peaked Mountain, 17 February; Keezletown, 24 February), and one Augusta congregation (Jennings Branch, 3 March). Afterward, he returned to Chambersburg to complete more studies with Philip Stock so that he might apply as a candidate for the Reformed ministry. Wust, *Family Data*, 8.

[6]Feete, 14 September 1856, p. 2.

[7]Weiss's [Weiß's] church was later renamed St. Michael's. The Augusta congregations were Zion's, St. John's, Salem, and The Branch. Letter of D[aniel]. Feete, 1 February 1852, Mt. Crawford, p. 2, ERHS. Pendleton County, now in West Virginia, was formed in 1787 from Rockingham, Augusta, and Hardy counties. Hening 12:637f (4 December 1787).

[8]Harbaugh, *Fathers*, 3:126; Braun was never able to preach in English, and for some time resisted the introduction of English in worship services. Yet, he did publish *A Short Instruction According to the Heidelberg Cateschism [sic] in German and English,* a parallel bilingual volume. Harrisonburg: Printed by Lawrence Wartmann, Rockingham County, Virginia. 1830, EMU; Feete, 14 September 1856, p. 7; Hensell, "Brown," p. 3, both ERHS.

The previous month, the United Brethren had formed their own denomination, the United Brethren in Christ, with its first two bishops Martin Boehm and William Otterbein. Funkhouser, *Virginia Conference*, 41. Christian Newcomer would eventually be ordained a bishop in the new denomination, while Henry Boehm would accompany the Methodist, Bishop Asbury.

[10]Newcomer notes that John Peters lived 3 miles from New Market and 16 miles from Keezletown. He is travelling what fifty years earlier was called the Indian or Waggon Road, the main north-south route through the Valley through the 1820s. Newcomer, *Journal*, 73, 123. *Rockingham Register*, 5 October 1876 referenced in Wayland, *Rockingham*, 221. John Peters was appointed a militia captain in 1784. RCMB 1:352 (28 June 1784), in Levinson, *Minute Book*, 1:243.

[11]Newcomer, *Journal*, 71.

[12]Newcomer "was not a great preacher except in earnestness of purpose. He had a slight impediment in his speech and his voice was but moderately strong." Funkhouser, *Virginia Conference*, 53.

[13]Newcomer, *Journal*, 71.

[14]At this home Martin Boehm baptized young Daniel Strickler and his wife. Newcomer, *Journal*, 72. In April 1863, United Brethren minister George Snapp stopped for dinner "at old Bro. Stricklers" near Mountain Valley [now United Methodist] just north of Keezeltown. "The Civil War Diary of George H. Snapp," transcribed by Roger Sappington, *The Rockingham Recorder* (April 1985), 3(3):107.

[15]One hundred acres was set apart as "Keissell's-Town" on 7 December 1791. Hening 13:297. A meeting house open to all denominations had been built in Keezletown by the fall of 1790. RCDB/Burnt 0:467ff (25 October 1790: "Beginning at a stake near the northeast corner of the meeting house…Lot No. 0").

[16]Joseph Travis, *Autobiography of the Rev. Joseph Travis, A. M.* Edited by Thomas O. Summers, D.D. Nashville, TN: E. Stevenson & F.A. Owen, Agents, for the Methodist Episcopal Church, South, 1856, p. 21. In 1799, itinerant Methodist minister Enoch George returned to Rockingham Circuit where he reported "the windows of heaven were again opened, and grace descended upon us." Apparently, these divisions were recent, though Asbury had reported even earlier that "Satan has been sowing discord" in Rockingham. Asbury, *Journal and Letters,* 1:759 (June 1793); Abel Stevens, *A Compendious History of American Methodism in History of the Methodist Episcopal Church.* New York: Carlton & Porter, 1867, pp. 344ff. Online at the University of Michigan's *Making of America* website, http://www.hti.umich.edu/m/moagrp/.

[17]An article from the *Rockingham Register* of 5 October 1876, says that "Fifty years ago Jas. Burgess occupied the house opposite Geo. O. Conrad's present residence," in 1885 located on the southwest corner of German and Bruce. Wayland, *Harrisonburg,* 338; Lakes 1885 Atlas. Yet by the census of 1810, James Burgess was already living in the growing town of Port Republic where he had purchased land the year before. and where he also became part of a Methodist class. RCDB/Burnt 1:347 (13 October 1809: Carthrae to Burgess), Port Republic Methodist Class book of Josiah Emmit for 1812 & 1813; May, Port Republic, 17f, 50f.

[18]"…most of the persons present were engaged either as subjects or instruments." Asbury, *Journal and Letters,* 2:360.

[19]Land for the old stone Presbyterian church building, located at the corner of East Market Street and Federal Alley in Harrisonburg, was deeded 25 September 1792 by Charles McClain. RCDB/Burnt 000:377; RCMB 2:93 (25 September 1792); *Rockingham Register*, 21 May 1885. During the early days of Asbury's visits, Presbyterians often attended Methodist meetings, having just experienced a similar revival of their own. Methodist historian and preacher Jesse Lee noted "At that time there was great union between the Presbyterians and the Methodists; and they frequently communed together, and united in holding camp-meetings, and in preaching together." Lee, *Short History,* 294. Just a handful of years later, this relationship seems to have changed. Travelling further south up the Valley, Asbury noted, "Friendship and good fellowship seem to be done away between the Methodists and Presbyterians; few of the latter will attend our meetings now: well, let them feed their flocks apart; and let not Judah vex Ephraim, or Ephraim, Judah; and may it thus remain, until the two sticks become one in the Lord's hands." 19 August 1806, Asbury, *Journal and Letters,* 2:515. The previous year when a woman in an Augusta county Presbyterian congregation began exhibiting the "jerks" — a sudden movement of the limbs sometimes seen in Methodist meetings — she was dragged out by another

Presbyterian in the belief that it "would not do to dance in meeting." Since her removal apparently violated a state statute against interference in religious worship services, the incident went to the county court. There the fellow who removed her was acquitted since his action met the approval of the congregation and pastor. Augusta County Judgments, September 1806, referenced in Chalkley, *Chronicles,* 2:37. In 1820, Rockingham Presbyterian Ananias Davisson published a songbook particularly for "his Methodist friends." Ananias Davisson, *Supplement to the Kentucky Harmony.* Harrisonburg, VA: Printed by Ananias Davisson, 1820, EMU.

[20]As the Presbyterians had agreed when they reunited after the Old Side/New Side split of the 1740s and 1750s, emotional experiences alone did not mean that a person had become a Christian. A personal commitment to Christ would be evidenced by a growing change of character. Lorenzo Dow, an itinerant minister associated with the Methodists, initially doubted the authenticity of "the jerks" — a sudden, involuntary movement of the body — as evidence of God's power. Dow paid a visit to Harrisonburg, where he preached in the northeast corner of the Court yard. Cathy Luchetti, *Under God's Spell: Frontier Evangelists, 1772-1915.* New York, NY: Harcourt Brace Jovanovich, 1989, p. 92f; Carr, *Rocktown,* 32.

[21]This could very well be the same Henry Shaver whom the itinerant Lutheran minister Robert Miller found living on Smith's Creek in 1813. "…rode to Henry Shaver's, on Smith's Creek, a kind man, raised a methodist in Harrisonburgh, and his wife a dunkard — She nor none of her children are baptized." Minutes of the North Carolina Synod 1813, p. 37, UVA-M.

[22]Travis, *Autobiography,* 23f. Asbury returned Tuesday to preach again, but then left once more for a rest. His sermon, on the transformation of the life of Jacob (Genesis 32:26, 27) — "his name and his nature were changed; his privileges were increased, and his power enlarged with God and man" — was a fitting description of Leonard Cassell. Those who knew the 18-year-old preacher marveled "how great a mind had been thus called from uncultivated darkness, to dawn forth. The improvement he made by watchful care and diligent attention to the Spirit and Word of Grace, were such as to astonish his pleased friends and to confound the adversaries of God, who were constrained to acknowledge the miraculous power, which alone could so soon, and with such depth and precision, instruct in the mystery of divinity a person so uncultured before." *Methodist Minutes,* 277, 445f; Asbury, *Journal and Letters,* 2:360.

[23]Lee, *Short History,* 286.

[24]Travis, *Autobiography,* 24.

[25]Travis, *Autobiography,* 24f. Large numbers of people coming to Christ were not unique to Rockingham County in these

days. In 1805, one historian reported, "The revival [referring to another one in Carolina] commenced on the first day of the meeting, and continued with increasing interest and power until Sabbath. Persons of all descriptions and all ages, from the child nine years of age to the hoary-headed sinner, were subjects. The revival did not close with the meeting, but spread abroad among the surrounding settlements until three hundred were converted. A camp-meeting was also held at a place called Hampton, belonging to General Ridgeley, about ten miles from Baltimore, which lasted four days. There were about thirty preachers present, and a large number of people were made the subjects of converting grace. Meetings of the same description were held at Linville's Creek, Rehoboth, and Big Levels in Virginia, and in the Mississippi territory, some of which lasted more than a week, and at all of which numbers were converted." W.P. Strickland, *The Pioneer Bishop: or, The Life and Times of Francis Asbury.* New York: Carlton & Porter, 1858, p. 363.

[26]This estimate is from Travis, but Jesse Lee says that on Sunday, the last day of the meeting, 107 joined Society, "most of whom lived in, or near the town." Throughout the nine days, Lee reported, "there was a constant crowd of people from the country….The number of those who lived at a distance, and shared in that gracious visitation, has not been ascertained; but it is probable it bore a proportion to those in the town." Lee, *Methodists,* 286.

[27]The Hoffman place was later the site of the first three United Brethren camp-meetings in Rockingham County, from 1819-1821. Hoffman eventually moved to Augusta county, where the Mt. Zion congregation gathered. Newcomer, *Journal,* 263, 270, 276; Funkhouser, *Virginia Conference,* 48f, 225, 232ff.

[28]Newcomer, *Journal,* 99.

[29]From 1802, the United Brethren ministers "decided not to keep a register of the members of the church," perhaps likening it to the time the Israelite king David took a census and brought judgment on all of Israel (2 Samuel 24; 1 Chronicles 21). They did not begin making their numerical statistics known until 1857. Funkhouser, *Virginia Conference,* 51; Drury, *Glossbrenner,* 103. In 1802 there were 260 white and 20 African Methodists in the Rockingham circuit. The following year there were 545 and 72, respectively. Between 1802 and 1805, more than 670 people would join the Methodists ranks in Rockingham, growing six times faster than the denomination at large. In 1805, the total "whites" in the Methodist circuit of Rockingham numbered 850; total "colored," 102. This ratio of Africans to Europeans was roughly proportionate to the general population. *Methodist Minutes,* 273, 291, 314, 345. Of the 12,753 people counted in Rockingham during the 1810 census, 213 were "free blacks," and 1491 were slaves.

[30]30 June 1774, *Virginia Gazette* (Purdie & Dixon),

Williamsburg, VA. Bacchus was aware of the Somerset case of 1770, which declared that any slaves brought to England were free, since there was no Parliamentary law establishing slavery there. The original of this advertisement and many others may be found in The Runaway Slave Database at http://www.wise.virginia.edu/history/runaways/. In 1790, there were 772 African slaves in the county out of a total population of 7,449. In this particular census, besides "whites," there were no other free persons enumerated. Netti Schreiner-Yantis and Florence Speakman Love, *The Personal Property Tax Lists for the Year 1787 for Rockingham County, Virginia.* Springfield, VA: Genealogical Books in Print, 1987. *Heads of Families at the First Census of the United States Taken in the Year 1790.* including *Records of the State Enumerations: 1782 to 1785, Virginia.* Baltimore: Genealogical Publishing Co., Inc., 1986, p. 9.

[31]Even the Mennonites, adamantly against owning slaves of their own, accepted the labor of slaves when work was exchanged among neighbors. Hartman, *Reminiscences,* 5. Hiring someone else's slaves became a familiar way of supporting the system in Virginia.

[32]Hinke, "Madison County," *VMHB* 14:145.

[33]Matthew 22:39. Dunkers had made statements about slavery as early as 1782. Zigler, *Brethren,* 79. At a later day, Mennonists would accept the labor of slaves when neighbors exchanged work with one another. Hartman, *Reminiscences,* 5. United Brethren in Christ would also take considerable abuse for their anti-slavery stand.

[34]"The Case of black Members or Slaves was consider'd, that is, whether they should be admitted to a Seat among us on Days of Business, when meeting with us on those Days; Resolv'd that they should." Minutes of the Linville Creek Baptist Church, p. 43 (12 November 1791), HSP. Giving African members a *seat* did not at all guarantee them the privilege to *vote.* On 1 August 1791, eastern Virginian Robert Carter, a wealthy slave-owner who had become a Baptist, manumitted (or "released") more than 500 of his 2400 slaves. From 1785 to 1795, the Baptist church meeting at Carter's home plantation of Nomini Hall was the largest Baptist congregation in the state. Carter's actions and attitudes towards Africans were certainly felt in every Baptist church — not to mention the rest of society — throughout Virginia. Louis Morton, *Robert Carter of Nomini Hall,* Williamsburg, VA: Colonial Williamsburg, Inc., 1941, pp. 234ff.

[35]Minutes of the Linville Creek Baptist Church, p. 54 (10 May 1794), HSP.

[36]Galatians 3:28. Both Cornelius Ruddle, a "person of quality" and former Church of England man, as well as their first minister, John Alderson, Sr., were dismissed from membership for their actions. Alderson was restored exactly 31 months later.

Minutes of the Linville Creek Baptist Church, pp. 20 (second Saturday in September 1773, 11 June 1774), 22 (13 August 1774: Alderson suspended), 23 (13 March 1777: Alderson restored), HSP.

[37]The case between Sister Margaret Harrison and Brother Joe is in the Linville Creek Baptist Church Minutes from 10 May - 9 August 1794, pp. 54-56, HSP. The Ketoc[k]ton Association, of which the Linville Creek Baptists were a part until 1801, crafted a plan for the gradual emancipation of slaves at its April 1797 meeting, but it met with such severe opposition from local congregations that the idea was abandoned by the following year. Minutes of the Ketockton Association, 1795, 1796, 1797, 1801, UVA-M; [Beale's] Semple, *Baptists in Virginia,* 392.

[38]There were apparently no significant numbers of Mennonists or Dunkers living in that part of Virginia at that time. Testimony in the Trial of Gabriel, 6 October 1800, by Ben Woolfolk. Transcript at http://www.lva.lib.va.us/whoweare/exhibits/DeathLiberty/gabriel/gabtrial17.htm. In 1784, the Methodist position was to expel any members who bought slaves "with no other design than to hold them as slaves." *Methodist Minutes,* 47. Yet, exceptions were repeatedly made for the citizens of Virginia, and this slavery ruling met with difficulty in the southern states. As Methodist historian Jesse Lee put it in 1810, "a long experience has taught us, that the various rules which have been made on this business have not been attended with that success which was expected." Lee, *Methodists,* 88, 101f (quote 102).

[39]*A Collection of All Such Acts of the General Assembly of Virginia of a Public and Permanent Nature as Have Passed Since the Session of 1801.* Richmond, VA: Printed by Samuel Pleasants, Jr., 1808, p. 229f; The first registration law for "free blacks and mulattoes" was passed in 1793. Shepherd 1:238f (10 December 1793); see also Shepherd 2:417 (25 January 1803).

[40]Out of 213 free blacks reported in the 1810 census, extant records give evidence that only 6 had registered. 1810 Census; Dorothy A. Boyd-Rush, *Register of Free Blacks, Rockingham County, Virginia, 1807-1859.* Bowie, MD: Heritage Books, Inc., 1992, 1ff.

[41]Peters lived near the (old stone) Presbyterian church beside another saddler, Peter Harry. In 1876, his residence was no longer standing, but was noted as being "where D. R. Clemm now resides." Joshua Peters was also described as the "father of 'Billy.'" *Rockingham Register,* 5 October 1876, quoted in Wayland, *Harrisonburg,* 344. Billy was William Peters, listed along with his family in the free inhabitants of Harrisonburg in 1850. Wayland, *Harrisonburg,* 276.

[42]Treasurer's Book, Rockingham Methodist Circuit, 1798-1820. Travis, *Autobiography,* 26. In 1809, two free blacks — "men of

color" — were baptized and received into the fellowship of the Linville Creek Baptist Church, one named Lewis, the other, John Peck. Minutes of the Linville Creek Baptist Church, 4 February - 15 April 1809, p. 78f, HSP.

[43]*A Form of Discipline, for the Ministers, Preachers and Members…of the Methodist Episcopal Church in America, Considered and Approved at a Conference Held at Baltimore…1784.* Sixth Edition. Philadelphia: Printed by R. Aitken & Son, 1790, p. 49, UVA-M. "The 1804 edition of the *Discipline* included a section on slavery adapted for Virginia and the states to the *north*, since none of these states raised any legal barrier to freeing slaves." Richard K. MacMasters, *Our Strong Heritage, 1778-1988, Asbury United Methodist Church, Harrisonburg, Virginia.* n.p.:n.p., 1988, p. 17, but see Baker, *Those Incredible Methodists,* 192ff.

[44]Practicably, the rule spoke against *life-long* enslavement of Africans. Treasurer's Book, Rockingham Methodist Circuit, 1798-1820. Reuben Harrison died 15 August 1840, at the age of 86 and was buried at the old Methodist graveyard on the corner of Water and South High Street in Harrisonburg. The graves were moved in the construction of the new road (Route 42), and now a marble slab at one of the entrances to today's Community Mennonite Church memorializes at least some of those who were apparently interred here. In 1813, Lucy, "a free negro girl lately emancipated by Reuben Harrison" married a black man by the name of Shadrack. Strickler, *Marriages,* 127.

[45]Their new building, about 40 x 45 feet, could hold between 1500 and 1800 people according to Asbury's estimation. At one person per square foot, he apparently was not counting on a lot of elbow room. Ever since he first saw the meeting house, Asbury wanted to have the conference here, but something prevented it. Instead, it was apparently held in the home of Samuel McWilliams, the future location of the Methodist parsonage, on the west side of German [Liberty] Street. *Christian Advocate,* 23 February 1842, p. 2, ABWC. Asbury, *Journal and Letters,* 2:515, 3:395, 567f. The Brown's Gap Turnpike was formally opened in 1806. Jean Stephenson, "From Browns Gap to Rockfish Gap," *Potomac Appalachian Trail Club Bulletin* (October 1936), online at www.patc.net/history/archive/browngap.html.

[46]Asbury, *Journal and Letters,* 2:593. James Burgess, the class leader whom Joseph Travis found praying in the stable that moonlit evening, was one of the trustees of the Methodist church to whom land was deeded on the South River in 1793. Burgess was a business partner with Reuben Wallace, as their account book indicates. The Methodists used this log structure for several years, but it was easily prone to flooding. One Sunday a heavy rain caused the river to rise, and the worshippers had to be taken out by horseback. Until the Methodists built their own house, they used the Presbyterian brick church building. RCDB/Burnt 6:451f (4 September 1824), May, Port Republic, 48ff, 60; 1833 Methodist Property Report, Joseph K.

Ruebush Collection, II-MS-8, Box 15, EMUA. Port Republic was established on 14 January 1802, but the town was not laid off until 1805. Nearby Newhaven, "on the head of Shenandoah river…opposite to where the South river empties into the North river and to Port Republic" was established in 1804. Shepherd 2:359f, 3:49. By 1840, the population of Newhaven was 49, half that of Bridgewater. 1840 Census.

[47]Boehm, *Reminiscences,* 225; Asbury, *Journal and Letters,* 2:593 (25-26 February 1809).

[48]At the United Brethren Conference of 1803, Newcomer had wanted to bring up the idea of a closer cooperation between the two groups, but had followed someone's advice to set it aside. Soon afterward, he wished he had gone ahead with his proposal. Newcomer, *Journal,* 105f (6 April 1803).

[49]Asbury and William McKendree wrote a long letter to the United Brethren on this subject, and reply was made two months later by Martin Boehm. Drury, *United Brethren,* 808ff. Asbury saw the need for greater order among the United Brethren and Newcomer agreed, but some of his colleagues found this "unnecessary; that the word of God alone was all-sufficient…" One of the letter's encouragements was that the Methodist discipline had already been printed in German, thanks to the work of Henry Boehm. Asbury, *Journal and Letters,* 3:372 (31 July 1807); and see *Lehre und Zuchtordnung der Bischöflich-Methodistischen Kirche.* Lancaster, [PA]: Gedruckt bey Henrich und Benjamin Grimler, 1808, UVA-M. Newcomer had almost decided to leave the United Brethren, but their decision to establish a correspondence with the Methodists encouraged him to stay. Newcomer, *Journal,* 175 (10 May 1809). This formal, annual correspondence was continued until 1814 when the Methodists broke it off since the United Brethren did not seem any closer to adopting a discipline of their own. Ironically, Newcomer had written a discipline for the United Brethren as early as 1813. The correspondence between the Methodists and United Brethren was renewed in 1826, but the strong anti-slavery stance taken by the United Brethren in their 1821 Discipline would have evidently pre-empted any potential merger. Newcomer, *Journal,* 212f; Boehm, *Reminiscences,* 387. *Minutes of the Annual and General Conferences of the Church of the United Brethren in Christ,* 24 (11 May 1809); Drury, *History,* 819f (22 March 1814); Edward Armstrong, *History of the Old Baltimore Conference, from the Planting of Methodism in 1773 to the Division of the Conference in 1857.* Baltimore, MD: Printed for the Author by King Bros., Printers, 1907, pp. 164f, 211; Drury, *Disciplines,* 90f.

The United Brethren experienced significant problems between 1810 and 1820, perhaps related to their practice of licensing "converts who felt it their duty to preach," including some who ventured into the ministry "immediately on their conversion." In 1815, the first general conference of the United

Brethren officially adopted their first Discipline. A revised form was first printed in English in 1817. Funkhouser, *Virginia Conference,* 42, 68. See also A. W. Drury, *Disciplines of the United Brethren in Christ, 1814-1841.* Dayton, OH: United Brethren Publishing House, 1895, reprinted Nashville, TN: Parthenon Press, 1996.

[50] Also during this conference, members mourned the death of Leonard Cassell, the teenaged preacher who had been in the pulpit when the revival of 1802 began in Harrisonburg. See *Methodist Minutes,* 277, 445f.

[51] Bourne left Rockingham and Virginia in January, 1816, after he was deposed by the Lexington Presbytery at their meeting of 27 December 1815. It was almost exactly three years since the new Presbyterian church at Port Republic had been dedicated (Christmas Day 1812). Christie and Dumond, *George Bourne* and *The Book and Slavery Irreconcilable.* Wilmington, DE: The Historical Society of Delaware and Philadelphia: The Presbyterian Historical Society, 1969, p. 53; Minutes of Lexington Presbytery, 27 December 1815. [Note: The minutes of Lexington Presbytery relative to George Bourne's case are transcribed in Christie and Dumond, cited above.]

[52] Bourne had "resided 18 months in a vacant part of our bounds; under his preaching a Congregation has been formed," read the minutes of Lexington Presbytery on 24 April 1812. The census of 1810 located a George Bourne in Amherst County. Index to the Census of 1810.

[53] The application to the presbytery did not indicate any change in Bourne's theology. He had been ordained by the Independent Churches of England, a group likely holding to what Bernard Manning described as "decentralized Calvinism" with a congregational form of church government. Many English reached by the Methodists eventually joined Congregational churches, whose ministers had often also been influenced by the evangelical revival. *Encyclopedia Britannica* 26:252f; Lexington Presbytery Minutes, 16 & 18 October 1811, 27 December 1815. Christie and Dumond, *Bourne,* 1, referencing Theodore Bourne, "George Bourne, the Pioneer of American Antislavery," *Methodist Quarterly Review* (January 1882) 64:71 [b. 13 June 1780]. George Bourne, *The Life of the Rev. John Wesley, A.M....* Baltimore: Printed by George Dobbin and Murphy, for themselves, John Hagerty and Abner Neal, 1807, p. 347, UVA-M. Here, Bourne expresses his disapproval of the Roman Catholic church. See also *Remarks Upon a Pamphlet entitled "An Inquiry into the Validity of Methodist Episcopacy."* Second Edition. Baltimore: Printed by Geo. Dobbin and Murphy, for John Hagerty, 1807, UVA-M.

[54] Lexington Presbytery Minutes, 16 & 18 October 1811, 24 & 25 April 1812; Christie and Dumond, *Bourne,* 5ff.

[55] Lexington Presbytery Minutes, 29 October, 25 December

1812. George Bourne, *The Majesty and Condescension of God. A Sermon Delivered at the Opening of the Presbyterian Church in Port Republic on Christmas Day, 1812.* Staunton, Isaac Collett, 1813, was referenced in a later Bourne and Davidson publication, but it is not known if a copy exists today.

[56] Christie and Dumond, *Bourne,* 20. Davidson was installed as the minister of the three congregations on 11 November 1809. "Sketches of Cooke's Creek Church," *The Young Virginian* (November 1875), 2:84f, UVA.

[57] In 1787, the neighbors Gabriel Jones, Peachy Gilmer, and Thomas Lewis together reported a total of 91 slaves, while others nearby added perhaps 50 more. Schreiner-Yantis and Love, *The Personal Property Tax Lists for the Year 1787 for Rockingham County, Virginia.* Springfield, VA: Genealogical Books in Print, 1987. *Heads of Families at the First Census of the United States Taken in the Year 1790.* including *Records of the State Enumerations: 1782 to 1785, Virginia.* Baltimore: Genealogical Publishing Co., Inc., 1986, p. 9. By 1810, the number of slaves in Rockingham was 1491, almost doubled from the 1790 tally, and more than thirty people in the county owned ten or more slaves. 1810 Census. Lexington Presbytery Minutes, 27 December 1815 ["at my house in Port Republic"], referenced in Christie and Dumond, *Bourne,* 37.

[58] Testimony of Robert Herron in Bourne's presence. Lexington Presbytery Minutes, 27 December 1815.

[59] In the early 1730s, the German Lutherans on the Robinson River believed if they kept their slaves better than those among the English people and instructed them in the Christian religion, that hundreds and thousands of Africans would come to Christ, "indeed that much good could thereby be accomplished among the English." Hinke, "Madison County," *VMHB* 14:145, 170.

[60] In his letter of 28 July 1815 to A. B. Davidson, now living near Lexington, Bourne declared, "*I shall attend no more sacraments,* but in my own congregation—where a Negro-thief is not numbered." Lexington Presbytery Minutes, 27 December 1815. Bourne may have been more restrained on these issues in public sermons previous to that summer, because it was not until 16 September 1815 that Bourne's pastoral relationship with his church was mutually dissolved.

[61] Bourne's friend and associate A. B. Davidson had left Rockingham almost a year earlier, on 19 October 1814. The pastoral relationship between Davidson and his Rockingham and Augusta charges was dissolved three and a half weeks later on Saturday, 12 November. Davidson had "become somewhat enthusiastic in advocating [the war of 1812 which] created some dissatisfaction among some of his people." D.C. Irwin, "Historical Sketch of the Church of Cook's Creek and Harrisonburg," in the minutes of the Old School (Rockingham)

Presbyterian Church, 1841-1867, PAM. After Davidson was settled in Lexington, Bourne upbraided his old friend and associate for his own entanglement with slavery. Christie and Dumond, *Bourne,* 34, 49. In 1816, Bourne published *The Book and Slavery Irreconcilable* (Philadelphia: Printed by J.M. Sanderson & Co., 1816), a manuscript he had nearly finished while living in Rockingham County, but which at one time he scarcely dared to publish. Sixteen years later, William Lloyd Garrison pronounced it "the most faithful and conclusive exposition of the cruelty and sin of holding the slaves in bondage, that we have ever seen." *The Liberator,* 17 March 1832, UVA-M. Letter to A. B. Davidson, 28 July 1815 in Lexington Presbytery Minutes, 27 December 1815. Bourne's dismissal from the ministry was overturned by the General Assembly in 1817. In 1818, the Lexington Presbytery retried and convicted Bourne in his absence, and their decision stood. The 1818 meeting of the General Assembly put forth resolutions condemning slavery, but in the eyes of one observer, "The grand error was that while the church declared to the world the great sin and guilt under which the church and country lay, no corresponding effort was made in the church or through the church, to put an end to the evil and lead to repentance and reformation." The quote is from Martha W. Paxton Lagow, editor, *A Memoir of J. D. Paxton, D. D.* Philadelphia: J. B. Lippincott & Co., 1870, p. 66.

Side 7 *The Publications, of the Virginia Religious Tract Society,* Harrisonburg, VA: Davidson and Bourne, 1813, EMU (p. 11 lists the directors and officers of the society including Rev. A. B. Davidson, President, and Rev. George Bourne, Secretary); Christie and Dumond, *Bourne,* 20f, 99f; George W. Snyder. *Christ, The True God: An Essay in which the Divinity of Christ is evinced to be a Scriptural Doctrine.* Harrisonburg, [VA]: George Bourne, 1815, p. 78f, UVA-M. His former partner, A.B. Davidson, had moved near Lexington the previous fall. Lexington Presbytery Minutes, 11? November 1814, 27 December 1815. Daniel Bryan, author of *The Mountain Muse,* also supplied a poem for Bourne's book against slavery, *The Book and Slavery Irreconcilable* (p. 4). Wartmann, who had first worked for the Henkel Press in New Market, had the press up and running by the fall of 1813. Klaus Wust, "A Virginia-German Printer: Laurentz Wartmann (1775-1840)," *American German Review* (August-September 1954), 20(6): 29f, 39; see also Christopher L. Dolmetsch, *The German Press of the Shenandoah Valley,* Columbia, SC: Camden House, 1984, pp. 22ff. Bourne's dedicatory sermon the preceding Christmas was printed by Isaac Collett in Staunton, but his fast day sermon of 9 September 1813 was published by Davidson and Bourne in Harrisonburg.

[62]Undated memorial in Quarterly Conference Records of the Rockingham Circuit, 1815-1828. Original at Asbury United Methodist Church, Harrisonburg, Virginia, transcribed in MacMasters, *Asbury,* 30ff. The 1816 General Conference eventually decided to tolerate slavery among their membership in States where emancipation was prohibited by law. James

Armstrong, *Old Baltimore,* 181.

[63]The Methodist memorial also protested against the hiring of slaves, which it claimed tended "Indirectly to encourage that sin which we long to be delivered from." Undated Methodist Memorial in Rockingham Circuit in Quarterly Minutes of Rockingham Circuit, 1815-1828, AUMC, quoted in MacMasters, *Asbury,* 32. Bourne himself had once hired a slave. "That I did wrong in *hiring* a slave I *contritely* admit," he wrote in a letter to A.B. Davidson on 10 August 1815. "I have repented; I have *made restitution*; and now I endeavour to counteract the influence of my former example." Lexington Presbytery Minutes, 27 December 1815, quoted in Christie and Dumond, *Bourne,* 39. The Methodists, whose position Bourne repeated in his opening to *The Book and Slavery Irreconcilable,* had once also stated that those involved in slavery should not "be admitted into society, or to the Lord's supper," until they met with the rules regarding emancipation. Lee, *Methodists,* 101f.

[64]Though Methodists were against *life-long* enslavement, they did allow slaveholders several years to recoup the monetary expense of buying and owning a slave, in effect reverting to a system of indentured servitude. In one case, Reuben Harrison committed to seeing that Dice, an African American child who would not be set free for another 22 years, could "read reasonably well in the Bible." Rockingham Circuit Quarterly Minutes, 1815-1828, AUMC. Another solution to the need for regular workers was a tenant system which contracted with people on an annual basis. See for example the account book of Stephen Harnsbarger, referenced in May, "Port Republic," 26 & others, JMU.

[65]Johannes Braun, *Circular-Schreiben an die deutschen Einwohner von Rockingham und Augusta, und den benachbarten Caunties.* Harrisonburg, VA: Printed by Laurentz Wartmann, 1818, EMU. The book was completed in December 1817 and published under the auspices of the Rockingham Bible Society. The Bible Society continued at least until 1827, when Johannes Braun was listed as its president. The society was apparently reorganized after the Civil War. *Rockingham Register,* 4 October 1866; Wayland, *Rockingham,* 160, 280. Johannes Braun also served as treasurer for the school commissioners for 1823. RCMB 10:251 (6 January 1823).

[66]"Treatise on Slavery and Serfdom," translated by Harriet Augusta Braun, p. 14. Typescript in the Brown Family Collection, SC #1751, Folder 5, JMU. This was the final section of Johannes Braun's *Circular-Schreiben.* Since the book was largely a justification of the importance of Bible Societies, this treatise seems to have been a late addition. Its German title — "Eine Ubhandlung wegen Sclaverey und Leibeigenschaft" — can be generally translated as "A Treatise on Slavery and *Soul Property* (or *Owning People*)." Translation courtesy of Lois Bowman, Archivist and Head Librarian, Menno Simons Historical Library, EMU.

[67]In an imagined discourse forming part of this treatise, Braun did say through the character Theophilus that a Christian could not with clear conscience "possess property in his neighbor's freedom, his body, his life." Braun, Treatise, 35.

[68]Braun, Treatise, 6, 24.

[69]Braun, Treatise, 41.

[70]There had not been a large-scale conspiracy in Rockingham, but especially in the wake of Gabriel's conspiracy, the fear of one was perhaps always in the back of everyone's mind. See also RCMB 1:11 (26 May 1778: conviction of Will), in Levinson, Minute Book, 1:9. The plan for ending slavery which Braun favored had been submitted to the Virginia General Assembly 18 years earlier by St. George Tucker. Among the problems of *immediate* and total emancipation of the slaves, Tucker noted an "irremediable general famine" as well as concerns for safety. Notwithstanding, Tucker was committed, as he put it, to "the abolition of slavery, the emancipation of every single slave." Braun, Treatise, 42f (quote 43).

[71]Letter to the Lexington Presbytery, 28 May 1817 in Lexington Presbytery Minutes, 1 September 1817. About this same time, the Presbyterian General Assembly made a resolution opposed to slavery. The United Brethren in 1821, their first denomination-wide gathering since 1817, included a measure about slavery in their Discipline, very similar to the position of the Dunker Church taken in 1782 and 1797. "Resolved, That all slavery, in every sense of the word, be totally prohibited and in no way tolerated in our community. Should some be found therein, or others apply to be admitted as members, who hold slaves, they can neither remain to be members or be admitted as such, provided they do not personally manumit or set free such slave, wherever the laws of the state shall permit it, or submit the case to the quarterly conference, to be by them specified, what length of time such slave shall serve his master or other person, until the amount given for him, or for raising him, be compensated to his master. But in no case shall a member of our society be permitted to sell a slave. 5. Resolved, That is any memer of this society shall publicly transgress as aforesaid, such member shall likewise be publicly reprimanded, and in case such member shall not humble, the same shall be publicly excluded from the congregation. Drury, *Disciplines*, 90f.

[72]Probably following the death of Martin Kauffman [II] in 1805, several associated with the "Kauffman church" emigrated to Ohio accompanied by three ministers, Martin Kauffman [III], Lewis Seitz, and Samuel Comer. Others who evidently remained in Virginia petitioned for reconciliation with the Orange Association as late as 1809. Though the reconciliation was rejected, several became part of the Mill Creek church [Page Valley] or the Smith's Creek congregation near New Market. [Beale's] Semple, *Baptists in Virginia*, 248f; Brunk, *Mennonites*, 1:38f; Stricker, *Page*, 274, 368

[73]The 1782 resolution stated: "Concerning the unchristian negro slave trade, it has been unanimously considered, that it can not be permitted in any wise by the church, that a member should or could purchase negroes or keep them as slaves." *Minutes of the Annual Meetings of the Brethren*. H. D. Davy and J. Quinter, eds. Dayton, OH: Christian Publishing Association, 1876, p. 8.

[74]In 1812, Dunkers declared slavery "a most grievous evil and should be abolished as soon as possible." The 1813 General Conference ruling reaffirmed their 1797 decision regarding slave owners who wished to join the church, yet allowed those who had purchased slaves to "hold them in a proper way so long as the church near which they live may deem it necessary for the slaves to earn the money they had cost, and then, they are to be set free, with a good suit of clothing…." Slaves who had been inherited were to be emancipated as soon as it was thought "proper," while children should be cared for until they had grown to adulthood (boys to age 21, girls to age 18). *Minutes of the Annual Meetings*, 40 (1812, Article 5), 41f (1813, Article 1). In a general council meeting of the "Brethren" [Dunkers] at Linville Creek on 2 March 1855, those assembled addressed the question "concerning those Brethren that are holding slaves at this time and who have not complied with the requisition of the Annual Meeting of 1854." Among the ordained elders signing the document were Benjamin Bowman [Jr.] and John Kline. Zigler, *Brethren*, 85ff.

[75]As noted above, some had viewed the earlier militia exemptions for these groups as favoritism which "evidently tends to destroy the harmony which should subsist, in society." But these petitions carried both English and German signatures. Shenandoah County, 21 November 1796. Virginia Religious Petitions.

[76]This observation was made during the 1809 special election at Harrisonburg between a Mr. Swope and a Mr. Smith. George Rockingham Gilmer, *Sketches of Some of the First Settlers of Upper Georgia*. Americus, GA: Americus Book Co., 1926 [reprint], p. 191.

[77]*The Christian Confession of the Faith of the harmless Christians, in the Netherlands, known by the name of Mennonists*. Amsterdam, Printed, and Reprinted by Ambrose Henkel and Comp. New Market, Shenandoah County, Virginia, 1810, EMU. The German press in New Market, thanks to the efforts of Paul Henkel's sons Ambrose and Solomon, had been active since 1806. Capon and Brown, *Check-List*, viii.

[78]The appendix was a translation and slight adaptation of T. T. van Sittert's 1664 apologetic for the Anabaptist-Mennonite tradition. After this 1810 imprint, it appeared one more time in English (Doylestown, Pennsylvania, 1814). Today it is read largely by the Amish. *T. T. van Sittert's Apology for the Anabaptist-Mennonite Tradition, 1664*. Translated and edited by J.C. Wenger. Privately printed, 1975, p. 2, EMU. Interestingly,

in the same year, the Dunker church put out their first English translation and American edition of Alexander Mack, Sr.'s *A short and plain view of the outward, yet sacred rights and ordinances of the house of God, as commanded to be observed by the true steward, Jesus Christ, and deposited in His last will and testament, arranged in a conversation between a father and son. By Alexander Mack: translated into English by a friend to religion*, BC/Brethren Heritage Room. These two books no doubt set the stage for any further discussions. In 1809, the Henkel press in New Market published *Eine kurze Betrachtung der Heil Taufe und Abendmahl, zum Unterricht des gemeinen Mannes…*, anonymously authored but attributed to a staunch supporter of Lutheran orthodoxy, Paul Henkel. Cappon & Brown, *Check-List*, 2f.

[79]This is another reflection of the legacy of *Die erste Liebe*, the book by Gottfried Arnold.

[80]Dunkers were not alone in their celebration of the Eucharist at night. On 6 November 1825, Lutheran minister Ambrose Henkel celebrated an "evening meal" at Armentrout's church just north of Keezletown.

[81]In part, this may have been a response to the 1809 publication — *Eine Betrachtung* — attributed to Paul Henkel.

[82]Peter Burkholder, *A Treatise on Baptism and the Lord's Supper.* Dale Enterprise, VA: Abraham Blosser, 1881, p. 4, EMU. A translation of *Eine Verhandlung von der ausserlichen Wasser-Taufe…* Printed by Laurentz Wartmann, Harrisonburg, Rockingham County, Virginia, 1816, EMU. On the inside back cover of the 1816 version, Wartmann printed a one-page version of the first annual (1813) report of the Virginia Religious Tract Society. With Davidson and Bourne now both gone, it is likely that Wartmann had hopes of reviving the endeavor. Off his press two years later came Braun's *Circular-Schrieben*, printed under the auspices of the Rockingham Bible Society.

[83]Burkholder, *Treatise*, 4. Burkholder later remarks, "So we have in part arrived in gloomy times: because so many divisions manifest and reveal themselves among the Christians; so much so that they can or will scarcely understand each other; so that it has almost become a Babylon, because of the many parties, and ideas, so that some scarcely know which party to follow or embrace." Burkholder, *Treatise*, 14.

[84]Funk's German songbook, in keeping with his non-denominational bent, included songs from the Reformed, Lutheran, and Mennonist traditions, as well as tunes from *The Kentucky Harmony*, an English songbook published by Ananias Davisson in 1816. This German songbook contains an afterword written by Funk and dated July 1816. *Die allgemein nützliche…* [Choral Music], Printed by Laurentz Wartmann, Harrisonburg, [1816?], pp. 48, 86, EMU. The Henkel Press in New Market had produced at least two songbooks, one in English (1816) and

one in German (1812). Cappon and Brown, *Check-List*, 6f, 10f. During the next decades, both Burkholder and Funk would become leaders for change and innovation in Rockingham, each in their own way.

The following year Wartmann printed a response to Burkholder, also in German and entitled *Ein Zeugniß von der Taufe* (translated, *A Testimony on Baptism*). This book has long been attributed to Peter Bowman, though the title page states only that it was "Written by a Lover of the Divine Truth, and submitted to the reflection of all those who seek their eternal welfare." Interestingly, this is the same moniker used for a book attributed to Benjamin Bowman, Sr. in 1823. According to one source, Brethren theologian Peter Nead — who married Elizabeth Youndt and lived in the Tunker House for a time — was convinced of the correctness of Brethren ideas by reading a book by Benjamin Bowman, yet Benjamin's 1823 treatise was on the last days. One owner of an 1831 English translation of *Ein Zeugniß* inscribed "Bro. B. Bowman" on the title page, while one copy of the 1817 German *Ein Zeugniß* has "Peter Bauman." Since Peter Bowman died suddenly from a hunting accident on 2 January 1823, it may be that Benjamin was using his same anonymous description of authorship in memory and honor of his friend. Sappington, *Brethren in the New Nation,* 139; "B. Bowman on the Millenium & c." *The Gospel Visitor* (February 1862), 13(2):50, BC. *Ein Zeugniß von der Taufe…geschrieben von einem Liebhaber der göttlichen Wahrheit; vorgestellet, zum nachdenken allen denjenigen welche ihr Heil suchen.* Harrisonburg, [VA]: Printed by Laurentz Wartmann, 1817 [JMU, UVA, BC]. The book was reprinted in Chambersburg, Pennsylvania the following year, indicating its usefulness to the Dunker church. In 1831, an English translation appeared, *A Testimony on Baptism, as practiced by the Primitive Christians, from the Time of the Apostles; and on the Lord's Supper, according to the Institution of Christ and His Apostles, and on the Washing of Feet, with regard to the right manner, in which the same ought to be performed, and also, on the Leprosy and the Sprinkle-Water, and the signification thereof. Written by a Lover of the Divine Truth, and submitted to the reflection of all those who seek their eternal welfare…* Baltimore, MD: Benjamin Eddes, 1831 [copy at Juniata College, Juniata, PA]; "Communicated," *Rockingham Weekly Register*, 18 January 1823, UVA; Emmert F. Bittinger, "Elder Peter Bowman of Virginia: Defender of Dunker Beliefs," *Pennsylvania Mennonite Heritage*, April 1996, pp. 19ff.

[85]Already to the south in Floyd County, there was an "English Arm" of the Dunker church, thanks to the preaching of William Smith, an English non-combatant who had come to the colonies during the war of revolution. Smith learned of Dunker beliefs through Elder Jacob Miller of Franklin County and was baptized by him. Zigler, *Brethren*, 52f, 152, 166ff.

[86]Henkel, *Tagebuch*, 61. As might be expected, German disappeared earlier in Lutheran churches located in areas of greater

English influence, such as Staunton and Winchester. Wust, *Virginia Germans*, 138f.

[87]By 1811, Henkel had already published his English translation of the Lutheran catechism. Cappon and Brown, *New Market Imprints*, 5. In the years to come, the Henkel Press would become a center for the publication of Lutheran texts in English.

[88]Virginia Special Conference meeting in Solomon's Church, Shenandoah County on 19-20 March 1815. Cassell, *Lutheran Church*, 93.

[89]4 July 1811. "The Journals of the Rev. Robert J. Miller, Lutheran Missionary in Virginia, 1811 and 1813," Edited by Willard E. Wight. *VMHB* 61:145. Johannes Braun was never comfortable preaching in English, and for a long time resisted the addition of an English preacher to his charge, likely hoping his son would one day fill that spot. In the interim, the English part of congregations began "scattering and going elsewhere." By the time an English preacher was received, "much was already lost, that will never be regained," wrote his colleague Daniel Feete. Feete, 14 September 1856.

[90]In 1805, the Lutheran Ministerium of Pennsylvania meeting at Germantown declared German the only acceptable language for use in synodical sessions. Many felt the Lutheran church could not exist apart from the German language since English was too shallow to furnish an adequate translation of doctrinal and devotional literature. Also, they saw German as the "bulwark of sound faith and evangelical theology." One congregation in Philadelphia demanded an English-speaking minister and sometime around 1815 took their case to court. They won apparently because the court saw the "necessity of cultivating an American spirit." The War of 1812 had only recently been decided, and patriotism was running high. Abdel Ross Wentz, *A Basic History of Lutheranism in America* (revised edition). Philadelphia: Fortress Press, 1964 [original copyright Muhlenberg Press, 1955], p. 72f.

[91]Thanks to Henry Boehm, Methodists had already preached in both English and German in the Valley.

[92]Funkhouser, *Virginia Conference*, 230, 232; *Methodist Magazine*, 1823; One of these Great Meetings was scheduled for 24-25 September 1807 at "Hohman's, in Virginia." *Minutes from 1800-1818*, 19 (21 May 1806). This may in fact be a misreading of "Hoffman," but the original manuscript is no longer extant, so far as is known. See also May, *Four Flags*, 333f.

[93]Asbury, *Letters and Journal*, 2:305 [5-6 September 1801: "The house could not at all contain the people, we therefore took to the woods; but we failed in shade, and felt some inconvenience in the sun."].

[94]Lee, *Methodists*, 279.

[95]In some cases Methodist, Presbyterian, and Baptist ministers would hold a meeting together. Lee, Methodists, 279f, 284.

[96]Lee, *Methodists*, 291f, 301. Lee cites a "letter from Harrisonburg" containing this information. Colonel Moffet's meeting house was in Augusta county, at this time still a part of the Rockingham circuit. Asbury, *Journal and Letters*, 2:128 (1797), 305 (1801).

[97]Lee, *Methodists*, 302; Rockingham Circuit Treasurer's Book (1798-1820) notes the Quarterly meeting held at Linville's Creek, 18 August 1804, and camp meeting collection on the same day. This is the first mention of a camp meeting collection in those records. The meetings mentioned (around 4 February 1803, 2-3 June and 18 August 1804) were all quarterly meetings, scheduled 3-day events that had now seemingly begun to resemble camp meetings. The old Methodist meeting house on Linville Creek sat upon the top of a hill on the east side of Route 42 across from what is now called the Williamsburg Road. A graveyard and a few trees mark its former site. Dale McAllister, personal communication. By 1833, a committee to report on Methodist property noted, "There is a small piece of land deeded to the Methodist E. Church on Lynnville's Creek, on which the brick work of a house was once put under roof — but is now fallen down." 1833 Methodist Property Report, p. 13, Box 15, J. K. Ruebush Collection, EMU.

Side 8 Uncle Jack had a back with "furrows like a plowed field" from his own "master's" ill treatment. [George Bourne, writing under the pseudonym] An Incindiary Fanatic, *Liberator*, 4 May 1833, quoted in Christie and Dumond, *Bourne*, 33; Mrs. Polly Kyle lived near the corner of German and Bruce Streets in 1826, not far from James Burgess according to an article in the *Rockingham Register*, 5 October 1876 transcribed in Wayland, *Harrisonburg*, 338; Boyd-Rush, *Register*, 1. For Joshua Peters' listing as a preacher, see Church Register, Harrisonburg Station, 1832-1835 at AUMC, in MacMasters, *Asbury*, 36. DBR says this is Joshua Peters, Sr., not Jr. 1830 Harrisonburg census figures quoted in MacMasters, *Asbury*, 38. Maria Graham Carr, *My Recollections of Rocktown*, Bridgewater, VA: Harrisonburg-Rockingham Historical Society, 1984, pp. 12f, 33. In addition, "Amos Herring, a free man of colour, was licensed as a local preacher. He and his wife Betsey Herring went to Liberia in 1833…" MacMasters, *Asbury*, 36. The 1819 law did not prevent masters from taking or allowing their slaves to attend public worship with them as long as the service was "conducted by a regularly ordained or licensed white minister…" *The Revised Code of the Laws of Virginia*. Volume 1. Richmond, [VA]: Printed by Thomas Ritchie, 1819, c.111, p. 425; *Autobiography of the Rev. Samuel Huber*, Chambersburg, PA: Printed by M. Kieffer & Co., 1858, p. 69f, EUB.

[98]This description here and in the following paragraphs was typical for many such meetings, but not necessarily exactly how the Linville Creek meeting proceeded. Officially, the

Methodists had not authorized camp meetings before this time, much less made specific rules about how they should be conducted. All of those details were left to the presiding elders and travelling preachers. Lee, *Methodists,* 360ff.

[99]Treasurer's Book, Rockingham Circuit, 1798-1822. Lee, *Methodists,* 360ff.

[100]Lee, *Methodists,* 361.

[101]Lee, *Methodists,* 302, 361f. Camp meetings usually began on a Friday and continued through mid-day Monday.

[102]Now called Massanetta Springs. Benjamin Harrison was appointed to the position of colonel of the county militia in 1781. RCMB 1:86 (26 March 1781), in Levinson, *Minute Book,* 1:80. The Treasurer's book for the Rockingham Circuit records the first camp meeting at Col. Harrison's on 11 September 1806, with subsequent meetings in August of 1809 and 1810. Treasurer's Book, 1798-1822, AUMC; Minutes of the Rockingham Circuit [Methodist], 1815-1828, 9 September 1816, Copy at AUMC.

[103]William W. Bennett, *Memorials of Methodism in Virginia, From Its Introduction into the State, in the Year 1772, to the Year 1829.* Richmond, VA: Published by the Author, 1871, p. 660.

[104]Advertisements for *The Kentucky Harmony* were included in the 26 May 1818 *Knoxville Register*: "…the second edition of the *Kentucky Harmony* Has lately been completed…" (subscribed by A. Davisson, May 20), and in the 23 August 1820 *Missouri Gazette & Public Advertiser* (St. Louis): "…having run through this large edition since the year 1817, the fourth will be out by spring." For an examination of melodies and texts used in Davisson's published volumes, see Rachel Brett Harley, "Ananias Davisson: Southern Tune-Book Compiler (1780-1857)." Unpublished doctoral dissertation, University of Michigan, 1972.

[105]Ananias Davisson, *A Supplement to the Kentucky Harmony.* Printed and sold by the author, in Harrisonburg, Virginia, 1820, preface, EMU. [The copy at EMU belonged to Rebecca Baker and is dated February the 4th 1830]. Also in 1820 Davisson printed John Firth's book, *The Experience and Gospel Labour of the Rev. Benjamin Abbott* for James A. Dillworth. Abbott had been an itinerant Methodist preacher during the days of the Revolutionary War. James Dillworth was a strong Methodist supporter who attended the old Methodist church on the hill in Harrisonburg. MacMasters, *Asbury,* 28, referencing an article in the 1888 *Old Commonwealth.*

[106]Conrad Speece, a Presbyterian minister in the Valley, made this comment in the 29 June 1815 edition of his regular column, "The Mountaineer," published for three years in *The Republican Farmer,* a Staunton newspaper. Speece's particular objection was to the fuguing tunes, in which as many as four parts with different words were sung at the same time — "such a farrago of confusion and absurdity, that I can only gaze with astonishment at the vogue which it has obtained." Davisson printed an early collection of these articles in 1818. Conrad Speece, *The Mountaineer,* Staunton, VA: Printed by I[saac]. Collett, 1823, p. 124f, UVA.

[107]Davisson, *Supplement,* preface [quote]. *The Kentucky Harmony* went through five editions, *A Supplement* through three. Harley, Davisson, 140f.

[108]Asbury's letter of 30 July 1807. Asbury, *Journal and Letters,* 3:372f; see also 2:551.

[109]Carr, *Rocktown,* 49. The scene is reminiscent of United Brethren preacher Christian Newcomer's remarks about a camp meeting in Brock's Gap at Jacob Lentz's (Lance's): "The number of people assembled on the present occasion was very numerous, but most of them remained hard and uneffected *[sic]* under the most powerful preaching of the gospel: may the Lord have mercy on them." Newcomer, *Journal,* 319 (12 September 1828).

[110]Lee, *Methodists,* 361.

[111]"Sunday was a day of divine power, more so than any sabbath at campmeeting I ever saw. Instead of it being a day of dissipation, it was a day of seriousness, prayer, mourning, weeping rejoicing & Christian exercise all through…" L.R. Fechtig, *Journal,* 1819-1822, p. 161 (12 August 1819), ABWC. The "dissipation" to which Fechtig referred probably reflected the general "county fair" atmosphere which heavily flavored the proceedings.

[112]Rockingham Circuit Quarterly Conference Records, 1815-1828, 17 September 1828, AUMC.

[113]The *Register* began publication in 1822 as a business venture of Lawrence Wartmann.

[114]"A Camp-Meeting," *Rockingham Register,* 11 August 1825, p. 1, UVA; Carr, *Rocktown,* 49.

[115]Fourteen years later, another petition to the General Assembly complained of "the great inconvenience and annoyance" posed by food vendors near the camp meetings. The Methodists hoped the Assembly would grant their meetings a three-mile buffer zone. Legislative Petitions from Rockingham to the General Assembly, 20 February 1839, LV.

[116]Funkhouser, *Virginia Conference,* 48f. During his visit in September 1828, Newcomer preached at a camp meeting in the neighborhood of Jacob Weitzel (Whitesel) and had a meeting at "old" Brother Weitzel's the night of 10 September. Newcomer, *Journal,* 319. This was in the neighborhood of

Hoffman's former place near Pleasant Valley. Moyers name is sometimes spelled "Meyers."

[117]Rhodes 500A farm was located five miles south of Harrisonburg along the current Valley Pike/Route 11. This Frederick Rhodes was the son of Mennonist Bishop Henry Rhodes. His uncle, for whom he was probably named, had moved further up the valley into Augusta. Brunk, *History,* 1:71, 81.

[118]There were about 80 members of the Mennonist church who met in 10 different places about this time. Yet since baptism (which made one a member of the church) was allowed only for adults, children are not included in this number. Families could be large. Joseph Funk, a Mennonist living in Mountain Valley (later Singers Glen) had 14 children by 1833, so the number attending services was perhaps closer to 300 or more. Blosser, "Church Dispute — 1825 Rockingham County, Virginia." also VMCA, HAB, Miscellaneous, Box 2, Folder 29, "Joseph Funk," article from *Daily News-Record,* 26 December 1930. Brunk, *Mennonites,* 1:79f; Zigler, *Brethren,* 43f. Dunkers also baptized only adults. "The usual pattern…was that adults became members of the church only after marriage, sometimes even later." Emmert Bittinger, personal communication, 18 January 2002.

[119]The deed for Trissels is dated 31 May 1823, from Abraham Neff and wife to the Mennon—- Church. Brunk Collection, Miscellaneous Box 2, Folder 26. Like the Moyers' Meeting House, it was named for an adjacent property owner, Joseph Trissel. Brunk, *Mennonites,* 66f; RCDB/Burnt 6:298 (31 May 1823).

[120]Zigler, *Brethren,* 60; RCDB/Burnt 9:501f (6 December 1829).

[121]Huber, *Autobiography,* 68f. After he had spent the night at the home of Rhodes' neighbor, Peter Moyers, Christian Newcomer attended this meeting from Wednesday, September 8 through its conclusion on Tuesday, the 14th and proclaimed it "one of the best meetings I ever attended; many were brought from darkness to light, from the power of sin and Satan unto God." Newcomer, *Journal,* 263.

[122]The story of Frederick Rhodes and this dispute comes through the daughter of Mennonist Bishop Peter Burkholder, Margaret Burkholder Blosser, who was about twenty years old when these events occurred. Mrs. Blosser related the story to her son a few years before her death and the account was transcribed by Bishop L.J. Heatwole. Virginia Mennonite Conference Archives. Harry A. Brunk Collection, I-MS-13 [hereinafter, "Brunk Collection"], Box 1, Folder 5, "Church Dispute — 1825 Rockingham County, Virginia," VMCA. The dispute and other details about Frederick Rhodes are related in Brunk, *Mennonites,* 1:71, 74ff, 79ff, 86f.

[123]Mrs. Blosser notes that eventually the "offended party" grew to forty, but "many of them were the children of those who were offended and joined their church after the Division." Brunk Collection, Box 1, Folder 5, "Church Dispute — 1825."

[124]The reference for "Moyers' Meeting House" comes from Mrs. Blosser's account, which also refers to the United Brethren as "Baptists." See also RCDB/Burnt 9:101f (29 August 1829: "beginning at a Sand Stone near the middle of the Stage Road at the mouth of the Lane of Peter Moyers…"). The two parcels of land were to be reserved for a meeting house and a school house. Mrs. Blosser says only that the meeting house was built "about this time" so it may not have been built before 1826. Burkholder's Meeting House church was later called Weaver's, after the man who moved into the area and became the church sexton for several years. RCDB/Burnt 8:387 (August 1828: for Burkholder's/Weaver's, "…on the North side of the Road leading from Harrisonburg to Dry River Gap…on which a meeting house stands…").

[125]An ironic twist, in that several years earlier another group of Pennsylvania ministers excommunicated Bishop Martin Boehm for associating with essentially the same group. The openness of the United Brethren to different denominational expressions was reaffirmed in their Discipline of 1837: "That no rule be adopted by General Conference, so as to infringe upon the rights of any, as it relates to the mode and manner of baptism, the sacrament of the Lord's supper, or the washing of feet, & c." Drury, *Disciplines,* 171.

[126]The phrase "and sometimes commune together," was added by transcriber Heatwole and probably refers to attending worship services together, but not necessarily sharing the communion meal known as the Lord's Supper. Yet at the 1802 meeting organized by United Brethren at Hoffman's barn, the communion service was celebrated by Mennonites, Dunkers, and a host of others regardless of their divisions.

[127]This is a loose translation. The original exchange was recorded as, "Shunst den ist es shicklich das mir bei der Gemeinde stehn," to which Bishop Eby responded, "Now sel es an schöner Fuhs."

[128]A fifth building used for worship by Mennonites at this time was "Plains Academy" which Brunk dates to 1826. As early as 1813 Lutheran minister Robert J. Miller "preached at a schoolhouse near the Plains Mills, to a very attentive people," and in 1822 Adam Miller, Sr., a Lutheran minister from Sullivan County, Tennessee, preached here. 1813 North Carolina Synod Minutes, UVA-M; 1822 Tennessee Synod Minutes, UVA. Groups that met in schoolhouses were as much of a congregation as those that met in buildings set aside exclusively for worship. Brunk, *Mennonites,* 1:69.

[129]The original building is no longer standing, but the site is now used by the Pleasant Valley Mennonite Church. Whitesel's was originally built around 1824, and later rebuilt around 1874

"after a great revival." Another new church was built here in 1893. Funkhouser, *Virginia Conference,* 202.

[130]At least three Dunker meeting houses were built during the 1820s — Cook's Creek (Garbers), Beaver Creek, and Linville Creek. The idea of building churches seems like it would have been more of a struggle for the Dunkers than the Mennonites, though there appears to be no record of this debate in the Dunker church. Zigler, *Brethren,* 59, 83, 187, 190, 194f.

[131]Later pictures of Dunker men in the 19th century show a full beard with no mustache, but in earlier times, one writer asserts, "no razor was allowed to touch their faces." Martin Groves Brumbaugh, *A History of the German Baptist Brethren in Europe and America.* Mt. Morris, IL: Brethren Publishing House, 1899, p. 548.

[132]Many years later, a notice in the local newspaper read as follows: "We, the brethren, members of the German Baptist Church, on behalf of the Churches in the Valley, respectfully give notice, that we shall, at all our meetings, claim the protection of the law prohibiting huckstering and trafficking within the prescribed limits of the law,—Our self-protection requires this. Solomon Garber / Jacob Thomas / In behalf of the Churches." *Rockingham Register,* 23 August 1872.

[133]Eating lamb for the Lord's Supper was traditional both in the sense of the New Testament story as well as Dunker practice. As late as the Annual Meeting of 1854, in response to a question about the use of beef Dunker leaders affirmed "that we would rather see a lamb prepared; but inasmuch as Christ has made us free from the ceremonial law, and as there is no command in the New Testament that it must be so, we should bear with each other in love in such matters." *Minutes of the Annual Meetings,* 172f (1853), 183 (1854). This was in keeping with Nead's 1834 assertion that "It is the least of our intention to eat or celebrate the Jewish Passover." Peter Nead, *Primitive Christianity, or A Vindication of the Word of God.* Staunton, VA: Kenton Harper, Printer, 1834, p. 139, EMU.

[134]*The Methodist Magazine,* January 1823, 6:3-4; Their comments are reminiscent of the words of Christ: "By this shall all men know that you are my disciples, if you have love one for another." John 13:35.

[135]Gottlieb Shober, *A Comprehensive Account of the Rise and Progress of the Blessed Reformation of the Christian Church.* Baltimore: Schaeffer & Maund, 1818, p. 210, UVA-M. Socrates Henkel's criticism of Shober, who had connections with the Moravian community, was perhaps exaggerated. Shober was not necessarily pressing for a human solution to disunity within the Christian church. "My friends," he wrote, "*at a proper season,* the Lord will unite us all…" and "In short, until all eyes are only fixed on him who was wounded for our transgressions, union cannot be expected." Yet Shober did see this union approaching by Bible, missionary, and tract societies,

Sunday schools, and frequent revivals of religion. Shober, *Account,* 208f.

[136]Abolitionism, though, began to take force in the 1830s in America and England. Through groups in New England, abolitionism made itself clearly felt in the Baltimore Conference of the Methodist church at least by 1836. That year, the conference passed a resolution affirming their strong conviction against "the great evil of slavery" and at the same time their opposition to "the proceedings of the abolitionists which look to the immediate, indiscriminate and general emancipation of slaves." Journal of the Baltimore Conference, 1835-1846, p. 68, ABWC; Armstrong, *Old Baltimore,* 248f.

[137]The millenial focus is reflected in the remarks of the Rev. Moses Gillett, a pastor in Rome, New York, who remarked, "My sermons have been prepared entirely for another state of things. And now so far as my people are concerned, the Millenium has come; my people are nearly all converted." *The Memoirs of Charles G. Finney: The Complete Restored Text.* Edited by Garth M. Rosell and Richard A.G. Dupuis. Grand Rapids, MI: Zondervan Publishing House, 1989, p. 544. Finney noted that "the house of worship was full to overflowing *of professed Christians.*" [italics mine] The people of Rome may be excused for their misunderstanding, since the presence of God seemed to pervade the whole atmosphere. A county sheriff who was skeptical of the revival and visiting Rome on business, noted that he had never had any conception of "such an awe, such a solemnity" as he experienced while there. Several times during his meeting, he had to leave the table and go to the window to distract himself just to keep from weeping. *Finney,* 166.

[138]This is Benjamin Bowman, Sr., although his son of the same name — Benjamin Bowman, Jr. — had been elected a deacon of the local Dunker congregations on 31 May 1818. Greenmount would not be officially designated as a separate congregational area until 1844, though the Dunker congregations north of Harrisonburg (Greenmount, Linville Creek, and Flat Rock) were "virtually independent of each other" prior to this time. Zigler, *Brethren,* 180, 185, 224; *The Gospel Visitor* (February 1862), p. 49, BC.

[139]Matthew 24:21 (quote), 36ff.

[140]Bowman's treatise, *A Simple Exhibition of the Word of God,* written in German, does not exist except in a brief excerpt translated in the Dunker magazine, *The Gospel Visitor* (February 1862), pp. 50-52, BC.

[141]Henkel, Tagebuch, 27, 55. *Documentary History,* 187 (16 June 1783: "A certain Mr. Paul Hinkel [sic], in the name of several congregations, earnestly asked for license to preach and baptize children. He was examined in Christian doctrine and found fairly proficient, and as he showed evidence of a Christian character and life, it was resolved futher to consider

his case."), 192f (7 June 1784: Letters from Rockingham, Shenandoah and Frederick requesting Henkel's ordination, "or at least extend his license. Mr. Hinckel [sic] was again examined in writing, and thereupon it was resolved to extend his license for one year, and to exhort the congregations by a circular letter, to prepare a call for a preacher and entrust it to the Ministerium, which will not fail to transmit it to Europe.").

[142]Henkel's first sermon at the "old Röders church" was on Wednesday, 11 December 1782. "The first Christmas [1783] I preached in the Röders Church the people came there from afar, unmindful of the snow and the cold. Although snow lay upon the earth and the air was cold, nevertheless the hearts of many people were warm and eager for the word of truth." Henkel, Tagebuch, 27, 53; "The Rev. Paul Henkel," translated by Wm. J. Finck, 1935-1937, edited by Melvin L. Miller, unpublished manuscript, p. 13.

[143]Henkel, Tagebuch, 33f.

[144]Socrates Henkel, History of the Evangelical Lutheran Tennessee Synod. New Market, VA: Henkel & Co., 1890, p. 8, offering an English translation of Paul Henkel's comments to the Virginia Special Conference of 1806. The original German version — Verrichtung der Special-Conferenz der Evang. Luth. Prediger und Abgeordneten…gehalten in der Neuen Röders-Kirche, Rockingham County, den 6ten October, 1806 — was the first imprint of the Henkel Press. See also Henkel, Tagebuch, 77f.

[145]The charge of lack of Scriptural teaching was apparently a real issue. One Rockingham Methodist said a local preacher "halloos them through whether he can [reason] them through or not." Henry Bear to John Bear, 4 August 1822. Transcript at http://homepages.rootsweb.com/~mdtaffet/bear_letter_1822_08_04.htm.

[146]The press was physically operated by two of Henkel's sons, Solomon and Ambrose, both of whom were also Lutheran ministers. Ambrose Henkel represented three Virginia churches at the Tennessee synod meeting in 1822. The Henkels also published the Valley's first German newspaper, Der Virginische Volksberichter Newmarketer Wochenschrift, which ran from 7 October 1807 to 7 June 1809. New Market, Virginia, Imprints 1806-1876. A Check-List. Edited by Lester J. Cappon and Ira V. Brown. Charlottesville, VA: University of Virginia (Alderman Library), 1942.

[147]One of their chief objections was to the creation of a General Synod among Lutherans, which they felt was decidedly ambiguous regarding the Augsburg Confession. The Henkel Press produced not only English translations of the proceedings of the Tennessee synod, but also an early translation of the Lutheran catechism (1811), sermons by Martin Luther (1827), the Augsburg Confession (1834), a church hymn book (1838), the Lutheran liturgy (1843), and two editions of the The

Christian Book of Concord, or Symbolical Books of the Evangelical Lutheran Church (1851, 1854), a massive translation effort which took six years to initially complete, and was the first English version of a standard Lutheran work. Cappon and Brown, New Market Imprints, x and following.

Side 9 Minutes of Harrisonburg (Old School) Presbyterian Church, 1841-1856, 17 (10 August 1849: "…Mrs. Ann Obrion presented a request to be dismissed from this Church on account of her remoteness from it or any other Presbyterian Church, with the view of connecting herself with the Methodist Church in Port Republic[.] Her request was granted."), PAM; A typescript of Pleasant Clarke's letter from [17 March] 1836 may be found at http://boards.ancestry.com. Clarke was one of the signers on an 1846 petition from the Mt. Crawford Methodist church indicating their solidarity with the Baltimore Conference ["Northern" church] after the Methodists' North-South split in 1844. Papers of the Baltimore Conference, 1846, AWBC. By 1848 he was involved in the Mt. Crawford Division no. 19 Sons of Temperance. Selected Rockingham County Petitions, 1800-1850, Harrisonburg, VA, 1983, p. 194 (26 January 1848). In July 1860, Pleasant Clarke was appointed as one of four delegates from Rockingham Methodist circuit to attend the Rockingham District convention at Harrisonburg the following month. That convention agreed that "the separation of Baltimore Conference [from the "Northern Methodist church"] is necessary to our peace." MacMasters, Asbury, 54.

[148]Röder's, along with three churches from Shenandoah County (Solomon's, Hawksbill, and Paul's), had petitioned the North Carolina Synod in 1813 to advance "their adopted minister, Peter Shmucker," and admit them into the synod. Paul Henkel had been instrumental in establishing this predecessor to the Tennessee Synod as well. Report of the Transactions During the Synod of the Lutheran Ministry: Begun and held in the state of North Carolina, in the year of our Lord, 1813. Raleigh: Minerva Press, 1814, p. 12, UVA-M.

[149]Henkel, Tagebuch, 60. It is surmised that the Tagebuch was completed sometime around 1824. Henkel, Tennessee Synod, 51, referencing the third annual meeting of the Tennessee Synod in 1822.

[150]It is perhaps around this time that the change of names from Armentrout's/Er[h]mentraut's to St. Phillips occurred. On 16 August 1826, Henry Miller and Henry Ermentraut advised the minister of the Tennessee synod to "take to heart and think for God's sake when you carry on your office, whether it is to please the great Jehova or the world." Müller and Ermentraut to "Rebublick Sinode von Tenesse," Tusing Collection, New Market, VA, quoted in Klaus Wust, The Virginia Germans. Charlottesville, VA: University Press of Virginia, 1969, p. 137. Phanuel's Church, in Brock's Gap, would also join the Tennessee Synod, but not until 1855, the same year it was organized. 1855 Tennessee Synod Minutes, LTSG.

[151]The minutes of the Virginia synod meetings of 1829 and 1830 can be found in Cassell, *Lutheran,* 99-104. Most of the annual minutes of the Virginia Lutheran Synod from 1829 on can be found at LTSG.

[152]Minutes of the Virginia Lutheran Synod, 1839, p. 7, LTSG. Also quoted in Eisenberg, *Lutheran Church,* 167.

[153]The Tennessee synod maintained churches in Rockingham through 1925, when their Virginia conference churches became part of the Lutheran Synod of Virginia, yet that did not mean relationships throughout this period were entirely uncordial. When Rev. John F. Campbell visited the Tennessee synod meeting in 1851 and asked to be received as a delegate from the Virginia synod, he was refused, owing to the actions of 1838 and 1839. He was, however, offered a seat as an "honorary member," which he graciously accepted. Henkel, *Tennessee Synod,* 123f; Cassell, *Lutheran,* vii.

[154]The building was apparently built jointly by Lutherans and Presbyterians, at least sometime before August 1829. Minutes of the Virginia Lutheran Synod, 1829, 1830, 1840, 1841, LTSG. Though many other churches were also "union" churches — built and used by more than one denomination — the Union Church here was known only by this name and no other. Lutherans had historically joined with German Reformed in their church-sharing ventures, but Presbyterians (English-speaking Reformed) were a fair substitute. The German Reformed had lost a number of their English-speaking members since there was no English preaching to be heard from Johannes Braun at nearby Friedens. His counterpart, Michael Meyerhoeffer, the very popular Lutheran minister who moved to Rockingham about 1821, preached in English as well as German. Feete, 14 September 1856.

[155]Session Minutes, Cook's Creek & Harrisonburg (*VL* 36), 1837-1851, p. 52 (24 December 1838). According to a church history written by D.C. Irwin in 1859, 144 persons were baptized between the end of 1831 and the beginning of 1833. Since Irwin notes there were 93 members in 1822, it was perhaps true that a number of these were on the rolls but not regularly attending. One count of membership from rolls around 1838 shows 210 members, but Irwin indicates that about 168 people were present when the church split. At least 108 signed the letter in support of the New School movement, and about 60 continued with the Old School congregation. Irwin, "Historical Sketch."

[156]Thompson, *Presbyterians in the South,* pp. 119ff, quoting Presbytery of Springfield, "An Apology for Renouncing the Jurisdiction of the Synod of Kentucky…" Lexington, KY, 1804, pp. 119ff.

[157]*Finney,* 190.

[158]"With regard to the doctrines preached in those revivals, I would say that the doctrine of total moral depravity was thoroughly discussed, and urgently pressed upon the people; the spirituality and authority of the divine law was also made prominent; the doctrine of the atonement of Christ as sufficient for all men, and the free invitations of the Gospel based thereon, were held forth in due proportions. All men were represented as by nature dead in trespasses and sins, as being under condemnation and the wrath of God abiding on them. Then they were pointed to the cross of Christ, and every inducement presented to lead them to a total renunciation of self-righteousness, and of all selfishness in every form, and to a present thorough committal of themselves and of their all to the Lord Jesus Christ. Ministers and Christians who had adopted the literal interpretation of the Presbyterian Confession of faith, had found it very difficult to deal with inquiring sinners. In general they did not like to tell them that they had nothing to do. They would therefore instruct them to use the means of grace, to pray for a new heart, and wait for God to convert them. In this revival we discarded all this teaching; and instead of telling sinners to use the means of grace and pray for a new heart we called on them to make themselves a new heart and a new spirit, and pressed the duty of instant surrender to God. We told them the Spirit was striving with them to induce them *now* to give him their hearts, *now* to believe, and to enter *at once* upon a life of submission and devotion to Christ, of faith and love and Christian obedience. We taught them that while they were praying for the Holy Spirit they were constantly resisting him; and that if they would at once yield to their own convictions of duty, they would be Christians. We tried to show them that everything they did or said before they had submitted, believed, given their hearts to God, was all sin, was not that which God required them to do, but was simply deferring repentance and resisting the Holy Ghost. Such teaching as this was of course resisted by many; but nevertheless the teaching was insisted upon, and greatly blessed by the spirit of God. Formerly it had been supposed necessary that a sinner should remain under conviction a long time; and it was not uncommon to hear old professors of religion say that they were under conviction so many months or years before they found relief; and they evidently had the impression that the longer they were under conviction the greater was the evidence that they were converted. We taught the opposite of this." *Finney,* 190f.

[159]On 2 April 1838, there were two meetings, one at 11a.m. at Cook's Creek, another at 3 p.m. in Harrisonburg. Those present at the Cook's Creek meeting unanimously chose Phillips, and the Harrisonburg contingent, being informed of the earlier proceedings, affirmed the decision. Session Minutes for Cook's Creek & Harrisonburg, 1837-1851, pp. 18ff.

[160]One of the four-day events was to be held at Cook's Creek, the other at Harrisonburg. The Harrisonburg meeting was postponed since it conflicted with the meeting of Presbytery that year. These were not the first protracted meetings held by the Presbyterians in Harrisonburg. A three-day meeting was held in

Harrisonburg on 18-20 November 1831, and another protracted meeting took place at Union Church in late 1832. Harrisonburg & Cook's Creek Minutes, p. 14, PAM.

[161]The strength of the New School movement lay in the North and West, areas of concentration for abolitionists as well. In August 1838, Cook's Creek session passed a resolution favoring union with the New School General Assembly [national body] "provided it can be done on a basis that would exclude by constitutional law the subject of domestic slavery from the deliberations and action of said Assembly." That October in Staunton, the Virginia Synod identified themselves with the Old School General Assembly. Minutes of Cook's Creek & Harrisonburg (*VL* 36), 1837-1851, pp. 32 (26 August 1838), 39 (6 November 1838).

[162]Minutes of the General Assembly, Philadelphia, 1838, p. 8.

[163]Irwin, "Historical Sketch." The Old School congregation, comprised of approximately 60 members, was then left to worship in the Court House or [perhaps later] in the old Methodist church on the hill.

[164]There were then perhaps as many as 220 members of the Cook's Creek and Harrisonburg congregation, but the 108 signatures, along with the concurrence of the session, comprised a majority.

[165]Wilson, *Lexington,* 105 quoting Lexington Minutes 10:257f, but this appellation was not included in the copy of the letter inserted in the Harrisonburg & Cook's Creek session records. In 1839, the New School Synod of Virginia was organized with about one-sixth of the membership of the old Synod of Virginia. Ernest Trice Thompson, *Presbyterians in the South,* Vol. 1 (1607-1861), Richmond, VA: John Knox Press, 1963, p. 407.

[166]With the key to the stone church gone, the Old School group had been meeting in the Court House and in the old Methodist church. On 27 August 1864, the two churches were "officially" reunited when the New School United Synod of the South — organized on 1 April 1858 over the issue of slavery — joined with the southern Old School General Assembly known as the Presbyterian Church in the Confederate States of America. Yet, the New School Winchester Presbytery to which Harrisonburg & Cook's Creek belonged did not consummate its reunion at the presbytery level with the Old School Lexington Presbytery until 31 August 1865. The two Presbyterian congregations in Harrisonburg did not reunite on a practical basis until December 1866, and the following January were known as the "the Presbyterian Church of Harrisonburg" meeting in the former Old School building. *Old Commonwealth,* 17 October 1866, UVA. Harold M. Parker, Jr. *The United Synod of the South: The Southern New School Presbyterian Church.* NY: Greenwood Press, 1988, pp. 177, 261f; Irwin, "Historical Sketch;" Rockingham Church Minutes

(9 January 1867), PAM.

[167]Both churches eventually built new buildings in town. The New School group was deeded the lot on the northeast corner of Main and Elizabeth Streets on 10 November 1840 by William McMahon. The Old School congregation moved into their new building about one half block south of the New School building in 1855, and from then on were known as the Rockingham Church. Minutes of Rockingham Church, PAM; cf. *Rockingham Register,* 28 May 1885.

[168]Lexington Presbytery published their December proceedings in the public papers, which the New School felt unjustly represented their case. Minutes of Cook's Creek & Harrisonburg (*VL* 36), 1837-1851, pp. 61ff (4 February 1839). This same meeting records the short-lived debate over church property. Phillips, according to Irwin, "soon fell out with his cong[rega-tio]n and removed in Nov 1839 not regretted by either party." Irwin, "Historical Sketch."

[169]Hensell, "Brown," undated ms. [1856?]. Though the affable Braun was said to be "averse to that 'fair show' in religion which loves to speak that it may be heard of men, and to do that it may be seen of men," the German Reformed Classis of Virginia heartily encouraged the use of protracted meetings. Garrison, *Reformed,* 67, referencing 1840 Minutes of the Classis of Virginia, held at Frieden's Church. Originals at ERHS.

[170]The recipient of the letter is unknown since page 1 is missing. It seems that Henry Bear must have left Rockingham sometime after the camp meeting that August or September. Letter of Henry Bear, 24 November 1832. Typescript at http://homepages.rootsweb.com/~mdtaffet/bear_letter_1832_11_24.htm.

[171]The "side-step toward the Methodists in doctrine and working with their tools" most likely had to do with protracted meetings and calling upon people to accept Christ then and there. This was seen as a departure from strict Calvinistic principles, which in and of themselves, probably represented a clear departure from what Calvin himself wrote and taught.

[172]Fristoe, *Ketocton,* 50.

[173]Again, the motive was seen as somehow trying to usher in the millenial reign of Christ by gathering large numbers of followers through whatever means. Fristoe, *Ketocton,* 50.

[174]Letter of Henry Bear, 24 November 1832. Typescript at http://homepages.rootsweb.com/~mdtaffet/bear_letter_1832_11_24.htm. Baptist historian Robert Semple writing in 1810 noted that wherever the Methodists had increased in numbers throughout the area served by the Ketocton Association (with whom the Linville Church had once been associated), the Baptists had decreased. "Does it arise from the Arminian doctrine being more palatable to the self-righteous

heart of man?" he questioned. "Or, have [the Methodists] succeeded, as in some places, in driving the Baptist preachers,
imperceptibly, to dwell too much upon high Calvinistic points,
the neglect of the more simple but more important principles
of Christianity?" [Beale's] Semple, *Baptists in Virginia,* 385.

175The Salem Church was officially organized in 1813 and
received as a member of the Shiloh Association. *Minutes of the
Shiloh Association,* 1813, p. 4 ("A letter from Salem, a newly
constituted church, on Cook's creek, in Rockingham county…"), VBHS. Tradition says that Joseph Coffman's father-in-law,
Jacob Lincoln, felt compassion on the young couple and contributed $100 to have a small building erected on their farm.
The deed for the church property was granted by Joseph's
parents, David and Elizabeth Coffman in 1819, a little less than
a year after the couple was married. David Coffman, according
to family genealogical information, was a cousin to the Baptist
minister Martin Kauffman who travelled and ministered with
John Koontz. *A Genealogy and History of the Kauffman-
Coffman Families,* compiled by Charles Fahs Kauffman
[1940], York, PA: Lawrence P. Kauffman, Jr. reprint 1980, pp.
228, 572; Strickler, *Page County,* 274, 368; RCDB/Burnt 4:306f
(18 September 1819); Wayland, *Lincolns,* 81f. Dayton, known
earlier as Rifesville or Rifetown, was legally established in
March, 1833. Wayland, *Rockingham,* 198. On 7 October 1830,
Samuel H. Coffman & Co. announced they had opened a new
store at "Rifesville (head of Cook's Creek)" and were offering
"Fresh & Seasonable Goods, purchased in the Philadelphia and
Baltimore Markets…" *Rockingham Weekly Register,* 6
November 1830, UVA. Sadly, for several years after the revival
of 1832-33, the burgeoning congregation had no pastor, and
membership slowly dwindled. By 1856, there were 35 people
associated with the church, the same number reported in
1823. *Minutes of Shiloh Association,* 1823, VBHS; *Minutes of
Ebenezer Association,* 1832, 1833, 1834, 1835, 1856, 1872,
VBHS.

176Those Baptists who did not go along with the new methods
were called Old School, a term they "were led to adopt…from
it having been applied to us by others." They used it to mean
"the school of Christ, in distinction from all other schools
which have sprung up since the apostles' days." Black Rock
Address online at http://www.pb.org/pbdocs/blakrock.html.
The Ebenezer Association (organized 1828) joined the Old
School camp sometime between May 1831 and May 1832.
Religious Herald, 11 November 1831 (reporting on the
Ebenezer Association meeting of 20-21 May 1831 at Salem,
Rockingham County), 11 May 1832, VBHS. Inasmuch as the Old
School practiced what the New School or missionary Baptists
referred to as "hyper-Calvinism" or the "do-nothing" approach
to evangelism, it is all the more amazing that the Salem church
grew so substantially following the 1831 meeting there. For
the formation of the Brock's Gap congregation, see Linville
Creek Minutes, 103ff (18 February 1843 & others from 15
October 1842 to 17 February 1844), HSP. Another record book
for this congregation begins on 4 February 1860. Copy at

HRHS. Other information about the Brock's Gap Baptist congregation, including the interim the church minutes do not
cover, can be found in the Minutes of the Shiloh Association
from 1824-1828, and the Minutes of the Ebenezer Association
after that year, both at VBHS. [Note: VBHS has only scattered
minutes of the Ebenezer Association beginning in 1832.] On 7
June 1813, Lutheran missionary Robert Miller visited "Mr.
Riddle's, in Brok's Gap, a baptist family—very kind and attentive people." Minutes of the North Carolina Synod 1813, p. 37,
UVA-M. Essentially, the original geographic center of the small
Linville Creek congregation was no more, the congregation
dispersing or dropping out probably between 1818 and 1823.
Minutes of the Shiloh Association, 1818-1824, VBHS; Minutes
of the Linville Creek Baptist Church, pp. 97ff, HSP.

177From the other side of the coin, Bible societies deliberately
steered away from choosing ministers on their Board of
Directors to avoid sectarian conflicts and to gather men with a
sound business sense. Creighton Lacy, *The Word Carrying
Giant: The Growth of the American Bible Society (1816-
1966).* South Pasadena, CA: William Carey Library, 1977, p. 9.

178Perhaps the most cogent position paper for the Old School
or Primitive Baptists is the 1832 Black Rock Address, presented
in a slightly modified form at
www.pb.org/pbdocs/blakrock.html.

179Coffman's frustration may have been highlighted by the
growth of the Methodists at Mt. Crawford in 1841. On 25
September a meeting began there with no special interest, and
the following Tuesday 43 persons came to the altar. The meet-
ing continued for three weeks. *Christian Advocate,* 23
February 1842, ABWC. The particular New School or
Missionary Baptist group visited by Coffman was the Salem
Union Association. John E. Massey, *Autobiography of John E.
Massey.* Edited by Elizabeth H. Hancock. New York: The Neale
Publishing Company, 1909, pp. 11 (Massey born on 2 April
1819), 23. See also Taylor, *Baptist Ministers,* 4:380ff.

180Massey does not mention the specific names of the localities
he visited that day, but the distance of 22 miles from the
Coffman place near Dayton would have been enough to reach
the Brocks Gap Baptists on Runions Creek. Another six would
have brought him back in the vicinity of Turleytown, perhaps
to the free church there.

181Massey, *Autobiography,* 24.

182This newer Salem congregation was officially organized on
15 November 1845, and was officially received the following
year by the Salem Union Association. By 1855, this Salem congregation had changed its name to Mt. Crawford, almost certainly to avoid confusion with the Salem Old School Baptist
congregation at Dayton affiliated with the Ebenezer
Association. *Minutes of the Salem Union Association,* 1846,
1847, 1854, 1855; *Minutes of the Ebenezer Association,* 1856,

1857, VBHS. According to the inscription on the front of the newer Mt. Crawford Baptist church at Mt. Crawford *Station* (by the train tracks east of I-81 at the Mt. Crawford exit), the Mt. Crawford congregation began in 1841. See also Wayland, *Rockingham*, 243. This earlier date may refer to an informal break-off from the Old School Salem congregation, a surmise which would explain why Coffman and others constituted their new church as "Salem." Robert Ryland, president of Richmond College (begun in 1832 as the Virginia Baptist Seminary, now known as the University of Richmond) which Massey had attended in 1836 and re-entered in 1841, visited the Valley sometime during the 1840s and had Massey appointed as a missionary of the Virginia Baptist Association. At the time, Massey was the only missionary Baptist preacher between Winchester and Lexington, a situation which would change little in the next twenty years. Massey, *Autobiography*, 17f, 24f; Taylor, *Virginia Baptist Ministers*, 4:350ff, 4:380ff, 5:477f.

[183]Stephenson, "Brown's Gap," PATC notes that in part the Brown's Gap Turnpike "followed one of the oldest trails from the west —from the Old Fields (in what is now Hardy County, W.Va.) through Brock's Gap, by Singers' Glen…" This is likely the bridle path requested by the petitioners of the 1740s.

[184]The new location is plainly seen on Lake's 1885 atlas, north along the old Greenmount Road.

[185]Massey's words were reported by Jacob Myers, who was present at the trial. C. S. Dodd, "Baptists of Rockingham County," *The Religious Herald*, 15 August 1912, p. 7. After Massey's marriage to Margaret Ann Kable on 30 August 1847, the couple lived in Harrisonburg, where Massey planted the seeds for the Baptist congregation organized after the Civil War (chapter 12). Massey, *Autobiography*, 25. John, Margaret, and their two-year-old son Llewellyn are listed in the Harrisonburg enumeration of 1850. Wayland, *Harrisonburg*, 297.

[186]By this time, too, a number of these groups had developed their own Virginia organizations.

[187]The Free Methodists, still an active denomination today, opposed the New School techniques of the Methodists, and held to what they called Wesleyan practices.

NOTES FOR CHAPTERS 10, 11, and 12 — CATARACTS

[1]The Greenmount Road then was *not* the same as Route 772, the current road by that name. In the mid-19th century and later, it essentially parallelled today's Harpine Highway/Route 42, and might be said to include what are now Crestview and Sunset Drive/617, Grist Mill Road/910, Fort Lynne Road/910, and Switchboard Road/910. Lake's 1885 Atlas; A. L. McKinney, *Memoirs of Eld. Isaac N. Walter.* Cincinnati: Rickey, Mallory & Webb, 1857, pp. 105 (referencing another incident, Walter mentions "the sermon you delivered on the stand near Antioch Chapel"), 245 ("The largest congregation assembled that I ever saw in that place. Upward of one thousand saddle horses were counted, beside carriages, buggies, etc."), UVA. The editor of Walter's journal does not mention the particular reason for this large gathering, but it is easily inferred from the journal of John Kline. Funk, *Kline*, 274f. The crowd gathered would have represented about one out of every twelve people in the entire county. 1840 Census: 17,344.

[2]McKinney, *Walter*, 68, quoting from the writings of Elder C. Sine.

[3]This was not the same Martin Burkholder who served as a bishop in the Mennonite church from around 1847 to 1861. That Martin would have been 11 years old at Walter's first visit. Brunk, *Mennonites*, 1:100f, 163f. In the winter of 1838, Burkholder drove his horse and carriage all the way to Winchester to meet the preacher and take him to Rockingham. McKinney, *Walter*, 83, 170, 231. Martin Burkholder's journal is located at Duke University, Durham, NC.

[4]McKinney, *Walter*, 83f.

[5]The deed for the property was made by Martin Croomer to John Kratzer, Sr., John Higgens, Peter Paul, Martin Burkholder, and Jacob Burkholder, trustees. The deed was dated 4 May, and the church dedicated 30 June 1833. McKinney, *Walter*, 99. Wayland, *Rockingham*, 247.

[6]The followers of Barton Stone, a contemporary of Alexander Campbell, actually preferred the name "Christian," while the Campbellites chose "Disciples of Christ." The two groups eventually united. See Samuel S. Hill, *Encyclopedia of Religion in the South*, Macon, GA: Mercer University Press, 1984, online at www.bible.acu.edu/crs/doc/doc.htm.

[7]Though Antioch was the only meeting house specifically set apart for the Christian denomination, Walter also preached in Bridgewater, Dayton, Harrisonburg, and Muddy Creek. At some point, probably at least by 1838, the church in Rockingham was under the leadership of Elder F. G. Miller and his wife. McKinney, *Walter*, 99, 170, 231 (15 June 1841), 298 (Union

Chapel in Harrisonburg and "some other points in the county").

[8]Bowman was elected a deacon on 31 May 1818 at the age of 33, and ordained an elder on 10 August 1837. The Bowman family homestead was just north of where the Greenmount meeting house would be built in 1859. The mill was torn down in the 1950s and the house burned later. Zigler, *Brethren,* 187, 224 (born 28 June 1785); Funk, *Kline,* 79; Emmert Bittinger, "The Jacob and Varena Bowman Family, Brethren Pioneers of Maryland and Virginia, Part II," *Mennonite Family History* (October 1997), p. 164; ACDB 11:553ff (14 November 1763: Daniel Harrison to Jesse Harrison, 400A on Linvulls Creek… Delivered to Benjamin Bowman by the order of Jesse Harrison Feby 18th 1783); Chalkley, *Chronicles* 3:409; Kline, *Stone Houses,* 56ff.

[9]Funk, *Kline,* 274. Walter, like many others of his day, had been convinced by the arguments of the "Adventists," who argued that Christ would return to earth sometime between 21 March 1843 and 21 March 1844. At one time there were as many as 50,000 Adventists in the United States. Frank S. Mead, *Handbook of Denominations in the United States.* New York: Abingdon-Cokesbury Press, p. 15.

[10]Benjamin Funk, *The Life and Labors of Elder John Kline, the Martyr Missionary.* Collated from his diary by Benjamin Funk. Elgin, IL: Brethren Publishing House, 1900, p. 139 (2 June 1842), UVA.

[11]Jesus, speaking of his return and second physical appearance on earth, said "But of that day and hour no one knows, not even the angels of heaven, nor the Son, but the Father only." (Matthew 24:36); Funk, *Kline,* 274.

[12]Funk, *Kline,* 220.

[13]Funk, *Kline,* 274f; McKinney, *Walter,* 28.

[14]Based on the published journal, this may have been July 1833. There was an article in the *Christian Palladium* about this debate, and perhaps also in the *Rockingham Register.* Both Walter and Lyon published pamphlets representing their different positions. McKinney, *Walter,* 88, 97ff.

James Smith, the 13th child of Col. Daniel and Jane (Harrison) Smith, had left the Valley for Ohio in 1807, "having conscientious scruples on the question of slavery." He later became a member of the Christian church and wrote several books on the Trinity. William Fletcher Boogher, *Gleanings of Virginia History,* Washington, DC, 1903, p. 364f.

[15]In 1836, the Conference declared it was strongly opposed to abolitionism, in "particular to the proceedings of the abolitionists which look to the immediate, indiscriminate and general emancipation of slaves." Journal of the Baltimore Conference, 1835-1846, p. 67f (quote 68), also pp. 229ff (22 March 1843: resolution on slaveholding), ABWC.

[16]Journal of the Baltimore Conference, 1835-1846, p. 230 (22 March 1843), ABWC.

[17]The added stipulation required that Hansberger and others not try to get around the resolution by "transferring the right of property to a third person." The Discipline then in force, page 196, answer 2 stated that "when any travelling preacher becomes an owner of a slave, or slaves, by any means, he shall forfeit his ministerial character in our church unless he execute, if it be practicable, a legal emancipation of such slaves conformably to the Laws of the State in which he lives." Journal of the Baltimore Conference, 1835-1846, pp. 220, 230 (22 March 1843).

[18]"…I am deeply convinced of the great error into which I was unwittingly drawn in the matter of the marriage contract," Hansberger wrote in his statement of 15 March 1844. Baltimore Conference Papers, 1844, ABWC.

[19]See for example the contemporaneous case of Baltimore Conference minister Nelson Head, whose wife purchased a slave girl at the girl's request so that she might not be sold to traders and sent away from family and relations. A Conference committee reported that after "having examined the law of 1831, and also the views of a legal gentleman, are of opinion that, the woman is free — but in consideration of the great uncertainty of litigating such cases in our courts beg leave to recommend the adoption of the following paper signed by Bro. Head." Head agreed to pay the girl, after ten years more enslavement, "a just and equitable remuneration for such services as she may render to my family," and if ever possible to free her along with any children she might have. Journal of the Baltimore Conference, 1835-1846, pp. 327f, 339ff (19-22 March 1845), ABWC. Papers of the Baltimore Conference, 1844, ABWC.

Side 10 Travis, *Autobiography,* 19f; "When on his way the vessel was overtaken with a terrible storm & captain & crew all gave up — & thought they were lost. At this time father B.['s] mind was very much exercised & he made a sacred vow to the Lord that if he spared him his future life should be more fully devoted to his services." At his death on 26 January 1850 he was 78 years, 6 months, and 5 days. The inscription on his tombstone read in part, "Laurels may flourish round the conquerors tomb/But happiest they who win the world to come." Feete, 14 September 1856, pp. 1f, 6; Harbaugh, *Fathers,* 3:134ff; D[aniel] F[eete], "Death of the Rev. Dr. John Brown," *German Reformed Messenger,* 13 February 1850 (Vol. 15, No. 23), p. 3003, ERHS.

[20]At their 1845 gathering, the Baltimore Conference directed that the obstructions to Hansberger's ordination be removed. Journal of the Baltimore Conference, 1835-1846, pp. 254, 256f, 264f (March 1844), 336 (21 March 1845), ABWC.

[21]Andrews situation was complicated by many circumstances. Some of his remarks are recorded in the Journal of the General Conference of 1844. *Journals of the General Conference of the Methodist Episcopal Church.* Volume 2, 1840, 1844. New York: Carlton & Phillips, 1856, ABWC.

[22]The split occurred on 3 June 1844, and the southern church was organized the following year. A similar scenario was happening with the Baptists, though the effects in Rockingham, where there was a small handful of Baptist congregations, received probably much less public notice. *Journals of the General Conference* (1844), 95, 135. The Presbyterian church, already split once over the New School/Old School controversy, was also reeling over the subject of slavery. The 1844 meeting of the Old School General Assembly in Louisville was in an uproar over the devision of the Bills & Overtures Committee to table twenty memorials on the subject. "It Happened in Louisville: General Assemblies of Yore," *Presbyterian Heritage* (Spring/Summer 2001), 14(2), p. 1.

[23]More specifically, the Virginia Conference was "bounded on the east by the Chesapeake Bay and the Atlantic Ocean, on the south by Albemarle Sound, Roanoke and Staunton Rivers, on the west by the Blue Ridge, on the north by the Rappahannock River, except Fredericksburg and Port [Front] Royal." *Journals of the General Conference* (1844), 95 (3 June 1844), ABWC. See also *The Christian Advocate and Journal,* 6 October 1847 (UVA-M) which details the struggle in Rockingham along the "border societies" and elsewhere.

[24]*Journals of the General Conference,* 2:1840, 1844, p. 135 (8 June 1844). Accusations were made against the M.E. Church, South that they had violated the spirit and letter of the plan by approaching congregations within Northern-aligned annual Conferences, such as Baltimore. Yet, the Southern church understood that the plan's wording of "societies, stations, and Conferences" along the border would apply to the individual congregations regardless of the decision of their Conference. *Journals of the General Conference of the Methodist Episcopal Church, South,* 1846, 1850, Richmond, VA: John Early, 1851, pp. 46ff (13 May 1846), RMC.

[25]Petition from the Bridgewater congregation to the Baltimore Conference, 1846, Papers of the Baltimore Conference, 1846, ABWC.

[26]Papers of the Baltimore Conference, 1846, ABWC. The Elk Run [Elkton] and Harrisonburg congregations were part of the Harrisonburg and Madison circuit of the M.E., South in 1848. Elk Run Class Book. Copy at HRHS; *Minutes of the Annual Conferences of the Methodist Episcopal Church, South,* 1855-56, Nashville, TN: Southern Methodist Publishing House, 1878, p. 615 (Elk Run and Keezletown, along with Harrisonburg and Woodstock, were two circuits part of the Charlottesville District of the Virginia Conference in 1855), RMC; *Minutes of the Annual Conferences of the Methodist Episcopal Church,*

South, 1859, Nashville, TN: Southern Methodist Publishing House, 1860, p. 141 (Bridgewater), RMC; *Minutes of the Annual Conferences of the Methodist Episcopal Church, South,* 1865, Nashville, TN: Southern Methodist Publishing House, 1870, p. 558 (Port Republic). A revival took place in Port Republic during the early part of 1851 under the ministry of Virginia Conference minister David Wood. Wood died in Port Republic at the age of 43 on 27 March 1851, and his grave is marked by an iron fence in the South River cemetery there. *Minutes of the Annual Conferences of the Methodist Episcopal Church South,* 1851, p. 334, RMC. On 4 May of that same year, the Harrisonburg, ME South congregation dedicated their new house of worship, Andrew Chapel in honor of the "slave-holding bishop." Dunker leader John Kline preached in the new M.E., South church building that August. MacMasters, *Asbury,* 48f; Funk, *Kline,* 295 (17 August 1851).

[27]Papers of the Baltimore Conference, 1846, ABWC (quote from Mt. Crawford petition); East Rockingham Circuit was divided off from Rockingham between 1844 and 1845, and the two circuits were roughly equal in size. In 1845, Rockingham had 331 "white" and 53 "colored" members, compared to 312 and 34, respectively for East Rockingham. Only one of the area's four local preachers was located in East Rockingham. Journal of the Baltimore Conference, 1835-1845, pp. 261 and others.

[28]Benjamin Denton. *Origin, Constitution, Doctrine, and Discipline, of the Separate Arminian Union Church, Rockingham County, Virginia.* Published for Benjamin Denton, By Joseph Funk and Sons, 1849, p. 3, EMU. Journal of the Baltimore Conference, 1835-1846, pp. 88 (18 March 1837), 90 (20 March 1837), ABWC. The Rockingham Quarterly Meeting was ruled as having no authority under the Discipline for their action. Denton is listed as a Methodist minister (local preacher) at the 25-29 August 1815 camp meeting held at Colonel Benjamin Harrison's. Quarterly Conferences of the Rockingham Circuit, 1815-1828, Copy at AUMC.

[29]Methodist Property Report of 1833, Box 15, J. K. Ruebush Collection, EMU. Virginia Lutheran Synod Minutes, 1845 (pp. 25, 27), 1846 (p. 28f), 1847 (pp. 12, 22f), LTSG. The property was deeded in 1820.

[30]Though Denton does not specify Blakemore's intention, the Virginia Lutheran Synod minutes do. Denton himself — through the agency of Schickel — applied for admission into the Lutheran group at this same time and was cordially, but firmly, refused in 1845. Blakemore's process was a bit more extended, and he did not receive final word that the synod would not license him until May, 1847. Denton, *Arminian,* 3; 1845, 1846, 1847 Virginia Lutheran Synod Minutes, LTSG.

[31]To put matters in perspective, there were perhaps no more than six members from Briery Branch and 25 from Dry River who joined Blakemore. There were evidently several different reasons why Methodists classes in this area were falling away.

The notation for Muddy Creek is vague: "This class may also be hard to find as some others: the circumstances of which you can soon learn in visiting the place." Rockingham Circuit Records, 1843-1858, AUMC. See also Rosser's book on Class Meetings, 1855. Much of the trouble may have centered on inroads made by members of the Virginia Conference, Methodist Episcopal Church, South. Members at Wesley Chapel, an early Methodist meeting house on the east side of Smith's Creek not far from Tenth Legion, had petitioned the 1846 Baltimore Conference in conjunction with members of Fellowship and Naked Creek appointments. Their concern was that the Conference not infringe on their rights to hold slaves, following the split in the Methodist Episcopal Church at large. The notation beside this class was, "These people have been left to follow their conscience and the Scripture." Yet, in 1854, the class at Wesley Chapel was 41 strong. Papers of the Baltimore Conference, 1846, ABWC; Rockingham Circuit Records, 1843-1858, p. 37, AUMC. Not far from Wesley Chapel was a new Christian (Disciples of Christ) congregation worshipping at Bethlehem church, a "free church" for which land had been deeded on 21 September 1844. RCDB/Burnt 17:381 (21 September 1844).

[32]Denton, *Arminian,* 5.

[33]Denton, *Arminian,* 5, 7, 20.

[34]On 11 February 1851, Denton and 24 others were "admitted on trial" as a re-organized class at Dry River. By 1855, Benjamin Denton appears on the list of United Brethren in Christ preachers as a "licentiate," and is described as a local preacher and farmer. He died shortly afterward, perhaps in 1856, and was buried at "Dry Run." Class Lists of Rockingham Quarterly Circuit, 1843-1858, AUMC; Funkhouser, *Virginia Conference,* 134, 257.

[35]Mountain Valley has since been renamed Singers Glen.

[36]Brunk, *Mennonites,* 1:112ff; Joseph Funk, *Genuine Church Music,* Winchester, [VA]: Published at the office of the Republican (J.W. Hollis, printer), 1832, UVA.

[37]*Genuine Church Music,* also more popularly known as *Harmonia Sacra,* would go through seventeen editions. The tenth was published in 1860, two years before Joseph's death.

[38]The "Do re mi fa sol la si do" scale first appeared in the 1851 edition of *Harmonia Sacra.* Brunk, *Mennonites,* 1:121. The shape-note system had appeared a year earlier in James P. Carrell's and David S. Clayton's *The Virginia Harmony* (Winchester [,VA], 1831). Carrell's first book, *Songs of Zion,* was published in 1821 by Ananias Davisson in Harrisonburg. William E. Chute, in the *Musical Million* 6 (1875), p. 71, referenced in George Pullen Jackson, *White Spirituals in the Southern Uplands,* New York: Dover Publications, 1965 [1933], p. 35.

[39]Taylor, *Virginia Baptist Ministers,* 3:330, 5:234. The Funks would also open a local music school on 1 November 1859, with prices set at $9 per month for board and tuition. *The Southern Musical Advocate and Singers' Friend* (August 1859), Vol. 1, No. 2, EMU; Brunk, *Mennonites,* 1:123; "Music in Education," *The Southern Musical Advocate and Singers' Friend* (December 1860), p. 274, EMU.

[40]"Music in Education," *The Southern Musical Advocate and Singers' Friend* (December 1860), p. 274f.

[41]It would not be until 1860 when official permission was given to Mennonite churches to have singing schools. Even then, musical instruments would not be allowed. *Minutes of the Virginia Mennonite Conference.* Published by the Virginia Mennonite Conference. Scottdale, PA: Mennonite Publishing House, 1939, p. 3 (28-29 September 1860 at Trissel's Church).

[42]During the occupation of Harrisonburg in April 1862 by Federal forces under General Banks, U. S. soldiers would visit the home of Mennonite Peter Hartman. "They must have been about the most orderly army in the war," Hartman recalled. "They did not molest anyone. They paid for the few things that they wanted. They would come out to our house, sit down and talk, and get us to sing." Hartman, *Reminiscences,* 20.

[43]Even at his death in 1860, after twelve or more years as bishop, there were reportedly some Mennonites who felt that Martin Burkholder had been "too progressive." Brunk, *Mennonites,* 1:101f.

[44]In 1860, each district of the Virginia Mennonite Conference was allowed to make their own decision regarding singing schools. *Minutes of the Virginia Mennonite Conference,* n.p.: Virginia Mennonite Conference, [1939] 1950, p. 3.

[45]Funk translated Heinrich Funk's *Ein Spiegel der Taufe* details, Philadelphia, 1744. The translation was *A Mirror of Baptism with the Spirit, with water and with blood. In three parts. From the Holy Scriptures of the Old and New Testaments. By Henry Funk Minister of the Gospel in the Mennonite Church… translated from the German,* Mountain Valley, Virginia (near Harrisonburg). Published by Joseph Funk and Sons, 1851.

[46]Joseph Funk, *The Reviewer Reviewed; or, Thoughts and Meditations on the Sacrifices, Offerings, Emblems, Figures, and Types of the Old Testament, compared, in their fulfillment, with the antitypes in the New Testament.* Mountain Valley, VA: Printed at the office of Joseph Funk & Sons, 1857, p. 5, UVA.

[47]Funk, *Reviewer Reviewed,* 3.

[48]Funk, *Reviewer Reviewed,* 6.

[49]Solomon Funk was a member of one of the classes of the Harrisonburg Methodist church in 1848. Records of Rockingham Circuit, 1843-1858, AUMC; Minutes of Cook's Creek and Harrisonburg Presbyterian church (*VL* 36), 1837-1851, p. 48f (2 December 1838: request "from Johnathan Funk (of Joseph) a member of the church of Turleytown, to be received into the Church of Cook's Creek & Harrisonburg"). Later, Benjamin, Solomon, and Timothy would all serve as ministers in the Baptist church. Solomon "was the pastor of Singer's Glen Baptist church, and often preached at places near this church." Solomon died 13 June 1880 at the age of 54. Taylor, *Virginia Baptist Ministers*, 3:329ff (Solomon); 5:234ff (Timothy); 5:239f (Benjamin). See also Dodd, "Baptists of Rockingham County," *The Religious Herald*, 15 August 1912, p. 7.

[50]Funk, *Reviewer Reviewed*, 7f, 305, 308f.

[51]Funk, *Reviewer Reviewed*, 7.

[52]John Kline, *Strictures and Reply to the Reviewer Reviewed: being a further defense of baptism…* Columbiana, OH: Henry Kurtz, 1858, BC.

[53]Kline had plans to build a bridge across the North Fork as it came out of Brock's Gap. His dream eventually happened, but not in his earthly lifetime. Funk, *Kline*, 217.

[54]Kline had many preaching points throughout Rockingham, including Seller's Schoolhouse in Brock's Gap, John Zigler's in Timberville, and elsewhere at Edom and Dayton, to name a few. Funk, *Kline*, 270 (3 March 1850: Seller's), 273 (16 May 1850: Zigler's), 328 (28 August 1853: Edom), 335 (4 March 1854: Dayton). Perhaps one of the most unusual places Kline held services was the home of Addison Harper. Harper, a Brock's Gap resident, "openly avowed his disbelief in divine revelation," yet politely tolerated the meetings. After the Civil War had ended, Harper gave his life to Christ and joined the Dunkers as a minister. Funk, *Kline*, 419f.

[55]Funk, *Kline*, 414.

[56]Funk, *Kline*, 213 (17 July 1847).

[57]For consistency, and to avoid confusion with the United Brethren, the term Dunker is used throughout this book, though Kline seemed to find that term annoying at best, preferring instead to refer to the church as "the Brethren." Funk, *Kline*, 192, 378.

[58]These were the results of the council meeting at Bowman's Mill (now the Linville Creek meeting house at Broadway) held Thursday, 11 September 1856. Funk, *Kline*, 212f, 381f. Though this meeting took place eleven years after the Coverstons' baptism, the Dunker church had always officially maintained their position against slavery.

[59]Funk, *Kline*, 382.

[60]Funk, *Kline*, 349f.

[61]The Methodist stance resulted practically in the avoidance of "life-long" enslavement, allowing — at least through the 1850s — for slaveholders to remain in the church. Despite the strong wording of the United Brethren ruling, there were some notable exceptions of slaveholders among the membership up to the time of the Civil War. Drury, *Disciplines*, 90f; Drury, *Glossbrenner*, 142.

[62]According to John W. Fulkerson, a United Brethen minister in attendance: "The fathers of the conference had a heavy conflict on their hands, for the formal churches had brains, education, and influence, and thought the United Brethren were fanatics, or fit subjects for a hospital for the insane. These formalists united to squelch the evangelical movement with all the powers they could command, and these were not insignificant." Funkhouser, *Virginia Conference*, 70.

[63]The story is related by a contemporary of Rimel's, John W. Fulkerson, a member of the Virginia Conference of the United Brethren from 1839 to 1852. Though Rimel is not listed in the abstracted minutes as being appointed to the Rockingham (Staunton prior to 1853) circuit during those years, he may well have been fulfilling his duty to the Home Missionary Society emphasized at the 1849 Conference, at which time Rimel was a presiding elder. Rimel was appointed to the Rockingham circuit in 1855 and 1856. Funkhouser, *Virginia Conference*, 78ff, 136, 143, 153, 253, 256.

[64]Funk, *Kline*, 420f.

[65]Massey, *Autobiography*, 26.

[66]*Staunton Spectator* (6 December 1859), p. 2, col. 5, quoting *The New York Observer* re: Thanksgiving sermons in the city. Peaceful abolitionists in the North had a difficult time dealing with the events, approving of Brown as a "moral hero" but not as a "soldier." Lucretia Coffin Mott in *National Anti-Slavery Standard*, 3 November 1860. Articles from the *Staunton Spectator* and related newspapers such as *The Vindicator* can be found online at The Valley of the Shadow website, http://valley.vcdh.virginia.edu.

[67]"Baltimore Conference," *Staunton Vindicator*, 9 March 1860, p. 2, col. 3.

[68]Matthew 7:12; Italics added. The rule was as follows: "*Question.*—What shall be done for the extirpation of the evil of Slavery? *Answer.*—We declare that we are as much as ever convinced of the great evil of Slavery. We believe that the buying, selling, or holding of human beings, to be used as chattels, is contrary to the laws of God and nature, and inconsistent with the Golden Rule and with that Rule in our Discipline

which requires all who desire to continue among us to 'do no harm,' and to 'avoid evil of every kind.' We therefore affectionately admonish all our preachers and people to keep themselves pure from this great evil, and to seek its extirpation by all lawful and Christian means." *Journal of the General Conference of the Methodist Episcopal Church,* NY: Carlton & Porter, 1860, p. 260, ABWC. The rule implied that all slave*holders* were to be expelled from the church. William Warren Sweet, *Virginia Methodism: A History.* Richmond, VA: Whittet & Shepperson, 1955, p. 264; D. W. Arnold, "Methodist Conference," *Staunton Vindicator,* 8 June 1860, p. 2, col. 6. ("Valley papers please copy.") The 1857 Baltimore Conference had agreed on the following two resolutions: 1) "...that we highly deprecate the agitation of the slavery question, which has already esulted to the great detriment of the political and religious interests of the country;" and 2) "...we will oppose with zeal any aggressions which shall be attempted by the abolition agitation of the country." The Baltimore conference held in Winchester on 29 February 1860 seemed to reaffirm the anti-abolitionist position of the conference. The Rockingham District included at least two circuits at least largely in the county itself, Rockingham, with seven churches claiming 382 white and 105 "colored" members, and East Rockingham, containing 228 white, but only 13 "colored" members in five churches. [In 1857, there was also a Rushville Mission as part of the Rockingham District.] The assignment of preachers was as follows: Rockingham: T. Hildebrand, George V. Leech; East Rockingham: R. Smith, J. N. Gray; and Lacy's Springs: Henry Hoffman. Neither circuit listed any local preachers. *Annual Minutes of the Baltimore Conference of the Methodist Episcopal Church.* March 4-18, 1857. Baltimore: Armstrong & Berry, 1857, pp. 14; *Annual Minutes of the Baltimore Conference of the Methodist Episcopal Church* (held in Winchester, VA), February 29, 1860. Baltimore: Printed by William M. Innes, 1860, pp. 10ff, 46, 51.

[69] The vote was 87 ayes, 1 nay, in addition to 41 who "declined to vote," and 3 who "reserved their votes." The single person "against" later sided with the majority. Those who stood against separation chose simply *not to vote,* perhaps intimidated by the sentiment in Staunton, where at the same time a Lay Convention was agreeing upon the same resolution. From Rockingham, both Henry Hoffman and Thomas Hildebrand voted in favor of the resolution to separate. Though the now independent Baltimore Conference in the Valley sent a delegate to the Methodist Episcopal Church, South, they did not join with the southern church until after the Civil War had ended. *Annual Register of the Baltimore Conference of the Methodist Episcopal Church* (held in Staunton, VA.), March 13-25, 1861. Baltimore: Printed by William M. Innes, 1861, pp. 6ff, 19. *Minutes of the Sessions of the Baltimore Annual Conference, Methodist Episcopal Church* (1862-1865). Staunton, VA: Stoneburner & Prufer, 1899, p. 5. For the remarks made at the Northern church's Baltimore Conference meeting on 10 March 1861 in Georgetown by former Rockingham residents John Bear and N. J. B. Morgan, see

http://homepages.rootsweb.com/~mdtaffet/bear_letter_1861_03_10.htm

[70] *Baltimore Conference* (1862-1865), 3f.

[71] When it formed in 1839, the New School General Assembly had left the question of slavery to the "lower judicatories," but in 1846 they proclaimed that "the system of slavery, as it exists United States...is instrinsically an unrighteous and oppressive system, and is opposed to the prescriptions of the law of God..." Finally, in April 1858, the United Synod of the Presbyterian Church in the U.S.A. was organized. Six years later, that new body was welcomed into the Presbyterian Church in the Confederate States of America. Thompson, *Presbyterians in the South,* 540f, 546, 550. Lutherans did not split until the outbreak of the war itself when they made reference to the "uncharitable and intolerant spirit and bearing of many of those who *[sic]* we once esteemed as 'brethren in the same faith' — that the interests of our church, loyalty to our Government, as well as the promprings of self-respect, imperatively demand that we should at once dissolve all ecclesiastical alliance with them..." Though at the outset the Virginia Lutheran synod was "fully persuaded that the present defensive war...is *just* and *righteous,*" two years later the same body was referring to the conflict as "This cruel and unjust war..." 1861 (p. 10), 1863 (p. 4) Minutes of the Virginia Lutheran Synod, LTSG. It should also be noted that the Northern Lutherans (General Synod, U.S.) had in 1862 passed some strongly-worded resolutions of their own, describing "the rebellion against the constitutional Government" as wicked, unjustifiable, unnatural, inhuman, oppressive and [lastly] "destructive in its results to the highest interests of morality and religion," and accusing the southern Lutherans of "open sympathy [to] and active co-operation [with]...the cause of treason and insurrection." Eisenberg, *Lutheran Church,* 218f, quoting Minutes of the General Synod, U.S., 1862, p. 30f. The German Reformed Classis of Virginia met only once during the war, in September 1861, and not again until 18 May 1866. Like the United Brethren in Christ whose congregations were also almost entirely in the Northern states, the German Reformed church seems to have avoided a denominational schism over the issues dividing the nation. Garrison, *Reformed,* 97, 100, 102.

[72] Funk, *Kline,* 438 (1 January 1861). Wayland, *Rockingham,* 133.

[73] John F. Lewis, like his popular father, General Samuel Hance Lewis, was a Whig. The other two delegates, S. A. Coffman (the youngest of the three) and A. S. Gray, were both Democrats. *Rockingham Register,* 8 February 1861; Wayland, *Rockingham,* 127; Mark W. Cowell, *The Family of John Lewis, Pioneer.* Compiled by Irwin Frazier, edited by Lewis F. Fisher. San Antonio, TX: Fisher Publications, Inc., 1985, p. 313f; Massey, *Autobiography,* 27 (In Rockingham "...there were, I think, at least ten times as many Democrats in the county as there were

Whigs.")

[74]Wayland, *Rockingham*, 133. The convention's decision was ratified in a general referendum on 23 May 1861, by a vote of 128,884 to 32,134.

[75]In 1865, Lewis would be an unsuccessful Union candidate for Congress, and in 1872 mentioned as a possible candidate for vice president under Ulysses S. Grant. He twice served as Virginia's Lieutenant Governor and once as a United States Senator. Wayland, *Rockingham*, 355f. Lewis was also active in the re-establishment of the Protestant Episcopal church in Rockingham. Though not really re-established in Rockingham by the war's start, the Episcopal Church would not have any "schismatical division" as a result of the secession of the Confederate states. Each state had its own diocese, which, "like each state, is sovereign and independent." The Episcopal church throughout the North had apparently maintained an anti-abolitionist stand. "The Episcopal Church," *The Vindicator* (12 April 1861), p. 1, col. 5; Wayland, *Rockingham*, 252.

[76]The operations and land of Mt. Vernon Forge extended over a wide area in this south eastern part of the county. Old Forge is in part now within the town of Grottoes. Cowell, *Lewis*, 314. Ananias Davisson moved to this area and set up a printing shop.

[77]Wysong was apparently not present to vote on the separation issue at the Staunton Convention of March 1861. The other minister at Port in 1861, probationer John N. Gray, was still serving in 1862 and later. May, *Port*, 61a; *Baltimore Conference* (1861), 19, 59f; *Baltimore Conference* (1862-1865), 20, 41.

[78]Funk, *Kline*, 440.

[79]*Baltimore Conference* (1862-65), 26f. Ironically, a letter in the *Staunton Spectator* of 2 August 1859, claimed the Methodists in their camp meetings "ignore the Sabbath [and] violate the peace and good order of society" by permitting or giving occasion for "drunkenness, profanity, huckstering, fighting, lewdness, and almost every crime." Replies and follow-ups were in the issues of 16 August and 2 September.

[80]Funk, *Kline*, 442f (19-22 May 1861).

[81]Funk, *Kline*, 446 (20 December 1861). The war was divisive even among the peace-loving churches, however. Six months earlier, "Gabriel Shank, who had been virtually excluded from the Menonite Church for joining a voluntary company, & who must start the next day to join the army, applied for admission to the [Cook's Creek and Harrisonburg New School Presbyterian] church. He was examined as to his knowledge & piety, & received into church communion." Minutes of Cook's Creek & Harrisonburg Presbyterian Church (*VL* 36), 1851-1886, p. 43 (17 June 1861).

[82]A. F. Roller, a soldier from Weyers Cave, reported that initially his army had no ammunition for their flintlock muskets which had been altered to percussion locks. They were sent to their first positions with nothing but bayonets and Bowie knives. A. F. Roller, "Lack of Equipments in '61," *Confederate Veteran*, 17 (1909), p. 123.

[83]Letter of I. D. Williamson to his wife, 20 July 1861, Williamson Family Papers, MS #405, VMI. Berkley, every thing {!} A first-hand account of the activities of the 10th Virginia by D. H. Lee Martz can be found in Wayland, *Rockingham*, 134ff. Martz, who later joined the Harrisonburg Methodist church, was "Converted in Confederate Camp under M. H. Balthis" in 1863. Chronological List of Members, 1882, AUMC.

[84]An African minister who was a slave once asked Dunker elder Jonas Graybill what he thought of the war. "It is an awful thing for a Christian nation to be engaged in," replied the pacifist-minded Graybill. "This is true," the slave agreed, "but there are thousandsof us poor slaves who are praying that the Lord will so overrule this war that we may be free." Zigler, *Brethren*, 77.

[85]Funk, *Kline*, 444 (21 July 1861).

[86]The 1860 census showed 2,388 enslaved Africans compared with 21,059 free inhabitants (including free blacks). Besides war-related difficulties, another trial for Valley residents was the diptheria epidemic, a plague which took the lives of many young children. Of the nearly 100 funeral sermons Kline would preach in 1861 and 1862, about half would be for children under 10 years old. "U. S. Census Rockingham County," *Rockingham Register and Virginia Advertiser*, 14 December 1860, p. 2 col. 2, UVA; Funk, *Kline*, 458, 467.

[87]Peter S. Hartman, *Reminiscences of the Civil War.* Lancaster, PA: Eastern Mennonite Associated Libraries and Archives, 1964, p. 8.

[88]Hartman, *Reminiscences*, 8.

[89]Hartman, *Reminiscences*, 10f.

Side 11 Funk, *Kline*, 490f; Hartman, *Reminiscences*, 9f; See also the correspondence between Henry Dedrick and his wife, Lissa. According to biographical material on the VMI website, Dedrick, a former resident of Rockingham, was wounded at the battle of Cross Keys. Throughout the correspondence Lissa expresses repeated concern for Henry's spiritual life and eternal destiny. Henry H. Dedrick Papers, 52nd Virginia Infantry, Manuscript #0332, VMI; http://new.vmi.edu/archives/Manuscripts/ms332.html.

[90]Major General T. J. Jackson to Col. S. Bassett French, 21 March 1862. OR, Series 1, 12(3):835.

[91]Zigler, *Brethren,* 104-111 has details on this incident from an account given by David Miller. *Olive Branch of Peace,* 59ff, contains a narrative of the group of 18 from J. M. Cline, and the story of the larger group from Joseph A. Miller. Another account mentions a "William Dunlap" among the group taken to Richmond. This may have been the same as Rev. Dunlap, a United Brethren minister whose name appears in the records of the Lacey Springs circuit. Records of Lacey Springs Circuit, UVA, published as *Record of the Churches of the Lacey Spring Circuit,* Bridgewater, VA: Beacon Printing, 1984. Organized in 1854, the Lacey Springs circuit included churches north of Dayton and Whitesel's to Mill Creek (Shenandoah county). Funkhouser, *Virginia Conference,* 256f.

[92]The smaller group of eighteen was taken just before Moorefield, then brought from Woodstock to Harrisonburg (via stops at Mt. Jackson and the Bethlehem church) and kept in the court house along with John Kline. *Olive Branch of Peace,* 63ff. United Brethren preacher, Benjamin Stickley, though he may not have been with the group of seventy, was imprisoned in Staunton during the war. Stickley was released on a writ of habeas corpus, but apparently his time in prison was a break-ing experience. "When liberated, he sacrificed his farm and other property, left the home and friends of a lifetime, and migrated to Iowa, where in no long time he died, never recov-ering his former spirit and ambition." Funkhouser, *Virginia Conference,* 74ff (quote 76), 84, 145.

[93]S[ydney]. S. Baxter, 31 March 1862. OR (2), 3:835.

[94]Elder Benjamin Miller helped collect money for the Dunkers. Zigler, *Brethren,* 113. A few in the group carried to Libby Prison were not members of either the Dunker or Mennonite churches and were forced to join the army. Hartman refers to "Brother Manassas Heatwole." In his report, Baxter notes two other persons, "Peter L. Goode, a broken legged man, whom I believe to be incapable of military duty, and…John Sanger, a youth of sixteen years," both of whom "seem to have partaken in the Tunker [Dunker] panic and fled with the others." Baxter, 31 March 1862, OR (2), 3:835; Hartman, *Reminiscences,* 16ff. The Virginia law, passed 29 March 1862, remained in limbo until a corresponding law was passed in the Confederate Congress in October of that same year. See Baxter, 2 April 1862, OR (2), 3:837. On 5 February 1863, the Virginia General Assembly authorized the auditor of public accounts to reim-burse those who had paid the fines. There were about 100 Rockingham County citizens who received the refund. In all over $50,000 was refunded to Dunkers and Mennonites in Rockingham and Augusta. Virginia. Auditor of Public Accounts (1776-1928). Military Service Exemption Fines, Certificates and Powers of Attorney, 1862-1863. Entry 472, R.G. 48, Box 1350, Military Exemptions, Powers of Attorney, Rockingham County, 1863; Roll of Names, LV. A number of others had avoided the fines altogether by getting through the lines to freedom. *Olive Branch,* 71. See also Christian B. Keller, "Pennsylvania and Virginia Germans During the Civil War," *VMHB* 109:65ff who

references the Rockingham County, Virginia Enrolling Office, Enrolling Books, 1862-64, two volumes, VHS.

[95]Funk, *Kline,* 374 (Kline was 59 on 17 June 1856), 448. A few months earlier, he had written, "Brethren, pray for us, and never forget us at the throne of grace. We feel as though perse-cution is right at the door. How long we will be permitted to write, or speak in public we know not. A few of our brethren have been taken before magistrates, but none condemned; no not even a charge preferred against them that could be estab-lished." Letter 10 December 1861 to the Dunker brethren in the Northern states. "Letter from brother Kline," *Gospel Visitor* (March 1862), 12(3):93. BC/Brethren Heritage Room.

[96]Kline's letter of 15 April 1862 makes reference to an article in the *Rockingham Register,* 11 April 1862. Zigler, *Brethren,* 109.

[97]Bethlehem church had also been a stop for the group of eighteen captured near Moorefield. While that group was at the court house in Harrisonburg, they "got a kind of epizootic [viz., a virulent illness] and had it not been for Brother John Kline, it did seem that we could not have lived. It did seem that the Lord had him to come there to take care of us. As a physician he took care of us in our sickness, and as a minister he preached for us several times at night, and on each Sunday." Gabriel Heatwole, Sr. (born 26 October 1789), one of those interned with Kline at the court house, was also a doctor. Five of his sons and two of his sons-in-law were among the group of seventy captured near Petersburg. *Olive Branch,* 62, 64 (quote from narrative of J. M. Cline), 108. Among the guard-house crew was United Brethren preacher George Snapp, but whether he was with the group of eighteen or arrested with Kline and Heatwole is not clear. "The Civil War Diary of George H. Snapp," transcribed by Roger Sappington, *The Rockingham Recorder* (April 1985), 3(3):107; Funkhouser, *Virginia Conference,* 262.

[98]Kline notes that Jackson came through Harrisonburg on 18 April, but Collins mentions 17 April as the date. Funk, *Kline,* 453; Darrell L. Collins, *The Battles of Cross Keys and Port Republic.* Lynchburg, VA: H. E. Howard, Inc., 1993, p. 7. In fact, Jackson began falling back via Harrisonburg to Swift Run Gap on the 17th, but he himself did not arrive until the 18th. Advance units from Federal forces would not enter Harrisonburg until 21 April. OR 12(3):853ff. A draft instigated by the Confederate Congress on April 16 overrode the Virginia exemption law. Mennonite Bishop Samuel Coffman announced from his pulpit that anyone who answered the call could no longer be a member of the Mennonite Church. Feelings ran high against Coffman in the community at large. With his life threatened, Coffman thought it best to leave Rockingham for a time. Brunk, *Mennonites,* 1:159, 163f.

[99]General Banks' forces camped in and around Harrisonburg for about two weeks, beginning on 26 April. Collins, *Cross Keys,* 8. "They must have been about the most orderly army in

the war. They did not molest anyone. They paid for the few things that they wanted. They would come out to our house, sit down and talk, and get us to sing. We got our families together to sing for them." Hartman, *Reminiscences*, 20. A United Brethren preacher, T. F. Brashear, prayed for the success of the Federal army while Banks was at Harrisonburg, but when Banks left, so did Brashear, to Iowa. Funkhouser, *Virginia Conference*, 97, 133. The first battle near Harrisonburg was on June 6 of that year.

[100]Letter from Rev. J. K. Hitner, Presbyterian, Private Rockbridge Artillery to J[ohn] William Jones, author and compiler of *Christ in the Camp; or, Religion in Lee's Army.* Richmond: B. F. Johnson & Co., 1888, p. 480ff (quote 481).

[101]In three months time, they marched 600 miles. General William C. Oates, *The War Between the Union and the Confederacy and Its Lost Opportunities with a History of the 15th Alabama Regiment and the Forty-Eight Battles in Which It Was Engaged.* New York: The Neale Publishing Company, 1905, p. 105f.

[102]Jones, *Christ in the Camp*, 481.

[103]Jones, *Christ in the Camp*, 94. R. N. Pool, a member of the Bridgewater Quarterly Conference of the Methodist Episcopal Church (independent Baltimore Conference), was appointed as a chaplain at the Baltimore Conference meeting held in Bridgewater in March 1865. *Baltimore Conference* (1862-1865), p. 97.

[104]Jones, *Christ in the Camp*, 35, quoting a correspondent of *The Louisville Courier* writing from Virginia.

[105]Jones, *Christ in the Camp*, 482.

[106]Oates, *15th Alabama*, 101.

[107]Samuel V. Fulkerson to his sister, Kate. 8 June 1862, Manuscript #0363 ALS, Fulkerson Family Papers, VMI. [Although this letter bears the heading 8 *May* 1862, it refers to the events of June at the Battle of Port Republic.] Text online at http://www.vmi.edu/archives/Manuscripts/ms363006.html.

[108]Jones, *Christ in the Camp*, 251, 481.

[109]As another chaplain advised his fellow preachers, "Let brevity mark these services. Let the words be few and well chosen. This is the principle: What are the few sentences that will save his soul if I never speak again? A great many useless appendages to sermons will be thus cut off, and we will leave the army better preachers than when we entered it. Long sermons weary and injure your usefulness. Be short and sharp; brief, but brimful of the Gospel." Jones, *Christ in the Camp*, 251, 519.

[110]Major-General T. J. Jackson to General Joseph E. Johnston, 6 June 1862, Port Republic, Virginia, in OR 12(3):906f; For a Union army perspective see Francis F. Wayland, "Fremont's Pursuit of Jackson in the Shenandoah Valley: The Journal of Colonel Albert Tracy, March-July 1862," *VMHB* 70:165-193, 332-354, esp. 332ff. Tracy notes that it was Robert H. Milroy's Federal brigade which was positioned around the Union Church.

[111]Since his marriage in 1858, George Boardman Taylor had been pastor of the "struggling, nascent church in Staunton, where Baptists were few and little esteemed." He wrote a series of children's books, two boys' books, and a historical novel about the early Baptists of Virginia entitled *Walter Ennis*, in addition to numerous tracts. During the war he penned *The Soldiers Almanac for 1863* (at http://docsouth.unc.edu/imls/almanac1863/menu.html), and *In the Hospital* (at http://docsouth.unc.edu/imls/taylor /menu.html). With the exception of a two-year chaplaincy at the University of Virginia (1869-1871), Taylor remained pastor of the Staunton church after the war until 1873 when he was sent to Rome as a Baptist missionary. Taylor, *Virginia Baptist Ministers*, 5:187-200.

[112]Accounts of the initial encounter at the Union church differ in various reports. See Oates, *15th Alabama*, 102f. "The ground was undulating, with much wood, and no extended view could be had," remembered brigade General Richard Taylor. Richard Taylor, *Destruction and Reconstruction*, New York: Appleton & Co., 1879, p. 72.

[113]The Union Army report indicates that the "sharp skirmishing" at Union church began at 9 a.m., though Col. Tracy's journal says the initial skirmish began an hour earlier. The 25th Virginia, Col. Walker in command, had reinforced Trimble's brigade by 10 a.m. and "assisted in the repulse of the enemy." OR 12(1), 655, 781; "Tracy," *VMHB* 70:332. Taylor's brigade had been called suddenly to march "double-quick to Port Republic." There, Jackson himself had barely escaped when one of Shields's guns managed to command one end of the bridge over the North River. Taylor, *Destruction and Reconstruction*, 72f. During the day's fighting, the 25th Virginia would suffer six fatalities and fifteen more wounded. Richard L. Armstrong, *25th Virginia Infantry and 9th Battalion Virginia Infantry.* Lynchburg, VA: H. E. Howard, Inc., 1990, p. 34.

[114]After hearing this report and other accounts of bravery by military chaplains, B. T. Lacy encouraged his co-workers, "Don't interfere with officers; consult them, and try to *work in* the Gospel. Don't *desert the men because they are in the trenches.* Go, speak a word to them, if you only say, 'I know you were ready to fight for your country; but were you ready to meet your God?' The Gospel hurts no man at any time under any circumstances." Jones, *Christ in the Camp*, 228 (Taylor's letter on the incident, 9 July 1862), 251, 518f (519: quote in endnotes).

Collins, *Cross Keys,* 49ff.

[115]"The War in the Valley," *Rockingham Register,* 20 June 1862, BC-Microfilm.

[116]"The War in the Valley," *Rockingham Register,* 20 June 1862, BC-Microfilm. Artist and author Benjamin J. Lossing returned to the battlefield in October, 1866 when he gave this description of the Union church and his artist sketched it. Lossing had also been present during the battles of Cross Keys and Port Republic. Though destruction of the church is sometimes attributed to Sheridan's army which devastated the Valley in the fall of 1864, Lossing's description indicates it is more likely that all or most of the damage was from the battle of Cross Keys. Oates, *15th Alabama,* 104; Benson J. Lossing, *Pictorial History of the Civil War in the United States of America.* Hartford, CT: Thomas Belknap, 1880, p. 396; Typed history part of Massanutten Cross Roads church records, *Lexington, VL* 64; *Rockingham Register,* 11 October 1866 (re: visit of Mr. Lossing and his artist).

[117]Colonel Samuel Fulkerson, Letter of 8 & 14 June 1862. Fulkerson also wrote of Jackson, "He is an ardent Christian. On the 8th when he ordered me to charge through the bridge and take the enemy's guns at the other end, he turned his horse around, raised both hands, closed his eyes and prayed till the guns were taken and the enemy put to flight. All this has at least a good moral influence over the men." Online texts at http://www.vmi.edu/archives/Manuscripts/ms363006.html and …/ms363007.html

[118]Funk, *Kline,* 457 (8 October 1862).

[119]The full lyrics to this piece can be found at www.goshen.edu/~lonhs/Practical_Musician/Shapenotes.html. The melody can be heard as a midi file at www.goshen.edu/~lonhs/Practical_Musician/Retreat.mid.

[120]According to his obituary, Parret "united with the Mennonite church when a young man." By the spring of 1862 when he was drafted, he would have been 19 years old [died 15 May 1905 at age of 62y., 8 m. and 15]. If Parret was a member of the church when drafted, he would have fallen under the exemption law, although many obeyed the draft and joined the army as teamsters. *The Gospel Witness,* 7 June 1905, p. 80 at http://freepages.genealogy.rootsweb.com/~mennobit/1905GW /jun05gw.html.

[121]Funk, *Kline,* 461ff.

[122]In 1862, Dunker minister David Thomas is said to have sold 1,000 gallons of molasses and several hundred gallons of flaxseed oil at a financial loss to himself in order to help his Rockingham neighbors. Wayland, *Rockingham,* 153.

[123]Samuel Coffman, born 2 June 1822, was ordained a bishop in the Mennonite church on 11 May 1861 and was officially exempted from military duty on 26 June 1861. During the war, the Coffman's were living "on the Leonard Jones place (1959) near Dale Enterprise." Coffman returned to Rockingham after the war and was later allowed $132 on his claim to the Federal government against wartime depredations. Later, he led the movement to have Sunday Schools in the Mennonite church. Brunk, *Mennonites,* 1:161f, 177, 199ff; 336 (ordination paper still preserved) and others; Nellie Coffman, "A Short Biography of Samuel Coffman," *Mennonite Historical Bulletin,* Vol. XIX, January, 1958, p. 4, EMU.

[124]Hartman, *Reminiscences,* 12ff. All of the cabins at Liberty Springs, two miles south of Rawley Springs, were burned to keep people from hiding there. Letter from D. B. Showalter, 14 December 1911 in Wayland, *Rockingham,* 397.

[125]*The Vindicator,* 8 July 1864. Hunter's advance to Harrisonburg interrupted the publishing of the Staunton paper on 3 June, since all the printers were called to arms. The paper of 8 July was the first published since 27 May and summarizes many events of the preceding weeks.

[126]Funk, *Kline,* 479.

[127]In late September, Brigadier-General Alfred T. A. Torbert, who had partially destroyed the railroad bridge at Waynesboro, fell back with his cavalry from Staunton to Bridgewater and Spring Creek, while drivining off livestock, destroying food supplies and burning mills. P. H. Sheridan, *Personal Memoirs of P. H. Sheridan,* New York: Charles L. Webster & Co., 1888, Volume 2, p. 49ff.

[128]Solomon Funk recorded in his diary that the "Yankees" were burning barns on 6 October 1864. Funk Papers, 1850-1918, Solomon Funk's Diary, BC.

[129]See also J. E. Taylor, *With Sheridan up the Shenandoah Valley in 1864: Leaves from a Special Artist's Sketch Book and Diary.* Dayton, OH: Morningside House, 1989, pp. 420ff. Not all who left were Mennonites and Dunkers. The family of young Susie Swank, who had four brothers in the Confederate army, were part of the refugee families who went north with Sheridan. Susie Swank, "Recalls General Phil Sheridan's Raid in Shenandoah Valley, and Visit of Soldiers in Her Home," *The Daily Examiner* (Bellefontaine, Ohio), 11 November 1927, p. 8, typescript at HRHS.

[130]*Staunton Spectator,* 17 October 1865, p. 2, col. 3. Black, a native of Scotland, had visited the Valley in June.

[131]The full list included 30 dwellings; 450 barns; 37 mills; 100 miles of fence; 100,000 bushels of wheat; 50,000 bushels of corn; 6,233 tons of hay; 1,750 cattle; 1,750 horses; 4,200 sheep; 3,350 hogs, 3 factories and 1 furnace in addition to a great deal of farm equipment and machinery. *Rockingham*

Register, 11 November 1864, quoted in "Rockingham's Losses," *The Vindicator,* 18 November 1864. The value was in Confederate currency and estimated at perhaps 20 percent higher than the government standard. In the 24 March 1865 edition of the *Register,* B. Hoover listed the names and losses of property owners in the Röder's church community. Garrison, *Reformed,* 98.

[132]Memories of Sarah Shank Zigler (1859-1952), "Shank Family" (vertical file), EMU.

[133]*Minutes of the Annual Meetings,* 301 (1865), 318 (1866). It is interesting to note that the 1866 meeting was held near the Antietam battlefield. Though the group decided not to have an open meeting where they would feed those who were not members of their church, the meeting was attended by 16,000 persons who were fed at a great tent, 1,000 at a time. This practice was at least suspended for the Annual Meeting in June 1867 at Pipe Creek, where there was to be no public preaching and no boarding tent "to entertain and feed a mixed multitude as before…" *The Old Commonwealth,* 29 May 1867, UVA; *Religious Herald,* 15 November 1866, p. 1.

[134]*Rockingham Register,* 20 September 1866.

[135]Yet, if they showed any feelings toward Virginia's plight, even those members of the peace churches who lived in northern states during the war might earn the displeasure of their neighbors. *Rockingham Register,* 9 August 1866.

[136]Though many of the initial leaders of the United Brethren came from the Reformed church, after 1800 when the group was officially organized, both preachers and members in general tended to come more from the Mennonites and other groups, if not outside denominational lines altogether. A. W. Drury, *The Life of Bishop J. J. Glossbrenner, D. D. of the United Brethren in Christ.* Dayton, OH: United Brethren Publishing House, 1889, p. 89.

[137]At their annual conference in 1852, "Resolutions of loyalty to the church law on slavery were passed, the institution being denounced as criminal." Funkhouser, *Virginia Conference,* 255. It was true, however, that "particular exceptions" to this slave-holding rule existed to the day Lincoln signed the Emancipation Proclamation. Drury, *Glossbrenner,* 77, 141.

[138]The United Brethren — wrote one of their bishops in language reminiscent of both Dunkers and Mennonites — had "endeavored to be a quiet people, interfereing *[sic]* in no way in the rights of others, and endeavored as much as possile, to live at peace with all men." Letter from United Brethren Bishop J. J. Glossbrenner, 27 September 1865 from Cora, Pennsylvania, appearing as "The United Brethren Church and Negro Equality," *Staunton Spectator,* 31 October 1865, p. 1, col. 6. Glossbrenner, a resident of Augusta throughout the war years, had always walked a careful line on this issue and Southern

fidelity. Once while visiting Confederate general Stonewall Jackson, Glossbrenner remarked, "I cannot wish you success, but my daughters who are with me can." Drury, *Glossbrenner,* 180.

[139]"Annual *[sic]* Conference of United Brethren," *Staunton Spectator,* 5 September 1865, p. 1, col. 6, quoting an article which orginally appeared in the *Western Religious Telescope* about the quadrennial General Conference of the United Brethren in Christ, held 11 May 1865 at Western College, Iowa. See also *Staunton Spectator,* 7 November 1865, p. 1, col. 6. At this meeting the United Brethren reported a loss of over 4,500 members. Some of these had been killed during the war, but others had withdrawn or were dismissed because of their "sympathy with treason" as the bishops' address put it. In spite of everything, and thanks to Glossbrenner's persistent leadership during the war, a southern United Brethren church was never founded. Drury, *Glossbrenner,* 189f.

[140]One writer believed the "political evil-doers of the North who wish to compel Southern submission to black suffrage…would like well to see the South driven to despair" with the hope that the Confederacy would once again take up arms and provide an excuse for its further destruction. *Staunton Spectator,* 24 October 1865, p. 2, col. 3.

[141]The stories and debate between United Brethren Bishop J. J. Glossbrenner and Major McCue, both of Augusta county, were carried in part in several issues of the *Staunton Spectator,* 5 September; 10, 24 & 31 October; 7 & 28 November; and 19 December 1865. Fifteen years earlier, as an Augusta magistrate, McCue had a postmaster publicly burn copies of the United Brethren newspaper, *The Religious Telescope,* which openly spoke out against slavery. Pressure from society to maintain the status quo was even stronger in a state which voted *viva voce* (out loud in a public meeting) until the election of 1867. Glossbrenner and his wife moved to Baltimore in 1868, but his 1865 correspondence was from Pennsylvania. Drury, *Glossbrenner,* 194, 200f.

[142]"Having been an official member of the Church of the United Brethren in Christ for twelve years, it is due the intelligent portion of the Church in the Valley of Virginia, to say that they indignantly and emphatically repudiate those resolutions and are utterly opposed to negro suffrage and negro equality…" *Staunton Spectator,* 10 October 1865. The letter is dated 1 October and was picked up from the *Rockingham Register.* The anonymous author also refers to the 22 September 1865 edition of the *Register.* One United Brethren minister from Rockingham, Joseph Funkhouser, switched to the Methodist Episcopal church, South in 1865. The letter quoted above was apparently not from Joseph Funkhouser, as his connection with the United Brethren extended further back than twelve years. Funkhouser, *Virginia Conference,* 136, 250ff.

Just prior to the outbreak of the war in 1860, the Virginia

Conference of the United Brethren reported 153 preaching places, 116 classes, 3354 members, 16 itinerant preachers, 24 local preachers, 57 meeting houses, and 50 Sabbath schools. John Lawrence, *The History of the United Brethren in Christ.* Dayton, OH: United Brethren Publishing House, 1888, p. 424.

[143]In 1819, the law attempted to discourage the fomenting of rebellion by declaring that "all meetings or assemblages of slaves, or free negroes or mulattoes mixing and associating with such slaves, at any meeting-house or houses, or any other places or places, in the night, or at any school or schools for teaching them reading or writing, either in the day or night, under whatsoever pretext, shall be deemed and considered as an unlawful assembly…" *The Revised Code of the Laws of Virginia.* Volume 1. Richmond, [VA]: Printed by Thomas Ritchie, 1819, c.111, p. 424. Legislation in 1831 read: "All meetings of free Negroes or mulattoes at any school house, church, meeting house or other place for teaching them reading or writing, either in the day or the night shall be considered an unlawful assembly. Warrants shall direct any sworn officer to enter and disperse such Negroes and inflict corporal punishment on the offenders at the discretion of the justice, not exceeding twenty lashes. Any white person assembling to instruct free Negroes to read or write shall be fined not over $50.00, also be imprisoned not exceeding two months." "It is further enacted that if any white person for pay shall assemble with any slaves for the purpose of teaching them to read or write, he shall for each offense be fined, at the discretion of the justice, $10.00-$100.00." June Purcell Guild, *Black Laws of Virginia,* Lovettsville, VA: Willow Bend Books, 1996, p. 176.

[144]German Street, on which corner the Brown's home was located, has since been renamed Liberty Street. Wayland, *Historic Harrisonburg,* 234, 323. At the close of the war, there were two distinct groups of African Methodists in the North. The African Methodist Episcopal (AME), and the African Methodist Episcopal Zion (AME Zion) denominations date from 1787 and 1796, respectively. On 30 May 1795, Asbury "met the Africans, to consult about building a house, and forming a distinct African, yet Methodist Church" in Baltimore. Mead, *Handbook,* 134; Asbury, *Journal and Letters,* 2:51. Many African Americans had been used to the Methodist order and style of worship. In the 1861 statistics of Baltimore Conference circuits in Rockingham county, there were no African American members on the East Rockingham Circuit. With the drop in African members of the Methodist Episcopal church in the Elkton area prior to the war, it is also a possibility that many began to meet independently of the official denomination even then. By comparison, African American membership in the Rockingham and Lacy Springs circuits (including those on trial) was about 11.5 percent in 1861, proportionate to the population at large. See Journal of the Baltimore Conference, AWBC.

[145]In a letter from Cora, Pennsylvania dated 27 September 1865 and appearing in the 31 October issue of the paper,

Glosbrenner clarified that he, too, had always abhorred the idea of social equality with the Negro, a process then termed "amalgamation," but firmly stood by the necessity of equality of every man before the law, including the right for freed slaves to vote. See also the Minutes of the Annual Conference of the United Brethren, May 1865.

[146]*Rockingham Register,* 2 August 1866. In addition to this fund raiser, African Americans put on "an entertainment at Thespian Hall" that October to help retire their debt. *The Old Commonwealth,* 17 October 1866. Albert H. Small Special Collections. University of Virginia.

[147]May, Port Republic, 63. May does not mention Pierce by name, but he does note there was preaching by the northern Methodists at this location.

[148]"A Disturbance—Rev. E. W. Pierce," *Rockingham Register,* 6 September 1866. The exact Sunday of the Court Square preaching is difficult to determine from the article. A follow-up article, including a letter from the Baltimore Conference's Presiding Elder are in the 13 September issue of the *Register.* Actually, keeping out the "meddling Northerners" was more complicated. By the fall of 1871, Mt. Crawford Methodist church, opposed from the start to the "uncalled for attacks of the Divisionists of the South," applied for a $300 grant from the Board of Church Extension of the Virginia Conference ["Northern" church] on which Pierce had served both as vice president and treasurer. Papers of the Baltimore Conference, 1846, AWBC; Minutes of the Church Extension Board, Virginia Conference, 16 October 1871, RMC. Though the Baltimore Conference listed the Rockingham District in its annual minutes of 1862 — its first meeting after the division — its *Virginia* District of 1864 was composed of churches behind the Northern lines. By 1866, the Rockingham District of the Northern church's Baltimore Conference noted only E.W. Pierce for the Rockingham Circuit. *Minutes of the Annual Conferences of the Methodist Episcopal Church,* Volumes 8-11 (1860, 1862, 1864, 1866), New York: Carlton & Porter, and Volume 12 (1868), New York: Carlton & Lanahan, RMC. When the Northern church created its own Virginia Conference in 1869, it was "composed of the Richmond, Abingdon, and Rockingham districts with 36 charges and a membership of something over 3,500." Sweet, *Virginia Methodism,* 285f.

[149]*Rockingham Register,* 18 October 1866; *The Old Commonwealth,* 28 November 1866. In 1870, a one-story, wooden frame schoolhouse was built in Harrisonburg for the use of African Americans. Bounded by Rock Street on the south and by Black's Run on the west and north the "little old school house by the creek" was used for a variety of purposes including church meetings and singing schools. Early that same year, the African American Methodists purchased the brick church on the hill originally built by the Baltimore Conference Methodists and used for a time by the Baptists. The *Rockingham Register* noted: "The Methodist congregation

of colored people here are thus giving proof that they are rising in the world, and that their pecuniary fortunes are improving. The Church they have occupied in Harrisonburg for the last four or five years has become too small for their increasing congregations, and we are pleased to see them securing a larger and more pleasant place of worship." The African American group, however, was not able to make their payments, so the trustees released them from their contract and leased the brick church for use as a federal courthouse. Early on, African American Methodists established a Sunday School in which many children learned to read. In 1880, African American Methodists purchased Andrews Chapel, recently vacated by the "white" Methodists. 3 February 1870, *Rockingham Register*; Wayland, *Harrisonburg,* 41, 346f; Lake's 1885 Atlas; 24 February 1870 (re: new brick church on the hill); 10 September 1874 (re: Sunday School, Rev. Mr. Leewood), *Rockingham Register*.

[149]*Rockingham Register,* 9 August 1866. The American Tract Society, a Northern group opposed to slavery, had established a depository in Richmond, Virginia which served Virginia, North Carolina, South Carolina, Georgia, Florida and Alabama. By this time, they had "employed about forty colporters, and have, from their benevolent funds, organized, resuscitated or aided over 700 Sabbath schools, with about 40,000 scholars, and some of these in the most destitute portions of the country." 11 October 1866, *The Religious Herald,* UVA-M. The following spring, G. W. Stanley wrote of "two [Sabbath] schools organized by him, which have been richly blessed, one reporting twenty-seven and the other thirty-five conversions. A third school was started in the face of some opposition, but the study of the Scriptures became interesting to many, and when the winter began, at which time these schools are usually closed, there was such a reluctance to suspend, that some of the teachers proposed a series of meetings. The Lord was present, and sixty souls found peace in believing in Christ." *Forty-Second Annual Report of the American Tract Society,* 8 May 1867, New York: American Tract Society, [1867], pp. 77, 89f, Archives of the American Tract Society, Garland, TX.

[151]Phil Siegrist, "Captured by Zenda: A Study of an African-American Community In Rural Rockingham County." May 14, 1997, [with supporting documents] EMU. Comparing the 1870 and 1880 censuses for that area, Siegrist noted that the names in Lake's 1885 Atlas do not appear together in the vicinity of Long['s] Chapel until 1880. Nevertheless, the *Rockingham Register* reported that African Americans comprised "a considerable element in that locality" near Mt. Tabor. *Rockingham Register,* 9 August 1866. It is likely that, during the process of geographical segregation which took place after the war, African Americans who had remained in Rockingham gathered together more closely into their own communities. The deed for the chapel was from Hannah and William Carpenter to trustees John Watson, Henry Frazier, and Reuban Dalan in order to give "the congregation of colored people" a tract of land which would be "theirs and their successors forever…for

the purpose of a church, burial ground and School house lot." RCDB 5:103 (23 September 1869). A separate school was built in this vicinity in 1882. Rockingham County School District Ledger, 1886 [photocopy],

[152]A Freedmen's Mission of the United Brethren also existed for a brief time in Vicksburg, Mississippi. Drury, *United Brethren,* 613. The only known records of the Virginia mission are in the abstracts of the minutes of the Virginia Conference from 1870-1879 in Funkhouser, *Virginia Conference,* 267ff, and bound volumes of the printed minutes from 1880 on, EUB.

[153]Legislation in March of 1832 regulated that masters have "slaves, employed or bound, and free Negroes to go with them to religious worship conducted by a white minister" and permitted religious instruction only "in the day time by a licensed white minister to slaves and free Negroes." According to a book proclaiming to be his confessions and published after his death, Turner, a self-proclaimed Baptist preacher, supposedly directed the massacre of several men, women, and children in obedience to "the voice of God." An 1848 law reaffirmed the restrictions on African American worship: "Every assemblage of slaves or free Negroes for religious worship, conducted by a slave or free Negro, and every such assemblage for the purpose of instruction in reading or writing by whomsoever conducted, and every such assemblage in the night time under whatsoever pretext shall be unlawful, and the punishment of any slave or free Negro not exceeding thirty-nine lashes." Guild, *Black Laws,* 106f, 167; There was also a report from Lynchburg of class distinction between Africans who were free prior to the war and those freed as a result of the war. *The Old Commonwealth,* 9 January 1867.

[154]It is uncertain how many of these freedmen were part of the United Brethren prior to the outbreak of the war. In 1880, there were 119 African Americans affiliated with the United Brethren in Rockingham. *Virginia Conference Minutes,* 1880, EUB.

[155]The Virginia Methodist Conference had organized a separate conference for African Americans four years before. Dwight Culver, *Negro Segregation in the Methodist Church.* New Haven: Yale University Press, 1953, p. 51f; C. H. Phillips, *The History of the Colored Methodist Episcopal Church,* Third Edition, Jackson, TN: Publishing House, C.M.E. Church, 1925, pp. 25ff, UVA-M. Baptist congregations could be formed very easily and were congregational, independent, and democratic in structure. The Virginia Negro Baptist convention was organized by 1867. Most former slaves left the Methodist church for the AME or AME Zion churches, although new congregations were formed by missionaries from the Northern church. In 1866, about 49,000 African members of the ME, South were organized into a separate conference. By 1870 they were "set adrift" as the Colored Methodist Episcopal Church. Hudson, *Religion in America,* 225. For discussions between the ME, South and the African M.E. denomination, as well as the official

reports of the Committee on Relgious Interests of Colored People, see *Journal of the General Conference of the Methodist Episcopal Church, South.* Nashville, TN: A.H. Redford, 1866, pp. 58f, 65f, 73, RMC.

[156]Hunter Farish, *The Circuit Rider Dismounts: A Social History of Southern Methodism, 1865-1900.* Richmond, VA: Dietz Press, 1938, p. 173. Of 207,000 African American communicants in the M.E., South church at the outset of there war, there were but 78,000 at war's end. Of these, 49,000 organized into the Colored Methodist Episcopal church. Phillips, *Colored Methodist Episcopal Church,* 71f; Phillips, an African American, was a bishop in this denomination. The reference to "kitchen church" does not appear in Phillips' account. May, Port, 68.

[157]A number of African Americans had left with Sheridan's army in the fall of 1864. *Rockingham Register,* 18 October 1866; Brunk, *Mennonites,* 1:298.

[158]*Rockingham Register,* 11 & 18 October 1866. The 17 adults who brought certificates of membership from the Northern Methodist church were by their own request organized into a separate congregation by the Presiding Elder of the Rockingham circuit. MacMasters, *Asbury,* 63f, referencing 1915 article by A. P. Boude. A church near Furnace was dedicated by members and friends of the Methodist Episcopal, South church in early August 1873. Milnes & Co. gave the land and contributed liberally to the building. "Dedication of a Church," *Rockingham Register,* 8 August 1873, p. 3, col. 1.

[159]William E. Montgomery, *Under Their Own Vine and Fig Tree: The African American Church in the South, 1865-1900.* Baton Rouge: Louisiana State University Press, 1993, p. 142. By the summer of 1867, several "freedmen" in Staunton had also accumulated enough money to purchase their own home lots. *The Old Commonwealth,* 5 June 1867. A few African Americans in Harrisonburg had begun to do the same at least by September of the following year. *The Old Commonwealth,* 9 September 1868, quoted in Wayland, *Harrisonburg,* 322.

Side 12 ACDB 11:826 (28 September 1764); Foote, *Sketches of Virginia,* 1:560f. The Virginia Temperance Society was formed in 1826, and grew to include 42 local societies throughout the state by the end of 1829. William Maxwell, "The Temperance Reform," *Virginia Historical Register* (1850), Richmond, VA, 1850, 3:100f; Rockingham's Temperance Society was represented at the first Temperance Convention of Virginia which met at Charlottesville on 30 October 1834. "The Temperance Reformation in Virginia," *Southern Literary Messenger* (July 1850), 16(7):431, online at Making of America [journals], University of Michigan, http://www.hti.umich.edu/m/moagrp/; *Rockingham Register,* 21 February 1835, page 2 (col. 2: "We have been requested to give notice that there will be a meeting of the Temperance Society, in the Presbyterian Church in this place, on Tuesday evening next at early candle light.

Several addresses may be expected on the occasion"), UVA. By 1839, after an infusion of ministers representing the New School movement, the Virginia Lutheran Synod changed its course and recommended that each minister establish Prayer Meetings, Sabbath Schools, and Temperance Societies in their parochial districts, and give an account of their results in their parochial reports. Minutes of Virginia Lutheran Synod, 1835, p. 7f; 1839, p. 11, LTSG; *Rockingham Register & Advertiser,* 19 July 1866, p. 1, (col. 5: Bridgewater described as a noble little *temperance* village); *Minutes of the Annual Meetings,* 120 (1847, Article 10), 323 (1867, Article 13); Drury, *Glossbrenner,* 130ff; The 1831 Conference of the United Brethren in Christ resolved that "if Conrad Weast don't quit making liquor and preach more, he shall have his license demanded." Six years later, it was ordered that "it be published in the Telescope that Conrad Weast is no longer a preacher among us." Funkhouser, *Virginia Conference,* 117ff; *Baltimore Conference Minutes, 1862-1865,* 26.

[160]The Moravians were at Schmidt's home on 8 December 1749, three days after they preached at Adam Mueller's. The Moravians recorded that despite the admonitions of the Lutheran minister and the general anger against them, Schmidt "believed that we were sincere and faithful followers of Jesus. We would always be welcome in his house." *VMHB* 11:129. Earlier the Moravians had described Schmidt as one "hungry to hear the word of the cross." *VMHB* 11:374 (21 November/New Style 1744); Craig, Baptisms, 21 January 1741/2, UVA (microfilm).

[161]*Pennsylvania Gazette,* (22 December 1790: dateline Baltimore, December 10, "On Tuesday last…") Quite a few ministers of other denominations met Bishop Carroll at the port and escorted him to his residence. Several editions of Antonio Gavin's early 18th century work *A Master-Key Against Popery* were published in Philadelphia in the 1850s. The issues then were perhaps more political, economic and social than theological. William Blackstone, *Commentaries on the Laws of England.* London: A. Strahan, 1809, 4:52ff. By 1866, the number of "religious sects" in the United States was said to be 53, including ten varieties of Baptists, nine of Methodists, and thirteen brands of Presbyterians. With 1,724,373 reported members, Baptists were the most numerous Protestant group, followed by Methodists with 1,651,732, yet both were dwarfed by the number of Roman Catholics, reported to be at least 3,177,140. *Rockingham Register,* 19 January 1866.

[162]MacMasters, *Asbury,* 35f; Carr, *Rocktown,* 17; Wayland, *Men of Mark,* 412.

[163]Bixio's brother was a general in the army of Giuseppe Garibaldi, who fought for a unified Italy. Abstract of a letter from Sister M. Teresa White, V.H.M., Georgetown, DC, to Ellen G. White, New York, NY, April 1861 at http://archives1.archives.nd.edu/calendar/cal1861d.htm. The first Catholic priest to serve the community in Harrisonburg

and Rockingham was apparently Daniel Downye, rector of St. Francis in Staunton. *Blessed Sacrament Catholic Church*, Harrisonburg, Virginia: 80th Anniversary, 1987, p. 3, MRL.

[164]Bixio preached and celebrated Mass on 23 September 1860. Even at this early date, Harrisonburg Catholics had plans to build a church of their own. Wayland, *Harrisonburg*, 230, probably referencing *Rockingham Register*, 27 September 1860; Georgetown University Archives, Maryland Province, Society of Jesus Folder. Card index describing a missing document: Box 20, Folder 4, Item 58 T3. Letter (10 February 1865) of Rev. McMullen. In one published history, Bixio was noted to have written several letters to Edward J. Sullivan announcing the times of his visits during the war. The letters may still be extant. *Blessed Sacrament*, 3. Sullivan was appointed postmaster at Harrisonburg on 14 July 1865. Record of Appointment of Postmasters, 1832–1971, UVA (Document Reading Room); *The American Union*, 14 April 1866, Private Collection.

[165]"Catholicity in the Valley of Virginia," *Rockingham Register and Advertiser*, 9 February 1866, p. 1, col. 5. Letter dated from Staunton, 10 January 1866 and signed by "A Catholic Virginian" reprinted from the Baltimore *Catholic Mirror*. "Reverend Father Maguire" was doubtless Bernard Maguire, S.J., president of Georgetown College from 1853-1858 and again from June 1866-1870. Personal communication. Lynn Conway, University Archivist, Georgetown University. 2 July 2001.

[166]*Rockingham Register*, 9 February 1866. Wayland says "In July, 1866, their chapel was on German Street,—a schoolhouse shortly before occupied by Miss Mary J. McQuaide." Wayland, *Rockingham*, 272.

[167]*Rockingham Register*, 9 February 1866.

[168]Georgetown University Archives, Maryland Province, Society of Jesus Folder. Box 19, Folder 3. Georgetown College-Corresp.-(1849-98) [56 M1-N7] Letter (11 February 1866) from Joseph Bixio, S.J., to C.C. Lancaster, S.J. By 1912, there were about 250 Roman Catholics in Rockingham. Wayland, *Rockingham*, 273.

[169]*Rockingham Register*, 2 March 1866.

[170]The Baltimore Conference Methodists had built this edifice by 1853, but no longer needed it since their reunion with the M. E. church, South in 1866. MacMasters, *Asbury*, 49, referencing N. J. B. Morgan, Sermon Book, Morgan Papers, AWBC. In Harrisonburg, both the independent Baltimore Conference and the Southern Methodists had begun holding joint meetings almost as soon as the war was over. "Religious Meetings in Harrisonburg," *Staunton Spectator*, 12 September 1865, p. 2, col. 3 from *Rockingham Register*. Similar happenings took place with the Presbyterians, as Old and New School Winchester Presbyteries united on 18 September 1865. It was the first meeting for business held by the Old School Winchester Presbytery since the early days of the war. The

paper noted that "Its proceedings were marked with great harmony, and its members appeared hopeful—resolved to enter vigorously upon the work of the Lord." "Winchester Presbytery," *Staunton Spectator*, 10 October 1865, p. 3, col. 3. It would not be until 1906, after the old Methodist church building had burned, that the Roman Catholic congregation would build on a lot along Main Street. Wayland, *Rockingham*, 272f.

[171] Two Jewish merchants known as Jacob and Raphael conducted business in Charlottesville, Stony Point, and Port Republic during the late 18th to early 19th centuries. Edgar Woods, *Albemarle County in Virginia*, Charlottesville, VA: Michie Co., Printers, 1901, p. 359f. Johannes Braun's 1818 circular encouraged mercy toward the Jewish people. Braun, *Circular-Schreiben*, 54ff. The Weiss and Herman Heller families came from Chodau, the Loewner and Joseph Heller families from Königswartha. "Congregation Beth El: Over 100 Years of History," in program for the 25th Anniversary Temple Beth El, September 10, 1989, pp. 5-6. The boundaries of Bohemia were not necessarily fixed, so both towns could have been located in Bohemia. Today Bohemia comprises the western and central portions of the Czech Republic.

[172]Lawrence Loewner, grandson of Samuel Loewner, reported that the family "came to America on a passport dated, Konigswart March 7, 1855" and according to tradition moved directly to Dayton where they lived for about four years before moving to New Hope (Augusta County), then to Harrisonburg. Louis Ginsberg, *Chapters on the Jews of Virginia, 1658-1900*. Richmond, VA: Cavalier Press, 1969, pp. 67, 70.

[173]It was not until the 1890s that leaders decided to change from Orthodox to Reform Judaism, a tradition which does not adhere as closely to the Old Testament law. Ginsberg, *Chapters*, 69f; "Many German-Jewish immigrants were part of the Reform Movement and the religious life of American Jews was colored by that connection. Founded in Hamburg, Reform Judaism aimed at winning civic equality and social acceptance in the modern world." http://www.jewishmuseum.net/American.htm

[174]Ginsberg, *Chapters*, 69; "25th Anniversary," 5. The first services were held on Rosh Hashanah, the Jewish new year and day of purification. Samuel Loewner carved the Ten Commandments in marble. The first building, torn down as part of Project R4 in the early 1960s, was also known as Hebrew Friendship Temple.

[175]Meade, *Old Churches*, 2:324.

[176]Wayland, *Rockingham*, 251ff; After a thirteen year stay in Winchester, Wheat and his family returned to the Port Republic area in 1887 where he became rector of the newly dedicated Grace Memorial church, established three years earlier. The Wheats daughter, Elizabeth, was helped to start the Lewiston Home School for Girls, and was "retained by the

Episcopal diocese to do missionary teaching and work with the 'mountain people' in the adjoining foothills of the Blue Ridge." Cowell, *Lewis*, 314, 322ff.

[177]Soon afterward, another meeting of the members and supporters of the Episcopal church was held at "Rev. Mr. Bell's Church" [New School Presbyterian on the northeast corner of North Main and Elizabeth]. *Rockingham Register*, 2 March 1866.

[178]*The Old Commonwealth*, 24 October 1866; Wayland, *Rockingham*, 252f. Wayland also notes that Shacklett's Hall was the location for Old School Baptist services once a month. Samuel Shacklett (1804-1886) was a successful businessman whose store was located in the rooms occupied by the Fletcher drugstore in the 1940s. *Men of Mark and Representative Citizens of Harrisonburg and Rockingham County Virginia*. Editor-in-Chief, John W. Wayland. Staunton, VA: The McClure Company, p. 428.

[179]This location is the current site of the new Massanutten Regional Library.

[180]Letter from J[ohn].W[illiam].J[ones]. Goshen Bridge, Virginia, dated 26 February 1866. "Baptists in the Valley of Virginia," *Religious Herald*, 15 March 1866.

[181]It is unclear whether or not Old School Baptists still met in the Dayton (Salem) and Linville Creek areas. Brock's Gap reported 35 members and Salem 36 in 1857, but there is no listing for the Salem church in 1870. The Salem congregation sent messengers to their Association in 1872, but did not report any numbers, and they are absent in the records from 1873-1877 and 1885. *Minutes of the Ebenezer Association*, 1857, 1870, 1872, 1873, 1874, 1876, 1877, 1885, VBHS.

[182]This was the newer Salem congregation organized in 1845 by John Massey. The church building at Mt. Crawford is no longer standing. By 1906, the Mt. Crawford Baptists met in a newer building at Mt. Crawford *Station*, along the rail line a little to the east. This building may still be seen on the south side of Friedens Church Road/682, heading east at the Mt. Crawford exit [240] off Interstate 81.

[183]Letter from A. B. Woodfin, 21 March 1864[?, reprinted from the *Southern Christian Advocate*?] in Jones, *Christ in the Camp*, 371.

[184]By 1870, and without a regular pastor, the membership numbers were back to their pre-revival numbers. *Minutes of the Albemarle Baptist Association*, 1865, 1866, 1868-1870, UVA; Letter 12 September 1866 from A. B. Woodfin, "Revival at Mt. Crawford," *The Religious Herald*, 20 September 1866; Letter 7 January 1867 from A. B. Woodfin, "A Query," *The Religious Herald*, 24 January 1867; Letter 14 January 1867 from J. William Jones, "Baptists in the Valley of Virginia," 31 January

1867; C. S. Dodd, "Baptists of Rockingham County," *The Religious Herald*, 15 August 1912, p. 7, UVA-M. After an absence of some seven years, Woodfin returned to Mt. Crawford in the late Summer of 1874 where there was another "series of interesting religious meetings" with preaching day and night for more than a week. *Rockingham Register*, 10 September 1874, BC.

[185]Harrisonburg Baptist church was constituted (organized) on 17 January 1869. After meeting for a time in the Northern (Independent Baltimore Conference) Methodist church on West Market, on 15 May 1871 they purchased the former New School Presbyterian church building which they owned for the next thirteen years or so. Wayland, *Harrisonburg*, 42. The Bridgewater church was begun in 1873, the Singers Glen church in 1876. The Baptist congregation at Turleytown was constituted on 25 September 1859, but is not mentioned in Jones's letter of 1866, due likely to the devastation of the war. Just after its constitution, Solomon and Benjamin Funk transferred their membership from Mt. Crawford Baptist to Turleytown Baptist, where their brother Timothy would serve as pastor. Records of Turleytown Baptist, in Swank 2:205 (25 September 1859: constituted), 209 (21 October 1859: Solomon), 212 (27 October 1860: Benjamin), 213 (1 November 1862: Timothy Funk set apart as pastor), EMU. Singer's Glen had received its new name around 1860. As evidence of the growing interest in the Valley, the Albemarle Baptist Association was scheduled to meet in Harrisonburg on Thursday, 21 August 1873. *Rockingham Register*, 15 August 1873.

The Baptist congregation at Turleytown met at a church shared jointly with the Presbyterians. Records of the Turleytown Baptist Church, in Swank, 2:222 (18 April 1881: New School Baptists "desiring to rebuild the Turley Town church," Presbyterian session of Broadway reserved right to use building one Sunday a month), EMU.

[186]Benjamin evidently got his start as a "licentiate" with the Mount Crawford church, Timothy was elected minister at Turleytown on 1 November 1862 following the resignation of Vincent T. Settle, and Solomon began preaching after the Civil War, giving his first sermon at Turleytown on 26 February 1866. On 15 November 1862, Benjamin Funk became a minister in the Greenmount Dunker church, but Timothy stayed with the Turleytown church until his resignation in 1889, and Solomon became pastor of the Baptist church at Singers Glen. *Minutes of the Salem Union Association*, 1855, p. 24, VBHS; Minutes Of Turleytown Baptist Church, Swank, 2:213 (1 November 1862), EMU; Funk Papers, 1850-1918, Solomon Funk's Diary, 26 February 1866, BC; Funk, *Kline*, 458 (15 November 1862: W. C. Thurman [also a former Baptist] was elected a minister alongside Benjamin Funk).

[187]*Rockingham Register*, 25 October 1866.

[188]The *Rockingham Register* for 1866 is filled with announcement and reports of Sunday School picnics throughout the county. "Nearly all the penitents and converts" at the fall 1866 revival at Fellowship Methodist church had been associated with the Sunday School the previous summer. *The Old Commonwealth*, 5 December 1866, UVA. Like the Methodists, the New School and Old School Presbyterians in Harrisonburg would join together as one congregation. Harrisonburg Presbyterian Minutes, 1866-1908, 3 (9 December 1866), *VL* 47; Cook's Creek & Harrisonburg Minutes, 1851-1886, 60 (15 May 1867), *VL* 36.

[189]Dunkers, though giving liberty to churches to hold Sabbath-schools, urged them to be careful in the books that were used and advised "that brethren avoid taking part in or encouraging the Sabbath-school celebrations, common in the world." *Annual Meetings* [1956 ed.], 204 (1857, Article 11), 255 (1862, Article 1), 261 (1862, Article 31), 333f (1868, Article 14, quote).

[190]The Rockingham Bible Society, initially formed around 1818 or earlier with the support of Johannes Braun and others, was active by 1866. *Rockingham Register*, 4 October 1866; Wayland, *Rockingham*, 159f, 280.

[191]*Rockingham Register*, 4 October 1866, 25 October 1866.

[192]Diary of J. W. Jones (February/March 1864), in Jones, *Christ in the Camp*, 365.

[193]The date was 11 July 1875. A second building would go up on the same site in 1907 and be demolished a few decades later as part of "urban renewal." Wayland, *Historic Harrisonburg*, 168, 240.

[194]*Rockingham Register*, 6 April 1876. Wells was from the Des Moines Conference and transferred to the East Pennsylvania Conference in 1880. Funkhouser, *Virginia Conference*, 146, 267ff. The "re-colonization" movement, which re-located freed slaves to Liberia, gained strong support from many during this time. Among United Brethren, the mission to Freetown, West Africa (now Sierra Leone) would become a focus. United Brethren had been sending missionaries to Africa since January, 1855. Drury, *Glossbrenner*, 152; Funkhouser, *Virginia Conference*, 135. The American Colonization Society had been organized in 1816, and there was activity in Rockingham as early as 1822. "American Colonization Society," *The Methodist Magazine* (1823), 6:349; "Notice to the Members and Friends of the Colonization Society," *Rockingham Weekly Register*, 5 October 1822.

J. A. Evans, appointed in 1880 as the Mission's first African American leader, was born in Michigan. In 1870, following his education, he went to Africa, and five years later was serving the Augusta Freedmen's Mission. In 1880, he returned to African soil in Freetown, West Africa [Sierra Leone] where he died in 1899. The year he left, there were six preaching appointments and five organized classes which were a part of the Rockingham Freedmen's Mission. Among them were likely groups at Linville, Dungee's Chapel near Pleasant Valley, Broadway, and Long's Chapel at Zenda. Funkhouser, *Virginia Conference*, 135. *Minutes of the Virginia Annual Conference of the United Brethren in Christ* (Edinburg, Virginia, March 3-8, 1880. Dayton, VA: Ruebush, Kieffer & Co., 1880.

Long-lasting stability for the Rockingham Freedmen's mission came through the person of Rev. Theodore K. Clifford, a free-born African American from West Virginia who had served in the Federal army during the Civil War, who was with the Mission by 1884 until his death on 16 March 1908. Funkhouser, *Virginia Conference*, 160f, 284; *Minutes of the Virginia Annual Conference of the United Brethren in Christ, Convened at Lacey Spring, Virginia.* March 5-10, 1884. Dayton, VA: Ruebush, Kieffer & Co., 1884, p. 5 ("Rev. T. K. Clifford, of Piedmont, West Virginia, took charge of the Freedmen's Mission within our bounds and has labored successfully.")

Long's Chapel and Linville groups both had buildings by 1885, as did a group meeting in Broadway on the northeast corner of Rock and Main. Dungee's Chapel, described by Wayland as "near Pleasant Valley," was undoubtedly the same congregation that used the second Whitsel's U. B. church building, moved to a location near Spader's in 1893. The building was still standing but rarely used as late as 1965. Wayland, *Rockingham*, 276; Glovier, *Pictorial History*, 176.

Even though the African Americans in charge of the Freedmen's Mission were included in the Virginia Conference and photographed in group pictures, it is said of Clifford that he "always attended the sessions of the conference, but never took part in its discussions unless called upon." The same writer further says that Clifford "so deported himself as to win the respect and esteem of the best people of both colors. His upright life was never questioned, and he manifested his appreciation of genuine kindness in every proper way." Funkhouser, *Virginia Conference*, 161.

In 1912, four out of the eight African American churches noted by Wayland were United Brethren. He located them at Harrisonburg, Linville, Long's Chapel near Lacey Springs, and Dungee's Chapel near Pleasant Valley. Wayland, *Rockingham*, 276. The Kelley Street United Brethren church in Harrisonburg, resulting from a split occurring in the African American Methodist church in that city, was not organized until 27 November 1892. Ruth M. Toliver, *History of Kelly Street United Brethren in Christ Church, Newtown, Harrisonburg, Virginia, 1892-1906.* Gaithersburg, MD: Signature Books, 1998, p. ii, UVA.

[195]William C. Thurman. *Non-Resistance, or, The Spirit of Christianity Restored.* Charlottesville, VA: The author, 1862. This 70-page treatise can be found at the College of William

and Mary, Williamsburg, VA.

[196]William C. Thurman, *The Sealed Book of Daniel Opened; or, A Book of Reference for Those who Wish to Examine the "Sure Word of Prophecy."* Philadelphia: J. Goodyear, 1864; and *The Ordinance of Feet Washing as Instituted by Christ,* Philadelphia: John Goodyear, 1864. A third book by Thurman, *The Christian Calendar for A.M. 5989* (Hausertown, Indiana: G. Long and I. Dell, 1864), was published that same year. The common theme of these 1864 publications seems to be to recover the lost facets of what Thurman believed was "true, primitive" Christianity. Funk, *Kline,* 458 (15 November 1862: Thurman was elected alongside Benjamin Funk).

[197]Essentially, this was an argument over the original way Christ washed the disciples feet, as opposed to traditions within the Dunker church. At least that is the way the Thurmanites saw the issue. After being deposed as a minister in 1865, Thurman appeared at the 1866 Annual Meeting and signed a statment that he would omit "to mention, in preaching on the doctrine of feet-washing…that the one who washes should wipe." This was often designated as the "single mode" as compared with the "double mode" where one washed and another dried. He was expelled in 1867 for not holding to his word. *Minutes of the Annual Meetings,* 300 (1865, Article 57), 318 (1866, Article 48: quote), 326 (1867, Article 27); *Brethren Encyclopedia* 1:396f, 481f, 2:1186, 2:1264; *Rockingham Register,* 6 January 1870 (letter dated 13 December 1869 and responding to editorial of the "19th [9th?] ult."); *Brethren Encyclopedia,* 2:1264.

[198]*Rockingham Register,* 22 April 1875. The newspaper of the group — *The Gospel Trumpet* — was published by John Flory and Benjamin Funk at Singer's Glen from April, 1873 to May, 1876. *Brethren Encyclopedia,* 1:561. Rockingham County historian John Wayland reported in his day book for 6 May 1911 that Joe Ruebush took him to the "the old Ben Bowman (Daniel Yount) place [near Dayton] where the Thurmanites in Sept 1868 assembled to await the Advent." John W. Wayland, Every-Day Book #1, p. 110, BC.

[199]Psalm 46:4-7

Note: Page numbers in italics indicate text in sidebars.

index